TRENDS IN LEGAL ADVOCACY

Interviews with
Prosecutors and Criminal Defense Lawyers
Across the Globe

Interviews with Global Leaders in Policing, Courts, and Prisons Series

International Police Executive Symposium Co-Publications

Dilip K. Das, *Founding President-IPES*

PUBLISHED

Trends in Legal Advocacy: Interviews with Prosecutors and Criminal Defense Lawyers Across the Globe, Volume One
By Jane Goodman-Delahunty and Dilip K. Das, ISBN: 978-1-4987-3312-0

Trends in Policing: Interviews with Police Leaders Across the Globe, Volume Five
By Bruce F. Baker and Dilip K. Das, ISBN: 978-1-4822-2449-8

Trends in the Judiciary: Interviews with Judges Across the Globe, Volume One
By Dilip K. Das and Cliff Roberson with Michael Berlin, ISBN: 978-1-4200-9978-2

Trends in Policing: Interviews with Police Leaders Across the Globe, Volume Four
By Bruce F. Baker and Dilip K. Das, ISBN: 978-1-4398-8073-9

Trends in Policing: Interviews with Police Leaders Across the Globe, Volume Three
By Otwin Marenin and Dilip K. Das, ISBN: 978-1-4398-1924-1

Trends in Policing: Interviews with Police Leaders Across the Globe
By Dilip K. Das and Otwin Marenin, ISBN: 978-1-4200-7520-5

Trends in Corrections: Interviews with Corrections Leaders Around the World
By Jennie K. Singer, Dilip K. Das, and Eileen Ahlin, ISBN: 978-1-4398-3578-4

Trends in Corrections: Interviews with Corrections Leaders Around the World, Volume Two
By Martha Henderson Hurley and Dilip K. Das, ISBN: 978-1-4665-9156-1

Trends in the Judiciary: Interviews with Judges Across the Globe, Volume Two
By David Lowe and Dilip K. Das, ISBN: 978-1-4822-1916-6

VOLUME ONE

TRENDS IN LEGAL ADVOCACY

Interviews with
Prosecutors and Criminal Defense Lawyers
Across the Globe

Edited by
Jane Goodman-Delahunty
Dilip K. Das

CRC Press
Taylor & Francis Group
Boca Raton London New York

CRC Press is an imprint of the
Taylor & Francis Group, an **informa** business

CRC Press
Taylor & Francis Group
6000 Broken Sound Parkway NW, Suite 300
Boca Raton, FL 33487-2742

Printed on acid-free paper
Version Date: 20161110

International Standard Book Number-13: 978-1-4987-3312-0 (Hardback)

Visit the Taylor & Francis Web site at
http://www.taylorandfrancis.com

and the CRC Press Web site at
http://www.crcpress.com

Printed and bound in the United States of America by Sheridan

Contents

Series Preface

The International Police Executive Symposium (IPES), in collaboration with CRC Press/ Taylor & Francis Group Publishing, has launched a series titled *Interviews with Global Leaders in Policing, Courts, and Prisons.* The objective is to produce high-quality books aimed at bringing the voice of leading criminal justice practitioners to the forefront of scholarship and research. These books based on interviews with leaders in criminal justice are intended to present the perspectives of high-ranking officials and private practitioners throughout the world by examining their careers, insights, vision, experiences, challenges, perceived future of the field, and the related issues of interest.

True, the literature is replete with scholarship and research that provides the academic interpretation of the field, its practices, and future. However, these publications often appear in journals, are difficult to access, and are written from the perspective of the academic, with little interpretation or feasible action items for those professionals working in the field. A comprehensive body of literature discussing on-the-ground, day-to-day understanding of how the criminal justice system works, does not work, and needs to be improved is lacking. This series provides "inside" information about the systems as told to respected scholars and researchers by seasoned professionals. In this series, the dialogue between scholar/researcher and practitioner is opened as a guided, yet candid, discussion between the two professionals, which provides the opportunity for academics to learn from practitioners, whereas practitioners also learn from an outlet for the expression of their experiences, challenges, skills, and knowledge.

Throughout the world, the criminal justice field is at a crossroads, and the time is ripe for change and improvements. Many countries throughout the world have long-standing policies that have been successful for their culture and political climate, or are in need of serious revamping due to budgetary concerns or corruption. Other countries are at a precipice and are beginning to establish new systems. In all of these situations, the international criminal justice field stands to benefit from an accessible, engaging, and enlightening series of frank discussions of the leaders' personal views and experiences in the field.

This volume, *Trends in Legal Advocacy: Interviews with Prosecutors and Criminal Defense Lawyers Across the Globe, Volume One,* sets the stage to enhance readers' understanding of legal advocacy in criminal trials and appeals used throughout the world from an insider's perspective. The legal advocates interviewed in this volume are seasoned contemporaries who practice their craft in a variety of disparate cultures, political environments, and economic and legal systems scattered across the globe in a total of 13 different countries.

Trends in Legal Advocacy: Interviews with Prosecutors and Criminal Defense Lawyers Across the Globe, Volume One, continues the work of the IPES and CRC Press series on *Interviews with Global Leaders in Policing, Courts, and Prisons* by advancing knowledge about criminal justice systems, examining comparative procedures and issues from the perspective of leading advocates in a variety of countries, and opening a dialogue between scholars/researchers and practitioners. It is anticipated that this addition to the series will facilitate discussions within and between countries' criminal justice systems to add value to their current operations and future directions. It is hoped that this series will also bridge the knowledge gap that exists between scholars and researchers in academe and legal practitioners in the field. I invite legal scholars and researchers and legal practitioners across the world to join in this venture.

Dilip K. Das
Founding President,
International Police Executive Symposium,
www.ipes.info

Foreword

Around the globe, movements to reform legal systems are in ascendance. Countries with newly minted legal systems and countries with systems of long standing have explored ways to reform trial practices to better meet the legal needs of their citizens. Democratizing movements in many nations have produced demands for more open, inclusive, and responsive legal practices. Growing internationalization and increased global connections of legal professionals and academic scholars have led legal reformers to look to the practices of different nations for alternative institutional frameworks and promising legal transplants.

This outstanding collection, based on interviews with legal practitioners from multiple countries, offers us invaluable insights from those on the front lines of legal change. Legal professionals, such as the prosecutors and defense attorneys interviewed in this book, often confront major challenges as a result of political and legal reforms. Trained in one system with one set of rules, they must reinvent themselves on how they approach their work to respond to shifts in the political, social, cultural, and legal domains.

The project that forms the basis of *Trends in Legal Advocacy: Interviews with Prosecutors and Criminal Defense Lawyers Across the Globe, Volume One*, aims to create a productive global and intercultural dialogue between the practitioners and scholars in law and criminal justice. The dialogue in this book is especially worthwhile because it draws from practitioners and scholars from diverse regions of the world. Comparative law scholars often focus on a small number of countries, deploying qualitative and quantitative methods to analyze and contrast different legal regimes. What makes this book so exciting and valuable is that it incorporates the perspectives of 14 practitioners in 13 countries. Such an approach holds significant potential for greater theoretical and practical understanding of the law in action.

The coeditors of this volume, Jane Goodman-Delahunty and Dilip K. Das, are both extraordinary leaders in their fields. Goodman-Delahunty is a renowned scholar of psychology and law who has spent decades studying legal decision making. Dilip K. Das, founding president of the International Police Executive Symposium, has devoted himself to incorporating the experiences of criminal justice practitioners into academic debates. Their model partnership as coeditors shows the promise of integrating perspectives from academia and legal practice.

The chapter authors, many from academic disciplines, spoke in depth with practitioners during semi-structured interviews. Their discussions covered the same set of substantive issues, yet they also had flexibility to pursue unexpected or unique directions. Interview topics included explorations of career trajectories, philosophies of legal advocacy, successes and challenges in legal work, and recommendations for justice system reform. In all but one country, just one practitioner is interviewed (the exception is New Zealand, in which both a prosecutor and a defense attorney participated in interviews). Of course, these individual interviews do not represent all legal practitioners in the country of origin, nor are they meant to. Instead, the interviews offer a particularized examination of a practitioner's life and work. This methodological choice nicely complements the qualitative and quantitative approaches adopted in other comparative law projects.

The chapters of this book are full of novel insights about law in action around the globe. We are treated to accounts of the personal, legal, and political lives of leading advocates. We hear, for example, from a prominent Belgian criminal defense attorney who finds it challenging to get timely access to the investigative file and other case documents in that country's inquisitorial justice system. In contrast, a Bolivian prosecutor, who played a key role in the justice system's shift from inquisitorial to adversarial procedure, describes how the adoption of oral trials gave prosecutors a better understanding of the facts and of the defendant. We learn about the influence of Canada's Charter of Rights and Freedoms on the practice of criminal law from a prominent criminal defense lawyer, and from New South Wales about the growing pressure on prosecutors to consult with victims of crime. We witness the courage of a human rights lawyer in Thailand before and after a military coup there, and we discover a Chinese prosecutor's experiences investigating and prosecuting corruption and bribery cases.

These and other examples tell us much about law in action. They vividly illustrate what academics can learn from practitioners, and vice versa. The many insights generated by these academic–practitioner dialogues offer a host of promising new directions for research. All those interested in legal practice around the world will benefit from reading this volume.

Valerie P. Hans
Cornell Law School

Acknowledgments

The editors thank the 14 criminal justice practitioners from around the world who agreed to be interviewed, and generously shared their experiences, views, and insights about their work to make this book a reality. We extend our appreciation to the 18 contributing authors from 13 different countries across all the major continents who so diligently undertook these collaborations with these leading lawyers to advance scholarship on this topic.

We appreciate the constructive comments from Dr. Scott W. Phillips, the IPES book editor at the Criminal Justice Department at SUNY-Buffalo State, New York, whose careful review of the manuscript improved its quality, and the excellent suggestions from Dr. Anna Bussu, assistant professor in social psychology at the University of Sassari, Italy, and the University of Guayaquil, Ecuador. Research assistant Ida Nguyen provided invaluable research support in compiling the manuscript and Jake Miyairi assisted with the Japanese translation.

Finally, the editors thank CRC Press/Taylor & Francis Group for their support in the production of this book, in particular Ellen Boyne, editor, Carolyn Spence, senior acquisitions editor, Eve Strillaci, and Jessica Vega.

Editors

Jane Goodman-Delahunty, JD, PhD, is a research professor at Charles Sturt University, Manly, New South Wales, Australia. Trained in law and experimental psychology, she joined academe in Sydney, Australia, in 2001. Her research is influenced by her experience as a litigator, an administrative judge with the U.S. Equal Employment Opportunity Commission, a mediator, a commissioner with the New South Wales Law Reform Commission, and general member of the New South Wales Civil and Administrative Tribunal. She is an elected fellow of the American Psychological Association, a former editor of *Psychology, Public Policy, & Law*, and a past president of the American Psychology-Law Society and the Australian and New Zealand Association of Psychiatry, Psychology, and Law. Her empirical legal studies have been funded by the National Science Foundation, the Australian Institute of Criminology, the Australian Research Council, the Royal Commission into Institutional Responses to Child Sexual Abuse, and the US High Value Detainee Interrogation Group. Her research applies psychological scientific methods to promote evidence-based policies to enhance justice. She is the author of more than 150 scholarly books and articles.

Dilip K. Das is a professor of criminal justice, former police chief, founding editor-in-chief of *Police Practice and Research: An International Journal*, and a human rights consultant to the United Nations. Dilip served in the Indian Police Service for 14 years. In 1994, he founded the International Police Executive Symposium (IPES), which enjoys special consultative status in the United Nations. He has authored, edited, and coedited more than 30 books and numerous articles. He is the editor-in-chief of two book series, *Advances in Police Theory and Practice* and *Interviews with Global Leaders in Policing, Courts, and Prisons* published by CRC Press/Taylor & Francis Group. Dilip has received several faculty excellence awards and is a distinguished faculty lecturer.

Contributors

Astrid Birgden is a forensic and clinical psychologist with 30 years of experience, working in courts, corrections, and disability services. In courts, she established family violence courts. In corrections, she managed a statewide sex offender treatment program, developed a statewide framework to reduce reoffending, and established and managed a drug treatment prison. In disability services, she worked with clients who exhibited behaviors of concern or who engaged in serious offending. As a consultant, she works in most Australian states in corrections and human services as well as in international work such as establishing a citizen-mediation program in New Orleans, preventing torture in police and military in Asia, and she is a moderator of an online course that trains judges internationally on problem solving courts. Dr. Birgden has a master's and PhD in forensic psychology from Australia and a master's in advanced mental disability law from New York Law School. She is published in offender rehabilitation, therapeutic jurisprudence, and human rights. Email: astrid99@hotmail.com.

Sarah Bishop, LLB (Hons), BAsSt (Thai) (Hons) is a PhD Candidate at the ANU College of Law, Canberra, Australia. Her primary area of research is Asian law, with a particular focus on Thai public law. Her previous research has focused on areas in which the country's newly established Constitutional and Administrative Courts have been particularly active—political party regulation and environmental regulation. Her doctoral thesis will focus on another aspect of the work of these and other Thai courts—the reception and interpretation of constitutional rights. Email: sarah.bishop@anu.edu.au.

Danielle Celermajer is a professor in the Department of Sociology and Social Policy at the University of Sydney, Australia. Her most recent project, funded by the European Union, interrogates the root causes of torture and seeks to design prevention strategies focusing on the police and military in Sri Lanka and Nepal. She was the founder director of the EU-funded Asia Pacific Masters of Human Rights and Democratisation. Her research focuses on transitional justice, the relationship between human rights and religious norms and institutions, human rights education, collective responsibility, conceptual frameworks for human rights, and the relationship between secular philosophical and theological thought. She received her PhD in political theory (*summa cum laude*) from Columbia University, New York. Prior to entering academia, she was the director of indigenous policy at the Australian Human Rights Commission. Her publications include *Sins of the Nation and the Ritual of Apology* (2009) and *Power, Judgment and Political Evil* (2010). She is the coeditor of a forthcoming volume on *The Cultural History of Law in the Twentieth Century*. Email: danielle.celermajer@sydney.edu.au.

Amita Dhanda is a professor of law at NALSAR, University of Law, Hyderabad, India. Her work on the rights of persons with psychosocial disabilities contributed to the discourse on legal capacity in the UN Convention on the Rights of Persons with Disabilities. Subsequently, she has actively engaged in the law reform process in her country to bring the Indian law in conformity with the UN Convention. Prof. Dhanda believes in the pluralizing of inclusion and multiplicity of voice. Her work on disability and gender is an effort in that direction. She views this book as an effort to vocalize the concerns of all players of the criminal justice system, thereby making a case for informed reform. In her book, *Legal Order and Mental Disorder* (2000) and all subsequent writings, Prof. Dhanda has foregrounded the plight of persons with mental illness in the criminal justice system. Email: amitadhanda@gmail.com.

Michael W. Gendler has practiced law in Seattle, Washington, since 1978, working in small, private law firms. His practice has emphasized representation of citizens groups and individuals challenging government and corporations in environmental, civil rights, and commercial litigation. He received his J.D. *magna cum laude* from Georgetown University Law Center, Washington, D.C., in 1978. He is a member of the American Civil Liberties Union of Washington Legal Committee. Mickey has been listed in "Best Lawyers in America" under Environmental Law and as a Washington "Super Lawyer." Mickey has the unique experience of having been a client in a major personal injury action and in a public records case decided favorably by the Washington Supreme Court, giving him valuable insight into the ways lawyers and clients can work together effectively to achieve the best result. Mickey is currently focusing on maximizing his recovery from a 2007 spinal cord injury. Email: gendler@mickeygendler.com, www.gendlermann.com.

Taryn Gudmanz is a barrister in Dunedin, New Zealand. A commercial litigator, Taryn was a finalist in the Rising Star Litigation category in the 2014 Euromoney Legal Media Group Australasia Women in Business Awards. She commenced practice in 2002 with *Bell Gully* in Wellington and moved to London to practice insurance and commercial litigation with *Barlow Lyde & Gilbert* (now *Clyde & Co*). After relocating to Dunedin in 2007, she practiced with *Gallaway Cook Allan* before moving to *Anderson Lloyd* in 2012 as a senior associate. Taryn was also seconded as legal counsel to the Pharmaceutical

Management Agency (PHARMAC) and has presented guest lectures at the University of Otago and Otago Polytechnic in Dunedin. She is a past convener of the Otago Women Lawyers Society, a current member of the Otago Branch Council of the New Zealand Law Society, and a trustee of its Benevolent Fund. Taryn is also a member of the Board of Trustees of King's High School. Email: taryn_gudmanz@yahoo.com.

Makoto Ibusuki is a professor of criminal procedure law in the Faculty of Law, Seijo University, Tokyo, since 2009. Previously he was a professor at Ritsumeikan School of Law in Kyoto (2002–2009) and associate professor and professor (1991–2002) at Kagoshima University, Japan. He has been a visiting scholar in the United States at the University of Hawaii (2014) and the John Marshall Law School, Chicago (1997–1998), and in Australia at the University of Sydney (2013) and the University of New South Wales (2002). He was also a visiting fellow at the University of New South Wales (2007–2008). Dr. Ibusuki has authored numerous scholarly publications, including six monographs, nine edited books (he was the supervisory editor of five of them), and many journal articles. He has also translated several books, most recently *Understanding Criminal Procedure* (5th ed.), Volume 1 (2014) by Joshua Dressler and Alan C Michaels. Email: ibusuki@seijo.ac.jp.

Nik Kiefer is a researcher at the Centre for International Law of the Free University of Brussels, where he works on issues of general public international law, international human rights law, international humanitarian law, and international and national criminal law. Previously, Nik was active internationally with the Office of the Prosecutor of the International Criminal Tribunal for the former Yugoslavia based in the Hague, the Netherlands, where he was part of the Hadzic Trial Team, and with the Criminal Law and Terrorism Unit of the Directorate-General Human Rights and Rule of Law of the Council of Europe, where he acted as a human rights consultant. In addition, Nik has worked for the Council of the European Union, Directorate-General Justice and Home Affairs, where he dealt with aspects of police and customs cooperation in Europe. Nik holds a master of laws (with high distinction) and a master of science in criminology (with distinction) from the Free University of Brussels. Email: nik.kiefer@vub.ac.be.

Nikolai Kovalev is an associate professor in the Department of Criminology at Wilfred Laurier University in Brantford, Canada. Dr. Kovalev's research is focused on comparative criminal justice, criminal law, criminal procedure, and human rights. He is particularly interested in the evolution of jury trials and reforms in the criminal justice systems of post-Communist transitional countries. Other research projects include study of jury bias in neo-Nazi skinhead trials and lay adjudication in military justice. His current research concerns the manipulation of juries in Canada and other countries. Dr. Kovalev has served as an expert on comparative criminal justice, law reform, and international human rights for the Organization for Security and Co-operation in Europe, the American Bar Association/Rule of Law Initiative, and the U.S. Department of Justice. He completed assessments of several draft laws on jury and lay assessors for Kazakhstan and Kyrgyz Republic, and the draft Criminal Procedure Code of Tajikistan. Dr. Kovalev is a frequent speaker at conferences, roundtables, seminars, and workshops on issues of human rights and criminal justice reforms in post-Communist states. Email: nkovalev@wlu.ca.

Lola Araujo Langthaler is a Bolivian lawyer with a bachelor of law and political science from the Universidad Mayor de San Andrés, La Paz, Bolivia, and a master of arts (sociology) from the Western University of Illinois, Macomb, Illinois. She coordinated the Program of Administration of Justice funded by USAID/Bolivia, designing and implementing the Bolivian Criminal Procedure Reform. She has a particular interest in anticorruption and transparency measures within the Latin American and Caribbean legal systems. In 2003–2006, she was a specialist senior adviser to an anticorruption program (USAID/Bolivia) that managed enforcement and policy development and provided general legal advice. In 2006–2008, she was the director of Transparency and Citizen Action Program (USAID/Dominican Republic), managing a three-year integrated transparency program. In Melbourne, Australia, Ms Langthaler has worked for the Department of Justice as a project manager in the Sex Offender Treatment Program, as manager of the Program Innovations Team at the Neighborhood Justice Centre, and as senior procurement officer at Courts and Tribunals Services of Victoria. Currently she provides governance support and advice to the Courts Services Victoria. Email: winaraujo@gmail.com.

Menaka Lecamwasam is a lecturer in the Department of Law, University of Peradeniya, Sri Lanka. She has an LLM in human rights (distinction) from University of Hong Kong and an LLB from the University of Colombo, Sri Lanka. A nonpracticing attorney-at-law of the Supreme Court of Sri Lanka, she has worked in collaboration with government entities and international organizations as an independent researcher on research endeavors pertaining to penal policy, delays in the law, human trafficking, and international humanitarian law. She teaches courses on international human rights law, international humanitarian law, law of international organizations, and the legal system of Sri Lanka. The author's research interests include human rights, refugees and International Development Programs, international humanitarian law, international organizations, and penal policy. She has served on the editorial committee of the *Junior Bar Law Journal* of Sri Lanka and as an assistant editor to the Sri Lanka Law Reports. Email: hasinilecamwasam@rocketmail.com.

Ai Ma is a professor in the Department of Psychology in the School of Sociology at the China University of Political Science and Law, Beijing, China. Dr. Ma is a distinguished scholar of legal psychology and the chief investigator of 20 research projects sponsored by the Ministry of Education, Ministry of Justice, and National Social Science Foundation of China. Dr. Ma is a recipient of the Distinguished Teaching Award of Beijing, and Excellence in Teaching Award from the China University of Political Science and Law. Dr. Ma has published more than 30 academic journal articles, and authored and coedited more than 20 books. Dr. Ma is the vice dean of the School of Sociology and director of the Criminal Psychology Research Center at the China University of Political Science and Law. Dr. Ma is the president of the Committee on Forensic Psychology of the Chinese Psychological Society. Email: chinafzxl@163.com.

Mark Nolan, BSc (Hons), LLB, MAsPacSt, PhD (ANU) SFHEA is an associate professor and interdisciplinary legal scholar with doctoral training in social psychology. Since 2002, Mark has been teaching and researching criminal law and procedure, law and psychology, advocacy, and military discipline law to undergraduate and postgraduate law students at the ANU College of Law, Canberra, Australia. Mark has also researched juries, citizenship law, human rights law, intergroup relations, social justice theory, and sentencing law. Mark has an interest in comparative legal research in Asia, having worked mainly on Japanese jury reform and Thai legal issues. He has made teaching and research visits to Chuo University (Japan), University of Yangon (Myanmar), Chulalongkorn University, and Thammasat University (Thailand). Mark recently completed a master's degree in Asia Pacific Studies at ANU, majoring in Thai language. He is also affiliated with the Myanmar Research Centre and the Thai Studies Centre at ANU. Email: mark.nolan@anu.edu.au.

Patricia O'Shaughnessy is a Queensland lawyer and barrister and solicitor of the High Court of New Zealand. Before moving to Queensland in 2014, she worked as a police officer in New Zealand for 24 years undertaking a variety of roles. Those roles included the investigation of serious crime as a detective, a prosecutor of criminal charges brought by the New Zealand Police in District and Youth Courts, and more recently, a strategic advisor to the police executive on a range of issues as an inspector at the Police National Headquarters. She is currently a consultant in Brisbane, investigating and reporting on workplace disputes and systemic issues within organizations.

She also conducts legal research for Queensland legal practitioners and universities within Australia. Email: trish_o@me.com.

Don Pinnock is an investigative journalist and a research fellow at the Centre of Criminology, University of Cape Town, South Africa. He is an associate of Southern Write, a group of writers and photographers working in Africa, and a former editor of *Getaway* magazine in Cape Town. He has been an electronics engineer, lecturer in journalism and criminology, consultant on youth justice to the Mandela government, a professional yachtsman, explorer, travel writer, and photographer. As a criminologist, he was one of the codrafters of the Youth Justice White Paper for the African National Congress government, which became the Child Justice Act. He is a specialist in adolescent deviance and was one of the founders of the Usiko Trust working with high-risk youths. He is presently its chairperson. He is also a trustee of the Chrysalis Academy working with youth from disadvantaged backgrounds. He has published 16 books and many papers and articles in the fields of criminology, history, biography, environment, travel, and fiction. Email: don@pinnock.co.za.

Anne Wallace, PhD, LLM, LLB is a professor and the head of the School of Law and Justice at Edith Cowan University in Perth, Western Australia. She has teaching expertise in criminal law and procedure, evidence, forensic evidence, and justice administration. From 1993 to 2006, she was deputy executive director of the Australian Institute of Judicial Administration, and in that capacity developed a keen interest in the theory and practice of case flow management in trials. Anne has researched and published widely on topics in the field of judicial administration including the development, applications, and implications of technology in criminal trials (interactive visual evidence, videoconferencing, and social media), judicial workload allocation, and court safety. Email: a.wallace@ecu.edu.au.

Shanti Nandana Wijesinghe has been the director of Social Development Affairs to the President of Sri Lanka since 2006. He was appointed senior lecturer in sociology at the University of Peradeniya, Sri Lanka, in 1985. He teaches undergraduate and postgraduate courses in sociological theories, peace theories, human rights, medical sociology, and sociology of reproductive health. He has conducted research and training in the fields of reconciliation, peace, conflict, and health. He is working on a PhD in the School of Global Studies at the University of Gothenburg, Sweden, holds an MA in health social sciences (1996) from Mahidol University, Thailand, and attended a study program at Bowdoin College, Brunswick, Maine (1992/93). For 20 years, he has served as the editor of *Samaja Vimasuma*

(Social Analysis), the annual publication of the Department of Sociology at the University of Peradeniya, and is the editor-in-chief of *Social Affairs.* Email: shanti_nandana@yahoo.com.

Zhuo Zhang is an associate professor in the Department of Psychology, the School of Sociology, the China University of Political Science and Law, Beijing, China. Dr. Zhang completed her PhD in the Department of Rehabilitation Science at the Hong Kong Polytechnic University and joined the China University of Political Science and Law in 2008. Dr. Zhang is the author of more than 10 academic journal articles and book chapters, and coeditor of two books. Dr. Zhang has obtained grants from the Beijing Municipal Social Science Foundation and the Ministry of Education of China to conduct research on the neuropsychological basis of criminal behavior. Dr. Zhang is a member of the Committee of Forensic Psychology of the Chinese Psychological Society and a member of the Branch of Drug Abuse and Criminal Psychology of the Chinese Association of Drug Abuse Prevention and Treatment. Email: gladzz@163.com.

Introduction

JANE GOODMAN-DELAHUNTY
DILIP K. DAS

1

Contents

Introduction to Legal Advocacy across the Globe

This book and series of interviews with leading prosecutors and criminal defense lawyers around the world is designed to foster a better understanding of the global challenges faced by criminal justice leaders, and of the successes that they achieve while functioning in an increasingly interconnected and democratized world. This chapter provides an overview of this innovative series on international legal advocacy and the use of legal life histories as a forum to explore trends and the latest developments in criminal justice from the perspectives of some of the foremost prosecutorial and defense practitioners.

Biographies of criminals and true crime stories are popular, in part because they deal with the intersection of the personal and the professional. Yet comparatively little is known about the legal professionals engaged in these cases. A few prominent lawyers, such as the French former prosecutor, Philippe Bilger (2003), and private practitioner and U.S. Attorney for the Southern District of New York, Robert Fiske, Jr. (2014), have successfully penned their own memoirs recounting the high-profile cases in which they were involved. Since legal advocates themselves rarely have time to write and reflect on their experiences, views, opinions, and perspectives, a series of interviews conducted by qualified criminal justice professionals contributes to fill that gap.

The aim of this book is to document trends and developments in criminal justice systems through interviews with outstanding prosecutors, public defenders, and defense lawyers as they speak about their lives and careers in law, their training, and the culture and societal context of their roles and activities. Since the late 1930s, the interview has been recognized as a reliable and useful research method, and has been increasingly used by social scientists (Platt, 2001). Leading scholars such as the French sociologist, Pierre Bourdieu (1984/2003), endorsed the interview as a dependable means to gain access to the lived everyday world of the interviewee (Brinkmann & Kvale, 2015). Today, in many disciplines, the interview has achieved the status of a key qualitative method (Morris, 2015).

Sources of knowledge on the criminal justice system, such as textbooks on criminal justice, rarely include information about prosecutors and criminal defense lawyers, creating a dearth of information about their careers and roles (Smith, 2012). Much of the focus in prior criminal justice research has been on the judiciary. Interest in the influence of prosecutorial discretion has increased, though often within a context where judicial decisions remain the primary interest. For instance, some research has examined prosecutorial overcharging practices that exert less readily perceptible influences on sentencing practices of the judiciary (Worrall & Nugent-Borakove, 2008). An internationally renowned Professor of Criminal Law and Policy, Michael Tonry, himself a former legal practitioner, recently drew attention to the paucity of available research on public prosecutors, and almost none comparing prosecutors across different legal systems within or across countries to foster scholarly critique (Tonry, 2013). The dearth of comparable research on criminal defense lawyers is more striking. Where brief individual profiles of leaders in the field have been compiled, these are not typically comparative in nature, and do not address both the prosecution and the defense in the same book or article (e.g., Smith, 2012; Williams & Hsiao, 2010). The inclusion in this book of interviews of six prosecutors and eight criminal defense lawyers redresses this imbalance, and has generated a uniquely rich set of resources on this topic.

Public interest in legal biographies was recently confirmed by the British Broadcasting Corporation initiation in the United Kingdom of a series of interviews with eminent legal professionals for television audiences. However, most legal biographies "have focused on the lives of the elite; most often white, male, higher court judges" (Sugarman, 2015, p. 13). Perhaps in a reaction to perceptions of the legal profession as male-dominated, the dissenting opinions of US Supreme Court Justice Ruth Bader Ginzburg, which stand in stark contrast to the views of her white, male counterparts, have garnered immense popularity, reflected in a Tumblr mini-blog, and a recent book celebrating "the notorious RBG" (Carmon & Kniznhnik, 2015). This book departs from the traditional focus in legal biographies on white, male members of the judiciary, and presents the biographies of leading male and female lawyers who have made their careers as prosecutors and as defense lawyers in a diverse range of cultural and multicultural societies.

The Interviewee Sample

An important feature of this particular volume is that it does not focus exclusively on legal practitioners in British and North American jurisdictions, while a leading Canadian and United States lawyer were represented among the practitioners interviewed. In all, a total of eight chapters focused on lawyers practicing in Asian countries: China, India, Japan, Nepal, Sri Lanka, and Thailand, providing unique insights into the evolution of legal rights and adversarial legal practices in countries drawing on non-Western values and traditions. Approximately, one-half of the interviews were conducted in countries that were formerly part of the British Empire, that is, Australia, Canada, India, Sri Lanka, New Zealand, and South Africa. These chapters will hold special interest for scholars of comparative criminal law and practice in postcolonial systems. Some practitioners work in an adversarial legal system, others in an inquisitorial legal system, and others in more hybrid systems that incorporate strengths of both adversarial and inquisitorial systems.

Notably, five of the legal professionals interviewed for this book are women; two working as prosecutors and three as criminal defense lawyers. Their stories fill additional gaps in the existing literature by focusing on the lives of lawyers who are often marginalized or treated as outsiders. For example, Judith Ablett-Kerr was the second of only two female barristers in Wales, and worked as a Crown prosecutor for nine years, before rising to prominence in New Zealand, her adopted country, as a leading defense barrister. Maria Teresa Rivero Gutierrez in Bolivia started her career as a public defense lawyer, and after seven years as magistrate, she was the first woman appointed President of the Superior Court. However, it is her work as Prosecutor of Appeals leading a series of criminal procedural reforms in Bolivia during a period of transition from an inquisitorial to an accusatorial model, which is highlighted in this book. Antoinette Ferreira conducts trailblazing work by applying criminal conspiracy theories to prosecute rhino and elephant poachers as her country turns its attention to environmental issues. The extraordinary dedication and resourceful use of human rights law by Yaowalak Anuphan and Mandira Sharma to change criminal justice practice in Thailand and Nepal have achieved global recognition.

Skilled Interviewer-Authors

The background and expertise of the 18 authors who contributed to this volume enhanced their capacity to engage the interviewees, to draw out fresh and innovative insights, and to capture the significance of their views. Among the authors are five current or former legal practitioners who established their own careers as successful litigators (Gendler, Gudmanz,

Kiefer, Langthaler, O'Shaughnessy, and Wallace). Five authors are non-practicing attorneys (Bishop, Dhanda, Ibusuki, Lecamwasam, and Nolan). Some authors have worked professionally in fields closely allied with the criminal justice system, such as court administration (Langthaler), corrections management (Birdgen), journalism (Pinnock), police investigations (O'Shaughnessy), and government administration (Wijesinghe). The majority of the contributing authors brought their extensive international practice or consulting experience to the interviews, and were sensitive to comparative criminal justice issues. Many of the contributors hold academic appointments in a diverse range of disciplines, including criminology (Kiefer; Kovalov, O'Shaughnessy, Pinnock), clinical, forensic, and legal psychology (Birdgen; Ma, Nolan, Zhang), law (Bishop, Nolan, Wallace), social policy (Celermajer), and sociology (Ma; Wijesinghe). Their biographies in the appendix provide further details of breadth and depth of their qualifications and expertise.

More than half of the contributing authors interviewed lawyers whose day-to-day work was conducted in a language other than English: the six Asian countries listed above plus Bolivia in South America and Belgium in Western Europe, and half of the interviews were conducted in languages other than English by the skilled contributing authors who translated the responses specifically for this book. As a result, this volume provides a wealth of fresh information not elsewhere accessible to the English-speaking world. These features enhanced the uniquely transnational set of comparisons offered in this book.

The Semi-Structured Interview Methodology

The prosecutors and criminal defense lawyers whose careers and lives are portrayed in this book were selected by the contributing authors based on their knowledge of the context in which the practitioners worked, the lawyer's reputation and field of expertise, and the author's interest in that lawyer's role, skills, and contributions to the criminal justice system. The individual interview responses are not intended to be representative of the views of other prosecutors and defense lawyers in each country in which the interviewees work. Instead, a theoretical sampling method was used to select interviewees to ensure that the relevant topics and concepts would be examined in sufficient detail (Yin, 1989). From a constructivist perspective, we fully acknowledge the collaboration of the contributing authors in the production of the knowledge gained through the interviews. Some authors chose to interview a prosecutor or criminal defense lawyer who could vividly convey a sense of his or her day-to-day work; others interviewed a lawyer with a reputation as outstanding in the field, or an intriguing or controversial figure in their legal landscape.

The goal in compiling the chapters for the book was to apply a method that allowed the interviewers to draw out the best of what each interviewee had to contribute. Life history interviews are a particular form of qualitative interview well-suited to obtaining a comprehensive account from legal practitioners of their reflections on their personal and professional experiences, and their understanding of those events. The 14 in-depth interviews in this volume comprise a form of life history, revealing each lawyer's views of the context in which he or she works, and their motivations. The topics to cover in the interviews were provided to interviewers in the form of 25 suggested interview questions, but interviewers were permitted to deviate if important in a particular country or context. By conducting semi-structured interviews using these 25 open-ended questions, the interviewers held directed conversations with each interviewee. This format allowed them scope to digress and to fully explore the responses given by the lawyers, by seeking clarification and explanations for the responses. Interviews are uniquely well-suited to explore these underpinnings (Morris, 2015, p. 8).

Institutional Insights

The 14 lawyers who were interviewed for this volume included seven practitioners employed by government or public agencies and seven private practitioners. The interviews provided a thorough and comprehensive account, from an insider's perspective, of how key prosecutors and defense lawyers viewed their roles, and the difficulties associated with the changing nature of their work.

Every interview report is preceded by a brief overview of the criminal justice system in the jurisdiction where the lawyer works. These synopses describe the essential aspects of the legal context in which the cases and issues described by the practitioners arose. To further elucidate the legal context, each chapter concludes with a brief glossary of key terms or concepts discussed by the legal advocate in his or her interview. The resulting chapters convey to readers how the law in the real world works (Genn et al., 2006).

By including the views of six prosecutors and eight criminal defense lawyers, this volume permits an exploration of the similarities and differences between prosecutors and defense lawyers across multiple international jurisdictions. These interviews also demonstrate how the public interest is served by the work of accomplished lawyers in private practice. Each chapter includes the same general topic headings to generate a comparative framework and foster comparisons across chapters. As a whole, this set of interviews fills a descriptive and theoretical void in the published literature on comparative criminal justice. The diverse range of jurisdictions in which these professionals work provides a rich, cross-cultural perspective on their practice that transcends any one of the local milieux.

Summary

In sum, the book provides engaging qualitative information detailing the perspectives of 14 legal professionals at the top of their field, and an overview of the criminal justice systems in 13 different countries across the globe. The result is a rich source of knowledge and information for readers interested in the role of prosecutors and public defenders or defense counsel, and their participation in global legal systems. A distinctive benefit of life writing is the accessibility of this form of scholarship to a wide range of audiences (Sugarman, 2015). Thus, the interactions between the personal and professional depicted in these materials will appeal to a wide readership. The book will be of interest to members of the public, legal professionals, criminal justice professionals, and students of law, policy, criminology, justice studies, policing, and forensic psychology.

Australia

ANNE WALLACE

2

Contents

The Criminal Justice Process of Australia

From 1788 onwards, Australia was colonized by British settlers, who brought with them the common law of England. Australia's indigenous peoples, Aboriginal and Torres Strait Islanders, had their own well-established systems of law that operated throughout the country. Those systems were significantly disrupted by European colonization, but continue to have considerable significance for indigenous people in today's Australia.

There are nine jurisdictions under Australia's Federal system of government, illustrated in Figure 2.1:

- Six states: New South Wales, Victoria, Queensland, South Australia, Western Australia, and Tasmania.
- Two territories: The Northern Territory and the Australian Capital Territory.
- The Federal, or Commonwealth, jurisdiction, which subsists across the whole country, but only in respect of those matters in respect of which the Commonwealth government has jurisdiction under the Constitution.

The states originated as separate colonies, established by Great Britain. They combined in 1901 to establish the constitutional federation of the Commonwealth of Australia, under a constitution enacted by the British Parliament. The Federal Government may make laws only with respect to matters that are specifically vested in it by the Constitution. All remaining matters are governed by state and territory law: either statute law or common law. Most criminal matters are governed by state and territory law, other than offenses created by Federal legislation or within the Constitution.

Criminal offenses are investigated by the police force of the relevant jurisdiction. There are also specialized criminal justice agencies that have investigation roles in relation to particular types of offenses, for example, in areas such as corruption, customs, taxation, and terrorism.

Less serious criminal offenses are often prosecuted by police prosecutors. More serious offenses are referred by the police, or other investigating agencies, to the relevant Director of Public Prosecutions (DPP) in the particular jurisdiction. The DPP is an independent statutory office, whose function is to carry out criminal prosecution on behalf of the State.

The court system reflects the British heritage and each court derives its authority from the relevant state, territorial, or Commonwealth legislation. Each jurisdiction generally operates at three levels (represented

Figure 2.1 The Commonwealth of Australia. (Courtesy of d-maps.com, http://www.d-maps.com/carte.php?num_car=3295&lang=en [accessed August 04, 2016]).)

diagrammatically below). This hierarchical system allows decisions made by one court to be re-examined by a higher court on appeal (Figure 2.2).

Less serious (summary) criminal offenses are heard and determined in the Local or Magistrates' Court and, if contested, the evidence is heard and the case decided by a magistrate. In more serious (indictable) criminal cases, the ultimate decision (guilt or innocence) is generally made by a jury of 12 citizens. In jury cases, the judge will usually give directions to the jury about the law and may issue determinations about the law in the form of written judgments if issues arise in the course of the trial. Most Australian jurisdictions also have provisions enabling an order to be made for a criminal trial to be heard by a judge sitting without a jury if the accused person elects or consents to that.

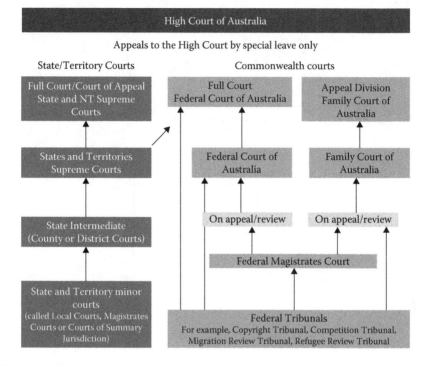

Figure 2.2 Australia—court system.

Mark Tedeschi AM QC, Senior Crown Prosecutor, Sydney

Introduction

Mark Tedeschi AM QC is one of Australia's most experienced prosecutors. Since 1997, he has been the Senior Crown Prosecutor for New South Wales, Australia's most populous state, with the largest criminal jurisdiction. He has prosecuted many difficult, high profile, and controversial criminal cases in the course of a career that spans over three decades.

In parallel with this legal career, Mark has pursued a passion for photography, exhibiting in both solo and joint exhibitions, nationally and internationally. His photographs have been widely published and are included in a number of significant public and private collections. A common theme in his subject matter is an emphasis on people—their lives, contexts, and environments. His work regularly appears as a finalist in major photographic competitions and has received a number of prizes.

More recently, Mark has developed a career as a writer. In *Eugenia: A True Story of Adversity, Tragedy, Crime and Courage*, published in 2012, he tells the story of Eugenia Falleni, a woman who spent 22 years living as a man and was prosecuted in 1920 for the murder of her "wife." The prosecution's case was based almost entirely on circumstantial evidence. Mark's detailed analysis of the evidence and the conduct of the trial bears testimony to his own forensic skills. His reconstruction of the accused's life story evidences an insight into the human condition borne possibly from both the variety of motivations and personalities encountered in his career in the criminal law, and from the individuals encountered in his candid photographic work. Mark's latest true crime book—*Kidnapped*—tells the story of the kidnapping and murder of Graeme Thorne in 1960 and the subsequent trial of his kidnapper, Stephen Bradley.

Mark's contributions to law and photography have been recognized by the governments of Australia and Italy (where his family originates and where he has frequently visited, photographed, and exhibited). He was awarded the Cavaliere della Republica (the Order of Merit of the Italian Republic) in 2009 for his services to photography and the law and made a Member of the Order of Australia (AM) in 2013 for his services as a prosecutor and to photography.

On the Friday afternoon I arrive at his Chambers in the Sydney Office of the New South Wales Director of Public Prosecutions, he is three and a half months into the trial of Robert Xie, who is alleged to have murdered five members of his extended family (including two children) in their Sydney home in 2009. The case has attracted a great deal of media attention, both in the investigation and in the trial stages.

This chapter traces the development of Mark's career, including coverage of some of the major criminal trials that he has prosecuted, cases that have been significant not only for the nature of their crimes, but also for exemplifying particular contemporary issues and concerns in the criminal justice system. It discusses significant issues that he identifies as facing the criminal trial process in his jurisdiction and some of the reforms that have been made that have benefited that system.

A glossary of legal terms is included at the end of the chapter.

Career

Mark has been a central figure in the New South Wales criminal justice system over a period that has been marked by some significant changes in the organization of the prosecution service and in criminal trial procedure. His forensic and advocacy skills, and his approach to the prosecution task, have had a significant impact on the criminal bar in New South Wales. He has also been able to balance a very successful career in law with one in the creative arts, two environments that might appear to require very different skill sets.

Mark was born in 1952 and raised in Sydney. His father and paternal grandparents, of Jewish background, immigrated to Australia from Northern Italy in 1939, and his mother, also Jewish, emigrated from Nazi Germany prior to the outbreak of the war. While none of his family came from the legal profession, he has credited the work that his father did as a court interpreter with sparking his initial interest in law.

After attending Sydney Grammar School, Mark went to the University of Sydney to study law, graduating in 1974. After graduating, he went overseas and obtained a part-time position as a lecturer in law at the then City of London Polytechnic (now London Metropolitan University) while studying for, and obtaining, a Master of Arts with a specialization in international commercial law. While he had initially envisaged a legal career as a suburban solicitor, during this period in London, living at a university college, he became attracted to the academic lifestyle, and, on his return to Australia, got a job in Sydney as an academic, teaching law. However, after two years, he found that the work was, in his words, "a little tame," and in 1977, he took up legal practice at the Bar.

Mark spent his first six years at the Bar in private practice. He took on his first criminal case at the end of his first year at the Bar as a defense counsel in what became known as the "Greek Conspiracy Case." This was the prosecution of a large number of individuals, most of Greek origin, for social security fraud. The case originated from an investigation by the Commonwealth Department of Social Security into an arrangement that was alleged to exist in sections of Australia's Greek community, whereby doctors accepted payment to assist members of that community to make fraudulent claims for invalid pensions. The lengthy legal proceedings took three years to complete, during which time Mark realized he enjoyed doing criminal trial work and at the end of which, in his words, "everybody thought of me as a criminal lawyer."

For the next two years, he did defense work in jury trials in the District Court. After deciding that he wanted to specialize solely in criminal law, he applied unsuccessfully for a job as a public defender. The next public sector job that came up in the criminal law field was as a Crown prosecutor. Mark applied and was appointed to that role in 1983. His subsequent success is evidenced by his appointment as a Queen's counsel in 1988, only 11 years after going to the Bar and only five years after becoming a full-time prosecutor. In 1990, he became a Deputy Senior Crown Counsel and was appointed as the Senior Crown Prosecutor for New South Wales in 1997.

As Senior Crown Prosecutor, Mark carries the responsibility for dealing with the state's most difficult and complex trials, which often attract high levels of media and public interest. He is renowned as a tough opponent and has been nicknamed "the prosecutor defense lawyers love to hate." A selection of the major cases he has prosecuted during his career is described in the following sections.

The Trial of Tim Anderson for the Hilton Hotel Bombing

In February 1978, a bomb exploded outside the Hilton Hotel in Sydney, where the Australian government was hosting the Commonwealth Heads of Government Regional meeting, resulting in three deaths. Eleven years after the event, Anderson was prosecuted, tried, and convicted of ordering the bombing on the basis of evidence from a former member of the Ananda Marga religious sect. The conviction was subsequently overturned on appeal to the New South Wales Court of Criminal Appeal, which criticized aspects of the way that the case had been conducted (*R v. Anderson*, 1991). The circumstances surrounding the bombing were highly controversial, involving allegations of threats made by the Ananda Marga against the then Indian Prime Minister (a delegate to the meeting). Anderson had been charged years earlier in connection with a conspiracy to murder Robert Cameron, the leader of the neo-Nazi National Front. That case gave rise to controversial allegations of involvement by Australian security agencies. The Hilton bombing has been subject of a documentary (Dellora, 1995). It and the Cameron case have been the subject of books published by Anderson and others (Alister, 1997; Anderson, 1985, 1992; Hocking, 1993; Jiggens, 1991; Molomby, 1986).

The Trial of Arthur Stanley ("Neddy") Smith for Murder

Neddy Smith is a notorious career criminal, with an extensive history of involvement in drug dealing, armed robbery, and corruption. In 1990, he received his second murder conviction for the murder of a tow truck driver that arose from a road rage incident. Smith subsequently turned informer, giving evidence against police to the Independent Commission against Corruption and the Wood Royal Commission into the New South Wales Police Force (Smith & Noble, 2005). Aspects of his career and his relationship with police were chronicled in *Blue Murder*, a television series produced by the Australian Broadcasting Corporation (Jenkins, 1995).

The Trial of Ivan Milat for the "Backpacker Murders"

In 1992 and 1993, a number of bodies, or body parts, were discovered buried in the Belanglo State Forest, near the NSW town of Berima. They were subsequently identified as those of seven missing Australian and overseas backpackers. Milat was tried and convicted for these serial killings in 1996, in a trial that took nearly four months to complete (Kennedy & Whittaker, 1998). The Milat investigation subsequently formed the basis of a television miniseries (Shine Australia, 2015) and was (in part) the inspiration for the feature film *Wolf Creek* (McLean, 2005). The case was significant not only for the horrific and repetitive nature of the crimes, and for suggestions (never proven) of involvement by other family members, but also for the attention it attracted overseas, given that a number of the victims were young international tourists to Australia.

The Trial of Phuong Ngo for Murder

In 2001, Phuong Ngo, a Vietnamese-borne Australian, was convicted of the 1998 murder of New South Wales politician John Newman, his political rival. Although Ngo did not carry out the killing himself, the jury accepted that the killing was organized and instigated by him (*R v. Ngo*, 2001). The conviction was achieved only after two mistrials and was widely publicized because of its political associations.

The Trial of Chew Seng Liew and Choon Tee Lim for Murder

Leading Australian cardiac surgeon and heart transplant pioneer Dr. Victor Chang was shot dead in 1991 during an attempt to extort money from him. Chew Seng Liew and Choon Tee Lim were both prosecuted and convicted in 1992 for his murder. This trial was newsworthy in part because of the high profile and popularity of the victim, and because the accused were foreign nationals.

The Trial of Kathleen Folbigg for Murder

Kathleen Folbigg was tried and convicted in 2003 for the murders of her four infant children between 1991 and 1999. The case against her was circumstantial, and she maintained the children had all died of natural causes. The case featured a great deal of scientific and medical evidence, both as to the possible causes of death of the children (including sudden infant death syndrome or "cot death") and as to the nature of Folbigg's psychological condition and motivations. The case has been analyzed in detail in a number of publications (Benns, 2003; Cunliffe, 2011). It is a good example of a case that might be likely to evoke significant prejudice among jury members and which required them to come to grips with conflicting and complex expert evidence.

The Trial of Sef Gonzales

Sef Gonzales, a 24-year-old student, was tried and convicted in 2004 for the murder of his parents and younger sister at the family home in Sydney in 2001. His actions were apparently motivated by greed and the threatened consequences of his parents' disapproval of his academic failure (*Gonzales v. R*, 2007; *R v. Gonzales*, 2004).

The Trial of Dr. Suman Sood

Abortion is illegal in New South Wales, unless a doctor finds on any "economic, social or medical ground or reason" that an abortion is required to avoid a "serious danger to the pregnant woman's life or to her physical or mental health" (*CES v. Superclinics ACES v. Superclinics Australia Pty Ltd*, 1995; *Crimes Act 1900* (NSW), ss82–84; *R v. Wald*, 1971). In 2006, Dr. Suman Sood was tried and convicted of two counts of performing an illegal abortion where she failed to enquire as to the existence of such a lawful reason (*R v. Sood*, 2006). The case attracted a considerable amount of media attention, partly because the issue of abortion on demand remains a controversial one in Australia, despite public opinion polls indicating that it attracts significant support.

The Trial of Gordon Wood

In 1995, model Caroline Byrne was found dead at the bottom of the cliffs at the Gap, Watson's Bay, in Sydney, a popular suicide spot. Wood, her boyfriend, was prosecuted for her murder in 2008 (*R v. Wood*, 2008). Expert evidence that the position in which Ms. Byrne landed indicated that she had been thrown, rather than jumped, was critical to the prosecution case. In 2012, the appeal court quashed Wood's conviction, casting doubt on that evidence and criticizing aspects of the way that the case was conducted (*R v. Wood*, 2012).

The Trial of Shirley Justins and Caren Jenning

Jennings was prosecuted in 2008 for manslaughter in relation to the death of Wylie, her long-term partner who was suffering from Alzheimer's disease and had lost decision-making capacity. The court found that his death had been brought about by the drug Nembutal, illegally imported into Australia by Jenning, a close friend (*R v. Shirley Justins*, 2008). The case illustrates the challenges that can arise in prosecuting individuals for acts that may appear merciful and attract sympathy from the jury, but are nevertheless illegal.

The Trial of Keli Lane

In 2010, Lane, a former Australian Olympic water polo representative, was tried and convicted for the murder of her baby, Tegan. The prosecution alleged that Tegan had been killed and disposed of by Lane in 1996 shortly after her birth; her body has never been found and the case against Lane rested entirely on circumstantial evidence. The trial, which lasted over four months, attracted significant media attention because of the mysterious nature of the crime, the extensive search conducted for the missing child during the investigation, and Lane's prominent sporting profile.

The Trial of Simon Gittany

In 2013, Simon Gittany was found guilty of the murder of his girlfriend, Lisa Harnum, by throwing her off the balcony of their 18th floor apartment building in central Sydney (*R v. Gittany*, 2013). The sensational nature of the facts attracted considerable interest from the public and the media, and the case highlighted the increasing use of social media to report on criminal trials.

Mark observes that entry to the Bar has become a lot more competitive over the years he has been in practice, not just in private practice, but also in the government sector. He observes, somewhat ruefully, that someone like him, who had no prosecution experience when he applied to become a Crown prosecutor, would not even be given an interview for such a position now.

He has declined several invitations to take on judicial appointments because he feels it would limit his ability, among other things, to pursue the sort of photography that involves taking candid shots of a variety of individuals and to write books about true crime stories. He views being a judge as a very isolating social experience, and doubts that he would be temperamentally suited to being confined to sitting and listening to the evidence. He comments: "I don't think I'd been a good judge because I'd want to hop down and do some of the advocacy, and I think I'd be impatient and irritable. I think I'm much better off being a counsel."

Along with the high profile, Mark has sustained his share of criticism, both from appeal courts and those he has prosecuted. However, it is clear, from our discussion, that though entering the prosecution service may have been a fortuitous career choice, rather than a carefully planned one, it has been very satisfying and a decision he says that he has never regretted.

Philosophy of Legal Advocacy

In Mark's view, the nature of the prosecution role in New South Wales has been very clearly established for a long time and has not really changed in nature over the time that he has been a prosecutor. While prosecution takes place within the context of an adversarial trial system, there are significant differences between the role of prosecution and that of defense. One of the major differences is that if, as a prosecutor, you do not believe that the evidence justifies a conviction you ought not to be put in a position where you are advocating that case in front of a jury. As a defense counsel, your belief in your client's guilt or innocence is irrelevant; you are obliged to do your best to defend your client. He sees it as one of the very good aspects of being a prosecutor that you do not have to put yourself in that rather invidious moral dilemma.

There has been a remarkable change in the oversight of prosecutorial decisions since 1983, when Mark became a prosecutor. At that time, Crown prosecutors reported to the Attorney-General, but the level of day-to-day involvement of the Attorney-General in the prosecutorial role was minimal and prosecutors had no obligations to consult in relation to decisions about matters such as pleas, plea negotiations, or sentence submissions. In 1986, the New South Wales Parliament enacted the *Director of Public Prosecutions Act* of 1986, which established the Office of the Director of Public Prosecutions (ODPP), headed by a DPP, as a separate authority responsible for the exercise of the prosecutorial function. The creation of the DPP was an attempt to enhance the independence of the prosecutorial function, and Mark views it as a success. In his opinion, it has lessened the risk of political interference in the prosecutorial function, by isolating the prosecution process from the political arena, as the DPP effectively acts as a buffer between prosecutors and politicians.

The establishment of the DPP has seen the establishment of published prosecution guidelines and extensive obligations to consult with victims, the police, and with the Director's Chambers. While that makes the job more involved, Mark believes that, overall, these changes have been good. While acknowledging that, in the past, not all his colleagues have shared this view, he sees victims and police as legitimate stakeholders in prosecution decisions and has always consulted with them. In his opinion, the prosecutor has to seriously consider their viewpoints, although they are not determinative. He also supports the requirement to consult with the Director on significant decisions, as providing prosecutors with additional assurance in terms of avoiding mistakes and being supported in difficult decisions.

He acknowledges the enormous pressure on the prosecutor, who in most trials is responsible for calling 90%–95% of the evidence. As he explains, being a prosecutor in a trial is a process of constant decision making and, in his view, to be a good prosecutor, you have to feel comfortable making decisions. Given the constant pressure, he acknowledges that it is difficult to get those decisions right all the time, commenting, "Look, if you get 98% of them right I think you're doing really well."

Prosecution of high-profile cases inevitably carries with it greater public attention and scrutiny of the way an advocate carries out their role. Mark has incurred his share of criticism, both from those he has prosecuted and, on occasion, from appeal courts. As a prosecutor, he is constrained from responding to those criticisms publicly, but must bear with the constant, and potentially distracting, presence of news media in the cases with which he deals. Another feature of the establishment of the DPP has been that the Director's office has become the liaison point between prosecution and news media. This has, in Mark's view, been beneficial in that it has alleviated the pressure on prosecutors of having to deal with those inquiries.

Mark has also seen an enormous expansion in the prosecution service, from approximately 30 prosecutors when he joined to over 95 at its peak, approximately five years ago (currently 82). He has also observed some significant changes in the nature of the work. One of these relates to the conduct of criminal trials, which have generally become much longer—by a factor of two or three—to the extent that it is now common to have a trial in the Supreme Court that takes 3–6 months.

On the topic of how difficult it is for prosecutors to relate to the living and social conditions of those from economically deprived backgrounds with whom they deal, Mark responds that he believes that to be a really good prosecutor, you have to be able to put yourself in the shoes of the accused and that it is really only possible to do that if you have contact with people from a wide variety of cultures and subcultures, and ethnic and financial backgrounds. He sees one of the great advantages of being a prosecutor, as opposed to being a judge, is that you can do a whole lot of other things that provide you with those experiences. One of the most striking features of his photography is the diversity of his human subject matter, which reveals an interest in individuals and their lives that spans a broad spectrum of society.

Successes and Problems Experienced

One major change to the criminal justice system in New South Wales during Mark's career has been the introduction of an option for an accused person to be tried by a judge alone (Criminal Law Legislation Amendment Act NSW, 1990, Sch 1). An order for trial by a judge alone can be made on the application of either the accused or the prosecution. The consent of the accused is required, but the court can override a prosecution objection to an order for trial by a judge alone if it is satisfied that it is in the interests of justice to do so. This option was introduced in 1990 in the face of concerns about the potential prejudice to an accused facing jury trial in cases that attracted high levels of pretrial publicity and dealt with particularly difficult subject matter.

Despite this reform, this highly experienced prosecutor is a great believer in the institution of trial by jury in criminal cases, which he describes as "the Rolls Royce of systems. It costs the most, but it's the best." His hope is that governments around Australia do everything they can to preserve it because he believes that jury decisions are generally more accepted by the community than outcomes of trial by judge alone. The reason for this, he believes, has to do with the way that the group dynamic operates to challenge the influence of factors that might influence the way individuals approach decision making. As he puts it:

> There's something about having a group of people that tends to soften the rough edges of each individual member of the jury, and, whether we're legally qualified or not, we all have our prejudices, we all have our preconceptions, we all have our bad experiences in life, which can influence us and if, if it's a trial by judge alone, there's nobody there to counteract those influences and say, "You must be joking! That's ridiculous!"

While he concedes that juries do not always get it right, in his experience, where they do make mistakes, those mistakes are almost invariably in favor of the accused. In a criminal justice system that operates on the presumption of innocence, that is the way that he believes it should be.

Mark also contends that most cases where there has been a travesty of justice that has resulted in a conviction have not been a failure of the jury system but a failure of some other part of the justice system, such as forensic science. He cites the conviction of Lindy Chamberlain for the murder of her daughter Azaria in 1980 as exemplifying his concerns about the potential influence of bogus forensic science being presented to a jury in a convincing way. (While the Chamberlain family was camping at Alice Springs in central Australia, Lindy alleged that the child had been taken by a dingo. The prosecution case relied heavily on forensic evidence that was later substantially discredited by a Royal Commission called to inquire into the case after new items of evidence were discovered six years later. Lindy was released from jail [after serving four years of a sentence of life imprisonment] and her conviction was overturned after the Commission released its findings [*Chamberlain v. The Queen* (No 2), 153 CLR 521 (1984); Government of the Northern Territory, 1987, pp. 310–321, 340–341; Vowles, 2010].)

He supports the introduction of majority jury verdicts in 2006 (Jury Act NSW, 1977, s 55F; Jury Amendment (Verdicts) Act NSW, 2006, Sch 1) as a good measure that has assisted in dealing with the reality that, as he puts it, "Your chances of getting one crazy person on a jury of 12 people randomly chosen

from the community are quite high." Changes introduced in 1997 that provided complete anonymity for jurors—giving them numbers instead of calling their names (Jury Act NSW, 1977, s 37; Jury Amendment Act NSW, 1997,
Sch 1)—have been a good reform that has obviated much of the risk of intimidation of jurors. This change was instituted after a juror with a distinctive
surname in a case that Mark prosecuted was identified through the phone
book and subjected to an attempt at intimidation. Another difficulty, that
of jurors dropping out during the course of long trials, was overcome by
amendments to the Jury Act in 2007 that allowed the empanelment of up
to 15 jurors in a long trial (Jury Act NSW, 1977, s 19(2); Jury Amendment
Act NSW, 2007, Sch 1). This is another reform that he believes has been very
worthwhile.

On being asked, Mark nominates the expansion in the length of criminal trials as one of the most significant problems facing the criminal justice
system in his state. He identifies two main causal factors: first, the enactment
of the Evidence Act NSW 1995, and second, a cultural change in terms of the
expectations of advocates.

He explains that, prior to the Evidence Act NSW 1995, the rules of
evidence laws were pretty well closely defined and well known, which made
it easy for both prosecution and defense to predict whether an item of evidence was likely to be admissible or not. That predictability was removed
by the Evidence Act NSW 1995, which introduced a number of judicial
discretions of varying kinds, so that even if evidence might be technically admissible, a judge still has a residual discretion to exclude it. As he
explains, these discretions were intended to overcome some of the limitations of the previous hard and fast rules that were thought not to make
sufficient allowance for justice in the individual case. However, the result
has been that all of these discretions have to be exercised, there is often
evidence to be called on the voir dire before the exercise of the discretion,
and then prosecution and defense have to make submissions in relation to
its exercise. Sometimes the judge will want to think about it and then the
judge will deliver a judgment, either extempore or sometimes reserved and
written, and all that takes time.

Mark has also observed a marked change in the expectations of appropriate advocacy on the part of judges, juries, clients, solicitors, and advocates
themselves, to a point where both defense and prosecution are expected to
explore in detail all possible aspects of a case, rather than focusing on the
issues that appear to be most relevant. Defense counsel will often range far
and wide in their cross-examinations of Crown witnesses in the hope of dis-
covering something, or getting an answer that is going to be favorable, and,
in his view, often for minimal return. Mark also makes the point that, in his
observation, defense counsel often lose the jury's attention when they stray
into areas of unnecessary detail:

When I see defense counsel going down every rabbit hole, which happens in many cases that I do, I look at the jury, and I think to myself, "You're bored out of your brain. You're not listening. Can't you see that, Mr. Defense Counsel, or Ms. Defense Counsel?" And often they don't; very often they're not aware of the fact that they've lost the jury.

On the prosecution side, delay has also been exacerbated by a growing belief on the part of prosecutors that one has to call the evidence about every single conceivable point that might provide some solid evidence against an accused, to "go down every rabbit hole." As a result, he believes that counsel in criminal trials go into much more detail and, as consequence, cases have become much longer. He gives as an example the case that he is currently prosecuting, which he estimates will take approximately 6–7 months to complete, but, if it had been heard in the early 1960s, would probably have taken only 3–4 weeks. He does not see this resulting in better justice, in terms of trial outcomes, and he is concerned about the cost to the community, both in financial terms, and in its impact on the waiting list for criminal trials.

In association with this development, he has observed that there are fewer trials being done by the public defenders as a percentage of trials, because there are only 25 or 26 public defenders and they are responsible for most of the defense appellate work. Mark clearly has great respect for public defenders, whom he describes as generally highly skilled, highly professional criminal law barristers who have no incentive to string out a trial and want to focus on the real issues. He believes that approach is not shared by all barristers at the private defense Bar and does not believe that there has been any satisfactory way that has been dealt with in New South Wales, as yet. Mark observes that very few judges are willing to take on counsel on either side and challenge them to substantiate the point of their questioning. He attributes this reluctance partly to a fear by trial judges of being overruled on appeal, but also notes that the provision in the *Evidence Act* that allows a judge to curtail cross-examination is inadequate for this purpose. (First, the provision applies only to individual questions, so that a judge would have to individually disallow each question. Second, questions can only be allowed on the grounds that the question is "unduly annoying, harassing, intimidating, offensive, oppressive, humiliating or repetitive." It is not a ground that the potential value to the cross-examiner is so slight that it is not worthwhile allowing the cross-examiner to pursue it [Evidence Act NSW, 1995, s 41(1)(b)].)

Hand in hand with the issue of lengthy trials, he also identifies court delays in New South Wales as a significant problem. At the time we speak, the wait for a District Court trial in New South Wales is more than a year, and it is at least a six-month wait for a Supreme Court trial. While waiting periods tend to wax and wane, Mark expresses concerns that currently the delays are getting longer. He is also concerned about the delay between conviction and appeal, which is generally about a year or more in New South Wales, a period he describes as much too long. This is also occurring at a time of government fiscal austerity when courts and prosecution services all have to manage with limited resources. He notes that Legal Aid New South Wales has probably suffered more than the courts and the prosecution service, a significant concern, given that the whole system depends upon legal aid being available in appropriate cases. The decision of the High Court of Australia in *Dietrich v. R* (1992) established that while there is no right under Australian law for an accused to be provided with counsel at public expense, a court has the power to stay or adjourn a trial where an accused is unrepresented and where representation is essential to a fair trial, as it is in most cases in which an accused is charged with a serious offense.

Mark acknowledges that the tendency to longer trials has also been exacerbated to some extent by increasing expectations by jurors about the availability of scientific evidence, the so-called "CSI factor." If you do not have some DNA evidence or fingerprint evidence or some sort of forensic science, juries think, "Oh what's the matter? Why haven't you?" He gives, as an example, the case he is currently prosecuting, which has eight different categories of forensic evidence, including DNA, blood spatter, fingerprints, shoe prints, forensic pathology, rope transfers, and forensic locksmith evidence. He describes how, as forensic science has become more complex and more common, it has become much more of a burden, particularly for the Crown, because, as he puts it, "If the jury does not understand the forensic evidence it may as well not have been called." Despite those concerns, Mark remains confident in the ability of juries to deal appropriately with forensic evidence when it is explained to them properly. He sees it as depending upon the skill of counsel to be able to digest the scientific material and to present it to a jury in a way that they will understand and remember. Part of what he describes as the incredible challenge of being a Crown prosecutor is to make complex evidence understandable and interesting, and to present it in a way that engages the jury. He also sees it as a responsibility of the judge to insist that the evidence is given in a way that the jury will understand.

The issue of social media and its influence on jury trials has emerged as a problem over the past few years. As Mark sees it, the main difficulty with social media, and with the Internet generally, is the potential for jurors to find out prejudicial information about an accused, a victim, a police officer, a witness, or anybody associated with a trial. While the law in New South Wales now requires them to be told that they cannot do that and that it is a breach of the law if they do, he believes that there is still that risk there that jurors will look up information on the Internet, particularly about an accused. If an accused has a prior history that has been reported in the media and there is information on the Internet about it, he believes it may be very difficult to ever know whether a juror has accessed that information and whether it has influenced their decision.

Mark believes that, in general, jurors take their oaths and directions from judges very seriously. In particular, he believes that they take very seriously the admonition that when they come to make their decision, that it has to be based on what is said in open court because the parties have a right to challenge the evidence, and to put it in its proper context, so that they should disregard anything that they might read outside the courtroom. However, he suspects that some jurors may view accessing the Internet as somehow different, and that while you can explain to them that the reasons why they should make a decision based only upon what they hear in court, he thinks that there are sometimes going to be jurors who feel that they should be able to do what they wish to in terms of searching the Internet in the privacy of their own home.

He also believes that, in general, jurors take very seriously the explanation that they should not go and conduct their own view of a scene associated with the case, or conduct their own experiments about matters to do with the case. He acknowledges some cases in the past in New South Wales where jurors have disobeyed that direction and have gone and looked at scenes of a crime on their own (*R v. Wood*, 2008); he believes that those have been situations where jurors have genuinely not realized that is an infringement of the judge's direction, and that, in all honesty, they have not appreciated that it is not a proper thing to do.

Theory and Practice

Dealing on a day-to-day basis with the preparation and conduct of criminal trials allows relatively little time for busy advocates to engage with aspects of legal theory that do not have immediate relevance to their work. Our discussion indicates Mark's awareness of broader debates about the criminal justice system—the influence of the therapeutic jurisprudence movement, for example, which has made a significant impact on the Australian criminal justice system in recent decades. Mark's view is that the New South Wales Drug Court has been a resounding success and is a very efficient way of dealing with drug-related crime.

During the past 10–15 years, there has been a great deal of focus in the Australian criminal justice system on facilitating the participation of vulnerable victims of crime in criminal cases, principally child and adult victims of sexual assault. Mark is supportive of the protections that have been introduced for victims, particularly sexual assault victims. These include measures to allow their evidence to be taken by video link or closed circuit television (CCTV) to spare them the ordeal of facing their attacker in the courtroom. While as a prosecutor he says one would prefer to have the victim in court, he endorses the need to take account of the victim's sensitivities and give precedence to their interests. He notes variation in the quality of the technology (CCTV generally providing a superior experience to videoconferencing), but in his experience, where the quality of the technology is good, it generally works well. However, when asked about its use for cross-examination, he comments that attempting to cross-examine by video link "lacks something. It's like having a Perspex wall between you and the witness. It's hard to exert the same sort of emphasis in your questions. You know, sometimes it's not just what you say, but the way you say it, and the way you're standing and the way you're looking, and all of that adds to the strength of your questioning. It's not quite the same over CCTV."

Mark also believes there would be great benefit in investigating the use of intermediaries to assist vulnerable participants to give evidence. A UK legislation makes provision for the use of registered intermediaries to assist witnesses who are deemed to be vulnerable on the grounds of age or incapacity, and where a court is satisfied that the quality of evidence given by the witness is likely to be diminished by reason of fear or distress (Youth Justice and Criminal Evidence Act UK, 1999, ss 16, 17). The latter category can include consideration of issues related to the witness's social and cultural background, ethnic origins, domestic and employment circumstances, religious beliefs, political opinions, as well as any behavior directed toward the witness by the accused, the accused's family or associates, and other relevant persons (Youth Justice and Criminal Evidence Act UK, 1999, ss 17(c), (d)). Where such a "special measures" direction is made, in effect, the examination and cross-examination of the vulnerable witness is conducted through the intermediary whose function

> is to communicate to the vulnerable witness, questions put to the witness, and to any persons asking such questions, the answers given by the witness in reply to them, and to explain such questions or answers so far as necessary to enable them to be understood by the witness or person in question. (Youth Justice and Criminal Evidence Act UK, 1999, ss 29(2))

The intermediary sits in court with the witness and alerts the judge if the person is experiencing any difficulties receiving communication or producing communication (Ministry of Justice, 2012, p. 13). An intermediary can also be used to provide the court with independent assessment of communication difficulties of the witness for the purposes of considering whether a special measures order should be made (Ministry of Justice, 2012, pp. 11–13). Intermediaries are not currently used in any Australian court, although a 2007 evaluation of their role in the United Kingdom was generally positive (Plotnikoff & Woolfson, 2007). Some recent Australian research has identified a preference on the part of relevant stakeholders to strengthen existing methods of providing support to vulnerable witnesses and complainants (Powell, Bowden, & Mattison, 2014).

Mark suggests that intermediaries could also be used to address communication difficulties arising from cultural, rather than language, factors and makes particular mention of the work of Eades (2010, 2013) and others in identifying the way that indigenous witnesses can be disadvantaged in this respect. While the UK legislation allows for the use of intermediaries for this purpose, there appears to be little data on the extent to which this is occurring and its effectiveness, an aspect which would certainly appear to warrant further investigation.

Similarly, the issue that Mark identifies as the influence of changing advocacy styles on the conduct and length of criminal trials appears to warrant further research. Case management has a long history in both Australian and U.S. courts, and there is extensive literature outlining the techniques that courts can employ to manage lists and assist the parties to focus on the issues prior to, and in the course of, the trial (see Steelman, Geordt, & McMillan, 2000). Despite this, Mark's concerns suggest that there may be additional obstacles to effective case management in criminal trials that warrant further research.

Transnational Relations

As a prosecutor in an Australian state jurisdiction, you would expect developments outside of Australia to have exerted relatively little direct influence on Mark's work. For example, there is no Bill of Rights in either the New South Wales or the Commonwealth Constitution, so that there is little scope for the importation of arguments based on international law into domestic criminal cases. However, as noted above, a number of cases he has prosecuted have attracted international attention for a variety of reasons.

It is also clear as our interview progresses that Mark has an interest in and an awareness of developments overseas. He has also undertaken a number of assignments outside of his domestic prosecutorial functions that have involved him in working in the Asia-Pacific region. These include his appointment as counsel assisting the New South Wales Coroner in a 2007 inquest into the deaths of five Australian journalists at Balibo in East Timor, who were found to have been killed by Indonesian special forces soldiers (Pinch, 2007). He also was seconded from the ODPP to prosecute the trials of a number of senior Fijian politicians for offenses arising out of the 2000 coup d'état by George Speight (see Lal, 2006). The first was in 2004, when he conducted the prosecution of the Vice President of Fiji and four other prominent leaders, including the Deputy Speaker of the House of Representatives, a government minister, and two other prominent citizens, who were charged with taking treasonous oaths of office as President and rebel ministers during the coup. Four of them were convicted and Mark returned to Fiji on their appeals, where the convictions were confirmed. In

2006, he conducted the prosecution of former prime minister and military commander Major General Sitiveni Rabuka on charges of inciting a mutiny soon after the 2000 coup. Rabuka was acquitted, and the trial was complicated by the fact that it took place during the 2006 military takeover by Commodore Bainimarama.

Mark has not observed any effects on his work of any developments arising out of the terrorist attacks in the United States on September 11, 2001. This is perhaps not surprising, as terrorism trials in Australia would largely be a matter for Commonwealth, rather than State, prosecution. Similarly, he has not experienced increased concerns about security in courts. He feels blessed that Australia does not have the same heightened levels of security situation that they have, for example, in the United States, around courts and public buildings. He hopes that will continue and that there will not be some terrible event that causes us to become hypersensitive to security.

General Assessments

It is clear from our discussion that Mark's most pressing concern about developments in criminal procedure in his jurisdiction relate to the time taken for jury trials. He is concerned about the imposition of asking members of a jury to give up their lives for significant periods of time and believes that there has to be a more efficient way of doing running jury trials that saves time on both sides and ensures that criminal trials focus on the real, substantive issues and the really important evidence.

He would like to see trial judges take more control and curtail cross-examination where counsel are exploring esoteric areas that appear unlikely to amount to anything of significance to the issues in the case and to encourage them to focus on the real issues. He notes that in some States in the United States, the courts place time limits on both counsel, in examination-in-chief, in cross-examination and in addresses, and suggests that is something that might be worth investigating as a solution in New South Wales. He also supports the idea of good advocacy training that encourages advocates to focus on the essence of their case.

An issue that he identifies as remaining to be dealt with are the provisions in the Jury Act that, in effect, require anybody who has a criminal record to disqualify themselves from jury service (Jury Act NSW, 1977, ss 6, 14, Sch 1). He suspects, very strongly, that there are many people who do not disqualify themselves as required and is concerned that there appears to be no effective measure to enforce that obligation.

Despite Mark's support for the jury system, he does not support the idea of involving jurors in sentencing decisions. He believes that would result in too much variation in penalties and that jurors would be more susceptible to making sentencing decisions on the grounds of emotion.

He is concerned that there is still a problem with the defense being able to access counseling records of victims in sexual assault trials. The current situation is that defense counsel can make an application for access to such records, and the judge does a weighing exercise, which in essence requires them to balance the probative value of the records against the public interest in preserving confidentiality (*Criminal Procedure Act* [NSW], 1986, Chapter 6 Pt 5 Div 2). Because this is determined on a case by case basis, sometimes access is given, sometimes it is not. Mark's view is that victims should be able to have counseling in the knowledge that those notes will never be accessible to anybody and should never be disclosed.

Conclusions

As one might expect, the interview with Mark Tedeschi centered mainly on issues of immediate and practical concern to prosecutors. Mark's responses to questions in the topic areas were thoughtful, but open and candid. Despite having some strong criticisms to make, he was careful not to attribute responsibilities for deficiencies in the operation of the process in a one-sided fashion.

Much of Mark's thinking is focused on the need for the effective and efficient operation of the criminal justice system. Underlying that core issue is a strong emphasis on the importance of access to the criminal justice system. Rather than seeing efficiency as a desirable goal in its own right, Mark's concerns center on the impact of lengthy delays on victims, witnesses, jurors, and defendants. The value of the institution of trial by jury was also a constant theme during our discussions, and it is clear that his experience has led him to believe that this is an institution that should be protected and nurtured.

Reflecting on his career, Mark states that it never occurred to him, as a law student, that he might become a prosecutor. He says he counts himself as "extremely blessed" in terms of the way that his career has turned out.

His success in pursuing his photography and writing also illustrates the way in which an individual with strong creative capacity has been able to nurture and develop that aspect of their life in association with their legal career. It is clear that the ability to do that is something he values highly, and it has perhaps contributed to ensuring he has the type of balance in his life that has enabled him to continue in such a demanding legal role for a long time.

Mark's legacy as a prosecutor will be written within the law reports, media articles, and books that have, and will in the future, chronicle the cases he has been involved in. He has perhaps not yet experienced the type of detailed analysis of his trial work that he was able to write in *Eugenia*, but that may come in the future. His documentation of the personalities and lives of those he has photographed will leave a legacy of a different kind, no less important, but one where the analysis and commentary will be left largely to the viewer.

Glossary

appeal: an appeal is an application to review the decision made in a case if one or more parties is dissatisfied with the outcome. In New South Wales, a person convicted of a criminal offense has a right of appeal in relation to conviction and sentence; the Crown has a right of appeal only in relation to the sentence. There is legislation governing the grounds that must be made out before an appeal can be upheld. Appeals from criminal trials are heard by the Court of Criminal Appeal.

Attorney-general: in countries like Australia, where the legal systems derive from common law, this is the title generally given to the minister in the executive branch of government who has responsibility for legal affairs and law enforcement. Traditionally, the Attorney-General was also the principal legal advisor to the government, although in modern day practice, it varies.

Bar: a collective noun used to refer to those lawyers who practice law as advocates in court (i.e. barristers) that is "at the bar." Originally, this refers to the "bar" or railing that separated the area of the courtroom where the public or observers sat from the area occupied by the advocates.

barrister: a lawyer who works as an advocate. Barristers are "briefed" or engaged by solicitors on behalf of clients, rather than approached directly by clients.

counsel: a generic term that can encompass any lawyer, but more commonly used to refer to an advocate.

Crown: refers to the representative of the State or the government, especially in relation to the prosecution or punishment of crime, hence usually the lawyer for the prosecution or "Crown prosecutor" (see below).

Crown witness: witness called on behalf of the prosecution.

Crown prosecutors: barristers who appear in court and perform other related functions related to prosecution matters on behalf of the New South Wales Director of Public Prosecutions (DPP). They are appointed under the *Crown Prosecutor's Act 1986* (NSW).

Director of Public Prosecutions: a statutory position created under the Director of Public Prosecutions Act NSW (1986). The director's functions are to prosecute criminal cases on behalf of the State and to deal with prosecution appeals.

District Court: the mid-level (or intermediate) court in New South Wales that deals with most of the serious criminal cases (other than treason, murder, or manslaughter). These cases are usually heard by a judge and a jury, but in some circumstances may be heard by judge alone (see definition below).

ex tempore: latin for "at the time," used to denote a decision delivered in court contemporaneously with the legal argument.

jury: a group of people (usually 12) who are tasked with giving a verdict in a case, based on the evidence that has been presented to them in the courtroom.

juror: person who serves on a jury.

judge alone trial: a judge sitting without a jury.

Legal Aid New South Wales: a government organization that provides advice, representation, and assistance to meet the legal needs of socially and economically disadvantaged people.

Office of the Director of Public Prosecutions: the office, created under the Director of Public Prosecutions Act NSW (1986), that supports the functions of the Director of Public Prosecutions and serves as the independent prosecuting authority for the State of New South Wales.

public defenders: salaried barristers appointed under the Public Defenders Act NSW (1995) who advise on and appear in serious criminal matters for clients who have been granted legal aid.

Queen's counsel (QC): a senior barrister who is considered to have achieved a high standing in terms of their professional expertise and reputation. QCs are appointed by the Crown and are known colloquially as "silks" because their robes include a gown made of silk.

sentencing: the process of determining and imposing penalties on persons convicted of criminal offenses.

solicitor: a lawyer who primarily undertakes advising and non-advocacy work, although in New South Wales, solicitors may also undertake advocacy in lower courts, such as the Local Court and some matters in the District Court, and appears before tribunals. Solicitors are engaged directly by the client.

Supreme Court of New South Wales: the highest court in New South Wales that deals with the most serious criminal cases (murder and manslaughter, major conspiracy, and serious drug matters). These cases are usually heard by a judge and a jury, but in some circumstances, may be heard by judge alone.

voir dire: literally "to speak the truth" (French). A smaller hearing held within a trial to determine the admissibility of evidence that is contested. In some jurisdictions, a voir dire can also be used to determine the eligibility of prospective jurors.

Belgium

3

NIK KIEFER

Contents

The Criminal Justice Process of Belgium

In terms of the fundamental distinction between common law countries where the system of law is based on judicial decisions and custom (e.g., the United Kingdom), and civil or continental law countries where the system of law derived from or was influenced by Roman law (e.g., Belgium), the current Belgian criminal justice system is best described as a hybrid system with mixed inquisitorial and accusatory features.

Typical of accusatory procedures is the horizontal structure in which the prosecution and the defense are on equal footing and have equality of arms. The suspect is not the object of the investigation but a full party to the procedure. Another defining feature is the comparatively passive nature of the judge whose task mainly consists of supervising the procedures and ensuring that the parties play by the rules.

Inquisitorial legal procedures are the opposite of those in an accusatorial justice system because of the vertical structure in which the government takes the lead and decides most of the procedures that are followed. The judge in an inquisitorial procedure has a more active role to play because his task is to uncover the truth. Although these days, pure inquisitorial justice systems are nowhere to be found, the legal procedures of many Western European countries, among which Belgium is included, still contain various inquisitorial features.

In line with the predominately inquisitorial nature of the Belgian criminal justice system, a pretrial fact-finding phase called the preliminary investigation or "vooronderzoek" precedes the appearance of the accused before the judge. This is a pretrial investigation to ascertain whether sufficient indicators of guilt can be found with regard to a particular suspect. In the Belgian system, this pretrial investigation can take one of two prescribed forms: a pretrial prosecutorial investigation is one conducted under the leadership and guidance of the Crown prosecutor, a public prosecutor (opsporingsonderzoek).

A pretrial judicial investigation is one conducted under the leadership and guidance of an examining magistrate (gerechtelijk onderzoek). Aside from the identity of the person leading the investigation, the main difference between these two types of fact-finding investigations is the fact that investigatory measures which have an impact on the fundamental rights and freedoms of the accused must be ordered by an investigative judge, and therefore, in theory, are not feasible during a prosecutor-led criminal investigation. In practice, however, it is possible for the public prosecutor to ask an investigative judge to issue a "mini-instruction" for action to be taken that might negatively impact fundamental rights and freedoms of the suspect. Certain investigative measures, however, such as a home search, are permitted only within the framework of a judicial investigation and therefore cannot be ordered by an investigative judge as part of a mini-instruction.

After this preparatory phase which is characterized by its inquisitorial nature, a second phase takes place in court before a judge. This phase is more accusatorial in nature, because the procedure itself is public, oral, and adversarial, in contrast to the investigation preceding the trial which is secret, written, and non-adversarial.

The court that has jurisdiction to adjudicate the merits of the case is dependent on the potential sentence for the crime prescribed by the law. A threefold distinction between crimes is based on the gravity or severity of the criminal misconduct. The lowest level of criminal conduct comprises minor infractions or transgressions (overtredingen) (such as public drunkenness); more serious but intermediate levels of offending comprise misdemeanors, (wanbedrijven); and the most serious offenses are crimes (misdaden), such as rape and murder. In correlation with this threefold distinction, three types of courts adjudicate these crimes.

The Police Courts have jurisdiction over minor infractions and traffic violations. For these more minor violations under the Belgian criminal code, punishment ranges from imprisonment from one to seven days, or a monetary fine of € 1–25 (currently multipliable by 6) and community service of 20–45 hours. The criterion used to distinguish between crimes is quantitative.

The Correctional Courts have jurisdiction over misdemeanors. In certain mitigating circumstances, however, it is also possible for a Police Court to adjudicate a misdemeanor and for a Correctional Court to adjudicate a crime. The Correctional Courts deal with most criminal cases in the Belgian judicial system. The majority of cases heard are misdemeanors, which are also the most common crimes committed. This court can preside over crimes where there are mitigating circumstances, which would normally be heard in the Court of Assizes.

The Court of Assizes has jurisdiction over other more serious crimes (misdaad) that in the Belgian criminal code are punishable by imprisonment of minimum five years and maximum of life imprisonment, and by monetary fines of €26 and above (multiplied by 6).

In the event that an appeal is lodged against a decision issued by a Police Court, the case will be brought before a Correctional Court and when an appeal is lodged against a decision of a Correctional Court, the case is brought before a Court of Appeal. No appeal is possible against the decisions of the Court of Assizes except for an appeal in cassation heard by the Court of Cassation. This court, however, does not rule on the merits of the case, and will examine only whether the law was appropriately interpreted and applied in a given case. An appeal before the Court of Cassation can be lodged against the appeal decisions of a Correctional Court and against the decisions of a Court of Appeal.

In the first instance, criminal cases are tried before either a Police Court or a Correctional Court in the case of more serious crimes. The decisions of a Police Court can be appealed before a Correctional Court and decisions of a Correctional Court can be appealed before a Court of Appeal. Once a decision is rendered in last instance by either a Correctional Court or Court of Appeal, a final appeal can be brought before the Court of Cassation (Figure 3.1).

As can be seen in Figure 3.1, the Belgian courts and tribunals are organized in a strict hierarchical structure. At the top of this pyramid is the Court of Cassation. This Belgian Supreme Court rules only on the legal merits of a case and not the facts, and has the power to repeal any judgment rendered by a lower court in last instance, namely those rendered by a Court of Appeal against the decision of a Correctional Court and by a Correctional Court against the decision of a Police Court.

Immediately below the Court of Cassation, there is the threefold distinction between the Courts of Appeal, the Labor Tribunals, and the Courts of Assizes. The Labor Tribunals are concerned with judgments rendered in first instance by the Labor Courts. The Courts of Appeal have criminal Chamber of Counsel which review the judgments of the Correctional Courts. The Courts of Assizes are a nonpermanent criminal court in Belgium which is only convened for the worst crimes under the Belgian Criminal Code. In this

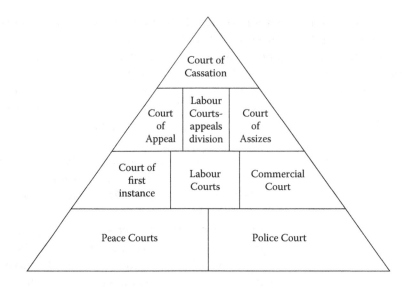

Figure 3.1 Overview of the Belgian courts.

court, questions of the accused's guilt are determined by a jury of the suspect's peers, namely ordinary lay citizens. The use of a criminal jury is exceptional in the Belgian criminal justice system as no other criminal courts rely on juries.

The third level in the pyramid is that where Tribunals of First Impression, the Labor Courts, and the Commercial Courts are situated. The Tribunals of First Impression can sit in a criminal or civil formation effectively forming either a Correctional Court or a Civil Court. The Correctional Court is the most important criminal court in Belgium as it deals with the vast majority of criminal cases. At the base of the pyramid are the Peace Courts that deal with minor civil cases and the Police Courts that deal with minor criminal infractions and traffic violations.

Raf Verstraeten, Attorney and Professor of Criminal Law, Leuven

Introduction

Raf Verstraeten is a leading Belgian criminal defense attorney. He specializes in white-collar criminal law including economic, fiscal, financial, and social criminal law, and also in cassation files, which deal only with legal (not factual) questions with regard to general issues of criminal law or criminal procedure. He is currently one of the founding partners (together with Dirk Dewandeleer and Benjamin Gillard) of the Leuven-based law firm *VDG Attorneys*. In addition to his activities at the Leuven Bar, he holds the position of Professor in Criminal Law, Criminal Procedure and White-Collar Criminal Law at the Catholic University of Leuven.

It was a great honor for me as an interviewer to have the opportunity to obtain his views on many current legal issues and the evolution of the Belgian criminal justice system. His position as both a practitioner and an academic makes him particularly well-suited for this book as he is able to tackle topics from both points of view, offering the reader dual perspectives on many contemporary Belgian criminal justice issues.

Career

After graduating from the Catholic University of Leuven in 1983, Raf Verstraeten registered himself at the Brussels Bar as a trainee lawyer with the law firm which was then called *Simont, Gutt et Simont*. It is important to mention that before a lawyer can qualify as a legal practitioner in Belgium, he or she must complete a three-year traineeship under the supervision of an experienced lawyer. One year into his legal traineeship, however, Raf Verstraeten chose to pause for an additional year of studies in Paris at the Panthéon-Assas University (Paris II) to obtain what was then called a Diploma of Advanced Studies in Theory and Practice of Criminal Law. Afterward, he resumed and completed his legal traineeship with *Simont, Gutt et Simont* in conjunction with his work as academic assistant at the Catholic University of Leuven.

In 1989, he earned the title of Doctor of Laws at the Catholic University of Leuven with a dissertation on the position of the victim in the framework of criminal procedure. He completed this during his traineeship with *Simont, Gutt et Simont* by reducing his traineeship to a limited type of legal advocacy which was focused on cassation files. This was possible because he had the privilege to do his legal traineeship with two lawyers who appeared before the Court of Cassation, namely Lucien Simont and Ludovic De Gryse. The files which he worked on offered him the advantage of combining his practical work as a lawyer with the preparation of a doctoral dissertation. In essence, Raf Verstraeten chose to limit his activities as a lawyer to concurrently complete his doctorate.

During the same year, he was appointed *docent* at the Catholic University of Leuven as the successor of Professor Raoul Declercq. A few years later, he was appointed as full professor. In essence, he has always combined and balanced his academic work with his work at the bar, an endeavor which he personally describes as "a permanent challenge."

Currently, Raf Verstraeten is an active attorney with a focus on cassation files and white-collar criminal law, and a professor of criminal law, criminal procedure law, and white-collar criminal law at the Catholic University of Leuven. Over the years, he has developed a significant practice specializing in white-collar crime.

In 2014, Verstraeten established a new law firm called *VDG Attorneys* together with Dirk Dewandeleer and Benjamin Gillard, two colleagues who were partners at *Eubelius* and also specialists in white-collar criminal law. *VDG Attorneys* is aptly named after its three main partners, Verstraeten, Dewandeleer, and Gillard. When asked what white-collar criminal law entails, Raf Verstraeten responded:

> White-collar criminal law can be seen as a branch of criminal law which is mainly relevant to businesses life, and can range from fiscal, financial, economic, and environmental to social issues. Commonly, white-collar criminal law deals with the reality that companies may be criminally liable or are the victims in a specific case. Raf Verstraeten together with his partners in *VDG Attorneys*, made a conscious choice to focus on cases which do not entail violent crime, sexual offenses or drug-related crimes. One exception in this regard, however, in which case I do work on those types of matters, is if it is from the purely juridical point of view specific to cassation.

Raf Verstraeten added that the law firm's focus is not a value judgment about the importance of financial over more common types of criminal cases.

> It is purely a question of which subject matter suits me best. As a law firm specializing in white-collar criminal law, we have a certain type of distinction. For us to be good at our work, bearing in mind that legal advocacy is very labor intensive, digging deep into a subject area and limiting ourselves to a specific area offers specific benefits. Considering that it is not possible to focus on everything and still achieve the required standards, it is necessary to make choices.

Specialization contributes substantially to the quality of the attorney's work product:

In Belgium alone, looking at the developments within the field of financial criminal law and taking into account the sheer magnitude of the files we deal with, it is clear that legal advocacy in this field is time-consuming and labor intensive. Consequently, it is important from a quantitative point of view to confine yourself to cases you are personally good at as a lawyer in order to find the right balance.

Philosophy of Legal Advocacy

When asked what motivated him to become a lawyer specialized in white-collar crime, Raf Verstraeten responded:

Traditionally, criminal law is considered as a person-oriented field of law. Because the financial and economic sectors have become more and more inundated with criminal law regulations and because criminal law is used more frequently as an enforcement tool in a fiscal, economic and social context, not only individuals but also corporations have become involved in criminal cases, either as victims, suspects or alleged perpetrators. This evolution towards punishment of the financial and economic sector has led to the realization by companies that criminal law really is a part of their daily concern. As a result, the questions we receive from corporations have increased exponentially. On May 4, 1999, the introduction in Belgium of the criminal responsibility of legal persons increased awareness of the importance of criminal law to individuals and businesses alike. In this respect, the choice of white-collar criminal law as an area of specialization seems to have been a good choice, and one that I have never regretted.

On the question whether his academic background as a university professor has had an influence on his choice to specialize in white-collar criminal law considering its inherent relation with other fields such as accounting, economics, and social law, he answered:

Without rendering a value judgment, it is true that I feel more attracted to and more challenged by this type of problem, which of necessity combines financial and economic expertise and the application of principles of criminal law. As an attorney, you deal with people who never imagined they would ever come into contact with criminal law. The fact that this does happen, through the application of financial and economic criminal law, can disconcert and even disorient these people, who then need guidance through the criminal justice process. Moreover, criminal law is not purely technical; it also involves an important strategic component, in the sense of how I approach criminal procedures in order to obtain the best results for my client. This combination of factors, namely the psychological, the strategic and the technical aspects, makes my job one of the most interesting jobs.

Based on this, I asked Raf Verstraeten if the psychological aspects of legal practice are an important aspect of his work, which he confirmed. He added:

> If you take your job seriously and you try to support people mentally, this will provide a lot of satisfaction, because you have the opportunity to support people involved in difficult criminal procedures which they can't avoid whether they are victims, suspects or defendants.

Raf Verstraeten did add the caveat, however, that "a lawyer cannot pretend to be scientifically versed in helping people psychologically because a jurist is not trained in this regard."

Nonetheless, lawyers who work primarily on criminal cases gather a certain amount of experience.

> This experience, which leads to a certain understanding of how you can guide people in the best way through a criminal procedure, is an important part of the job and can range from taking the time to explain to a client how a criminal procedure works, and what are the next steps, to preparing a client for interrogation, especially if that client is a suspect. Since the development of the Salduz jurisprudence of the European Court of Human Rights defense attorneys in Belgium have started to play a bigger role in providing assistance to their clients in the framework of interrogations. As an attorney, you learn how police officers do their work when they prepare to interrogate your client. This allows the attorney to offer certain advice to the client before the interrogation, which does not mean that the attorney tells his client what he or she should or should not say. Rather, the attorney tries to ensure that by providing the client with specific guidance, those things the client has to say are said in the best way possible.

When asked what he considers to be a well-functioning criminal justice system, Raf Verstraeten answered:

> That is a complex question. A well-functioning criminal justice system must try to link quality and a certain degree of speed, which is exceptionally difficult because quality requires thoroughness and thoroughness requires time. In a world in which fraud (such as tax fraud, economic fraud, and social fraud) is present to a large extent, the judicial system must carefully select cases for prosecution. It is an enormous challenge to know which cases to prosecute and which to drop when resources are scarce or because the case can be dealt with through an administrative procedure.

What Raf Verstraeten is referring to is a procedure whereby a Crown prosecutor will drop a case on technical grounds (e.g., no suspect can be found) or policy reasons (e.g., guidelines from the Minister of Justice). Raf Verstraeten further elaborated this point:

> A healthy policy with guidelines on when to drop a case and when to pursue it is essential for a well-functioning criminal justice system. In a way, this is a

frustrating idea because simply dropping a certain number of cases is always unpleasant. Nonetheless, to properly handle cases in which prosecution proceeds, one has to choose. In that sense, Belgium is a problematic country because the prosecution can be hindered at any moment by a victim compensation claim, a declaration of a civil claim filed by a crime victim, which is very taxing on the criminal justice system. An important policy question for Belgium is whether we want to retain this system, which allows individual initiatives to intercede.

A second challenge is securing well-trained magistrates. In the last decade, significant progress was achieved on this topic. Compared to before, magistrates are a lot more prepared for their work by the training provided at the magistrates' school. Time management remains a serious problem. Belgium struggles to manage the volume of cases which in turn has repercussions on the amount of time it takes to process cases and on compliance with the requirement of providing a hearing within a reasonable time pursuant to article 6 of the European Convention on Human Rights. There is room for improvement in this regard.

Actually I would like to add another two aspects, namely the necessity not only of a good training for the magistracy, which will lead to good magistrates, but also training for police. After all, the police investigate criminal cases on the ground, and in that regard, the proper management of a financial and economic investigative service is essential. In fact, this is a quite hot topic right now. One way or the other, the expertise of the fiscal, social and economic administration has to be harmonized with traditional police and prosecution services. In my practice this is of crucial importance. If one does not succeed in structuring and managing the police properly, the investigation and prosecution of white-collar crime will remain problematic. In my opinion, insufficient attention has been paid to resolve this problem. There is certainly room for improvement in this regard.

The second point I would like to add is closely correlated to the aspect of time which I mentioned before. Belgium needs a thorough evaluation of its criminal procedure law in general. The current Minister of Justice is calling for examination of and possible rationalization and acceleration of the criminal procedure. The big challenge in this regard is to meet the call for rationalization and acceleration without compromising the rights of the accused. Nowadays we live in a climate in which everyone is demanding more speed and efficiency but efficiency, no matter how well I understand it, must never be prioritized at the expense of the essential safeguards, and therefore, a balance needs to be struck.

Before continuing, it is important to explain that Belgium's Minister of Justice, Koen Geens, has launched a plan that may fundamentally alter the Belgian criminal justice field. I asked Raf Verstraeten his thoughts about this justice plan and if he expected the proposals to contribute to an improved criminal justice system. Raf Verstraeten responded as follows:

Yes, although the correct balance I mentioned earlier (between speed/efficiency and procedural safeguards for the accused) will have to be found. Nonetheless, it is a very healthy and very ambitious plan. Compared to the ideas of the predecessors, one has to admit this plan is, in the broad strokes at least, very well developed and consists of a good projection of the difficult context in which criminal law and criminal procedure law exist. There are a few very important courses of action which he proposes. Two closely related examples are the place of the investigative judge in our criminal justice system and the question whether or not the Chamber of Counsel must continue to exist as an intermediary agent. These questions are closely related because if you remove the investigative judge from his current function, in which he is the nerve center of the judicial investigation and he is placed above the investigation instead, then a number of functions which at the moment are entrusted to the Chamber of Counsel can possibly be shifted to the investigative judge in a new job profile. This of course implies shifting some of the main actors in the criminal justice system, which is a very delicate operation, where crucial choices have to be made. However, one has to admit that Belgium has a system that is more top-heavy and more cumbersome than the systems in many of our neighboring countries. If you look at France by comparison, you will see that they abolished the Chamber of Counsel as we know them as early as 1856. In that sense, a number of the courses of action that Minister of Justice proposes really are worth investigating further. I have spoken with Koen Geens and have told him that in the framework of criminal procedures many subjects are interrelated, which means that if you reform, you must look at things globally. It is my understanding that he wants on relatively short notice, by the end of this legislature, which ends in 2019, to prepare a proposal for a new code of criminal procedure.

Raf Verstraeten added that the investigative judges were saying in unison that they provide the best guarantee, even an indispensable guarantee, for a democratic society, but he perceived that this statement should be taken with a grain of salt. This is because in Belgium approximately 95% of criminal cases are initiated by a police investigation without any involvement of an investigative judge, and only the remaining 5% are initiated by a judicial investigation led by an investigative judge. While it is unlikely that all the cases investigated without input from an investigative judge are unfairly or unjustly handled, it is important, to dare to think about certain sacred cows, such as the role of investigative judges.

The main difference between investigative judge and the judge of the investigation is that the latter does not participate in the gathering of evidence. His or her sole responsibility is to assess the necessity of certain investigatory measures which have repercussions on certain fundamental rights and freedoms, in light of the facts of the case. Generally, the advantage of having a judge of the investigation over an investigative judge is that he or she is more neutral, and this arrangement enhances the protection of the rights of the accused (Van den Wyngaert, 2014). A possible remedy regarding investigative judges is to convert them into judges of the investigation.

Problems and Successes Experienced

On the topic of the problems and successes he has experienced in his career, Raf Verstraeten gave an example of a change he regards as truly positive:

> Without any doubt, the most important evolution in my area of practice was the initiative in 2011 to enlarge the system of amicable settlement. This was a very important step and also a sensitive social choice by Parliament. Practice has shown in only four years that expansion of criminal cases eligible for amicable settlement contributes to a more manageable and efficient prosecution system. However, I am not trying to say that amicable settlements are a cure-all or should be the cure-all. It is one instrument, within a wide range of options that the prosecution has at its disposal. If you look at it from this perspective, and also take into account that the goal is not for every financial criminal case to end with an amicable settlement, but to acknowledge that the prosecution has at its disposal more options than before, in my view, this is a very good law. Of course, it is imperative that the correct application of this law be carefully safeguarded, and this is a question of careful investigation policy. In principle, I am a big proponent of expanding the possibilities of amicable settlement and I notice in practice that most divisions of the prosecution service share this view.
>
> This provides an opportunity to developing a negotiation relationship within criminal law, which has been a bit of an adjustment. The classic criminal law specialist was mainly preoccupied with pleading, but today, as a criminal lawyer, you must also develop skills in the field of negotiation, balancing of the interests of the victim, the prosecution and the suspect to come to an equitable resolution. This opportunity gives a lawyer more options to defend his clients. Personally, I believe this is also a benefit for the system. In an ideal world, the criminal justice system must be able to react very rapidly to prosecute cases in an expeditious and efficient manner. Unfortunately, this ideal world does not exist. Therefore, a manageable system has to be developed in which amicable settlements have a place. In the past, sentences were imposed involving high sums of money which in a certain number of cases were "paper tigers" because they could not be executed financially, or because certain assets which were to be confiscated could not be located or recuperated. An amicable settlement where the suspect has to repatriate his assets in Belgium in order to relinquish them to the Belgian state offers the possibility of recuperating assets which otherwise would be lost. To me this is a question of whether we want a pragmatic justice system that succeeds in recuperating large sums of money, or a justice system that is focused only on obtaining a criminal conviction, which may not be executed in the end. I personally choose the former, I prefer the pragmatic solution.

One factor to take into account are certain risks associated with amicable settlement. For example, the system is vulnerable to abuse by an accused person seeking a fast amicable settlement to avoid a heavy sentence if the case were adjudicated by a judge. Another disadvantage is that the deterrent effect of court procedures can be lost considering that amicable settlements can give offenders the impression that they can easily get away with their crimes. In practice, amicable settlement critics have noted that its preventive effects and relapse avoidance effects are as good as nonexistent (De Ruyver & Van Impe, 2000).

I asked Raf Verstraeten whether the new "filter" in the procedure before the Court of Cassation also increases the efficiency of the system, considering the fact that the Court of Cassation is currently quite overloaded. He was less optimistic:

> The filter that they have in mind is to require all attorneys who work on criminal cassation files to attend a brief course on the basis of which a certificate will be issued. He preferred a screening mechanism based on something less superficial. I was informed by a reliable source that approximately 600 lawyers have obtained this certification after a mere 20 hours of training. If 600 lawyers already have this certificate, this filer will certainly miss its mark. To obtain appropriately selected cassation files, more far-reaching measures are needed. For example, the Court of Cassation itself is hesitant about the abolition of the ex officio appeals on behalf of the defendant on its own motion. Personally, I have no problem whatsoever with a procedure before the Court of Cassation whereby the appellant must express his grievances. It is not sufficient to expect the Court of Cassation to conduct this analysis on its own motion.

I asked Raf Verstraeten if raising arguments on its own motion was not a way the Court of Cassation helped defendants who do not have the financial means to hire a highly specialized and often more expensive lawyer to defend them, especially since a guilty verdict can have a dramatic impact on a person's life. He responded:

> That is correct and a pertinent consideration. However, the process has to be manageable. Right now, delays in cassation decisions are on the increase, sometimes one year or more before a verdict is rendered. This unhealthy situation requires improvement. Moreover, Belgium has a system which allows a full appeal against every decision on the merits. It is possible to start with a guilty verdict in first instance and obtain a full re-evaluation on appeal. In the Netherlands or the United Kingdom, by comparison, to be allowed to appeal you have to pinpoint very specific errors and/or seek leave to appeal. Procedures of this nature were unknown to us.* In Belgium, there is already a double evaluation across the board

* In March 2016, the law changed. The party lodging an appeal must specify the errors in the first judgment.

of both the facts and the law of the case. Allowing the Court of Cassation to raise arguments on its own motion adds no particular value. If, after the case has been evaluated by the Court of Appeal, legal questions about the decision persist, that party should have the opportunity to proceed to the Court of Cassation.

I asked whether seeking leave to appeal was compatible with article 14 of the International Covenant on Civil and Political Rights and Protocol 7 to the European Convention for Human Rights and Raf Verstraeten confirmed that the European Court of Human Rights took the position that a convicted offender has the right to have a conviction reviewed by a court of higher instance. He noted that the jurisprudence of the European Court of Human Rights also stipulated that limitations within an appeal system were common. Understandably, the European Court in Strasbourg approved these limited rights of appeal, or the English system would be considered highly problematic. Raf Verstraeten implied that the Belgian system went further than what the European Court of Human Rights expected from member states.

> Belgium could actually fulfill its obligations with a less elaborate system as far as legal remedies are concerned. It could certainly curtail the possibility of reacting to a judgment rendered in absentia. This procedure allows defendants to avoid appearing in court without providing any reasons for their absence, in combination with an unconditional right to set aside or vacate a default judgment reached in their absence. This procedure is high on the list of priorities among those that the current Minister of Justice wishes to abolish, and is quite justified in my opinion.*

To sum up, a problem which plagues the Belgian criminal courts is the unmanageability of the system which leads to protracted procedures with a burdensome impact on the parties.

When asked about other problems in the Belgian criminal justice system, Raf Verstraeten emphasized "the system of legal remedies. This, I believe is of the utmost importance. And the training and specialization of police officers who investigate white-collar crime."

Next, I shifted attention to Raf Verstraeten's personal perspectives as a lawyer and his daily practice. I asked what problems he encounters which make it hard for him to carry out his day-to-day job. He answered:

> What can be improved in Belgium at this point in time is the way in which access is granted to the investigative file. In very big cases, starting around 2014, you could obtain a CD-ROM, but in the vast majority of cases, paper remains the main information carrier. Even now it is very difficult while the

---

* In March 2016, the law changed so that the absence of the defendant must be justified on the basis of a legitimate reason or "force majeure."

investigation is ongoing to obtain a copy of the key documents. Sometimes it is rather grotesque how much time is spent writing notes on, dictating or scanning certain documents. There is room to improve this very practical issue. It is somewhat ludicrous for example, how things proceed in Belgium regarding the scanning of documents. In some parts of the country, it is no problem to scan documents the moment you are granted access to the dossier, while in other parts, no scanning is permitted, and in other parts of the country you are only able to scan if the registrar does not know. It is unbelievable that no uniform regulation exists on this point and it is sad to see that in a way every registry functions as a separate kingdom. At a certain point in the procedure, the defense is granted obligatory access to the files, and receives a copy of the investigative file to be able to prepare its defense. At that moment, you suddenly receive thousands of pages which create a time problem. A more transparent system involving more participation by lawyers during the investigative phase would be beneficial. Theoretically, this would be legally possible because the criminal procedure code provides for it but in practice, in many cases, access to files is refused. I am a proponent of a more participatory model whereby lawyers can get a lot more and a lot faster access to the documents, as is the case in France. This would obviate lawyers from trying to win time later because they did not have adequate opportunity to fully study and prepare the case. If the parties had access sooner and were allowed to make suggestions, to ask questions, to request certain things, it will be easier later on to speed things up.

Hearing this, I asked if this created a risk of violating article 6 of the European Convention on Human Rights that contains the principle of equality of arms, or the constitutional principle of equality considering the differences that exist between the registries of various judicial departments. Raf Verstraeten responded that every case was different and that one could invoke article 6(3)(b) of the European Convention on Human Rights which provides that the defense should have sufficient time and facilities to prepare its defense. He noted that lawyers used this article when they needed a few weeks or even a few more months to prepare a case. He said they had to use every weapon at their disposal including the safeguards of the European Convention on Human Rights.

Theory and Practice

I asked Raf Verstraeten what lawyers could learn from academics and vice versa? As both a practitioner and an academic, he saw a certain cross-fertilization between these two activities as perfectly possible. He noted that a high quality defense required practical experience but also thorough knowledge. As a professor, he had to keep abreast of scientific advances, which in turn, he could use in his cases. While lawyers should not give a scientific exposé before a judge in court, it was of the utmost importance to ground a plea on thorough knowledge: "Based on my experience, I try to combine theory and practice in the right proportions."

Next I asked Raf Verstraeten whether academic theories on criminal justice issues were useful in his activities as a practicing lawyer. He responded that:

A number of scientific studies in the past have undoubtedly contributed to practical developments, not in concrete cases, but more from a conceptual standpoint. For example, the law expanding options for amicable settlement was preceded by a number of studies and publications which clarified for legislators that this was the best way forward. In that sense, science contributes to concrete practical developments. In individual cases, experience built by practicing as a lawyer is more valuable than science in guiding one through the pitfalls of a specific case.

This discussion indicated that a certain symbiosis between theory and practice contributed not only to a higher quality defense but also to positive developments in criminal law and procedure.

For me, the combination of the two has always been a beautiful experience, aside from the fact that it sends your schedule into disarray on a daily basis. Looking at it purely from the impact on my professional practice, the combination has always added value. I'm not trying to imply that lawyers who do not have an academic career are not equally able to support their clients. An attorney without an academic career who does his work thoroughly and who reads, analyses, and studies his cases can do his job as well as me. However, the benefits from this cross-fertilization are obvious in both directions. A number of articles I have written are inspired by my practical experience, because you try to make use of what you have learned in practice to substantiate your article.

Transnational Relations

In light of the fact that nowadays, the European Union has become omnipresent in our daily lives, I asked Raf Verstraeten whether European law had become a field of law of major importance for him, considering especially the regulatory impact of Europe on national jurisdictions. He agreed that the interface between European law and criminal law had increased.

We observe the penetration of European regulation in national legislation, in social and economic criminal law, and customs and excises regulation. Over the years, I have also noticed that legal cooperation between the different member states of the EU has increased substantially. This in itself gives rise to questions about transnational procedures. We are dealing a lot more now with problems associated with legal cooperation and the prosecution of foreign legal persons in Belgian criminal jurisdictions. This generates work in explaining to foreign clients how the Belgian system operates, and guiding them through the Belgian cases in which they are involved. This transnational component has grown in importance.

I asked if it would be fair to say that developments from outside Belgium, such as legislative actions by the European Union or the jurisprudence of the European Court of Human Rights, had influenced his work. He answered that it was the duty of every lawyer who dealt with criminal cases to follow these developments closely and use them. He added:

> The fact that I am active academically necessitates that I follow what happens in Europe. No lawyer at this time can afford not to attend to developments on the European front. I'll give you one example. If you look at changes in the jurisprudence of the European Court of Justice regarding EU law, the European Charter, Schengen and as far as the European Convention on Human Rights is concerned, you will observe that the way in which Europe has enlarged its interpretation of the *ne bis in idem* principle in the last decade has had an enormous impact on Belgian practice. Therefore, taking lessons from Europe is an absolute necessity for anyone who deals with white-collar criminal law.
>
> A second example is that Europe has made it clear that a number of so called nonpenal administrative procedures intrinsically have a sanctioning effect. Thus a number of safeguards inherent in traditional criminal law must be present in so called administrative sanctioning systems. Consider the famous case *Engel* (1976). This led to the fact that when we pursue procedures before certain administrations or, for that matter, before the Belgian Financial Services and Markets Authority concerning insider information or market abuse, basic principles of criminal law have to be applied. Europe has done groundbreaking work in this area. Lessons which can be derived regarding competition law, from the jurisprudence of the European Court of Justice, or from the case law of the European Court of Human Rights regarding administrative procedures, can also be very useful in the framework of Belgian judicial practice. These are two illustrations of Europe's impact on the Belgian judicial practice.

When asked whether the jurisprudence of the European Court of Justice and of the European Court of Human Rights had a positive influence on Belgian criminal law and criminal procedure law and on his work as a lawyer, Raf Verstraeten affirmed that in the last few years, progress was made in this regard and the system had improved.

> Without a doubt, they have had a positive influence on Belgian criminal law, as reflected in the prior example of administrative sanctioning, which was previously underdeveloped in terms of necessary safeguards. Thanks to the influence of the European Court of Human Rights we have certainly seen a big improvement in this regard.

However, the question did arise as to whether Europe's influence created an increasingly complex and alien system to persons subjected to criminal prosecution. Raf Verstraeten considered this a fair question and commented that the European Court of Human Rights in Strasbourg had proven that its interceptions were needed to fully develop adequate safeguards in the framework of criminal procedures. Raf Verstraeten views one of the challenges for a lawyer nowadays as making what has become an enormously legalistic justice system understandable to a client. He further added that this made the job very labor intensive, but that it was also very satisfying to explain the benefit of certain national or international safeguards to a client.

He is fully up to date with all recent developments in the law in his field, both national and international. Given the acknowledged complexity of the system, I commented that few lawyers were as highly specialized as he is. Many are general practitioners who have less in-depth knowledge. Considering that people with less financial means have to consult a less specialized, less expensive but also less knowledgeable lawyer, I wondered whether this was a possible perverse effect of the European influence? Raf Verstraeten responded as follows:

> That is correct. However, not every criminal case is highly technical. People who have a general practice are well equipped to take on many criminal cases. On the other hand, it is true when you are dealing with a complex financial criminal case, and a client has the means to allow his lawyer to achieve the best possible result, that that is a comfortable position to be in. I will not deny that. This is a factor that leads to inequality, but inequality is inherent in every aspect of life, and also in legal advocacy. Belgium does not have a fantastic system of legal aid to provide people with the best defense possible. Article 6(3)(c) of the European Convention on Human Rights provides that anyone has "the right to defend himself in person or through legal assistance of his own choosing or, if he has not sufficient means to pay for legal assistance, to be given it free when the interests of justice so require." The concept of legal assistance mentioned in this article refers to circumstances when a defendant has no means to pay for legal assistance, in which case the state is obliged to provide a *pro bono* lawyer. Other countries, notably the Netherlands, have a better-developed system of legal assistance. Until Belgium has a better system, inequality will persist.

In Belgium, the legal aid system relies on newly qualified lawyers, who are paid by the state during their legal traineeship, to support clients to the best of their abilities. Unfortunately, this deprives people of specialized legal assistance. Notably, in the Netherlands, more experienced lawyers who have built a certain reputation within their specialization are compensated by the state. I asked Raf Verstraeten his opinion of a system in which experienced lawyers are obliged to take cases *pro bono* to remedy the foregoing problem. He viewed that more as a political question, given the limits as to how far can you go in imposing an obligatory service to society on members of a liberal profession. He noted that some lawyers, but not all, were already crumbling under the weight of their workload. While he empathized with people who lacked high quality legal support, he thought provision of those services was the responsibility of the state.

General Assessments

When asked to reflect on the changes he has witnessed in the Belgian criminal law and criminal procedure in the course of his career had been positive, negative, or in between, he responded:

> When looking back over my career, one thing that has struck me is the substantial growth of white-collar criminal law. I have personally witnessed this exponential development. When I started my career in 1983, the sector, especially financial criminal law, was rather marginal, and there were not many financial criminal cases. Of course, now and then, there was a case of financial fraud, but that was rather exceptional. Today, this area of practice has grown enormously in importance, which I think is justified. By looking at the numbers published in scientific studies on the prevalence of fiscal and economic fraud, one can see a very positive change in that the prosecution pays a lot more attention to prosecuting cases of fraud than used to be the case. Of course, as I mentioned before, attention should always be paid to ensure that these cases are handled properly and professionally. In this regard, as far as the police administration is concerned, there is still room for improvement. Belgium would benefit from a competent system of police investigation with multidisciplinary teams to ensure that fraud is dealt with in the best way possible.
>
> The other important development I have witnessed is the broadened extent of the possibility of negotiation in criminal cases in recent times, thanks to the law which broadened opportunities for amicable settlement. If Belgium could succeed in making its system more manageable, starting with the influx of cases, by in part working preventively (this is another evolution I have witnessed with the creation of the preventive anti-money laundering law whereby the goal is to act fast by targeting the source itself), and additionally, by obtaining high quality results from police investigations, then I see a positive future for our criminal law and criminal procedure.

The preventive anti-money laundering law obliges members of certain professions among others to disclose possible cases of money laundering to a specialized institution.

A specific critique made by other lawyers specialized in this field is that the quality of the legislation on white-collar criminal law is not up to par. Specifically, the use of the so called "blank criminal laws," whereby all clauses of a law are criminalized by the addition of an article specifying that every violation of the stipulations of that law is penalized without distinction, but also the fragmentation of penal provisions in the field of white-collar criminal law, which are scattered across numerous legal instruments, are often considered as major shortcomings. In the Netherlands, however, a different system pertains, whereby all penal provisions of economic and financial criminal law are grouped in a single law. I asked Raf Verstraeten whether he shares the opinion that a unitary system would be an improvement for Belgium. He answered:

Belgium has the ability to create such a law. The best example of course is the Social Criminal Code of 2010, which is a beautiful example of the thorough work that a specialized commission can achieve, even on a hypertechnical subject matter. In terms of progress, this is laudable. It does remain, however, limited to the sector of social criminal law. While it is perfectly possible to do the same for economic criminal law, unfortunately, this has not happened yet. Regarding fiscal criminal law there is another problem: In that field, the necessary penal provisions are present, but unfortunately, the legislators have never thought about delimiting what is worthy of criminal prosecution and what is not, and the latter category being cases which it's perfectly possible to handle administratively. Criminal law benefits from a healthy selection of those acts that warrant criminal punishment, and those that do not. Again, the social criminal code serves as a prime example of a codification in this regard.

Koen Geens, the current Belgian Minister of Justice, has stated that he wants to implement certain changes based on his justice plan by the end of this legislature, in 2019. This is a tight time frame. Therefore, I wanted to know whether Raf Verstraeten thought this objective was feasible.

A lot of very hard work both in the preparatory phase and during the parliamentary evaluation will be needed to achieve the goal of implementing his justice plan by 2019. I have the feeling that the minds of all the actors in the criminal justice process, a lot more than before, have ripened, and are ready for change. It is felt in almost all echelons that reform is necessary, and thus, the willingness to engage in thinking about reform is there. Nonetheless, you notice that when the time to reform comes, all the actors have their own positions in mind. For example, the investigative judges are extremely sensitive the moment that transformation of their roles is mentioned. However, the spirit of the time is one of reform.

Conclusion

To conclude the interview I asked Raf Verstraeten whether, if he could change one thing immediately in the Belgian criminal justice system, what it would be. After pausing to think, he came up with the following answer:

To make the system more manageable, questioning the current system of victim compensation claims is a necessity because of the high numbers of these claims and the trial delays they cause. This is a very sensitive issue because it impacts the participation of crime victims in the criminal justice process. Nonetheless, in a modern system of criminal justice, it is imperative to have a competent/professional public prosecution service which demonstrates that it can function well. The current unbridled option for every victim to initiate a criminal cause of action is simply not tenable.

Now that I have had a chance to think about this, although you asked me for one example, I'll give you two. Another feature of the Belgian criminal justice system I would change is the Court of Assizes, which I would abolish immediately. This is an equally sensitive subject. Ten years ago, I was the chair of the Commission for the Reform of the Court of Assizes. I tried to make clear to the Minister of Justice at that time (Laurette Onkelinx) that abolishing the Court was probably the best solution. Ten years later, I am still convinced of this. I do not believe that the Court of Assizes contributes to a healthy justice system. Convening this court consumes enormous resources on the part of the magistrates, and as a consequence, many other cases are not dealt with, which only causes our judicial backlog to grow. In my view, sloppy solutions whereby certain cases, such as crimes of passion, are still brought before the Court of Assizes offer no solution. Belgium needs to make a radical choice in this regard. Abolishing the Court of Assizes is simply the best solution.

This was the final question and therefore also the end of the interview. I expressed my deep-felt gratitude to Mr. Verstraeten and told him it had been a pleasure and an honor to be able to share in his experiences. He responded that the pleasure was all his and that he was looking forward to reading the book.

Glossary

amicable settlement: a negotiation procedure available under criminal law whereby the public prosecutor proposes to a person suspected of committing an offense which has not caused any serious physical harm and which is eligible for a jail sentence of less than two years, to pay a certain sum of money in exchange for which the public prosecutor will drop the charges. Additionally, the relinquishment of certain goods which have been or will be confiscated can be requested. Recently, use of this system has been significantly expanded, making it possible to achieve an amicable settlement after the proceedings have been officially initiated.

arguments on its own motion (ambtshalve middelen): the Court of Cassation may initiate arguments on its own volition against the judgments under its scrutiny.

Chamber of Counsel room (raadkamer or chambre du conseil): at the conclusion of a judicial investigation, an investigative court will decide on the appropriate follow-up to the investigation depending on the outcome of the investigation (e.g., where there are sufficient indicators of guilt, transferring the suspect to a criminal court).

case closure (seponeren): where a public prosecutor determines based on either technical reasons (e.g., no suspect can be found) or policy reasons (e.g., the guidelines of criminal policy of the Minister of Justice) to dismiss or terminate processing of a matter.

cassation files: cases heard at the Court of Cassation which involve only legal questions of a procedural nature or the interpretation of the law.

court of appeal: within the criminal jurisdiction, this court deals with appeals lodged against the decisions of a Correctional Court rendered in the first instance. It reconsiders the facts of the case and will adjudicate on points against which the appeal has been lodged.

court of assizes: it is a nonpermanent court which only convenes to handle the most serious crimes under the Belgian criminal code. For example, certain homicide cases because of the gravity of the offense and the facts. It is the only court in Belgium where a jury of lay citizens decides the question of guilt.

court of cassation: it is the apex of the pyramid in the Belgian judicial system. To ensure legal development and uniformity, the Court of Cassation will not examine the facts of cases but only review whether the laws have been correctly applied by the lower courts.

Crown prosecutor/public prosecutor: the prosecution refers specifically to the *"openbaar ministerie"* or *"ministère public,"* which is the name for the Belgian prosecution service.

default judgment: a judgment rendered against the defendant in his absence due to his failure to appear at the trial.

docent: an academic appointment and the lowest rank of professor in the Belgian academic system.

economic criminal law: the rules and regulations which penalize violations of the rules regulating economic activity including the rules concerning consumer protection.

European Convention on Human Rights: an international treaty to protect human rights and fundamental freedoms in Europe, which entered into force in 1953 and was implemented in Belgian law in 1955.

financial criminal law: the rules and regulations which penalize, among others, violations of the rules regulating the financial markets and their transactions.

fiscal criminal law: the rules and regulations which penalize violations of the fiscal code. In essence, therefore, fiscal criminal law deals with the prosecution of tax-related crimes.

investigative file (strafdossier): a collection of redacted reports documenting the pretrial investigative acts. These documents are the primary resource relied upon by the trial judge to adjudicate the case.

investigative judge (onderzoeksrechter): a judge who, before the actual trial, seeks the truth by collecting evidence both beneficial and detrimental to the position of the accused person. His task may involve, search and seizure, interviewing a suspect, investigation of the body, interception of telecommunications (telephone), and forensic research. Generally speaking, to uncover the truth, the investigative judge is allowed to take any necessary measure permitted by law that does not contravene the dignity of his function.

judicial investigation (gerechtelijk onderzoek): this is one of the two possible forms the pretrial investigation in the Belgian criminal justice system can take. It is characterized by its secret, written, and noncontradictory nature and is led by an investigative judge. It is used most frequently in more serious cases where violations of fundamental rights and freedoms may be necessary in order to uncover the truth about a case.

misdemeanor: a crime more serious in nature than a transgression, punishable by imprisonment of not more than five years, monetary fines of €26 and above, and community service of 46–300 hours. Examples of misdemeanors include theft, scams, assault, and battery.

*ne bis in idem***:** a legal principle to the effect that no legal action can be instituted twice for the same cause of action, similar to the common law doctrine of "double jeopardy." This principle is incorporated as a human right in article 4 of the 7th Protocol supplementing the European Convention of Human Rights and in article 14(7) of the International Covenant on Civil and Political Rights. See *Zolotukhin/Russia* (ECHR, February 1, 2009) and *Aklagaren* (ECJ, February 26, 2013).

police court (politierechtbank): is the lowest ranking of all Belgian criminal courts and it deals primarily with small infringements and traffic violations (see overtredingen).

prosecutorial investigation (opsporingsonderzoek): a criminal investigation conducted by the public prosecutor, without the intervention of an investigating judge (except in specific circumstances).

Salduz jurisprudence: the European Court of Human Rights stipulates that a suspect has the right to assistance by his attorney starting from the first interrogation.

social criminal law: the rules and regulations which penalize violations of the social code. In essence, this concerns labour- and social security law related crimes.

vacation of judgment: a legal remedy open to defendants who have had a default judgment against them because the defendant or his lawyer was not present at the hearing. The same judge who tried the case initially will re-evaluate it.

victim compensation (burgerlijke partijstelling): anyone who has suffered damage as a consequence of a crime can submit a compensation claim before an investigative judge (*onderzoeksrechter* or *juge d'instruction*). A complainant can also directly subpoena the alleged perpetrator of the crime to court.

Bolivia

4

ASTRID BIRGDEN
LOLA ARAUJO LANGTHALER

Contents

The Criminal Justice Process of Bolivia

Bolivia is a unitary, independent, free, sovereign, multiethnic, and multicultural republic in Latin America. A new Constitution was established in 2009 by President Morales, changing the country's name to the Plurinational State of Bolivia, in recognition of its multiethnicity and to enhance the position of its indigenous peoples. In particular, the rights of the original indigenous peasant communities (naciones y pueblos indigenas orginariocampesinos) were recognized to administer justice in any civil or criminal dispute and apply their own principles, cultural values, norms, and procedures (Faundez, 2011). That is, the Constitution placed indigenous community justice at the same level as state courts, while including the right to life, the right to legal defense, and other constitutional rights and guarantees. More specifically, the criminal law excludes from indigenous community justice the crimes of murder, rape, violence against children and adolescents, against state security, war crimes, against humanity, drug offenses, corruption, and infringement of customs regulations.

Under the Constitution, the key State organs are the Legislature, the Executive, and the Judiciary. The judicial powers are exercised by the Supreme

Court of Justice, the Constitutional Court, and the Superior District Courts, corresponding to each department based on the country's geographic distribution. Establishing exceptional courts or tribunals is not allowed. The Supreme Court is the highest court of justice for regular, contested, and administrative matters. Constitutional review is entrusted to the Constitutional Court, which is made up of five judges previously designated by the National Congress, but more recently elected. In addition, there is the Judicial Council that serves as the administrative and disciplinary organ of the Judiciary.

The current Criminal Procedure Code was enacted by a previous government in Bolivia by Law No. 1970 in March 1999 and operationalized in 2001. It had been enacted in response to the extremely slow administration of criminal justice within an inquisitorial system, with trials taking an average of five years, utilizing a system that was written (not oral) and rather secretive, resulting in a justice service that was inaccessible, expensive, and corrupt with low juridical security, and with no constitutional guarantees; "the rich found justice, the poor not." These systemic weaknesses impacted negatively on the community's trust in the system.

The Criminal Procedure Code was part of a broader suite of reforms that included the passage of a Law of Judicial Organization and reforms of the Bolivian Constitution in 1993. The Judicial reform of the criminal justice system had been occurring throughout Latin America, ostensibly to enhance democracy, improve the protection of human rights and social justice, and develop the economy and enforce international law (Domingo & Sieder, 2001). The reforms were designed to place time limits on investigations, institute speedy trials, and establish greater judicial oversight in all stages of the criminal justice system (Barry, Cano & Chambers, undated). In particular, the shift from an inquisitorial to an accusatorial system weighted the power of Bolivian judges (who had conducted the investigations and then ruled in all cases) against defense lawyers who could take on a more active role and it allowed the defense and prosecution to test the evidence in court.

However, with a change of regime in 2002, the Bolivian government established a punitive crime prevention policy with tougher penalties, new offense categories, and expanded powers of judicial officers to request and implement preventive detention. This shift between 2003 and 2012 was in response to rising crime rates, excessively lengthy criminal proceedings, and a weak response of the criminal justice system to the demands of citizens. This shift has served to stall the restructuring of the criminal justice system and resulted in prosecution of misdemeanors overloading the courts and prison system and delaying justice without the required infrastructure and resources being made available.

Faundez (2011) noted that international development agencies had initially focused on state institutions when wanting to initiate legal and judicial reform, but after disappointing outcomes in numerous failed states, the focus shifted to nonstate justice systems that operate outside the state framework. However, in countries such as Bolivia, nonstate justice systems need to work together with state authorities, which become more openly challenging than merely improving court management systems or updating the legal skills of lower court judges. In particular, Faundez noted that governments such as Bolivia are well versed in manipulating the rights of traditional communities and indigenous peoples.

Relevant to this chapter is the position of indigenous peoples in Latin America who are among the poorest and most discriminated groups, whose exclusion dates back to colonization that continued after independence under the guise of false republicanism calling for their assimilation. Bureaucratic legal obstacles to indigenous rights reflect underlying social and economic conditions, encompassing in Bolivia's case, drug trafficking issues. However, the activities of the nonstate justice systems were considered to have raised the political and legal awareness of indigenous communities.

Maria Teresa Rivero Gutiérrez (Esq.), Attorney
at Law and Former Prosecutor, La Paz

Introduction

Maria Teresa Rivero Gutiérrez is a Bolivian lawyer with a 40-year career within the criminal justice system. In this time, Ms. Rivero Gutiérrez has fulfilled the roles of defense lawyer, Magistrate, prosecutor and was one of the four members of the Judicial Council (in charge of the corporate administration of the Judiciary). The focus of the interview was on the role of the prosecutor within a period of legal reform within Bolivia.

Ms. Rivero Gutiérrez grew up in Beni located in the Bolivian Amazonia in a conservative, united and religious family. She attended a private Catholic school "Mother Elizabeth Setton" in Trinidad, Beni. Beni, despite its natural beauty and its vast natural resources, has always been relegated by governments and did not develop at the same pace of other Bolivian States. From a very young age, Ms. Rivero Gutiérrez questioned social inequity and discrimination. She was very fond of her hometown and with sadness witnessed poverty and underdevelopment. She developed a vocation to help the unprivileged and became an enthusiastic advocate of social justice. Later she moved to Cochabamba and enrolled at the University of San Simón where she obtained her Law degree. Living in a patriarchal society in which professional opportunities were scarce for women, especially in the justice sector, Ms. Rivero Gutiérrez, with her strong and outgoing personality, firm convictions, and self-confidence, found her first job as a Public Defense Lawyer in La Paz (political capital of Bolivia) and since then she has developed a career in the criminal justice system with hard work and leadership. Retired from the Judiciary, she now works as a private barrister and consultant. Ms. Rivero Gutiérrez has been a witness of, and an actor within, important changes within the administration of justice. These changes include the establishment of the Constitutional Tribunal, the Criminal Procedure Reform, the Judicial Council, and the Public Defense.

Ms Langthaler conducted the interview in Spanish, and transposed the notes into English. The interview was conducted via Skype between Australia and Bolivia on two occasions. Ms Langthaler's reflections are at the end of the chapter.

Career

Ms. Rivero Gutiérrez initiated her career as a public defense lawyer in 1980. In 1984, she was appointed as a Magistrate of the Superior Court of the Department of Beni for seven years. In 1989, Ms. Rivero Gutiérrez became the first female to be appointed to the position of President of the Superior Court of Beni. Later in 1991, she was appointed as Prosecutor of Appeals (investigating, recommending, and representing the State in cases that went to the Supreme Court on appeal) and assigned to the Drug Court (for narcotic-related crimes only). Finally, Ms. Rivero Gutiérrez was appointed by Parliament as a member of the Judicial Council, a position that she held for 10 years. In addition, Ms. Rivero Gutiérrez has actively contributed to the education of legal practitioners in her role as an Adjunct Professor of Criminology and Criminal Procedure Law in various Bolivian public and private universities.

In Bolivia, prosecutors are faced with a citizenry with substantial economic and social deprivation. Bolivia is the poorest country in South America where 59% of the population is living in poverty and 45% is living below the poverty line. Bolivia also has a high indigenous population resulting in 36 indigenous languages, besides Spanish, recognized in its current Political Constitution. In the 2012 census, 41% of the population identified themselves as indigenous, and have historically been deprived and living in or below the poverty line.

Ms. Rivero Gutiérrez was a key actor in the implementation of structural criminal procedure reform in Bolivia while the country transitioned from an inquisitorial to an accusatorial criminal procedure system. This process of Criminal Procedure Reform was of a duration of approximately six years and was mainly assisted by the Program of Administration of Justice funded by American and German cooperation. This transition required enormous institutional and cultural change across the system in the administration of justice. In particular, it required a change in the practices of legal practitioners as the reform incorporated new legal institutions that were previously unknown in the Bolivian justice system. These changes included the implementation of oral trials; the creation of tribunals of sentence that integrated lay citizens' views into the criminal justice system; the recognition of indigenous justice, the introduction of alternative measures to preventive detention, and so on. In this reform initiative, Ms. Rivero Gutiérrez played a key role initially as responsible for liaison and reform coordination at the Attorney General's Office, and later from within the Judicial Council until 2008.

Ms. Rivero Gutiérrez was asked to focus on her previous career as a prosecutor for this chapter. She agreed but clarified that her view of the criminal justice is the result of her combined experience in her different roles.

When asked what had been surprising in her career, Ms. Rivero Gutiérrez indicated the fact that Bolivian justice operators had been willing and able to do their work to their best ability in the absence of available resources and in the context of far from ideal conditions. Within the role of prosecutor, performed in a period of legal reform, Ms. Rivero Gutiérrez noted the capacity and willingness of prosecutors and other justice operators to adjust rapidly to a very different criminal procedure system to guarantee its success. The new system required intensive training, change of investigation and prosecution techniques and practices, and what is more important it required a change of mentality not only of legal practitioners but of the citizens as well. The implementation of a new approach to criminal justice—particularly the oral trial in 2001—unexpectedly accelerated the delivery of justice, made trials more transparent, and met the principle of immediacy (where the magistrate or prosecutor is able to address and interrogate the accused directly, rather than via the magistrate within the tribunal hearing). This principle of immediacy allowed the prosecutor to gain a better appreciation of the facts, as well as the personality and character of the accused that would allow for the identification of the underlying causes of the crime. Ms. Rivero Gutiérrez highlighted the establishment of the collegiate tribunals, as part of the reform, made up of three technical judges (legal practitioners) and two citizens. Ms. Rivero Gutiérrez was of the view that these tribunals served to provide a better understanding of the facts and evidence, resulting in fair sentences based on an objective and efficient assessment of the facts and the law. These tribunals decided both culpability and sentences.

When asked whether she felt that her work as a prosecutor proved as rewarding as she had expected, Ms. Rivero Gutiérrez reported that while she had previously fulfilled the role of defense lawyer and magistrate, she had not known what to expect when she accepted the position of prosecutor. What she found appealing was to be the defender of society and the prosecutor of crimes of "public action" (criminal offenses that can be prosecuted by the State automatically as they are against national security, life, property, and other areas such as espionage, terrorism, embezzlement of public funds, homicide, robbery, abortion, abduction, and rape). Ms. Rivero Gutiérrez had found the function of prosecutor to be very different as she was involved in investigation and coordination with other agencies such as the Police, the Forensic Institute, and the Comptroller Officer (an Auditor-General). In the role of prosecutor, she found her experiences to be very rewarding, particularly when her decisions and recommendations ensured fair sentences and contributed to the protection of society. Ms. Rivero Gutiérrez reported that being part of the design, development, and implementation of the required Criminal Procedure Reform made her work as a prosecutor even more rewarding as she was able to contribute with her practical experience to the drafting of the new policy. The new system enhanced and delineated better the function of the prosecutor, and it established the need for interagency coordination that in the past had been almost nonexistent. Further, the Criminal Procedure Reform allowed magistrates and judges to accelerate the delivery of justice for victims and detainees who had, in many cases, previously waited for years to be sentenced. Therefore, Ms. Rivero Gutiérrez concluded that to be a prosecutor in a time of fundamental change had been a privilege.

Philosophy of Legal Advocacy

Ms. Rivero Gutiérrez described herself as advocating for a criminal legal system that was respectful of constitutional rights and democratic principles. She believed that the Criminal Procedure Reform responded to the aforementioned principles and was demonstrating a significant change in the efficiency and effectiveness of the justice administration. However, she warned that the Criminal Procedure Reform, that had previously occurred, is currently at risk as the justice administration has been once again politicized. Improvised legal reforms have been introduced to respond to the interests of the new political regime without proper research to the detriment of Bolivian citizens, who for years fought for the fair, secure, and efficient administration of justice.

When asked about the role of the prosecutor in society, Ms. Rivero Gutiérrez stated that her role had been established within the Criminal Procedure Code as the advocate of society and the director of the criminal investigation in cases of public action crimes (described above). As the advocate of society, the prosecutor therefore guarantees respect for the constitution and human rights of both the accused and the victim, and oversees the integrity and legality of the criminal investigation. As director of the investigation, the prosecutor is in charge of coordinating and planning the investigation. The prosecutor is to establish the strategic direction of the investigation, effectively coordinate with the police investigator, ensure the legality of the collection of evidence and the integrity of the investigation, and keep the victim informed of the development of the investigation. A very clear division of responsibilities between the prosecutor directing the investigation, the police officer investigating, and the judge/tribunals judging and sentencing is crucial. In addition to these functions, the prosecutor is to be in regular contact with the community to identify crime "hot spots." For society in particular, the prosecutor is to be the guarantor of the respect of human and constitutional rights and is to be fair and objective. This means that the prosecutor will guarantee the rights of the victim and of the defendant. In the investigation, the prosecutor should take into account not only the evidence against the defendant but also that evidence could absolve him/her of guilt.

In considering the role of the prosecutor in relation to other justice operators, Ms. Rivero Gutiérrez emphasized that while the assigned responsibilities of the prosecutor by law cannot be delegated, she advocated for a team work approach while working on investigations. In the past, the prosecutor had worked in isolation from the police officer in a parallel investigation, as both within their institutions had been reluctant to give up their perceived authority. Since the Criminal Procedure Code reform, it has become evident that a joint approach, particularly for the investigation of organized crime using a task force, has been far more effective. Ms. Rivero Gutiérrez indicated that an efficient prosecutor requires skills in planning and management and investigative techniques, in addition to receiving regular training.

In considering workable and unworkable organizational arrangements, Ms. Rivero Gutiérrez indicated that there had been various attempts to strengthen the Prosecutor's Office and the Police in Bolivia. As considered above, the investigative roles of the prosecutor and the police investigator had not previously been clearly defined and separated. As a consequence, there was a conflict of power in the investigation; police investigators considering that the prosecutor was ill-equipped to conduct an investigation as they were lawyers rather than trained investigators and, conversely, prosecutors considering that police officers did not understand, nor protected, the legality of the investigation and did not understand the law adequately. As a consequence, many rules, manuals, agreements, and other documents were prepared when Ms. Rivero Gutiérrez was a prosecutor that contributed to increasing the efficiency of the delivery of justice. Agreements between the Attorney General's Office and the Police to facilitate a more coordinated approach provided what she described as "excellent results." In this process, joint and specialized training was provided to prosecutors and police officers to enable the preparation of investigations and presentation of results. This training contributed to the development of a more collegiate and collaborative relationship among the agencies, contributing to organizational change. In clarifying the roles in the Criminal Procedure Code and supporting them through interinstitutional agreements, these problems were slowly resolved. The implementation of the Prosecutor's Career training system in 2003 was another positive change in that graduate lawyers had to complete this training to qualify as candidates for a prosecutor role.

Under the direction of the prosecutors, unique Anticorruption Task Forces were also established in 2004. These teams consisted of full-time and highly trained prosecutors, police investigators, forensic auditors, Financial Investigations Unit officers, and Comptrollers' Office auditors, working together in the same office. In 2005–2006, these teams investigated crimes against the public function (e.g., corruption offenses such as bribery and fraud) initially in two states before the model was replicated across all Bolivian States. For the first time, condemnatory sentences against public officials for corruption crimes were obtained in Bolivia.

In considering working relationships with agencies, groups, and the community, Ms. Rivero Gutiérrez noted that in Bolivia, as in most countries, one of the problems with the justice system is the lack of community trust.

However, with the reforms that were enacted between 2001 and 2010, the levels of community trust increased when the new criminal procedure system was put in place because prosecutors were appointed based on merit and prosecutors, legal defense lawyers, and magistrates received regular training. To support these reforms, there was a significant investment from international aid funds as well as technical assistance. An example of an interesting project within this period was that of the implementation of the Network for Justice and Participation established in 2004 that helped to establish a precedent for civil–society oversight of the selection of justice officials. The Network allowed community-based, professional, and not-for-profit organizations, over a period of time, to have input into the appointment of prospective candidates. This process legitimized to some extent the appointment of justice operators and increased trust in the justice system. Ms. Rivero Gutiérrez believes that Bolivia should have continued with this practice in order to effectively manage the risk of political interference and guarantee that appointments continued to be by merit. However, since 2010, as a subsequent result of the new political environment, international aid agencies were excluded by government to the detriment of the justice institutions. As a consequence, community trust in the prosecutor function lowered significantly as new prosecutors became political appointments rather than merit-based appointments, possessing no skills and with no funding for training provided.

Poverty and inequality is clearly evident in Bolivia and so it is not difficult for a prosecutor to witness the living and social conditions of the deprived every day. However, that ongoing situation can "immunize" justice operators against poverty and Ms. Rivero Gutiérrez noted that prosecutors should be aware of that risk. Courts and prisons are overloaded with people who are economically deprived, uneducated, illiterate, and often speaking an indigenous language rather than Spanish, due to the rich diversity of the country. The prosecutor has to adjust services to this reality and consider at all times the social conditions of the accused before issuing recommendations. Nevertheless, Ms. Rivero Gutiérrez emphasized that prosecutors cannot subscribe to the fallacy of viewing poverty as the sole cause of crime.

In considering how prosecutors can develop empathy for socially and economically disadvantaged individuals, Ms. Rivero Gutiérrez was of the view that it would be ideal to have multidisciplinary professional teams to assess the social and psychological conditions of the accused to gain an understanding of the possible circumstances that had led them to committing a crime. However, currently prosecutors do not have access to such resources. At present, the evaluation is ad hoc and mostly based on the prosecutor's experience with the exception of expert reports that are provided by private defense. It is therefore difficult for prosecutors to recognize that people from disadvantaged backgrounds may be motivated to commit crime to survive or do so because of ignorance of the law and legal processes. For example, there are accused who have confessed to a crime because they did not understand the language. As previously stated, Bolivia recognizes 36 languages but does not fund interpreters at police stations, although they are available in the courts. This lack of support in police stations leads to the increased risk of false confessions. There also examples of entire families, who are extremely disadvantaged, whose children are working in cocaine laboratories under extremely poor working conditions. However, those that organize the drug-related industry are rarely brought to account. As a result, the underlying causes of crime related to the lack of basic rights such as food, education, housing, and transport remain unresolved. As a consequence, the prosecutor can only attempt to apply the law with humanity and integrity while prioritizing the safety of society.

In considering what strategies Bolivia ought to be implementing, Ms. Rivero Gutiérrez believed that crime prevention should be prioritized. In Bolivia, the trafficking of narcotics is expanding at an alarming rate. Because of this issue, more laws were passed creating new types of legal responses and increasing penalties and prisons sentences. However, this hard-edged crime control approach has proven to be ineffective as drug-related crimes are still escalating. As a consequence, prisons are becoming overcrowded with preventive detention in a country that is not equipped to adequately maintain detention facilities. Ms. Rivero Gutiérrez believes that crime prevention strategies in coordination with the community would be more effective with support services for the accused and the victim. The implementation of a proper community corrections system would also assist. A current priority is to increase the capability and resources for the administration of justice to increase community access and trust in the justice system. Instead, prosecutors have reverted to conducting investigations with poor skills and very limited resources, ultimately to the detriment of victims and society.

Problems and Successes Experienced

Ms. Rivero Gutiérrez was asked to reflect upon problems and successes she had experienced. In considering which policies had worked and had not worked, she emphasized that it was important to note that there were policies that worked very well while she was a prosecutor, but these policies are currently being revised within a political climate in which new legislation has been introduced that in her view is not well considered. Rather than improving the efficiency of the administration of justice, these changes are making justice more complex and inaccessible.

Ms. Rivero Gutiérrez provided two examples of policy developments that had worked well: the abbreviated procedure and the oral trial.

The abbreviated procedure is a legal process allowing a contested trial to be avoided when the accused was willing to accept responsibility for the crime and his or her participation in it. The sentence in this instance was rapid and the punishment did not exceed what the prosecutor had requested. This reform had worked well and had contributed to relieving case overload in courts and to improving the efficiency of sentencing. This reform is still in place.

The oral trial is a contested trial in which the evidence and interrogation occurs within a hearing. For decades, Bolivia had relied upon a written and inquisitorial system with the evidence presented to the Court Registry filed in a folder. While there were hearings previously for confessions and witness declarations, both the prosecutor and legal defense could only address questions to the accused through the judge. Thus, the principle of immediacy in sentencing was not optimal as the spontaneity of the interrogation was lost in the translation and formality. As a consequence of the written system, the delay in sentencing was unacceptable with some cases taking 20 years to resolve. Against all expectations, the implementation of the oral trial resulted in substantial improvement: justice was delivered faster, the presentation of evidence and conclusions became more efficient in taking less hearings to form a decision, and the transparency of the trial was more controlled.

Ms. Rivero Gutiérrez considered the greatest problems and issues facing the criminal courts in Bolivia at present. A high caseload has been, and continues to be, the greatest problem in the criminal courts. There have been suggested strategies and policies to manage this problem. However, any suggested solutions have been impossible to implement due to resource restrictions and lack of political will. The accumulation of legal cases and obstacles to justice has had an impact on preventive detention. Due to the criminalization of 12 new offenses related to corruption, discrimination, racism, and customs tax evasion, the rates of preventive detention have increased, and eight out of ten persons in detention have not yet been sentenced. With the hard-edged crime control approach that is advocated by the current government, the accused is being apprehended and placed in detention facilities to protect society before proper investigations are conducted. Citizens are detained based upon minimal evidence and, unfortunately, the pace of going to trial and being sentenced is very slow taking sometimes even six years. According to a report presented in 2014 by FundacionConstruir to the Inter-American Commission of Human Rights, Bolivia has become the first country in the American Continent with a majority of preventive detainees; of 14,415 prisoners in Bolivia, 11,996 (83%) are on remand awaiting sentencing. Among others, the obstacles to speedy justice include lack of resources and lack of skills in current operators. Operators are applying preventive detentions as a rule rather than as an exception. As a consequence, prison detainees are deprived of their freedom in the most deplorable living conditions in which the violation of human rights is high due to lack of minimum standards. For example, detainees have to pay for their cell accommodation and food, the space is very limited, safety cannot be guaranteed, and there is no access to support services.

Ms. Rivero Gutiérrez considered the issues faced by the courts. In general, with some exceptions, the capability of appointed judges is characterized by lack of expertise. This issue creates the foremost obstacle that prosecutors and defense lawyers have to overcome. In other words, it is very difficult to argue a case with doctrine and jurisprudence when judges, who have not necessarily been the result of merit-based appointments, do not have specialized knowledge or training to administrate criminal justice effectively. The lack of respect for procedural terms (times established for different procedures to guarantee procedural celerity) and the constant adjournments of hearings do not allow prosecutors to complete their work effectively. Another problem is political interference within the legal process that is very difficult to control at present. Political interference has generated fear among community members resulting in distrust in the administration of justice. The application of community justice, legalized by the criminal procedure reform with respect to constitutional rights as its basis, was preferred by the community. Unfortunately, corruption is present within the system of administration of justice with bribery to justice officials being very common as well as traffic of influences.

Ms. Rivero Gutiérrez considered what organizational change or reforms may assist in dealing with poorly selected legal actors, political interference, and corruption. She was of the view that if the prosecutor's career strategy were to be efficiently implemented, it would improve the capabilities of the judiciary and prosecution. With the addition of adequate and periodic training, the culture of the organization could be changed toward more efficient, ethical, and accountable functions. Further, improving the work conditions of judges, prosecutors, police, forensic staff, and public defense lawyers would improve their motivation and commitment. Last, improving and maintaining the interinstitutional coordination and expanding the network of operators with international peers to learn of new developments, innovation, and lessons learned would greatly assist. Ms. Rivero Gutiérrez concluded that "although not easy but not impossible" is the avoidance of political interference that is dependent upon the assertiveness and integrity of legal actors: actively avoiding external pressure of any nature and engaging in decision making based only on what the law prescribes and with respect for human rights.

Theory and Practice

We asked Ms. Rivero Gutiérrez to consider the relationship between theory and practice in legal advocacy. She indicated that while she and her colleagues learned theory in their university education, they enriched that knowledge throughout their careers in reviewing new legal trends and theoretical developments in practice. Ms. Rivero Gutiérrez indicated that theory provides the conceptual framework to engage in daily legal advocacy practice; theory poses the question of *why*, while the practice poses the question of *how?* Ms. Rivero Gutiérrez indicated that in her career applying a theory-based approach gave her the purpose, the argument, and the reasons she would choose a particular pathway to investigate, or to sentence, or to defend (in the various roles she has held). She emphasized that it is very important to expose law students to practical work as part of their education, so they can learn applied law. While theory sets up principles for legal practice that should be the reference for any action or decision taken as part of legal functions, the administration of justice cannot be merely theoretical or empirical as such an approach can lead to chaos or injustice. In other words, theory needs to be adjusted to reality, to the dynamics of life in society, and to human nature. In practice, this means that legal actors have to understand the underlying causes of crime and apply the law accordingly.

In considering the interaction between theory and practice, Ms. Rivero Gutiérrez stated that theory is evidenced-based and therefore legal practitioners should learn from it. Regardless of their approach, her view was that legal practitioners should review the latest trends and theories so as not to implement practices that may have been proven wrong. In turn, theory-builders enrich their work if, through consultative methodologies, they gather the experience from people who are in the field and are dealing daily in courts with suspects, victims, and legal actors. Theory-builders should therefore learn about organizational dynamics, court management, budget issues, and so on, prior to developing policy.

Ms. Rivero Gutiérrez believed that the relationship between theory and practice is currently becoming weaker because in the current delivery of justice, prevailing political views are losing touch with legal doctrine. The delivery of justice is therefore at risk of becoming too empirical and in cases ad hoc, as theory and doctrine are relegated as secondary. In short, the current political climate in Bolivia is an obstacle to collaboration between theory and practice.

In considering what kind of research would assist legal advocacy practice, Ms. Rivero Gutiérrez suggested that it would be useful to establish an institution that would observe and carry out comprehensive research regarding crime trends in Bolivia related to social living conditions, and then propose strategies to counteract these crime trends to create resilience and effective prevention mechanisms. Therefore, systems that capture accurate crime and court statistics are necessary.

In seeking theory-based information, Ms. Rivero Gutiérrez consults classic books of criminal law that continue to be good sources of theoretical information. She also consults specialized articles and publications of universities and juridical centers, such as CIEDLA-Konrad Adenauer, CEJIP-Centre of Justice Studies and Participation, and Institute of Comparative Studies of Criminal and Social Science (Argentina). The Internet also provides information that is very accessible and has made a big difference to her practice. When she was a prosecutor, Ms. Rivero Gutiérrez consulted information on investigation strategies for specific cases especially when the crime was novel for the Bolivian justice system such as trafficking of people, terrorism, and human organs. Unfortunately, for decades Bolivian justice officials have not had easy access to good libraries because of lack of resources and access to Internet services. It is in the last 10 years that finally the Courts and the Attorney General's Office have introduced more modern technology and communications systems.

Transnational Relations

Transnational relations include international developments outside Bolivia. Ms. Rivero Gutiérrez reported that new crime threats such as the trafficking of persons and other organized crime challenged Bolivian prosecutors and other justice operators, as they had not been trained to investigate such crimes. In particular, as the accused in many cases were foreigners, they were required to implement coordinated investigations with other jurisdictions that were costly and complex. Nonetheless, Ms. Rivero Gutiérrez considered the interaction with international jurisdictions as beneficial, although costly and sometimes difficult, because of distance, communication issues, and language barriers. However, the terrorist attacks in the United States on September 11, 2011, had not affected her work.

General Assessments

In general, when asked whether she was satisfied or dissatisfied with developments in Bolivian criminal law and criminal procedure, Ms. Rivero Gutiérrez responded that she felt "very satisfied" as an actor within the criminal procedure reform that occurred in Bolivia in 2003. This reform had resulted in the implementation of the adversarial system and oral trials. The result had been a fundamental reform that established a more transparent and efficient criminal procedure system, mostly because it advocated and guaranteed respect for constitutional rights. However, as previously noted, the structural reform that had benefitted the administration of justice and legal practitioners has been perverted by the current political system that has subsequently passed new and improvised legislation that create obstacles to justice and impunity. This new system is not satisfying for professionals like Ms. Rivero Gutiérrez who had fought and defended a fair and timely trial, an unrestricted right to legal defense, and, most importantly, the principle of procedural celerity or alacrity in the criminal justice process.

Finally, Ms. Rivero Gutiérrez spoke about what developments she would like to see. She stated that she would like the courts to conduct a comprehensive assessment of the Criminal Procedure Reform and its current implementation to identify gaps and opportunities for improvement. She would also like to see the Judicial and Prosecutors Career Systems is re-established in order to develop and implement a much needed specialized training program for current prosecutors, public defense lawyers, and judges. Ideally, the current government should prioritize the budget to improve the labor conditions of justice operators as well as the courts, enhance investigative laboratories and equipment, and ensure delivery within the correctional system.

Ms. Rivero Gutiérrez listed the following requirements to improve legal advocacy and the justice system in Bolivia to:

- Deliver immediate and improved education and training for justice operators, not limited to technical and specialized training, but mainly to inform justice operators regarding ethical principles, commitment, and greater respect for human and constitutional rights.
- Eradicate political interference or influence in the appointment of judges and prosecutors as well as interference in investigations and sentencing.
- Promote true independence of the judiciary and the Attorney General's Office.
- Provide an adequate budget for the administration of justice and better investigation and sentencing conditions.

Conclusion

As the interviewer, I had an interesting experience doing this interview as I could hear the evidence on how the culture and the context of a country can determine the way one approaches different topics. Maria Teresa has been very open, genuine, and critical in her opinions. I appreciated her objectivity, as well as her lack of fear, in revealing the weaknesses of the current Bolivian criminal justice system, at a time when those opinions can have negative repercussions for her. I appreciated her conviction and her passion to discuss these topics. The awkward time zone difference made the setup of the interviews quite challenging. However, Ms. Rivero Gutiérrez made herself available, and was willing to clarify and provide additional information via email.

It was difficult to bring her to think just as a prosecutor. As a professional, she is the product of the combined experiences gained in her former roles. Within those roles, she has always gone the extra mile, and incorporated project work to contribute to the improvement and reform of the Bolivian criminal legal system. I sensed her mixed feelings toward the criminal administration of justice; that of satisfaction and pride in the reforms implemented in criminal procedure, but also of frustration with the current Bolivian political environment that has impacted negatively on the administration of justice. However, I also perceived hope and optimism as she identified some simple tasks to be executed to improve the current situation.

I appreciated that during the interview she also asked me questions and wanted to know my views on different topics. She showed professionalism and remained very engaged in the interview.

Glossary

Judicial Council: created by the Act of December 22, 1997, to December 31, 2011, it was the administrative and disciplinary body of the Judiciary of Bolivia. It was part of the modernization of the judicial system in the country, as a cornerstone of strengthening democracy. The new institution was based in the capital city of Sucre. The Council was chaired by the President of the Supreme Court and it was composed of four members named Councils of the Judiciary, each with a law degree and 10 years of suitable professional practice, or experience as a university professor. This council transitioned into the Magistrates' Council on January 3, 2012.

Criminal Procedure Reform: the reform process that began in 1993 with the passage of a Law of Judicial Organization, reforms of the Bolivian Constitution and other rules that allowed the transition from a written and inquisitorial system to an oral and accusatorial procedural model through the enactment of a new Criminal Procedure Code by Law No. 1970 on March 25, 1999, that entered into effect in 2001.

oral trial: a trial that allows oral and public arguments and uses accusatorial procedures.

principle of celerity: a right to be tried without undue delay. This principle identifies the differentiation of procedures depending upon the seriousness of the case. For petty crimes, the procedures would be simplified as opposed to cases of more serious crimes.

principle of immediacy: this legal principle refers to the direct interaction that should exist between the judge and the parties in the adjudication of facts based on direct evidence presented to the judge to render a verdict and determine a sentence. This principle is closely related to the principle of orality in the trial. Immediacy requires an adjudicator to decide a case only on the evidence seen with his/her own eyes, not, for example, on the basis of hearsay evidence.

tribunals of sentence: tribunals that integrate views from two technical judges who are legally trained practitioners, and three lay citizens. These tribunals are appointed to hear and resolve criminal disputes by determining the culpability of the accused and also the applicable sanction.

Canada

5

NIKOLAI KOVALEV

Contents

The Criminal Justice Process of Canada

Canada is a constitutional monarchy and parliamentary democracy based on the Westminster model. The current Queen of Canada is Elizabeth II. The essential elements of the Canadian criminal justice system were inherited from England in the form of common law tradition of an independent judiciary, adversarial trials by jury, a strong criminal bar, and a system of law based primarily on judicial decisions. However, unlike many common law jurisdictions, Canada codified criminal substantive and procedural law in one single statute—the Criminal Code of Canada. Canada is a federal state consisting of 10 provinces (Alberta, British Columbia, Manitoba, Ontario, Prince Edward Island, Quebec, New Brunswick, Newfoundland and Labrador, Nova Scotia, and Saskatchewan) and three territories (Nunavut, Northwest Territories, and Yukon) and powers are divided between the federal and provincial governments. While the federal government has an exclusive jurisdiction over the criminal law and procedure (s. 91(27) of the Constitution

Act, 1867), the administration of justice in the provinces, including the constitution, maintenance, and organization of provincial criminal courts, is within the jurisdiction of the provinces (s. 92(14) of the Constitution Act, 1867).

In 1982, Canada amended its constitution to include the *Charter of Rights and Freedoms*, which had a profound impact on the development of the criminal justice system (Constitution Act, 1982). It provided for new safeguards of rights of accused in the criminal process at the pretrial investigation stage and trial stage. It changed the role of judges and gave them the power to exclude illegally obtained evidence and to use other remedies to rectify violations of the constitutional rights of defendants (Sharpe & Roach, 2013).

The Canadian system of criminal courts consists of the nine-member Supreme Court of Canada, which is the highest judicial authority; courts of appeal of provinces and territories, which hear appeals from the superior and provincial courts; superior courts (in some provinces they are called Supreme Courts or Courts of Queen's Bench), which adjudicate the most serious crimes, with or without juries, and sometimes hear appeals from provincial courts; and provincial courts that try the vast majority of criminal offenses and do not hear any appeals. There are also special federal courts such as the Federal Court of Appeal, Federal Court, Tax Court of Canada, and Court Martial Appeal Court and courts martial, which do not usually consider criminal matters, with the exception of court martial, which have the power to try military personnel and civilians accompanying such personnel abroad for crimes and offenses against the Code of Service Discipline. In order to become a judge, a candidate must have at least 10 years of experience practicing law. All federal and superior courts judges are appointed formally by the Governor General in Council (a representative of the Canadian monarch in Canada) and in fact, selected by the Prime Minister of Canada. Judges of provincial courts are formally appointed by the Lieutenant Governor in Council (a representative of the Canadian monarch in provinces), and in fact by the premiers of provinces. In 2013, there were 70 federal judges, 109 court of appeal judges, 721 superior court judges, and 1,042 provincial court judges in Canada (Hausegger, Hennigar, & Riddel, 2015, p. 38).

Only a small proportion of cases go to trial because the vast majority of criminal defendants in Canada plead guilty. If the person is charged with a crime punishable by at least five years in prison, he or she is eligible for a trial by jury consisting of 12 members. As opposed to some common law jurisdictions, which allow majority verdicts, jury verdicts in Canada must be unanimous. In cases where defendants are either not eligible for a jury trial or waived their right to the jury trial, they are tried by a judge alone sitting in either provincial court or superior court, depending on the seriousness of the crime and election by the accused.

Upon a guilty plea or a guilty verdict, the trial judge sentences a convicted person to one of the sentencing options: absolute or conditional discharge, probation, fine of up to $5,000 for individuals and unlimited for corporations, imprisonment for a fixed term up to 20 years or life imprisonment, with a possibility of parole determined by statutory provisions. There is a special form of punishment of indeterminate sentence that may be imposed on a convicted person if he or she has been found by the court to be a dangerous offender. In addition to fine and imprisonment, the sentencing judge can order a convicted person to abide by certain terms or conditions that are not part of a probation order or a conditional sentence such as, for example, a firearms prohibition order, or prohibition to operate any motor vehicle, vessel, aircraft, or railway equipment.

A person convicted of an indictable offense may appeal to the court of appeal from either the conviction or the sentence or both. One of the unique features of the Canadian criminal justice system, as opposed to other common law jurisdictions, is that the Crown has a right to appeal acquittals, including those that are based on jury verdicts. Although these cases are rare, the court of appeal can order a retrial in case of jury acquittal or enter a guilty verdict in case of judge alone acquittal if the Crown satisfies the appellate court that the verdict would not necessarily be the same if no error had been made at trial (Penney, Rondinelli, & Stribopoulos, 2011, pp. 747–748). A panel of three, or sometimes five, judges hears appeals at the court of appeal. A person, who is convicted or acquitted of an indictable offense where the conviction was confirmed or the acquittal set aside by the court of appeal, may in some cases appeal to the Supreme Court.

Provinces regulate legal professionals through independent professional corporations called law societies (in Quebec, the *Barreau du Québec*; in Nova Scotia the Barristers' Society), which set the standards for admission to the profession and the conduct of members in a particular province or territory. Currently, there are more than 100,000 lawyers practicing in Canada (Federation of Law Societies of Canada, 2015). As opposed to the United Kingdom, Canadian legal professionals are not divided into two separate legal professions of solicitors and barristers. All Canadian lawyers in common law provinces have the title of barrister and solicitor and can practice any type of law and appear in any court of the province in which they are admitted to the bar, and at any level of federal courts. In Quebec, however, legal professionals are divided between *Avocats,* the equivalent of barristers, and *Notaires,* who practice notarial law and are equivalents of solicitors. Upon admission to the bar, lawyers who choose criminal law as their practice can either work as private lawyers, representing defendants in criminal courts (defense counsel) or join the Crown Attorneys' Office in a province and work as Crown attorneys (prosecutors), responsible for prosecuting the vast majority of criminal offenses in provincial and superior courts. They can also join the Public Prosecution Service of Canada (PPSC), which is responsible for prosecuting offenses under more than 40 federal statutes (Public Prosecution Service of Canada, 2015).

Brian H. Greenspan, Defense Counsel, Greenspan Humphrey Lavine, Toronto

Introduction

Brian H. Greenspan is one of Canada's leading trial and appellate criminal lawyers whose career in criminal law spans over 40 years. As legal counsel, Mr. Greenspan has argued hundreds of cases at all levels of Canadian courts, including more than 20 cases before the Supreme Court of Canada. He has represented numerous high-profile and celebrity clients including fashion model Naomi Campbell, singer Justin Bieber, child-soldier Omar Khadr, and founder of the National Hockey League Players' Association Alan Eagleson. Mr. Greenspan's achievement and influence has been recognized through his ranking by the Canadian Lawyer Magazine as one of the top 25 most influential lawyers (2010 and 2013) and one of the best lawyers in Canada between 2007 and 2014. He is a recipient of the G. Arthur Martin Medal, which is the most prestigious award in Canadian criminal law given for outstanding contribution to criminal justice in Canada. He was awarded an honorary Doctor of Law degree by the Law Society of Upper Canada in 2012. He was recently named in Chambers Canada first listing of white-collar crime as one of three Band One lawyers in Canada.

Mr. Greenspan belongs to a renowned dynasty of legal professionals: his late brother, Edward Greenspan (1944–2014), was a celebrated criminal defense lawyer. His sister, Dr. Rosann Greenspan, is a criminology professor at the University of California at Berkeley. Mr. Greenspan is a partner in the Toronto law firm *Greenspan Humphrey Lavine*, which specializes in criminal and related regulatory and administrative litigation. This chapter provides an account of Mr. Greenspan's career as a criminal lawyer and his philosophy and attitudes towards crucial issues in the Canadian criminal justice system.

Career

At a very young age, both Mr. Greenspan and his brother, Edward, decided to pursue careers as criminal defense lawyers, inspired by the example of their father. As an immigrant to Canada, their father received his B.A. in Law from the University of Toronto in 1939 and entered Osgoode Hall Law School. He was unable to complete his studies because both WWII and the personal circumstances of his family required him to take on the family business in Niagara Falls, Ontario, which turned his career path to business. However, Mr. Greenspan's childhood was influenced by the law in many ways. His mother was a legal secretary to a Toronto lawyer for whom his father had worked for during his first year of law school. It is remarkable how in the 1930s and 1940s, one's ethnicity often determined career opportunities and choices: Jewish students were only able to land jobs with Jewish lawyers, and Jewish lawyers had Jewish secretaries. On March 31, 1957, when Mr. Greenspan was 10 years old, his father died of a heart attack. As part of his legacy Mr. Greenspan's father left a collection of law books that included works by Clarence Darrow, Edward Bennett Williams, and other great criminal barristers.

It was in the context of this early exposure to the world of law that the desire of Mr. Greenspan and his siblings to pursue a career in law emerged. Although Rosann Greenspan attended law school for one year, she soon realized her academic vocation and subsequently became a prominent criminologist. For a while, the Greenspan brothers followed the same path. Edward, the elder of the two brothers, enrolled at University College of the University of Toronto in 1962. In 1965, when Edward began his studies at the Osgoode Hall Law School, Brian followed his footsteps to University College, and lived in the same residence hall where Edward had lived several years earlier. In 1968, Edward graduated from law school and articled at the Ministry of the Attorney General, while Brian graduated in 1971 and was also scheduled to article at the Ministry of Attorney General. During their studies at the law school, both Greenspan brothers worked for the same criminal lawyer, who was also their second cousin: Edward started to work with that lawyer after his admission to the bar in 1970 and Brian worked with the same firm briefly during law school. In 1971, when Brian Greenspan graduated from law school, his mentor and friend, Professor Johann (Hans) Mohr, who taught law and psychiatry at Osgoode, encouraged Mr. Greenspan to apply for the Laidlaw Foundation Fellowship to pursue graduate studies. He was accepted by three different universities, but decided to do his LLM at the London School of Economics and Political Science, which he completed in 1972. During that year, Mr. Greenspan, who had never previously been able to afford travel to Europe, traveled extensively on the continent, to Israel and to the Soviet Union. That year was very fascinating for Mr. Greenspan, and shaped his further professional path.

When he returned to Canada and completed his articles at the Ministry of Attorney General, Mr. Greenspan joined *Pomerant & Pomerant*, a law firm where his brother Edward was junior counsel at the time. At the start of his legal career, Mr. Greenspan wanted to focus on appellate advocacy to translate his academic training into practical work. Because he was one of the few, if not the only practicing criminal lawyer with an LLM degree, the Osgoode Hall Law School invited Mr. Greenspan to teach a course on administration of criminal justice in Canada. After one year with *Pomerant & Pomerant,* Brian Greenspan left the firm against his brother's strong advice. Years later, both brothers recognized that Brian's departure was a wise decision because it enabled them to become closer brothers, grow stronger professionally, and collaborate on many cases. The Greenspan brothers built a tradition of working on important cases together, and were co-counsel on some very significant criminal cases, such as the "Blood Trial" (*R v. Armour Pharmaceutical Co.*, 2007) and Livent (*R v. Drabisky and Gottlieb*, 2009). This personal and professional bond evolved over the years with daily phone conversations, frequent meetings, and sharing of common topics and issues.

Beyond his professional tandem with his brother, Brian Greenspan's legal career has been marked by long-lasting professional relationships with his colleagues. When Brian Greenspan was leaving *Pomerant & Pomerant* in 1975 his assistant, Ms. Betty Bolter, also left the firm, continued to support him for the next 27 years and remains Mr. Greenspan's great friend. When Mr. Greenspan decided to expand his practice he hired his first articling student in 1977. His third articling student, Jane Arnup, became his first junior and later partner. Having experienced the challenges and pressures of a private defense practice, Ms. Arnup decided to move to Ottawa to take a position at the Law Reform Commission of Canada. Since 1977, Mr. Greenspan's firm has had 60 articling students with equal gender representation: 31 women and 29 men. In 1985, the firm became *Greenspan Humphrey* when David Humphrey joined Mr. Greenspan and continued as a partner for over 30 years. After Sharon Lavine joined the firm in 1993, it became *Greenspan Humphrey Lavine.*

Criminal law firms in Canada are typically small or are solo practitioners who frequently share space and administrative and clerical support. *Greenspan Humphrey Lavine* has eight lawyers and can boast outstanding collegiality within the firm, team spirit, and loyalty of staff.

As his practice was growing and flourishing, Mr. Greenspan continued to teach at Osgoode Hall and the University of Toronto for a period of over 20 years, between 1977 and 1998. Alongside his brother, Mr. Greenspan enjoyed teaching a criminal law course at the University of Toronto from 1984 to 1998. Edward and Brian were good teaching partners because of their frequently opposing views on many legal issues. Eddie Greenspan had more politically conservative views than his younger brother. Although both brothers shared the same views on fundamental justice issues, they often disagreed on issues of origin of crime. Mr. Greenspan jokingly admits that they stopped teaching that course when they realized there were no more disagreements, and the thought-provoking tension in the room had disappeared.

One of the things that has fascinated Mr. Greenspan during his career as a lawyer was policymaking by the government in relation to the justice system. He observes that in the last 40 years, despite an increasing number of criminal lawyers, Canada has consistently experienced a declining crime rate, making many criminal lawyers question their career prospects. While the reasons for this decrease are not clear, it is obvious from

Mr. Greenspan's perspective that there is no link between a "war on crime," tough anti-crime measures, and a reduction in crime. His view derives from a history of declining crime rates both during the eras of liberalization and eras of a more penal approach to crime. Mr. Greenspan suggests that the policies of the Canadian government have had little influence on crime trends in the country, and he questions the rationale and effectiveness of changes in policy directions and attitudes with each change of government. Policymaking with regard to crime should be based on social attitudes on how people who have committed crimes should be treated rather than a rational model, which hypothesizes that a tougher approach to crime, for example, will result in better outcomes.

Another topic that has provoked Mr. Greenspan's interest has been the interpretation and the influence of the Charter of Rights and Freedoms. In his 1987 lecture on the influence of the Charter jurisprudence on the criminal law in Canada, which was delivered at Cambridge University (Greenspan, 1987), Mr. Greenspan predicted that Canada would end up with a typical Canadian compromise. He believed that Canadian courts would be liberal in their declarations of rights and interpret those rights in a liberal fashion. He also suggested that while a violation of a Charter right would be recognized, no exclusion of evidence would be made in accordance with s. 24(2) of the Charter, which states:

> Where, in proceedings under subsection (1), a court concludes that evidence was obtained in a manner that infringed or denied any rights or freedoms guaranteed by this Charter, the evidence shall be excluded if it is established that, having regard to all the circumstances, the admission of it in the proceedings would bring the administration of justice into disrepute.

From Mr. Greenspan's viewpoint, this would be the usual compromise between American principle and British inaction, which has always been a tension in Canadian law. At the time when the lecture was delivered Mr. Greenspan thought that his interpretation of the Charter was right and insightful. It turned out that for some time his prediction was wrong. When Justice Antonio Lamer (1933–2007) was appointed to the Supreme Court in 1980 and served as a judge and, subsequently, Chief Justice up until 2000 (Dodek & Jutras, 2009), it gradually became an activist court, which both interpreted the Charter liberally and created remedies. It was astonishing for Mr. Greenspan and many other lawyers to see the creation of new remedies, which had never existed in Canadian law. Over the following decade, however, the new composition of the Supreme Court put the brakes on, and Mr. Greenspan's interpretation of the Charter offered in his lecture back in 1987 was becoming true again. During that period, the decisions of the Supreme Court of Canada became unpredictable, and it was almost impossible to foresee the outcome of one's Charter challenge. What Mr. Greenspan has observed is a consistent trend toward retrenchment as a result of a new conservative philosophy: not only there is no remedy but also there may not be a recognition of a Charter's breach. Mr. Greenspan has witnessed how, within several decades, Canadian jurisprudence has gone through a roller coaster experience with Charter interpretation and the impact of the Charter.

Another groundbreaking event for Mr. Greenspan was the Supreme Court's *R v. Stinchcombe* (1991) judgment written by Justice John Sopinka (1933–1997) in 1991. When *Stinchcombe* was released Mr. Greenspan would not have predicted that it would become the most transformational case in the history of criminal procedure in Canada as it changed the entire nature of the practice of criminal law. Mr. Greenspan started his career in the era when defense lawyers would go to the prosecutor's office to ask for disclosure and the Crown attorneys would orally share selected information from their files, which was written down by defense lawyers. Simple photocopying was unusual, and the process of disclosure was time consuming and very selective. *Stinchcombe* helped criminal defense lawyers better prepare for their cases. It became particularly helpful for the purposes of conducting cross-examination. After *Stinchcombe*, defense lawyers were constitutionally mandated to receive all materials; any attempts to conceal relevant evidence would become a significant issue within the current justice system. Mr. Greenspan believes that in comparison with the rest of the common law world, Canada is far advanced with respect to disclosure requirements as a result of Justice Sopinka's judgments.

Mr. Greenspan professes that he loves his work today more than he did 42 years ago for a variety of reasons. First of all, there is a sense of growth and professional maturation which enabled Mr. Greenspan to build a team of excellent legal professionals and provide them with opportunities to develop professionally, while staying focused on aspects of the practice that he truly enjoyed. Second, Mr. Greenspan has a romantic view of his and his colleagues' practice and of the role of defense lawyers. He strongly believes that without a vibrant, energetic, and strong defense, democracy fails and that the adversarial system is a very effective way to seek out the truth, be fair and have a civilized democratic society. He compares the defense lawyer with the "little boy with his finger in a dike" making sure that democracy does not erode. It is this view of the role of defense lawyers that makes Mr. Greenspan feel privileged to be part of the profession; it is a role that he envisioned at the beginning of his career and continues to adhere to.

Philosophy of Legal Advocacy

Brian Greenspan's philosophy about legal advocacy is underpinned by the basic principles of the justice system: in the adversarial process, rather than in the accusatorial process, a vigorous defense minimizes the mistakes that the justice system makes. A vigorous defense calls on the state to perform its duties responsibly, play by rules and fairly, and investigate and prosecute crime in an appropriate way. There should be a clear division of responsibilities between different players in the criminal justice system. First, the police are tasked with investigating crime: they gather evidence and then reach the point when they have a case to present on a low standard, based on reasonable and probable grounds to believe that the offense has been committed. Some parts of Canada are disadvantaged by the fact that these decisions are not first vetted by professionals with legal training. In Ontario, for example, the Crown does not vet charges. Mr. Greenspan suggests that while not every charge needs to be vetted, serious charges ought to be vetted. In the province of British Columbia, on the contrary, charges are vetted.

The second function or role in the criminal justice system belongs to the Crown attorneys who, when the case is passed to their office, make a decision on whether there is a reasonable prospect of conviction. By then, at least in Ontario, suspects are already charged and already impacted by these events. The fact of the charge, particularly against someone with any public profile, may inflict significant reputational damage even if the charges are subsequently withdrawn.

For example, Mr. Greenspan's firm represented a popular singer, Justin Bieber, who was charged in Toronto with a common assault on a taxi driver. The police station where Justin Bieber surrendered was crowded and a police escort was required to walk him through the crowd. This mayhem was the result of an information leak to the press from within the police division. In this case, the Crown subsequently vetted the case after the client was charged and decided that there was no reasonable prospect of conviction.

The next role in the justice system emerges at the time when the Crown vets the charge and the case goes forward. At this point the tension between the defense and the Crown intensifies, while both parties are expected to conduct themselves honorably, honestly, and with integrity. This tension and adversariness is part of the rules of engagement. In this adversarial environment, the defense lawyer vigorously and energetically defends his client's position with the ultimate objective of defending the client's liberty. Many criminal lawyers were, and continue to be, challenged by this high-pressure environment and are at risk of mental health issues and addictions.

Mr. Greenspan sees the profession of criminal law as a community of independent people who have strong moral and political views, including the view that people who are engaged in crime are part of the socioeconomic underbelly of the society and those who are generally underprivileged and marginalized. This philosophy leads many lawyers to participate in organizations defending rights and freedoms of such people. Mr. Greenspan himself is a Director of the Association in Defense of the Wrongly Convicted, a foundation that funds cases where lawyers believe there has been a miscarriage of justice. Mr. Greenspan is also on the Board of the Book Club for Inmates, a nonprofit project, which aims to help inmates develop their literacy skills and appreciation of literature. Mr. Greenspan is also involved in Peacebuilders, a great contribution to youth justice through which young people are diverted before they get into the criminal justice system. There is an opportunity for criminal lawyers to make significant impact by getting increasingly involved in such projects and initiatives.

Another opportunity for criminal lawyers to influence the criminal justice system is to express their views about proposed legislation. In 1992, Mr. Greenspan was the founding president of the Canadian Council of Criminal Defense Lawyers, an organization representing Canadian defense counsel, with a view to providing a forum for the defense to voice their views. There is an obligation of the leaders of the bar to speak up the way in which Eddie Greenspan did in the 1980s against the proposed reintroduction of capital punishment in Canada. Brian Greenspan is himself a frequent speaker at various events around Canada. He talks about vital criminal justice issues that concern Canadian society today, such as civility in advocacy and the war on crime. Public outreach is an indispensable part of a criminal lawyer's role in society.

Collegiality of the criminal bar is a very significant part of who Canadian criminal lawyers are. *Greenspan Humphrey Lavine* has been committed and active in the work of the Criminal Lawyers Association. Mr. Greenspan is a proponent of reinstatement of the Bench and Bar Council of Ontario, which served as a liaison between judges and Ontario legal profession in 1980–1990s. Mr. Greenspan's firm also collaborates with international lawyers' associations, such as the National Association of Criminal Defense Lawyers, the American College of Trial Lawyers, and the International Society of Barristers. Programs and conferences organized by these and other associations provide great lifelong learning and knowledge sharing opportunities for new and experienced criminal defense attorneys. Mr. Greenspan taught for 25 years in the National Criminal Law Program, organized by the Federation of Law Societies of Canada, which brings together around 700 Canadian judges, defense lawyers, and prosecutors.

Mr. Greenspan challenges the effectiveness of the crime control model adopted by the former conservative government. The so-called "war on crime" and establishment of mandatory minimum punishments that do not vest judges with healthy discretion are erroneous. Restricting parole release and keeping offenders in custody for longer periods are counterproductive. Mr. Greenspan is a proponent of the rehabilitation model of punishment, as he believes that the increase in punishment does not have influence on general deterrence. This view is based on a simple premise that people who are going to be involved in criminal activity do not estimate the number of days or years they are going to serve as a result of their criminal activity before they engage in criminal activity. The failure of a universal policy of "war on crime" is illustrated by the example of a prominent business person who commits fraud causing many victims to lose their life savings. If this businessman has a significant public profile, his business career is over, which is a significant punishment in itself. If this offender has any assets, he can be compelled to forfeit them as a punishment. After his reputation and financial position are destroyed, the state may consider the appropriate period of incarceration, for example, 2, 4, 10, 25, or 50 years. However, there is no rational basis for these decisions. From a rational perspective, once someone's career and wealth are destroyed, whether he goes to jail for two years or ten years is unlikely to discourage from committing the crime. Examples like this indicate that the criminal justice system and society in general should be looking for more effective ways to reduce crime.

Problems and Successes Experienced

From Brian Greenspan's perspective, one of the main developments in Canadian criminal law was the introduction of diversion rather than prosecution. Diversion programs focused on alcohol and drug addiction are particularly successful. Mr. Greenspan described a case in which he represented a lawyer who, near the end of his career, at the age of 67 became addicted to crystal meth. He went to the United States for a holiday and tried to smuggle the drug across the border in his briefcase. Although this case was captured by the criminal justice system, it should not have has a criminal law resolution.

Mr. Greenspan sees more challenges associated with mental health diversion programs. Sharon Lavine, one of the partners at *Greenspan Humphrey Lavine*, is an Alternate Chair of the Ontario Review Board, an agency that annually reviews the status of every person who has been found not criminally responsible or unfit to stand trial for criminal offenses on account of a mental disorder. Ms. Lavine and her colleagues in the firm regularly discuss cases that come for her review. Mental health and its relationship to crime has always been a difficult topic, complicated by a range of professional opinions on the application of imposed treatments. There are many psychiatrists who argue that imposed treatment is not very effective, and a strong public opinion that people who suffer from mental disorders should be willing to be subjected to treatment. While there is no consensus on imposed treatments, Mr. Greenspan believes that the mental health diversion program is a very important element of the criminal justice system in Canada.

Effectiveness of the parole system is another topic of importance to Brian Greenspan. The idea of keeping people in custody until the bitter end, and then releasing them, is counterproductive. Bringing people back into the society through a phased program is more successful and rational. Transferring people from the penitentiary to a prison with a lower level of security, then to halfway houses, is much more effective in terms of reintegrating offenders into the community. Conversely, transferring people from a violent and traumatic environment directly into the community is doomed to failure. One of Mr. Greenspan's most recent cases involved an appeal against conviction of two counts of second-degree murder based on a guilty jury verdict. The court of appeal allowed Mr. Greenspan's appeal on the ground that the jury verdict was unreasonable, and acquitted the client (*R v. Dodd*, 2015). After six years in custody, his client was released into the community as a free man. Mr. Greenspan has a tremendous sympathy for the difficulties confronted by individuals in trying to control themselves responsibly after confinement and restriction for a lengthy period of time. Full release into the community after a long sentence is a very traumatic experience, and current parole policies in Canada do not support a gradual transition from lengthy custody to freedom.

The biggest issues facing Canadian criminal courts should be viewed from a cyclic perspective rather than as an isolated topic or hot issue of the month. For example, there are two categories of preventive detention in Canada: dangerous and long-term offenders. For a period of time, there were many attempts to label people as dangerous or long-term offenders but as time passed, this approach has either weakened or there is simply no attention to the topic. The frequency with which dangerous offenders come into the criminal justice system is quite low. However, if the Crown starts treating this as a hot topic, all of a sudden there would be an increase in applications to declare offenders as dangerous or long-term offenders. This and other similar examples reflect that it is frequently the latest pronouncement or a hot topic of the month as opposed to a continuing policy issue that burdens the criminal law.

Mr. Greenspan is also very concerned with issues related to bail. About 20 years ago because of the extensive bail caseload, Ontario shifted the responsibility for conducting bail hearings from the jurisdiction of professional judges to the jurisdiction of justices of the peace, many of whom are not legally trained. While justices of the peace are undoubtedly very capable and dedicated people, they may not have sufficient legal training in order to make what is arguably the most significant decision about an offender in the criminal justice system. This first decision in the process is so important because the suspect can be detained in custody for several years before the process moves any further. Bail issues dictate the conduct of the trial. If the suspect does not receive bail, there is more of a tendency across the board to try to resolve the case in a less favorable way than when lawyers have the freedom to conduct a full defense. In Mr. Greenspan's opinion such a crucial decision as bail should be made by legal professionals.

Throughout his legal career, Mr. Greenspan has observed the evolution of relationships between judges and defense counsel. In the mid-1970s, when Mr. Greenspan became a lawyer, stereotypical old-fashioned, crotchety judges were prevalent. All of sudden they were replaced by thoughtful, highly qualified, courteous, and generous professionals who dealt with counsel in a dignified and very civil way. These attitudes dominated over the next 20 or 30 years, and the overall environment in Ontario courts was dictated by thoughtful and civilized lawyering and judging, and great courtesy. However, in recent years there has been some retrenchment from that trend, and Mr. Greenspan has observed a reemergence of judges with poor communication skills. In the circles of legal professionals, there is a notion that dignity and respect shown to counsel should be earned, not assumed, while in the past it was assumed: unless counsel or the participants in the courtroom were somehow offensive, judges showed them respect. Mr. Greenspan observed that today, legal professionals are more impatient, less friendly, and collegial. In this environment, there are occasions when counsel may justifiably think that he has not had a thorough and unbiased opportunity to present his case before the judge.

Theory and Practice

In terms of the relationship between theory and practice in legal advocacy, Mr. Greenspan believes that because of the adversarial nature of the criminal justice system, the objectives of the defense are not to alienate the tribunal of fact, jurors, but to persuade them and bring them around to the defense counsel's way of thinking. Between the two, practical considerations should prevail over theory because of the objectives. Lawyers should always have a view of what they are trying to achieve in a particular case. If the lawyer can achieve this objective by applying a principled approach or a legal argument that is based on the position of the Supreme Court of Canada on a particular issue of law, then he or she should do it. At the same time, the focus on objectives of the case should never compromise a defense lawyers' honesty and integrity. For example, defense counsel should never advance a position that was overruled by a binding authority that would not be only bad advocacy but also wrong and professionally irresponsible. It is often said that if there is a case that a lawyer thinks is arguable against his or her case, the lawyer should always include it in their factum or written arguments to the court. If this information is not included, it may come to light in the opponent's factum and the defense lawyer would end up strategically disadvantaged, as the judge would have doubts about the defense counsel's candor and integrity. Failure to adhere to the principles of candor and integrity can be self-defeating for a lawyer. By including a case against one's own case, and arguing it effectively, reflects a lawyer's professionalism and integrity.

Today almost every legal problem is examined and analyzed through the prism of the Charter. Therefore, lawyers and policymakers need to understand the dynamic behind Charter jurisprudence, which is often very theoretical. *R v. Ryan* (2013), was one of Mr. Greenspan's recent Supreme Court of Canada appeals in the case of a woman who made six attempts to hire a contract killer to murder her abusive husband. In that case, a different trial lawyer used the defense of duress, which may not have been the ideal defense, but was successful both at trial and in the Nova Scotia Court of Appeal. The case was appealed by the Crown to the Supreme Court of Canada and Mr. Greenspan appeared with his colleague from Nova Scotia. Although it was not the case of duress, but more a matter of self-defense, as an appellate lawyer, Mr. Greenspan was confined by the initial defense theory of duress. This case manifested the real challenge between legal theory and practice: the defense team placed a strong emphasis on compassionate understanding of actions of the accused, who feared continued threat of physical violence against her and her daughter from her abusive husband. Mr. Greenspan and his team tried to convince the court not to expose the accused to a new trial that would lead to continued trauma and potential for violence against her person. Mr. Greenspan believes that the defense team succeeded in their strategy, although it was a surprising result for him and his colleagues. While they lost on the principle of duress, as they should have, according to Mr. Greenspan, the Supreme Court of Canada stayed the proceedings against the client because of the lengthy timeframe and state neglect. Interestingly, it was an eight to one decision, with all conservative judges in favor of a stay. In this case, the Supreme Court of Canada made a decision that was not based on principles, but rather practical considerations, as the defense team had worked tirelessly to find a practical solution for the client because the case did not fit with the principle.

There is an interrelationship between theory and practice, and it is governed by the lawyer's commitment to advance the client's causes as effectively as possible. The lawyer has to figure out a strategy consistent with legal principles and consistent with professional obligations to be honest and candid. At the same time the lawyer must remember that his or her main objective is to serve the client's interests.

Transnational Relations

Mr. Greenspan and his colleagues do a lot of work that touches on cross-border issues, including numerous cases involving extradition, mutual legal assistance, immigration issues that relate to Canada and the United States, as well as some cross-border prosecutions. Mr. Greenspan was involved in the first if not the only transborder resolution, the case of Alan Eagleson, a former lawyer, hockey agent, and promoter who was charged with a variety of serious fraud allegations both in the United States and Canada. Alan Eagleson was facing up to 20 years in jail in the United States and 10 years in Canada. This case required a team of lawyers in both countries to engage in concurrent negotiations with both American and Canadian prosecutors. After reaching a resolution in both United States and Canada, all other charges in both countries were withdrawn by the prosecutors in Canada and the United States.

Other clients of Mr. Greenspan included, for example, a U.S. pharmaceutical company charged and acquitted of providing contaminated hemophilia blood products and the U.S. Tobacco Corporation charged with contraband of tobacco products into Canada. Mr. Greenspan also observed how the consequences of the September 11, 2001 terrorist attacks in the United States affected his work particularly due to activities of the U.S. Homeland Security, which retrieved all historical records on Canadians who had been charged or convicted of criminal offenses. As an example, Mr. Greenspan cited the case of an elderly woman with children and grandchildren in the United States, but who lives in Toronto. She was prohibited entry in the United States due to her 1979 conviction for fraud of under $500. After 2010 she had to apply for a waiver even though she had traveled to the United States between 1985 and 2010 on numerous occasions. Such cross-border work and the ability to effectively collaborate with the U.S. legal professionals require Canadian lawyers to have a solid understanding of the U.S. process.

General Assessments

Mr. Greenspan has numerous observations on problematic or challenge-ridden areas of law and some retrenchment trends. For example, he is deeply concerned with the existence of mandatory minimum punishment, recent developments in the area of early release on parole, and the use of incarceration in Canada. He challenges the general attitude in the Canadian society about a less active role of judges. He argues that the common law has been a remarkable patchwork of judge-made law and that the common law has advanced through judges' interpretation of the law. The Canadian public may have misleading messages and opinions about the role of courts. According to Mr. Greenspan, judges should continue to interpret codified law in order for it to stay current and responsive to the issues that Canadians think are important.

With regard to future developments in the Canadian criminal justice system, Mr. Greenspan hopes to see the reinstatement of the Canadian Law Reform Commission. Research studies and papers prepared by the Law Reform Commission in 1970s and 1980s had an enormous impact on the Canadian criminal law and justice system. An objective, independent study, analysis, and testing of the effectiveness of the Canadian criminal justice system should continue to be available to Canadian society.

Conclusion

In the interview that formed the basis of this article Mr. Greenspan raised important issues, which Canadian legal professionals are currently facing in the criminal justice system. Mr. Greenspan's openness revealed that practices in Canadian criminal courts are significantly influenced by the government's crime control and *tough on crime* policies. The Conservative Government that was in power in Canada for the last 10 years stacked higher courts with conservative judges who are willing to implement the *tough on crime* agenda. As a result, criminal lawyers observe how constitutional rights of the accused have been diluted by conservative jurisprudence. Mr. Greenspan's deep insights and rich experience as a criminal defense lawyer help the reader understand the meaning and implications of policies and initiatives advanced by the current Canadian government.

Glossary

American College of Trial Lawyers: an association composed of the best of the trial bar from the United States and Canada, widely considered to be the premier professional trial organization in North America. Founded in 1950, the College is dedicated to maintaining and improving standards of trial practice, the administration of justice, and the ethics of the profession. http://www.actl.com.

Association in Defense of the Wrongly Convicted: a Canadian, nonprofit organization dedicated to identifying, advocating for, and exonerating individuals convicted of a crime that they did not commit, and to preventing injustices in the future through legal education and justice system reform. http://www.aidwyc.org/.

Book Club for Inmates: a registered charity that organizes volunteer-led book clubs within federal penitentiaries across Canada. By fall of 2015, it will be facilitating 22 book clubs inside 15 different penitentiaries in seven provinces.

Canadian Council of Criminal Defense Lawyers: an association formed in 1992 to represent defense counsel and to offer a national voice and perspective on criminal justice issues. Its representatives frequently appear before the Senate the House of Commons Standing Committees. http://www.cccdl.ca/.

Canadian Law Reform Commission: the Law Reform Commission of Canada (1971–1993, 1997–2006) served as a permanent independent body to study and undertake a systematic review of Canadian law. The Commission was permanently disbanded in 2006 by the Conservative Government of Stephen Harper.

Charter of Rights and Freedoms: part of the Constitution Act of 1982, which introduced a bill of rights into the Canadian constitution.

Criminal Lawyers Association: one of the largest specialty legal organizations in Canada, with more than 1,200 members. http://www.criminallawyers.ca/.

Federation of Law Societies of Canada: the national coordinating body of Canada's 14 provincial and territorial law societies.

G. Arthur Martin Medal: an annual award presented by the Criminal Lawyers Association for outstanding contribution to criminal justice. G. Arthur Martin was Canada's greatest criminal advocate before he became a leading jurist with the Ontario Court of Appeal.

International Society of Barristers: a private organization created in 1965, dedicated to preserving trial by jury, the adversary system, and an independent judiciary. Membership is by invitation only after a rigorous screening process by lawyers and judges to identify trial lawyers who meet its standards. http://www.isob.com/.

National Association of Criminal Defense Lawyers: the largest US *organization of criminal defense attorneys.* It generally advocates for legislation and court rules to protect defendants. http://www. nacdl.org/.

China

6

AI MA
ZHUO ZHANG

Contents

The Criminal Justice Process of China

The judicial system of China comprises subsystems for investigation, prosecution, trial procedures, jails, judicial administration, arbitration, lawyers, public notaries, and state compensation (China Internet Information Center, n.d.). In conducting criminal proceedings, the public security agencies, the People's Procuratorates, and the People's Courts perform their task independently; however, cooperation between these three divisions may be necessary for some cases. The public security agencies are responsible for investigation, detention, execution of arrests, and preliminary inquiry in criminal cases. The People's Procuratorates are responsible for procuratorial work, authorizing approval of arrests, conducting investigation, and initiating public prosecution of cases directly accepted by the procuratorial agencies. The People's Courts are responsible for adjudication. The People's Courts and the People's Procuratorates are elected, report to, and are supervised by the People's Congress at various levels. The People's Courts, the People's Procuratorates, and the public security agencies divide responsibilities, coordinate their efforts, and check each other to ensure correct and effective enforcement of law.

Modern History of the Legal System in China

The history of the legal system of China can be traced back to the Xia Dynasty (c. 2070–c. 1600 BCE) (Zhang, 1999). The Imperial era came to an end in 1911 following the overthrow of the Qing dynasty. After the First Opium War in the 1840s, feudal China gradually developed into a semi-colonial and semi-feudal country (China, 1983). No government was strong enough to establish a legal system until the foundation of the People's Republic of China (PRC) in 1949, which marked the transition from the centuries-old dictatorial system of feudalism to the system of people's democracy (Chen, 2016).

China's current justice system was formed and developed gradually after the founding of the PRC. The Common Program of the Chinese People's Political Consultative Conference, which functioned as a provisional Constitution, and the Organic Law of the Central People's Government of the PRC were both promulgated in September 1949 and laid the cornerstone for legal construction in New China. The Constitution of the PRC was enacted in 1954. The Organic Law of the People's Courts and the People's Procuratorates of the PRC were among the other laws and regulations that defined the organic system and established the basic functions of the People's Courts and Procuratorates. Additionally, the Organic Law established the systems of collegiate panels, defense, public trial, people's jurors, legal supervision, and civil mediation, hence providing the basic framework of China's judicial system (Information Office of State Council of the People's Republic of China, 2012).

Toward the end of the 1950s, especially during the tumultuous 10-year "Cultural Revolution" (1966–1976), China's judicial system suffered severe damage and its legislation almost came to a standstill. Since the introduction of Reform & Opening up in 1978, China, after summing up its historical experience, established the fundamental policy of promoting socialist democracy and improving socialist legal construction. This restored and rebuilt the judicial system, and formulated and amended a range of fundamental laws. In the 1990s, China established the fundamental principle of governing the country in accordance with the law and quickened the step to build China into a socialist country under the rule of law. Currently, China has established a socialist system of laws with Chinese characteristics, headed by the Constitution. The Constitution has laws relating to civil, commercial, administrative, and local regulations and other tiers of legal provisions, which has ensured that there are laws to abide by in economic, political, cultural, ecological, and social development (Chen, 2016). During the process of promoting social progress, democracy, and the rule of law, China's modern judicial system is continuously improving and developing.

People's Procuratorates of China

The People's Procuratorate is the prosecutorial agency in China. The state has set up the Supreme People's Procuratorate, Local People's Procuratorates at different levels, and special People's Procuratorates such as military procuratorates and railway transportation procuratorates (Organic Law of the People's Procuratorates of the People's Republic of China, 1979, art 2). The Supreme People's Procuratorate directs the work of the Local People's Procuratorates at different levels and that of special People's Procuratorates. A People's Procuratorate at a higher level directs the work of a People's Procuratorate at the level below it. Procuratorates are established at levels corresponding to those of the courts so that cases can be prosecuted in accordance with legal procedures. The People's Procuratorate exercises legal supervision over criminal, civil, and administrative litigations in accordance with the law (Organic Law of the People's Procuratorates of the People's Republic of China, 1979).

As shown in Figure 6.1, People's Procuratorates at various local levels are divided into the following:

- People's Procuratorates of provinces, autonomous regions, and municipalities directly under the Central Government.
- Branches of the People's Procuratorates of provinces, autonomous regions, and municipalities directly under the Central Government, and People's Procuratorates of autonomous prefectures and cities directly under the provincial governments.
- People's Procuratorates of counties, cities, autonomous counties, and municipal districts.

According to the Constitution and other laws, the People's Procuratorates exercise the following functions and duties:

- Directly accepting and handling criminal cases involving corruption, bribery, violations of citizens' democratic rights, and allegations of misconduct in office, placing them on file for investigation and deciding whether to initiate prosecution or not.
- Performing legal supervision over the judicial proceedings of courts and investigations of criminal cases.

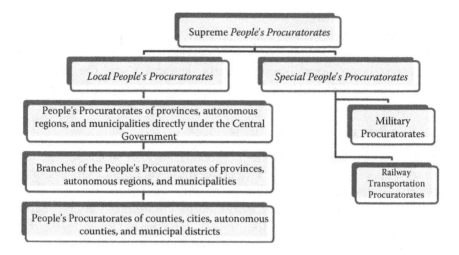

Figure 6.1 The structure of the People's Procuratorates in China.

- Deciding on arrests and prosecution of criminal cases according to law and performing legal supervision over judicial activities in criminal cases.
- Performing legal supervision over the judicial proceedings of courts and investigations of the civil cases.
- Performing legal supervision over the administration of litigation.

Huisheng Zong, Senior Prosecutor of the
Henan People's Procuratorate Beijing

Introduction

Prosecutor Huisheng Zong has served as a public prosecutor with The People's Procuratorate of Henan Province, China, for over 30 years. Henan Province is one of the most populous provinces in China, with approximately 95 million permanent residents (National Bureau of Statistics of China, 2014a). More than 80,000 defendants per year are prosecuted by the Henan People's Procuratorate (People's Procuratorate of Henan Province, 2015). Having previously served as an assistant prosecutor, in 2007, Prosecutor Zong was nominated to Senior Prosecutor of the Henan People's Procuratorate.

With a career spanning 30 years in the procuratorial system, Prosecutor Zong has primarily focused on corruption or duty-related crimes, such as embezzlement, bribery, misappropriation of public funds, and distributing state-owned property to individuals. His seniority and his vast experience in this area have made him a pioneering prosecutor and expert since the position of public prosecutor on duty-related crimes was first created.

This chapter traces the development of Senior Prosecutor Zong's legal career and provides an overview of his engagements and reflections on the development and operation of the contemporary legal system in China. A glossary of legal terms is provided at the end of the chapter.

Career

Since the introduction of corruption crimes in the 1980s, Prosecutor Zong's career advancement has been closely linked to the development of China's legal system. In the 1970s, during the Cultural Revolution, Prosecutor Zong spent two years in the countryside as an educated youth. From 1976 to 1981, he served as a literary and artistic soldier at a communication unit, stationed in Xi'an and Chongqing. After his retirement from the army, Prosecutor Zong started work as a police officer in the Railway Public Security Division of Zhengzhou, the capital city of Henan Province. During his four years of service in the Railway Public Security Division, Prosecutor Zong further pursued his education at the Party School of the Zhengzhou Railway Bureau and completed an undergraduate degree in Law, Philosophy, and Political Science. Prosecutor Zong complemented his education further by under-taking advanced training in interrogation and criminal investigations at the renowned China University of Political Science and Law in Beijing. With a university degree and advanced specialist training in law, Prosecutor Zong embarked on his legal career as a clerk at the Zhengzhou Railway Transport

Procuratorate in 1985. After a year of prosecutorial work, he was appointed as assistant prosecutor. In 1988, when he became a prosecutor, he began to conduct investigations and initiate public prosecution of cases independently.

At the end of the 1980s, China underwent a rapid series of Reform & Opening up policies (Shirk, 1993). The success of China's economy resulted in immense changes in the Chinese society (Fang, 2009; Yu, 2002). Duty-related crimes emerged as a result of the open market policy (He, 1999). The student protests of 1989 against corruption attracted extensive attention from the Chinese government (Jiang, 2010). In that same year, Prosecutor Zong led an investigation into an organized group that gained excessive illegal profits by bribing railway officials to obtain difficult transportation resources. During his investigation, it was proven that the deputy director of the Zhengzhou Railway Bureau at that time was involved with this group. This led to a subsequent joint investigation by Zhengzhou Railway Transport Procuratorate, the Railway Transportation Department, and Economy Department of the Supreme People's Procuratorate. Prosecutor Zong spent two years investigating this case, and ultimately, more than 20 high-ranking officials were convicted and dismissed from their positions. The highest-ranking official, the former director of the Transportation Department, Ministry of Railway, was convicted of embezzlement and accepting bribes, and was sentenced to death, commuted to a life sentence. This was the first major corruption case implicating top-ranking leaders after the founding of New China. It marked the beginning of the era of investigation into duty-related crimes.

In tangent with the success of China's economic reforms, duty-related crimes evolved into more intelligent and subtle forms. For example, only a few economic crimes appeared in the first Criminal Law of the People's Republic of China in 1979. Numerous additions of crimes related to embezzlement and bribery appear in the latest amendment (Amendment (IX) to the Criminal Law of the People's Republic of China, 2015). Such crimes included embezzlement, misappropriation of public funds, and acceptance of bribes. These changes not only impose more challenges on the prosecutorial system, but also place further pressure on individual prosecutors.

Reflecting on his past work in this area, Prosecutor Zong believes that duty-crime investigations must be more systematic and scientific to meet new challenges and developments required by the modernization of the Chinese legal system. In 2007, as the lead prosecutor, Prosecutor Zong established a collaborative training program between the People's Procuratorate of Henan Province and the Institute of Criminal Psychology at the China University of Political Science and Law. The goal of this program was to explore the psychological and social factors associated with duty crimes, develop theories on the processes of investigation and interrogation of duty-related crimes, and improve the application of psychological methodologies in analyzing cases and conducting investigations. Professors from the China

University of Political Science and Law and legal practitioners who teach at the National Prosecutors College of PRC are invited to develop training materials and deliver lectures. This program fosters collaboration between academics and legal practitioners in researching duty-related crimes. About 1,000 trainees from the duty-related crime investigation department of the People's Procuratorates of Henan Province participate in the program every year.

Philosophy of Legal Advocacy

The work of procuratorates comprises two essential parts: first, the supervision of criminal and civil investigations, and second, the supervision of court procedures. In accordance with the Criminal Procedure Law of the PRC (Criminal Procedure Law of the People's Republic of China Amendment, 2012), the role of the People's Procuratorates is to exercise legal supervision over criminal proceedings. The People's Procuratorates also have the right to exercise legal supervision over civil proceedings, in accordance with the Civil Procedure Law of the PRC (Civil Procedure Law of the People's Republic of China Amendment, 2012). The People's Procuratorates' tasks further extend to prosecutorial power over cases seriously endangering state and public security, infringing upon citizens' personal and democratic rights, and other important criminal cases. In addition, they have the power to examine the cases scheduled for investigation by public security agencies, decide whether a suspect should be arrested or not, discretion over whether a case should be prosecuted, institute and support public prosecution in criminal cases, and oversee activities in public security agencies, people's courts, jails, and prisons.

Chinese courts are divided into a four-level court system, including the Supreme People's Courts, Higher People's Courts, Intermediate People's Courts, and Basic People's Courts (Organic Law of the People's Courts of the People's Republic of China, 2006). The People's Procuratorates, as well as the People's Courts, independently exercise their powers without interference from any administrative organ, social organization, or individual person. Possible corruption of People's Courts, procuratorial agencies, and public security agencies, especially at basic levels, is the uppermost concern of Prosecutor Zong. He noticed that some of these agencies at the basic level might collude for some mutual benefits.

Prosecutor Zong observed that the supervision of procuratorates became increasingly transparent and effective after the Supreme People's Procuratorate issued and rigidly enforced the Implementing Regulations of the Criminal Procedure Law (Provisions of the Supreme People's Court, the Supreme People's Procuratorate, the Ministry of Public Security, the Ministry of State Security, the Ministry of Justice, and the Legislative Affairs Commission of the Standing Committee of the National People's Congress on Several Issues concerning the Implementation of the Criminal Procedure Law, 2012). For instance, according to the Implementing Regulations, video and audio recordings of interrogation are mandatory from the time when a suspect is first arrested and detained. The suspect's defense team has full access to all these recordings. Procuratorates from all levels are subject to annual random internal inspections by higher-level People's Procuratorates. This is aimed to curb the admission of forced confessions and forged evidence. In spite of the above measures, misconduct still occurs during the process of investigation and interrogation. Prosecutor Zong has conducted empirical surveys on this issue for the anticorruption training program. Surprisingly, 3 or 4 participants per 100 endorsed "extorting a confession by torture."

Prosecutor Zong believes that two basic qualities make a good prosecutor. First, a good prosecutor not only requires practical and theoretical legal competence, but also needs to be familiar with the work of police, attorneys, and judges. In many cases, prosecutors need to coordinate and interact with their counterparts and peers in public security agencies and courts. Evidence is what prosecutors and attorneys pursue when processing a case. Trials in Chinese courts are traditionally conducted in an inquisitorial manner. In court, after the public prosecutor has read out the bill of prosecution, the accused and the victim will make statements on the crimes alleged in the bill of prosecution, and the public prosecutor may question the accused (Criminal Procedure Law of the People's Republic of China Amendment, 2012, art 155). Prosecutors usually have a passive position, whereas defense counsels scrutinize all the materials submitted by prosecutors, trying to find a minor flaw to undermine the foundation of the entire case. For this reason, it is essential that prosecutors understand the perspectives of criminal defense attorneys and the standpoints of judges.

Second, a good prosecutor always treats all the parties impartially, without any presumptions or resorting to stereotypes or default judgments. During the investigation, interrogation, and preliminary hearing, defendants or suspects in custody usually have needs, both reasonable and unreasonable. For example, Prosecutor Zong recalled one embezzlement case in which a corrupt official from Shanxi Province was arrested and refused to confess. When he was transferred to Shanxi Province for trial, the official asked if he could travel along a road where his daughter's school was located. His request was granted, but his daughter did not arrive. Although he failed to see his daughter, after this, the official began to show great remorse and cooperated with the investigators. Only with a rational perspective can the defendants' needs be understood so that effective countermeasures can be taken. Maintaining an unbiased attitude is also necessary to restore the truth as much as possible. Conversely, too much eagerness by a prosecutor to combat crime or produce a significant outcome may only taint justice. The bias induced by a prosecutor with a prior hypothesis and emotionally driven judgment will inevitably lead to the loss of evidence. Prosecutor Zong believes that the goal of a prosecutor is to uncover facts rather than secure a confession or admission of guilt.

His experiences as an educated youth working with local villagers on a farm during the Cultural Revolution and for five years as an ordinary soldier with young men from different social strata have given Prosecutor Zong invaluable insights into the living and social conditions of persons from economically deprived backgrounds. From his own experience at the Procuratorate, Prosecutor Zong found that defendants with three deficits, namely limited education, a low socioeconomic background, and low ethical standards, were common features of the most time-consuming cases for prosecutors. For instance, in one of the most remarkable cases in his experience, the defendant was a housewife with these three deficits. She was the childhood sweetheart of a corrupt official and was married to him for many years. During investigation and interrogation, she denied everything, even in face of solid evidence. It was almost impossible to communicate with her or to establish any rapport with her. The investigation progressed only after tracking down the embezzled bribes. Prosecutor Zong commented that the frustration arising in investigating cases with these three deficits required extreme patience.

Successes and Problems Experienced

Over the past 30 years, Prosecutor Zong views the increasing recognition of the value of procedural justice as the greatest achievement in the field of investigation and prosecution. Previously, there used to be a tradition to value substance and devalue procedure in Chinese legal practice (Chen, 2000), especially in the field of criminal investigations. Procedural justice and substantive justice were completely isolated from each other. In the past decade, more progress and significance have been placed on procedural justice. Measures have been taken to assure procedural justice at all levels, from the Supreme People's Procuratorate to basic-level procuratorial agencies, including amending practices of extended custody (Notice of the Supreme People's Procuratorate on Issuing Several Provisions of the Supreme People's Procuratorate on Preventing and Redressing the Extended Custody in Procuratorial Work, 2003), the disposal of items seized by police (Notice of the Supreme People's Procuratorate on Issuing the Provisions on the Management of Property Involved in Criminal Proceedings by People's Procuratorates, 2005), and compulsory measures before and after case filing (Notice of the Supreme People's Procuratorate on Issuing the Eight Prohibitions of the Supreme People's Procuratorate on the Duty-Related Crime Investigation, 2015). Over the years, Prosecutor Zong has observed a gradual decrease in reliance on forced confessions and in the rates of wrongful convictions. These changes could be attributed to the widespread shift in views and values about the importance of procedural justice.

Prosecutor Zong acknowledged that one of the most difficult problems to deal with in the courts was to keep up with legal and social developments. He noted: "For a prosecutor, learning never ends." On the one hand, arguments between prosecutors and defense attorneys in court are never limited to the contents of legal articles or regulations. It is equally important to comprehend why laws, amendments, and judicial interpretations are enacted, revised, or abolished. Rapid social and economic development in China over the last 30 years has given rise to new problems, and thus new types of crimes, especially after the Reform & Opening up policy (Information Office of State Council of the People's Republic of China, 2012).

For example, in the 1980s, Prosecutor Zong filed the first case of misappropriation of public funds in China after the prohibited conduct was first introduced in 1985 (Criminal Law of the People's Republic of China (97 Revision), 1997). In this case, a railway station official loaned money that belonged to the station to a businessman without any authorization and for personal benefits promised to him by the businessman. At that time, the only judicial basis for the crime of misappropriation of public funds was a judicial interpretation of the prohibited conduct issued by the Supreme People's Court and the Supreme People's Procuratorate. As the criminal act and the trial occurred before any detailed judicial guidance or case was available, the defense attorney entered a plea of not guilty and the arguments in court were intense. The official was sentenced to five years in prison at the first instance, but several months later on appeal, he was acquitted because the misappropriated funds were identified as collectively owned property rather than public funds. With the benefit of hindsight, Prosecutor Zong noted that this case reflected the unsynchronized development of legislation and the judicial system following the profound social changes and rapid economic transition after the Reform & Opening up. It was this experience that led to Prosecutor Zong to realize how important it is for prosecutors to be capable of understanding and applying the latest laws and policies.

The work of prosecutors is hard, trivial, and often distressing, especially due to spending numerous days inside jails and prisons. A further challenge for prosecutors is to spare no effort in pursuing evidence with extreme caution in every case. In the process of obtaining and adducing evidence, a prosecutor needs to review not only the quality of the evidence itself, but also the nature of the investigative methods and the sources of the evidence. The goal of a prosecutor is to forge links in the chain of evidence. Integrating and mutually corroborating items of evidences is the basis of fact reconstruction. If the evidentiary chain is incomplete, or the evidence is too simple or is fabricated, factual reconstruction cannot be plausibly and reliably achieved. Pursuing evidence in this fashion in each and every case is time and resource consuming, especially in China, which has a huge population of 1.37 billion (National Bureau of Statistics of China, 2014a), but justice cannot be achieved otherwise.

Prosecutor Zong emphasized that the integrity of every prosecution is essential to reinforce confidence in the judicial system. He mentioned the nationally well-known Zhao Zuohai case, which was prosecuted by a local procuratorate in Henan Province. Zhao was a villager from Shangqiu, Henan Province. He was sentenced to death, commuted to a life in prison, for the murder of a fellow villager in 1999. After serving 11 years in prison, after the purported murder victim was found alive, he was acquitted. Zhao was compensated 650,000 yuan (USD 96,000) under the State Compensation Law (1994), and six police officers who were responsible for Zhao's case were investigated and convicted of extorting a confession by torture. The case of Zhao Zuohai aroused nationwide attention due to the heavy-handed tactics applied by the police during the investigation. Prosecutor Zong noted that the integrity of every prosecution can only be strengthened by evidence review processes, and in this way, miscarriages of justice can be avoided in future. He advocated that evidence should be admissible only when qualified by exclusivity, uniqueness, legitimacy, and completeness in the evidentiary chain.

Theory and Practice

Regarding the question of the relationship between theory and practice in prosecution, Prosecutor Zong believes that it is important for legal practitioners to learn from theories espoused by different disciplines. From his experience, research on criminal psychology and penology are useful and beneficial to the practice of interrogation and investigation. Prosecutor Zong recalled that the first time he came into contact with criminal psychology in the 1980s, it was underappreciated, and even denigrated as a pseudoscience. Nowadays, research findings from criminal psychologists are valued more by procuratorial agencies and public security agencies. For example, at a training program held by the Supreme People's Procuratorate last year, the theme topic was emotional control in interrogations. The training focused on how to apply psychological methods when confronting a criminal suspect in an interrogation.

Prosecutor Zong noted: "With multidisciplinary research findings providing theoretical and methodological guidance, prosecution practices can make great strides in development." He advocates that information and findings about prison culture and rehabilitation should be integrated into earlier phases of the criminal justice process, including interrogations and preliminary hearings. Prosecutor Zong gave the example of a child molester who had refused to confess his crime even after he was repeatedly taken into custody for multiple offenses. The suspect obstinately denied all charges despite all of the prosecutor's efforts. It was not until he was detained with an inmate who was also a convicted child molester that the suspect freely confessed. His fear of the responses within the prison subculture toward child molesters was the primary reason progress in this case was hindered.

Prosecutor Zong emphasized the need to integrate theory and practice. For instance, young prosecutors usually found criminal psychology interesting and helpful, but did not pay much attention to this course at school. As a result, more systematic training and guidance on theories and methods other than the law are needed in practice. He believes there is still room for improvement to properly integrate theory and practice in day-to-day work. Some theories that have been empirically tested might be useful, but have not been well operationalized, making it difficult to apply them in prosecuting. The integration of theory and practice in a detailed operational manual may assist in showing a prosecutor what to do, how to do it, why it is done, and why not.

Regarding theory, Prosecutor Zong recommends that prosecutors keep up with the newest developments to update their theoretical systems to guide the prosecution process systematically. For instance, the contemporary textbook *Evidence Science* (Chen & Wang, 2013) is quite different from the one Prosecutor Zong learned in the 1980s. In the new textbook, assessment of facts is no longer limited to the elements of a criminal case. Other aspects, such as psychological elements, including emotions, and the language interaction between both parties, are also relevant. Investigations that focus only on the elements of the crime are often fragmented, which might lead to a miscarriage of justice, as occurred in the case of Zhao Zuohai.

In practice, Prosecutor Zong found it was critical to make full use of information technology in the Internet age. For example, the work of anticorruption, formerly known as economic supervision, was closely associated with administrative departments. Previously, it took great effort to collect information from public security records, employment archives, and certificates of identification. Prosecutors had to search manually and had no electronic recording devices. Nowadays, new investigation methods such as retrieving communication records, monitoring, and tracking are adopted. Data queries and data reconstruction dramatically increases the efficiency of an investigation, especially for crimes such as money laundering. Training in database establishment and application is necessary for prosecutors. He noted: "If the Internet and information technology could be called the advances in hardware, then new theory and methods are the advances in software."

Transnational Relations

On the topic of how his work has been affected by influences outside of China, Prosecutor Zong observed that some universal codes of ethics have been specified and strictly followed. As mentioned above, the tradition to value substance and devalue procedure in China has been fundamentally changed.

Prosecutor Zong confirmed that: "Some principles such as the principle of legality, the presumption of innocence, and human rights, which have existed in the Constitution of China as guidelines for years, are now concretely implemented." Prosecutor Zong believes that these global interactions have been beneficial for the Chinese legal system. For instance, certain forms of police misconduct during suspect searches and arrests were ignored in the past, but have ultimately come under scrutiny and changed. Considerable suppression of illegally obtained evidence has been achieved since illegal evidence extraction and self-incrimination were prohibited by the revised Criminal Procedure Law (2012).

Through communications with his counterparts in Europe and Hong Kong, Prosecutor Zong observed some significant differences between the legal systems in China and other developed countries. First, the number of legal cases prosecuted each year in China is far higher than that in any European country. In all, in 2014, a total of 879,615 criminal suspects were arrested and 1,391,225 defendants were prosecuted by the People's Procuratorate in China, including 41,487 cases of duty-related crimes involving 55,101 persons (Jianming, 2015). Although the rate of crime in China is lower than that in many other countries, the absolute number of prosecuted defendants is vast because of the huge population.

Second, in the last 30 years, the laws in China have undergone far more extensive changes and revisions than the European laws. After 1976, China summarized the experience and lessons during the Cultural Revolution and legislation in this period, focused on restoring and re-establishing state order, and carrying out and advancing Reform & Opening up. In 1979, the Second Session of the Fifth National People's Congress passed a resolution to amend several provisions of the Constitution. The meeting marked the beginning of the large-scale legislation reform in the new period. For example, the Criminal Law of the People's Republic of China has been revised nine times since 1979, and the Amendment IX came into effect on November 1, 2015 (Amendment [IX] to the Criminal Law of the People's Republic of China, 2015).

Third, the cultural history of China is very different from that of Western countries. Prosecutor Zong believes that a strong culture is required to establish a legal system: "A people-oriented precept is rooted in Chinese culture, which has lasted uninterruptedly for thousands of years. Laws can rule a country as well as disrupt a country. Our goal is to establish people-oriented laws, that is 'good laws.'" To elaborate on the idea of good laws, Prosecutor Zong referred to democracy as an example. For members of his generation, the notion of modern democracy could be traced back to the Paris Commune in 1871 (Gluckstein, 2011, p. 5). For people with different cultural backgrounds, the definition and interpretation of democracy might be diverse and lack consensus. Prosecutor Zong observed that: "The coexistence of diversified views is genuine democracy, rather than a uniform definition from one culture. Good laws need to limit rights as well as democracy. Neither extreme rights nor extreme democracy conforms to the spirit of good laws." He further commented that China is still exploring her own legal institutions, striving for harmony without uniformity, at an increasing pace. With the huge population and rapid social changes, China's regional development has lagged, causing tremendous imbalance. For instance, in 2014, the gross domestic product (GDP) of Henan Province was 3493.938 billion yuan (approximately USD 548.31 billion) and ranked number five, with Guangdong Province in the lead with a GDP of 6779.224 billion yuan and the lowest GDP of 92.083 billion yuan recorded by the Tibetan autonomous region (National Bureau of Statistics of China, 2014b). Regional economic inequality contributes to great variation in the legal development of different regions of China in terms of judicial transparency, legal awareness, and the level of law enforcement (Li & Tian, 2014). Based on these differences, Prosecutor Zong advocates that China could absorb lessons from developed countries, and at the same time, remain cautious about dramatic innovation in a single step and avoid emulating other systems blindly and indiscriminately.

General Assessments

Reflecting on whether he was satisfied with the developments in criminal law and criminal procedure in China, Prosecutor Zong responded that remarkable achievements have been accomplished during the last 30 years, and these changes had created a virtuous cycle: "Public confidence in the rule of law became mainstream, and legal awareness and self-protection awareness of the people also improved." Such positive changes established a solid foundation for future reform and improvement.

Although the overall progress is satisfying, Prosecutor Zong expressed concerns that serious reforms were needed at lower levels of the procuratorate administration. He pointed out that the need to protect the rights of the common people is a bottleneck in the development of legal institutions. It is comforting to note that the main trends are positive and that defects are corrected as soon as they are exposed.

The ongoing sweeping anticorruption campaign in China began in 2012. The anticorruption campaign made great efforts to root out corruption, and hundreds of officials across the nation have been investigated and prosecuted, including Zhou Yongkang, the former member of the Politburo Standing Committee, of the highest Council of Communist Party of China (Zheng & Chen, 2015). Although the campaign is powerful, effective, and popular with the public, Prosecutor Zong pointed to the challenges in institutionalizing good governance. Institutional improvement and standardization are crucial to successfully restraining power within the limits of the law.

Prosecutor Zong also emphasized the importance of cultivating young law practitioners in the lower-level institutions such as the courts and offices of the public prosecutors. He noted that "old habits die hard" in spite of new rules and regulations, and that the "rule of man" was traditionally preferred in China. The transformation to the "rule of law" will take time and generations. Prosecutor Zong believed that it is the young college graduates with a solid educational foundation and systematic training at the undergraduate levels who will gradually accomplish the transformation and become the mainstay of support for the legal system of the entire country.

Prosecutor Zong has witnessed the development of anticorruption law over the past 30 years in China. Before the nation's Reform & Opening up, within local government departments, there was a section responsible for economic supervision. Charges of economic crimes surfaced for the first time, and the laws were improved alongside this prosecutorial work. The work of anticorruption started from scratch in 1989 (Jiang, 2010), the Department of Economic Supervision was renamed the Department of Embezzlement and Bribery in the Supreme People's Procuratorate, and specific agencies for the investigation of embezzlement and bribery were established at various levels of the People's Procuratorates. In the same year, the first Anti-Corruption Bureau was also established in the People's Procuratorate of Guangdong Province. Prosecutors in this field initially fumbled, and developed their practice through trial and error. Looking back upon his 30-year career, Prosecutor Zong noted that the learning experience was most rewarding and valuable. This learning process helped expand the knowledge structure, law enforcement capacity, and personality traits of a prosecutor, which in turn contributed to the development of the legal field of anticorruption and refinement of the Chinese legal system. Prosecutor Zong stated that: "Tenacity is the advantage and value of our nation. Continued learning and innovation is also the foundation of legal development." The opportunity to contribute to the development of the nation was the factor motivating his accomplishments, rather than securing social respect and financial compensation. Prosecutor Zong looks forward to improved legal institutions and greater benefits for all people in the long term.

Conclusion

In this interview, Prosecutor Zong shared his views and experiences in the investigation and prosecution of criminal cases involving corruption and bribery. Prosecutor Zong reflected on developments, issues, and trends in the criminal justice system of China. In particular, he focused on the development of the supervision of the People's Procuratorates, strengths and weaknesses of today's anticorruption practices, and differences between Chinese and other legal systems.

The interview summarized his 30-year legal career, starting from his employment as a legal clerk in a county procuratorate and ending with his accomplishments as a Senior Prosecutor of one of the most populous provinces in China. The successes, failures, joys, temptations, and frustrations in his career were closely linked to the development of the current legal system in China. Prosecutor Zong shared his personal philosophy of legal advocacy and identified critical qualities that make a good prosecutor. His insights on the relationship between theory and prosecution practice focused on the positive collaboration between prosecutors and psychological researchers. His reflections on transnational relations were intriguing, especially the exploration of modern legal institutions of China, as well as his concerns and anticipation to improve procuratorate administration in the future.

Glossary

Chinese economic reform: see Reform & Opening up, below.

Cultural Revolution: this 10-year period in China's history, between 1966 and 1976, was initiated by Mao as a means to revive the revolutionary spirit in the nation's youth, which led to the victory of the Civil War that formed the People's Republic of China. However, the underpinning of the revolution was for Mao to assert his control over the Chinese government. He was concerned that current party leaders had embraced bourgeois values, and a privileged and intellectual class was developing in China. During this tumultuous period, Mao encouraged the youth to attack those who did not fully support his ideal of a classless society. The Cultural Revolution continued in various phases until Mao's death in 1976. Its tormented and violent legacy resonated in China's politics and society for decades after.

educated youth (zhiqing): a special term used to describe the urban youth during the Cultural Revolution. The urban youth were called on to leave school and travel to rural areas to learn from local workers and farmers. The annual National Higher Education Entrance Examination was officially canceled from 1966 to 1976 during the educational turmoil. Estimates are that a total of 20 million educated youth were impacted during the period from the 1950s to the end of the Cultural Revolution, including most of China's top leaders today, such as President Xi Jinping and Premier Li Keqiang.

legal clerk: an assistant who works under the guidance of the judge or the procurator. Most judges and procurators began their careers working as legal clerks.

New China: the formation of the People's Republic of China, also known as New China, marked the great transition from the centuries-old dictatorial feudal system to the system of democracy. It marked the end of the period of semi-colonialism and semi-feudalism in China that existed from the 1840s.

People's Courts: local courts of the first instance, handling both criminal and civil cases. Three levels are distinguished: (a) Superior People's Courts: at the level of the provinces, autonomous regions, and special municipalities; (b) Intermediate People's Courts: at the level of prefectures, autonomous prefectures, and municipalities; and (c) District People's Courts: at the level of autonomous counties, towns, and local municipal districts.

People's Procuratorate: the office of public prosecutors who conduct prosecutions on behalf of the State. They have wide discretion and power as to whether or not to prosecute after considering the circumstances, evidence, and nature of the crimes in question. Additionally, they have the power to investigate criminal cases.

pretrial detention: lengthy pretrial detention is not a systemic issue in China because of the mandatory requirement that the People's Court issue a judgment within a month of accepting the case. In extraordinary circumstances, a six-week extension may be required.

procuratorial system: public prosecuting offices known as People's Procuratorates employ procuratorial personnel who exercise the procuratorial authority of the State according to law. Public prosecutors are organized in a hierarchy that corresponds with the levels of the courts, including Chief Prosecutors and Deputy Chief Prosecutors. At the highest level is the Supreme People's Procuratorate, which handles matters within the jurisdiction of the Supreme People's Court and oversees all other public prosecutions.

Reform & Opening up: also known as the Chinese Economic Reform, the Reform & Opening up was initiated by the former Chinese leader Deng Xiaoping at the Third Plenary Session of the Eleventh Party Central Committee in December 1978. The Communist Party of China implemented the Reform & Opening up policy in 1979, setting in motion the transformation of China's economy. In the two decades that followed, China's economic and social development has been crowned with remarkable success. The Chinese people have reaped vast material benefits. In 2011, with one-fourth of the world population, China became the world's second-largest economy.

Supreme People's Court: located in Beijing, this is the premier appellate court in China with oversight responsibility for the administration of justice by all subordinate local and special People's Courts.

India

7

AMITA DHANDA

Contents

The Criminal Justice Process of India

India attained independence from the British on August 15, 1947. The Constitution of India came into force on August 26, 1950. India is a union of 29 states and seven federally administered union territories. India has adopted a federal system of governance; however, Article 1 of the Constitution describes the country as a Union of States to underscore that the federal system was adopted for administrative convenience and not as part of any agreement between the center and the states. The federal arrangement as incorporated in the Constitution divides legislative and executive responsibilities between the center and the states. The legislative division in criminal law allocates some dedicated domains in the union list to the center and in the state list to the states. The subjects mentioned in the third list can be legislated upon by both the center and the states. Both the Indian Penal Code (IPC) and the Code of Criminal Procedure (CrPC) are mentioned in this list. Consequently, both the substantive and the procedural law can be modified to meet the local requirements of a State, provided the President, who acts on the aid and advice of the Union Council of Ministers, accords assent to such a proposal.

India has a federal legislature but a unitary judiciary. Consequently, the same set of courts adjudicates on both the central and state legislations. The judicial hierarchy is formed by the magistrates' courts with different degrees of authority and varied territorial jurisdiction at the base. Next are the assistant sessions judges and the sessions courts at the next level; followed by the High Court of the State and at the apex is the Supreme Court of India (see Table 7.1). Other than the territorial differences, there is a difference in the punishment that can be awarded by different categories of courts. The varied class of magistrates and the assistant sessions judges can only award imprisonment of different periods of time and varied quantum of fines (see Table 7.1). The sentence of death (as India is a retentionist country) can be imposed by the Sessions Court, and becomes operational only if confirmed by the High Court. Both the High Courts and the Supreme Court can impose the death penalty (see Table 7.1). For the death penalty to be executed, the Supreme Court has to dismiss the appeal against it, and the petition for clemency must be rejected by the governor of the state and president of the country (Figure 7.1).

Law and order is a state subject and every state government establishes its own police force that is formally enrolled. The authority for settling the

Table 7.1 Hierarchy and Sentencing Powers of Criminal Courts in India

Court or Judicial Officer	Sentencing Powers
Supreme Court	Any sentence authorized by law
High Court	Any sentence authorized by law
Sessions Court	Same as above except that death sentence to be confirmed by High Court.
Assistant Sessions Judge	Up to ten years imprisonment and/or fine
Chief judicial Magistrate or Chief Metropolitan Magistrate	Up to seven years imprisonment or fine
Judicial Magistrate Class I or Metropolitan Magistrate	Up to three years imprisonment and/or fine up to Rs 5000
Judicial Magistrate Class II	Up to one year imprisonment and/or fine up to Rs 1000

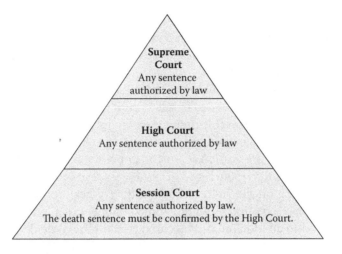

Figure 7.1 Hierarchy of the courts in India.

strength of the cadre in terms of officers and other junior staff resides with the state government. This force is required to maintain order and detect crime. In addition to the state police establishments, the central government under the Delhi Special Police Establishment Act of 1946 has constituted a special force, which investigates specified offenses in the union territories and in any state with the concurrence of the state government. Due to its image of impartiality and independence, especially in sensitive matters, there is a public preference for investigation by the Central Bureau of Investigation (CBI) over the state police. In 2003, a Central Vigilance Commission (CVC) was established to inquire into charges of corruption (Pillai, 2014).

In recognition of the fact that a crime is committed against society and not just a particular individual, the state as representative of the people prosecutes the accused. The public prosecutor or the assistant public prosecutor acts as counsel for the state in criminal trials. Under Section 301 of the Code of Criminal Procedure 1973 (CrPC), the prosecutor has authority to appear before any court in any case entrusted to him or her. Under Section 321 of CrPC, the prosecutor can also withdraw any prosecution with the consent of the court. The prosecutor can also, if asked, advise the police or any other government department.

Prosecution of cases in sessions and high courts is undertaken by the public prosecutors whereas assistant public prosecutors pursue prosecutions in the magisterial courts. Cases filed on the strength of police reports are pursued by the prosecutors, whereas cases initiated on private complaint are pursued by the complainant either in person or through authorized counsel. If a case initiated on private complaint is considered to have a public interest, then it can also be pursued by the public prosecutor. The courts while expounding on the role of the prosecutor have stressed that the prosecutor should be indifferent to the result of the case and only be intent on presenting all the evidence in the case to enable the court to reach a just and accurate decision. In practice, however, the criminal trial operates on adversarial terms with the prosecutor intent on obtaining convictions.

Article 22 of the Constitution of India entitles an accused charged of a crime to consult and be defended by a lawyer of his or her choice. Section 303 of the CrPC also recognizes this right to legal representation. The right has little meaning unless the accused has the resources to hire a lawyer. Section 304 of the CrPC enjoins the Sessions Court to appoint a pleader at state expense if an accused lacks the resources to hire a lawyer. The Indian Supreme Court while expounding on the right to life and liberty has pronounced the right to free legal representation as an integral component of a fair trial that must be guaranteed to all individuals if accused persons are to be denied personal liberty according to procedure established by law (Basu, 2015). In furtherance of this obligation, a number of legal aid schemes have been floated by the legal service authorities: Bar associations and state governments. Notwithstanding these arrangements, the question on the quality of service provided by state paid defenders survives, especially when this service is compared with the defense that can be accessed by people with capacity to pay.

Article 22 of the Indian Constitution enjoins that no person shall be detained in custody without being informed, as soon as may be, of the grounds of arrest. The Article also requires an arrested person to be produced before a magistrate within a period of 24 hours and prohibits any detention beyond such period if magisterial permission has not been obtained. The CrPC has provisions whereby a person apprehending arrest can obtain directions, from courts having the requisite jurisdiction, that the investigation authorities shall release them on bail and conduct its inquiries without taking the accused into custody. There are provisions in the CrPC whereby bail for all manner of offenses can be granted by all courts. In practice, however, bail for the more severe offenses has to be obtained from the higher courts and the magisterial courts are not as willing to provide relief. Stringency in relation to the grant of bail is also demonstrated by statutes that direct courts to hear the objection of the prosecutors before granting bail. The statute on prohibiting narcotics and psychotropic substances is one such example.

If curtailment of the right to bail is one strand of the crime controlling criminal justice regime, then reversal of burden of proof in certain instances of sexual violence, and terming an act a crime if harm is caused even if intention is not proved, are further components of a crime controlling criminal law. There are provisions in the Indian Constitution, which unequivocally mandate that the criminal justice system shall operate in accordance with fair process. In more recent times; however, with larger emphasis on crime control, the presumption of innocence is being displaced in both legislative and adjudicative expositions.

Dinesh Mathur, Senior Advocate of High Court, Delhi

Introduction

A friend working in Tihar Jail, the largest jail in Delhi, once informed me that the prisoners there wished to install a statue in honor of Mr. Dinesh Mathur (hereafter DM), a leading criminal appellate defense lawyer in the country, due to the competence and commitment with which he defends their cases even though he does not always win. I was so fascinated with this nugget of information that I always wanted to know more. What was his *modus operandi* in constructing the case for the defense? How did he prepare his cases? What in his opinion were essential qualities for a good criminal appellate defense lawyer? Prior to this interview, I recommended that DM write about his defense strategies; but with characteristic modesty, he dismissed my suggestion. This interview provided an opportunity to effectuate a long-pending objective.

Initially, DM's self-deprecatory manner and innate modesty made him reluctant to speak about his professional life as a criminal appellate defense lawyer. Ultimately we had four conversations each about 90 minutes in length, in May 2015, in which we discussed his most challenging cases: defense strategies that worked, the qualities of a good defense lawyer, and reforms to the Indian criminal justice system to make it more fair and efficient.

Career

DM started his career as a practicing lawyer in 1964 after graduating from the Faculty of Law, University of Delhi. In 1990, he was designated as Senior Advocate of the High Court of Delhi. His father, Tara Chand Mathur, was a highly respected and successful criminal defense lawyer. To forge an independent identity for himself, DM avoided criminal law and started his professional life as a civil law practitioner. Within a year of starting his practice, he lost his father. This tragic occurrence left his father's clients without a lawyer. After unsuccessfully trying to manage both his own and his father's practice, he gave up his own practice of civil law to take over his father's pending cases and thereafter, exclusively practiced in criminal law. Despite this transition early in his career, his training in civil law greatly influenced the manner in which he practiced criminal law. He employs as rigorous a process of pleading in criminal law as is undertaken by the civil lawyers. Whether preparing an application for exemption or bail or an appeal, he has always drafted his pleadings by referring to the relevant provision of the CrPC. This approach led him to differentiate between the various remedies available under the CrPC and consider the distinct nature of each remedy. If the constitutional mandate is that no one can be deprived of their life and liberty except according to procedure established by law, it is imperative that a criminal defense lawyer understands the demands of procedure in its full plenitude. The significance of procedural knowledge was reiterated when DM elaborated the qualities of an effective criminal defense lawyer.

The Operational Backdrop

Three primary concerns were repeatedly voiced by DM in the interview and provide an overarching backdrop to his opinions on the topics we discussed, namely, corruption, competence, and resources. A rule of law society, DM opined, needs to act in accordance with the law. Thus, the registration of a first information report (FIR) by a police official should not depend upon who lodges the report—prince or pauper—but whether the facts disclose a *prima facie* case. To determine whether a *prima facie* case has been established, police need education and training to exercise this judgment. At the next stage of investigation, the investigation officer must be equipped with requisite technological support to evaluate the veracity of the complainant's account and, on the strength of the investigation, determine whether a charge should or should not be framed. The appointed officer must possess requisite knowledge about the type of technical expertise that will ensure credible factual conclusions, and must have the resources to access this expertise, for example, for a range of technical expertise for scientific investigation. Upon the strength of the charge sheet, the public prosecutor needs to independently determine whether the evidence is sufficient to prosecute and convict the accused. The law requires the best evidence to be produced before the court, and on the strength of the best evidence, the judge must determine the guilt or innocence of the accused.

This description underscores the need for competent, well-trained personnel to administer the system. The dearth of such training was a continuous refrain of the interviewee, as in its absence, when pressure is mounted whether political, financial, or even departmental, the person on the receiving end of the pressure cannot resist and corruption prevails. Then, recording of crimes is not dictated by the plausibility of the account but by the status of the narrator; and investigation is not about fact-finding but about constructing a story that holds up in court. For example, where the veracity of a reported crime can be established by forensic or ballistic expertise, investigating officers prefer to rely on oral evidence from witnesses and confessions. The dividing line between investigators and prosecutors becomes blurred, and prosecutors act in concert with investigating officers to shore up the inadequacies in the evidence to obtain a conviction at any cost.

DM acknowledged the existence of corruption in the criminal justice system, but maintained that a lack of knowledge, competence, and resources at each level in the criminal justice system was the reason corruption flourished. With characteristic candor, DM conceded that inadequacies in investigation and prosecution allowed the defense systemic shortcuts. For instance, where the prosecution case was not controverted by a counternarrative or technical expertise, the defense resorted to winning over the prosecution witnesses. Ideally, and also because they have access to more extensive resources, he placed greater burden on the state and its agencies to comply with the law. Since two wrongs could not make a right; he also emphasized the need for accountability from defense lawyers. The initiative for change need not come only from state agencies but equally from legally well-informed, technically aware, and procedurally cognizant defense lawyers. In outlining this standard for defense lawyers, he acknowledged that the task was tougher for the current generation of defense lawyers, as crime control models and strict liability laws had greater currency.

DM pointed out that the most critical task in preparing a defense arises at trial. The job of a criminal appellate defense lawyer was largely to rectify errors committed by the lawyer and judge at the trial stage. This experience was edifying in terms of what an effective criminal defense lawyer needs to know.

Philosophy of Legal Advocacy

Knowledge of Criminal Procedure

The prosecution is obligated to prove the guilt of the accused by following procedures established by law and devised to ensure that accused persons are not surprised or trapped into making admissions. A defense lawyer must know the procedural entitlements of the accused. Any departure from this procedure means that the accused is hindered from meeting the prosecution case. Any finding of guilt reached without allowing the accused a full and fair opportunity to meet the case against him is vitiated, as it breaches the requirement of fair procedure. This omission can be relied upon only if the defense lawyer is abreast of requirements of fair process such as Section 226 of the Indian CrPC which requires that "when the accused appears or is brought before the Court in pursuance of a commitment of the case … the prosecutor *shall* open his case by describing the charge brought against the accused and *stating by what evidence* he proposes to prove the guilt of the accused" (emphasis added). The direct effect of this section is that the prosecutor cannot rely upon any evidence that is not included in the opening statement.

The prosecution must inform the defense of the nature of the case against the accused and the evidence on which it relies upon to prove it. Failure to provide this information can nullify the prosecution case. The appellate defense lawyer needs to scrutinize the record to confirm that the prosecutor has not relied upon any evidence that did not feature in the opening prosecution statement. An omission is a breach of natural justice established through documentary evidence on the record, not deduced from fact narratives, which are a weaker form of defense. Prioritization of this sort is vital when the criminal justice administration is plagued by manipulation, but is weak on investigation.

To exemplify the importance of fair procedure, DM referred to Section 313 of CrPC, which requires that the accused should be provided an opportunity "to explain any circumstances appearing in the evidence against him." The accused has to be confronted with all the incriminating circumstances to ensure that the opportunity to defend is real, not notional. If the prosecution fails to draw attention to the circumstances, then the judge is mandated to do so. The importance of this protection has been stressed in several apex court decisions. Again, the trial record discloses whether or not the incriminating circumstances were put to the accused, and whether by the court or the prosecution. Failure to obtain explanations from the accused comprises denial of a fair trial.

The foregoing examples bring home DM's opinion that effective criminal practice requires examination of the demands of procedure for every factual allegation. Since the prosecution often relies upon testimony of witnesses to establish its case, cross-examination to test this testimony is critical. However, in preparing an appeal, he looks for the link between the witness testimony and the procedural legal requirements.

Illustratively, Section 45 of the Evidence Act 1872 states that a court may accept the opinion of handwriting experts to establish the source of a disputed sample of handwriting. Testimony of persons other than experts who are acquainted with the handwriting is also admissible if the lay witness observed that person wrote or has exchanged correspondence with or received many written documents from the alleged source. Any testimony from a nonexpert must meet the requirements of Section 47 of the Act. To utilize those protections in practice, defense lawyers must subject the facts to the scrutiny of the law.

The Importance of Forensic Sciences and Ballistics

Proving of facts is critical to establish culpability or innocence. In a system that operates more on manipulation than investigation, DM values forensic science. He continually exhorts lawyers to mount a defense by drawing upon the relevant forensic science to examine the authenticity of the prosecution case. For example, the difference between entrance and exit wounds can determine whether the person accused of the crime could have caused the injury with the weapon allegedly used from the place where he was allegedly located. For instance, in a case in which the deceased had spindle wounds on his body, and the sole weapon recovered was a side knife, incapable of causing the observed injuries, the accused had to be acquitted. In a system where the testimony of witnesses is often suspect, DM strongly advises lawyers to study the alleged weapons of crime and to seek ballistic expertise to determine whether the alleged injuries could have been inflicted by the weapon specified as the source.

The Significance of the Factual Context

In a country as diverse as India, no prototypical standard of probable and expected conduct exists. Conduct is influenced by the caste, class, region, religion of the parties involved in a transaction. A good criminal defense lawyer studies the facts because the law has to be applied to the facts (Hall, 1947). Inadequate appreciation of the facts can lead to a miscarriage of justice. For instance, when a woman filed an FIR of cruelty against her father-in-law, an official who worked in the courts, all reported incidents of cruelty occurred on dates of important festivals when either the court was closed or the accused could have been on leave. The perfect match of festival days and dates of the reported quarrels led DM to question the genuineness of the complaint (*Raj Kumar Khanna v. State*, 2002).

A further example of contextual interpretation of facts in a criminal case is an accused who described an amicable meeting where he was offered betel nut and leaf by the complainant at his residence. The prosecution asserted this was improbable, until it was pointed out that the customary mode of greeting a visitor to a Muslim household is by offering betel nut.

While noting that it is not unique to India that a competent criminal defense lawyer should be familiar with procedural law, forensics, ballistics, and the peculiarities of the facts and circumstances of the case defended, in India, considering the diversity of the country, it was necessary for a defense lawyer to also know the social and cultural context. These competencies are of special relevance for any lawyer who wishes to practice ethically as a defense criminal lawyer in India.

Significance of Precedents in Criminal Justice Adjudication

Since India is a common law country, and DM did not list knowledge of judicial precedents among the mandatory competencies for defense counsel, I asked him about this (Waluchow, 2007). In line with the emphasis he places on facts, DM was of the view that the theory of precedents was of little importance in criminal defense practice. Although every court decides the guilt or innocence of an accused by citing some basic principles, the principles must be applied to a set of facts. In criminal cases, even small differences in facts can cause courts to depart from an earlier ruling. Thus, the presence of a precedent or even a catena of decisions can be distinguished by both judges and lawyers if the facts so merit. Thus, he considers a precedent-based strategy as both lazy and unstable. It is lazy because it discourages advocates from applying their mind afresh to each case, and it is unstable because the judge can always distinguish the precedent quoted and decide differently.

Criminal defense lawyers should examine the demands of the relevant legislation anew in the light of the facts that come to the fore in every case.

However, legal precedents are not irrelevant in criminal justice advocacy. DM described precedents as powerful narratives. Whenever a judicial decision is encountered where the fact situation is broadly similar to the case at hand, the earlier decision can guide how the facts on hand should be presented, how the evidence should be sequenced, and the law argued. Precedents, which lay down propositions useful for the case at hand, provide guidance on devising the larger strategy for an appeal. Used in this way, precedents provide advocates with much needed support without becoming mental strangleholds that discourage independent thinking.

Problems and Successes Experienced

DM classified as his best cases those resulting in judicial decisions where his arguments contributed to the growth of criminal law.

Suspension of Conviction

DM first mentioned a decision wherein his arguments formed the basis of a clarification issued by the Court on a point of law, which had contributed to the development of the law. The dispute in *S. M. Malik* and others *v. State and another* (1990) arose on the construction of Section 389(1) of the CrPC which states that "pending any appeal by a convicted person, the Appellate Court may for reasons to be recorded by it in writing, order that execution of the sentence or the order appealed against, be suspended and, also, if he is in confinement, that he be released on bail, or on his own bond."

Mr. Malik the appellant was held jointly liable of the offense of abetment to suicide by the Sessions Court and sentenced to five years in prison along with fine. He challenged the decision on appeal and the High Court admitted his appeal, and suspended his conviction and sentence until the appeal was decided. On the strength of this order, the appellant obtained a direction to his employers that since the order of conviction was suspended, the employers could not dismiss the appellant but would have to pay him a subsistence allowance during the pendency of the appeal. The employer then filed a revision application in the High Court contending that Section 389(1) did not envisage suspension of conviction but only the order of sentence. DM in his arguments raised the fundamental question of what a person challenges when he files an appeal. He asserted it was necessarily the conviction as the sentence flows from the conviction. Consequently, the order appealed against is the order of conviction and by terms of Section 389 the execution of this order can be suspended pending decision of the appeal. This interpretation put forth by DM was first accepted by the Delhi High Court. Subsequently in another case (*Rama Narang v. Ramesh Narang*, 1995), the same contention was acceded to by the Supreme Court of India. Acceptance of this argument allowed appellants to carry on with the everyday business of their lives, despite the conviction, during the pendency of the appeal.

In a subsequent decision of *Shanti Behal v. State* (1993), DM successfully persuaded the Delhi High Court that the power of suspension could also be extended to persons who were convicted of murder and sentenced to death. DM's contention was that the statutory provision did not limit this power of the court to specific offenses, and the court should not restrict it by interpretation. The court accepted this argument in principle, but did not provide relief to the appellant.

Partial Use of a Dying Declaration and Trial by Media
Another matter that DM handled successfully illustrated the proposition that an accused person needs the full panoply of fair process. Inmates in Delhi's largest prison advised the father of the accused that DM was his best bet. The case revolved around a young woman who suffered fatal burns a few years after marriage following demands by her spouse's family for a larger marriage portion or dowry. The woman had made three prior statements on the cause of her burns prior to her death, one of which supported a claim of accident, one a suicide, and one a homicide. The first statement referred to an accident, the other two statements implicated the husband and his family. The second statement was made to a judicial magistrate. The third and last statement was video recorded and given to a major television journalist who broadcast it on national television, after the woman's death and before the bail application of the accused husband was listed for hearing. Ten women's organizations intervened in the case to oppose the grant of bail to the accused. The public prosecutor allowed them to be parties to the proceedings, provided they agreed to function under his general supervision. The critical question that DM put to the court was how the State Broadcasting Channel Doordarshan could be permitted to broadcast a program on the incident, which included the dying declaration of the woman and statements of other friends and relatives, when the matter was pending before the court and the culpability of the accused husband was yet to be decided. He submitted that the broadcast severely jeopardized the accused's right to a fair trial, especially as the dying declaration was not televised in its entirety, but edited and sequenced to make the program more watchable. DM used the multiple versions of the dying declaration to show that the facts of the case did not speak only of the culpability of the accused and argued that his application for bail could not be determined on parameters that were appropriate to decide on his culpability. Further the broadcast of a television program on the case prior to a courts adjudication operated like a trial by media, which infringed the fair process rights of the accused. The arguments won the day and DM secured bail for the accused.

The challenge noted by DM in *Praveen Malhotra v. State through Delhi Administration* (1990) was to see the facts from the standpoint of the accused and to convey this to the court. This had to be done against all odds as both public opinion and the media were against his client. He overcame this challenge by closely scrutinizing the facts in the light of the rules that governed proof by dying declarations. On this basic scaffolding, he placed the constitutional right to a fair trial and passionately argued it in court over several days, so that the accused could get his day in court.

Facts Should Show Offense in Accordance with the Law

DM referred to *Anil Sharma and others v. S. N. Marwah and another* (1994) to distinguish lay from legal understanding of crime. Only if the act complained of meets the legal definition of proscribed behavior can legal proceedings be initiated. In this case, a woman filed a criminal complaint of cheating against her husband four years after their marriage. She made this allegation because one year after their marriage she discovered that her husband was already married and had a son from the previous marriage. Subsequent to this discovery, the complainant conceived and gave birth to a daughter. Two and a half years after the birth of the daughter, she filed a criminal complaint of cheating against her husband and of criminal conspiracy against his family. On the basis of this complaint, the subordinate court issued a summons against the husband and his family under Section 420 of the Indian Penal Code 1860 (hereinafter IPC). DM moved the Delhi High Court to quash the proceedings primarily because the alleged wrongful conduct in no way came within the four corners of the legal definition. Section 420 of the IPC defines cheating as follows:

> Whoever cheats and thereby dishonestly induces the person deceived to deliver any property to any person, or to make alter or destroy the whole or any part of a valuable security, or anything which is signed or sealed and which is capable of being converted into a valuable security, shall be punished with imprisonment of either description for a term that may extend to seven years, and shall also be liable to fine.

Since in that case, no one had dishonestly induced any person to deliver any property or to alter or destroy any part of a valuable security, the offense of cheating under Section 420 could not be made out. After demonstrating to the court that the accused could not be charged under Section 420, DM combined the substantive and procedural law to construct the second limb of the defense whereby he told the court that the accused could not also be charged under Section 417 of the IPC, since his conduct was not covered by Section 415 of IPC. Then, he argued, without conceding that even if an offense under Section 417 could be made out, the applicant could not be prosecuted for the same, as the case was barred by limitation under Section 468 of the CrPC. Section 468 lays down that any offense punishable with imprisonment up to one year needed to be prosecuted within a period of one year of commission of the offense. Since the complainant had overshot that time limit, the summons issued against the applicants were canceled by the High Court. The case of Anil Sharma showed that courts can issue a summons even if the wrong complained of does not meet the substantive requirements of the law.

Strict Construction in Favor of the Accused

Harking back to his advice that the competent practice of criminal law requires counsel to re-examine the mandate of the law afresh with every case, DM note that this can result in the evolution of the law and keep it in tune with the times, provided judges keep an open mind. To illustrate the importance of close and connected reading, DM referred to the case of *Sanjeev Nanda v. CBI* (2008) where he sought bail for accused persons who had allegedly criminally conspired to commit an offense under the Prevention of Corruption Act (1988). Section 120B of the IPC in its two subsections prescribes punishment for criminal conspiracy. While Section 120B(1) prescribes punishment for offenses that are liable for capital punishment or life imprisonment or rigorous imprisonment exceeding two years; Section 120B(2) lays down the punishment for offenses that are not covered by Subsection(1). The accused was charged with an offense under Section 13(2) of the Prevention of Corruption Act, punishable with minimum imprisonment for one year, which could be extended up to seven years. The section did not specify whether the nature of the imprisonment was simple or rigorous even though Section 53 of the IPC (1860) distinguishes between simple and rigorous imprisonment. DM contended that for the accused to be covered by Section 120B (1) it was necessary that the offense for which he was charged to be legislatively included within the list of offenses punishable with rigorous imprisonment. If such legislative enumeration was absent, while it was well within the powers of the judiciary to award rigorous imprisonment on completion of trial, such discretion could not be taken into account while deliberating the matter of bail.

Since the offense with which the accused was charged could not be included within Section 120B(1) of the IPC, it was necessarily covered by Section 120B(2). A Section 120B(2) offense was only punishable with imprisonment for six months and offenses punishable with less than six months imprisonment were categorized as bailable under the CrPC. The contention was accepted and the accused were released on bail.

The Power of Forensic Science and the Missing Corpse

The last case of high moment that DM described was that of *Shibhu Soren v. CBI* (2007) in which a high-profile politician of a regional political party became embroiled in a major criminal case. Mr. Soren was first in the eye of the storm when he was alleged to have accepted illegal gratification from the ruling party in order to vote in their favor in a parliamentary no confidence motion. The Indian Supreme Court refused to examine the matter of his guilt on grounds that the voting behavior of a legislator was protected by parliamentary privilege, reasoning that many perceived as highly questionable. Mr. Soren was next arrested for entering into a criminal conspiracy to murder his own private secretary who was handling all his finances and had insider knowledge of Mr. Soren's affairs. Mr. Soren was convicted of this offense by the Sessions Court, whereupon Mr. Soren filed an appeal in the Delhi High Court and simultaneously sought the suspension of his conviction and a stay. The High Court did not accept the plea qua the suspension of conviction, keeping in view the seriousness of the offense and the short period for which he had been in detention.

On appeal, DM sought to demonstrate the mismatch between the evidence on the record and the conclusion of the trial court. He persuaded the appellate court to revisit the entire record and determine whether the appellant could be convicted of criminal conspiracy to murder. He demonstrated an absence of evidence on motive and although the accused were charged of criminal conspiracy, there was no evidence on the record to show where and when any of the conspirators met to hatch the alleged conspiracy. The court was convinced that disjointed snippets from here and there could not be the basis to infer a sinister design. DM drew attention to the loopholes in the testimony of each witness as the failure of the court to fulfill its duty under Section 313 CrPC to provide an opportunity to the accused to explain circumstances that implicated them. The defense of false implication was sealed by the DNA profiling report which concluded that the alleged corpse was not that of the deceased private secretary. Because the so-called skeleton produced as corpus delicti had not been proven to belong to the deceased, the accused was prosecuted for the murder of a person with a corpse other than that of the person who was murdered. If the defense had not proactively sought reconsideration of the entire evidentiary record and pointed to the inadequacies of the prosecution case, in a crime controlling political climate, the prosecution would win by default.

Cases Involving Political Celebrities

Reversal of a conviction in a murder trial is a matter of some moment, especially when a political personage is involved. Considering that DM had represented several political personages in cases alleging money laundering, it seemed appropriate to ask him about the challenges posed by representing a political celebrity. With characteristic modesty DM opined that representing a celebrity did not turn the lawyer into a celebrity, even if the media seemed to think otherwise. Except for the media glare there was nothing different to report. DM pointed to the strong sense of entitlement with which political personages operated. Ho noted that since their political ideology dominated their psyche, it was rare for political leader to admit an error of judgment.

The political consequences and not the letter of the law rules when financial institutions are charged with cheating having folded up without paying the promised astronomical interest on public deposits. In DM's view, the depositor had paid the money voluntarily and has not been deceived into parting with the money. The greedy acceptance of the depositor is not taken into account and all fault is found in the financial institution. The greed of the depositors is converted into their gullibility and the entire wrath of the law is unleashed on the financial institution. All DM's arguments on the benefit that the complainant had derived from the contract before the institution failed just got no takers either because the depositors were small savers or defense personnel. The vulnerability or political standing of the depositors prevailed over legal definitions of cheating. Similarly, when a speeding BMW car trampled a number of persons standing in the middle of the road in the wee hours of the day, DM's contention that the driver had adapted his driving to what he expected to be the conditions of the road at that hour, and that duties of safe behavior also applied to pedestrians, were not accepted.

Theory and Practice

DM reflected on some systemic changes introduced in Indian criminal law, such as the enhanced use of the crime control model that altered presumptions of innocence, and restricted access to bail. He noted an exponential increase in behavior that was designated as criminal and the extent to which criminal law was progressively used as a vehicle of social change. For instance, several sharp economic practices were being regulated through criminal law, as were crimes against women and wrongful conduct within the family (Hart, 1958; Simester & Hirsch, 2011).

DM perceived that the change in criminal law from a due process to a crime control model would increase inequities in an already unequal society. Restrictions on the grant of bail or placing impossible standards for the grant of bail, such as that in Section 37 of the Narcotics Drugs and Psychotropic Substances Act of 1985, disproportionately disadvantage persons from economically and socially disadvantaged classes. The section permits courts to grant bail when the public prosecutor opposes the grant, only if the courts believe that the accused has not committed the charged offense and is not likely to commit such an offense when on bail. In effect, the statute expects the court to stand surety for the conduct of the accused when granting bail. It is unrealistic to expect courts to assume such responsibility in order to protect an under trial's right to freedom.

DM anticipated that the introduction of normative changes on the burden of proof would create problems by substituting one prejudice for another. The classical presumption of innocence until proven guilty benefits all. When the onus of establishing innocence is shifted to the accused, then a culture of accusation replaces the quest for truth. Use of this heavy-handed instrument to usher gender parity and restore balance in domestic life is fraught with danger, as the negotiation between the oppressed woman and her matrimonial family occurs in the shadow of criminal law. Since legislation lays down a general norm, it requires the courts to treat all marital relationships similarly, even when it is known that all marriages are not the same. The consequence of this one-size-fits-all criminal law is that a number of men who have done no wrong find themselves within the clutches of criminal law as the new norm views all men with suspicion (Feiberg, 1984).

DM did not approve of using criminal law to usher in social change, as criminal law lacks the subtlety and nuance required for this task and this approach could further complicate social relations.

Transnational Relations

DM discussed this area primarily around the Bofors gun case, wherein he defended Ottavio Quattrocchi (*Ottavio Quattrocchi v. CBI*, 1998) who was accused as part of criminal conspiracy to cheat because he facilitated the payment of commission for an arms procurement deal contrary to the terms of the agreement that the Indian government had with the Bofors Company. DM questioned the jurisdiction of Indian courts in the matter. How could breach of this term of the agreement be termed criminal when the commission was paid outside India by a foreigner to another foreigner? Courts in India could have jurisdiction if an Indian breached Indian law in foreign territory. How could such jurisdiction arise in the case of a foreigner? DM regretted the fact that the courts were unwilling to engage in such foundational questions. And yet the CBI obtained a warrant of arrest to extradite Quattrocchi from Malaysia. The Malaysian courts rejected the extradition request in 2003. With this rejection, DM emphasized that the warrant stood exhausted. However, in 2007, on the same warrant, the CBI effected Quattrocchi's arrest in Argentina. DM filed an affidavit before the Argentinean courts informing them that the accused had been arrested on the strength of an expired warrant. The Argentinean courts granted Quattrocchi bail on February 12, 2007, yet the CBI obtained a fresh warrant of arrest from a metropolitan magistrate in Delhi on February 24, 2007. The letter of request for extradition stated that the accused was wanted in a case of cheating, whereas he had been charged of the conspiracy to cheat. There was thus an evident discrepancy between the letter of request and the charge sheet. India lost the extradition case in June 2007. Yet it was only in 2009 that the Attorney-General of India advised the CBI to write to Interpol to have Quattrochi's name removed from the red corner notice list as two foreign jurisdictions had found that there were no good grounds for extradition. Ottavio Quattrocchi's case exemplified the conflation of executive and judicial roles in prosecuting cases beyond the national borders.

DM stressed the need to distinguish between municipal and international boundaries in criminal prosecution, in the light of several Indian investigations trying to trace the deposit of Indian money in foreign banks, with the aid of orders obtained from Indian courts.

General Assessments

With respect to suggested reforms to the criminal justice system, DM dismissed the proposition as in his view, questions about changing the system should only be raised if the existing normative system has first been tried and tested. Absent empirical evidence to inform any reform proposal, the next set of reforms were also doomed to fail. Consequently, DM took the line that the need was not to replace the existing system with a new one, but to make the existing system work.

To make sure that this happens, DM favored investments at all stages and in all branches of the criminal justice system. Law schools needed to introduce a strong practical component in the teaching of criminal law, abandoning the present mode of teaching the law of evidence and substantive and procedural criminal law as disparate areas and replacing them with course curricula that integrate these fields. Students should be inducted as interns but only after completing comprehensive theoretical training.

All actors of the criminal justice system should be comprehensively educated on the theoretical components of their work, followed by practical training that enables them to utilize their education. Training should not be limited to acquiring the knowledge and skills needed for the job to be performed but should include an understanding of their roles and responsibilities in the criminal justice system. Thus, honest policing should be accorded greater value than forcibly solving cases. Prosecutors should mount cases only against those accused persons against whom credible evidence is produced by the police. And judges should accord a fair trial to every individual who is arraigned before them and not be guided by ideology or policy. The right to fair trial should inform every stage of the criminal process.

Aside from building the capacities of the various players who run the criminal justice system, DM placed great emphasis on investing in state-of-the-art forensic and ballistic resources. A scientifically conducted investigation geared to trace the actual wrongdoer increases crime prevention while building people's trust in the system. Unless investments in scientific crime detection are made, criminal investigation will continue to operate by performing its duties of crime control by trapping people within its snares. Those with private resources may effect a lucky escape, but such recourse is unavailable to the defenseless. The fairness of a system has to be judged on how it treats those who cannot defend themselves.

In DM's view, crime prevention, detection, and punishment have to be responsibly performed by all players of the criminal justice system be it police, prosecutor, defender, or judge. Unless all these players perform their duties for the benefit of all, the just administration of criminal justice is infeasible. Accountability systems must apply to all. It is not enough to point to the self-serving ways of police officials when they try to escape the consequences of their actions by striking *quid pro quo* deals with investigation officers who are also police officers. Questions of accountability need to be raised for all players in the system: prosecutors, defense lawyers, and judges (McEwan, 1992).

Conclusion

This interview documented how one of the doyens of the Indian criminal justice system perceives the system. What is the work ethic that earns him such adulation from people who find themselves on the wrong side of the law? The encounter taught me the difference between being realistic and being cynical. DM was unsparing in his critique of the system. His awareness of the corner cutting practiced by all players in the system was astounding, but used this knowledge to save his clients from the snares of the system. The professional ethic of a committed defense lawyer is to protect the interests of his client even if it resulted in personal loss. When DM found that judges started to draw adverse inferences against his clients when he appeared in the subordinate courts, he stopped practicing in the lower courts.

His large-heartedness is displayed not only to his clients but also to his colleagues. DM was first elected as President of the Delhi High Court Bar Association in 1982 and subsequently in 1983–1984, 1990–1991, 1994–1995, and 2002–2004. Affectionately called Dada or "elder brother" by his colleagues, DM has never flinched in providing personal or professional support whenever near or distant colleagues have asked. DM may hold some kind of record on the number of colleagues he has mentored who were subsequently designated senior advocates.

In a system where people do not play by the rule book, it is the duty of a defense lawyer to proactively safeguard the interests of his client by closely studying the evidence produced by the prosecution to see whether it establishes the prosecution case.

The Indian criminal justice system is meant to function in accordance with the enacted substantive and adjective law. The vast body of DM's work includes innumerable cases before the High Court because the requirements of the law were breached by the prosecution or the subordinate courts. The fact that the prosecution has ignored or is ignorant of the law was used by DM to devise his defense strategies. A major component of that strategy is an unrelenting insistence on observance of the law, that a person can be denied life and liberty only if convicted in accordance with the law. Any conviction which is in breach of this tenet he has questioned.

If knowledge of the law is one signal aspect of DM's defense strategy, then knowledge of facts is the other. A defense lawyer must critically examine how the facts have been construed by the prosecution and the subordinate courts, and whether the construction was informed by the perspective of the prosecutor and judge, or the sociopolitical reality of the alleged perpetrator. DM maintains that only the latter construction comprises an acceptable basis for conviction. Defense lawyers do not just need to know the law; they need to understand the social milieu, the cultural practices, the geography, and history of the persons whose cases they take on.

DM has practiced criminal law in various courts in India for more than 50 years. As a full-blooded defense lawyer, he disapproves of the current mode of obtaining convictions where legal presumptions replace hard evidence. This change dismays him as he believes the law is being stacked against the defenseless that most need its protection. Society should be as concerned when people lose their liberty on flimsy grounds as when they escape conviction. Notwithstanding these systemic inadequacies, he soldiers on. DM is an exemplar of a competent, committed professional who has the courage to practice criminal law ethically, even in a malfunctioning criminal justice system.

Glossary

betel nut and leaf or paan: betel leaf with betel nuts and other ingredients rolled into small packets, which is used as mild stimulant and mouth freshener offered as greeting food to guests when they are entering or leaving the house.

Code of Criminal Procedure: it is the central statute prescribing the procedure by which crimes are reported, investigated, tried, and judged in India.

common law: a judicially created law developed on a case-by-case basis; however, similar cases may be bound by previous judicial decisions.

Central Bureau of Investigation: the crime investigation agency of the country, which was firstly established by executive order and later set up by the Delhi Police Special Establishments Act 1946 to investigate crimes in those territories of the Union that are under control of the central government. The Bureau can investigate cases occurring in the states with the consent of the state government. By Section 3(1) of the Act, the central government can from time to time refer cases for investigation by this national agency.

Delhi High Court Bar Association: an association of advocates practicing in the Delhi High Court and registered as members with the Association.

dowry: money or property brought by a wife to her husband at marriage.

High Court: the highest court in a state that has a constitutional status. The court can be approached in original and appellate petitions.

Indian Penal Code: the principal statute laying down the acts and intentions that substantively constitute offenses in India.

judicial precedent: a principle whereby in a similar fact situation, courts are bound by their earlier decisions.

legal aid: a system whereby the state provides legal representation, especially in criminal cases, at state expense.

legal services authorities: bodies set up under the Legal Services Authorities Act 1986 at the national, state, and district level to provide legal assistance for economically weak and socially deprived persons. These authorities provide legal assistance through various schemes and programs.

parliamentary privilege: a legal immunity extended to legislators whereby they are protected from civil and criminal liability for any speech made or action done in the fulfillment of their parliamentary duties. The Indian constitution has drawn from British parliamentary practice to extend this protection to Indian legislators.

pleaders: lawyers who were allowed to practice in courts below the High Court for at least a period of one year before they were registered by the High Court. This system no longer exists and the term is used just to signify a practicing advocate. However, lawyers who represent the government on the civil side are called government pleaders.

prima facie: a legal term that means presumed to be correct on the basis of first impression unless proved otherwise.

rule of law: it means rules of law and not personal whim and caprice informs public policy.

ruling party: the political party which is in the majority in parliament and thus entitled to form the government.

senior advocate: an honor conferred by the judges of the High Court or Supreme Court upon lawyers practicing before them on the strength of their specialization and seniority. Once a lawyer is declared a senior advocate, he is not permitted to directly deal with clients; he can only accept briefs from other lawyers who are briefed by the clients.

sessions courts: district-level courts that hear criminal matters. Previously, they heard cases continuously in sessions until pronouncement of judgment, hence the name.

Tihar Jail: it is a prison complex in New Delhi, India.

Japan

MAKOTO IBUSUKI

8

Contents

The Criminal Justice Process of Japan

Historical Overview

Almost 150 years ago, the Japanese criminal justice adopted the German inquisitorial model of trial and court practices. Following the Second World War, under the occupied forces of the Allied Powers, criminal procedural law changed from the inquisitorial to the adversarial model. Human rights protections were introduced under the Japanese Constitution in 1946. Concurrently, a basic three-tier court structure was established with approximately 50 District Courts (Chihō Saibansho), eight Courts of Appeal (Kōtō Saibansho), and the Supreme Court (Saikō Saibansho).

Since 1945, the Supreme Court has consisted of 15 judges who are nominated by the Prime Minister of the Cabinet, and recognized by the Emperor. There is no official public screening process, but following their election, Supreme

Court judges are confirmed by a public vote at the first election of the lower National Diet of Japan—the bicameral supreme legislative body in Japan. The Supreme Court is divided into three petty benches. Four or five judges work for the petty bench for the ordinary national criminal and civil jurisdictions and the full bench of 15 judges discuss only unprecedented constitutional cases.

Each District Court has a criminal and civil division. The Family Court has jurisdiction over juvenile and family matters. Nationally, eight courts of appeal are positioned in major cities in Japan for access to the appellate process.

The Japanese legal education system has remained the same for many years. While the majority of people who take the Bar Examination to be admitted as legal practitioners are law graduates, anyone with a four-year college degree may also sit the examination. Currently in Japan, there are approximately 35,000 attorneys, 2,700 prosecutors, and 2,800 judges.[*] Fewer than 400 registered foreign lawyers are eligible to work in Japan on matters such as nondomestic legal services and specific legal services approved by the Japanese government.[†]

Criminal Procedure and Trial Procedures

Japanese criminal procedure is an adversarial system. The Constitution guarantees the defendant due process of law, a fair trial, the right to an attorney, and the right to a speedy trial.[‡] The law prohibits cruel punishment, the use of coerced confessions as evidence, and torture by a public servant. The prosecutor bears the burden of proof at trial, and a trial judge issues a judgment.

Prosecutors have wide discretion in determining which indictments to pursue. Depending on the circumstances, they drop many cases even when there is sufficient evidence to prosecute. In Japan, the primary penal policy of the Prosecutor's Office is not to punish criminals but to deter repeat offenders. In light of this policy, the Office averts the indictment of many first-time offenders and petty offenders, such as shoplifters. Because of this screening function by the prosecutor, the conviction rate at trial is high, at approximately 99%. The high conviction rate is often shocking to foreign observers, as it seems almost inevitable that a defendant who proceeds to trial will be convicted, and hence that Japanese trials appear to be a formalistic proceedings. On the other hand, because the prosecutor has discretion to drop a large number of cases, the prison population in Japan has been very small compared to that of many other developed countries.[§]

---

[*] http://www.nichibenren.or.jp/jfba_info/membership/about.html
[†] http://www.nichibenren.or.jp/jfba_info/membership/about.html
[‡] Arts 37, 34, 31.
[§] http://www.nytimes.com/1996/07/08/world/prisons-in-japan-are-safe-but-harsh.html

During the pretrial phase, Japan has a unique facility for detaining suspects at the police station in a "holding cell." The prosecutor may detain the suspect for up to 20 days prior to trial. During this detention period, suspects have no access to a lawyer, even during interrogation. The Supreme Court has ruled that police and prosecutors can interrogate the suspect without attending lawyers. Many exonerated suspects have reported that the experience of being held for so many days without right of access to a lawyer was the main cause of their wrongful conviction.

Strong criticisms of the Japanese interrogation process have been elicited due to procedures that place suspects in critical and vulnerable circumstances. Mandatory video recording of suspect interrogations was one of the hot topics on the recent criminal procedural reform agenda.

Recent Reforms to the Japanese Criminal Justice System

Recently, the Japanese criminal justice system was the subject of two judicial reform movements, one in 2002 and the other in 2014. In the first reform period, the government introduced civilian participation into the criminal trial system for a limited category of crimes, such as murder and manslaughter cases. Six lay jurors are appointed to work alongside three professional judges who together decide whether the defendant is guilty or not, and on an appropriate sentence for convicted defendants. The reformers expected that the presence of the lay judges in the trial process would promote greater understanding of judicial system.

Another notable reform is the introduction of a new legal education system modeled on North American law schools.* Since April 2004, approximately 70 law schools have been established.† After four years of undergraduate training, the students spend two or three years completing coursework at a law school. Upon graduation, they are eligible to take the Bar Examination. These reforms are expected to significantly increase the number of lawyers available to provide adequate legal services to Japanese society.

Recent dramatic reforms have also been made to a suspect's right to an attorney. Although the Constitution guarantees all defendants a right to counsel in the trial process,‡ prior to the reform era, suspects were not able to receive any support from public attorneys in pretrial proceedings. In 2004, an official scheme of duty solicitors for defendants was implemented. In 2009, a public defender program was launched. Now, a person who is suspected of committing any crimes except for petty offenses (such as simple theft, shoplifting, and traffic violations) has the right to attorney from the preindictment stage.

---

* http://www.hg.org/law-schools-japan.asp
† http://www.japantimes.co.jp/opinion/2013/10/03/editorials/law-school-and-bar-exam-reform/#.Vr1TW9JMvVg
‡ Art 34.

Punishment and Prison

One notable feature of criminal sentencing in Japan is the small proportion of incarcerated offenders per population compared to that in other developed countries (Figure 8.1). The homicide rate in Japan is the lowest among 17 developed countries, as is reflected by comparative data for 2011 homicide rates from 17 developed countries (Statistics Canada and United Nations Office on Drugs and Crime, 2011).

In spite of a low overall crime rate in Japan, the country retains the death penalty. Although statistically the number of capital sentences and executions is very small, Japanese death row inmates are executed every year. The total number of executions in Japan in the past four years is 16 (Japan Today, 2016). In response to criticism from overseas commentators, the Japanese government maintains that strong civilian support for the death penalty persists although recent survey research has challenged that view (Sato, 2015, 2016). In September, 2016, for the first time, the Japanese Federation of Bar Associations announced a proposal to move toward the abolition of the death penalty by 2020 (Japan Today, 2016). A Supreme Court ruling in 1948 declared that capital punishment was not unconstitutional, and that it did not amount to cruel and unusual punishment (Schmidt, 2002).

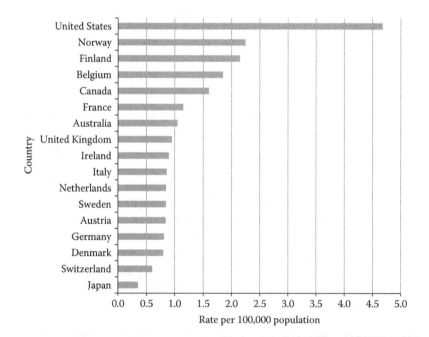

Figure 8.1 2011 National Homicide rates, by Country. (United Nations Office on Drugs and Crime, *2011 Global Study on Homicide: Trends, Context, Data.* United Nations Office on Drugs and Crime, Vienna, 2011.)

Naoya Endo, Attorney, Fairness Law Firm, Tokyo

Introduction

Attorney Dr. Naoya Endo was born in 1945 in Gunma Prefecture, which is located right at the center of Honshu, the largest island of Japan. The year 1945 is a memorable for the end of the Second World War. The early period of Dr. Endo's life corresponds with the history of democracy in Japan because in 1946, Japan established sovereignty of the people by enacting a new Constitution.

As a practicing lawyer, in a career that spans 40 years, Dr. Endo has worked in several different fields. Although it is typical among Japanese non-government legal practitioners to confine their practice to one specific legal area of expertise, Dr. Endo's practice has encompassed criminal defense, personal injury litigation, consumer rights, medical malpractice, and he developed a practice focused on complex litigation involving expert evidence. His diverse legal career and breadth of interests are evident in the personal library maintained by Mr. Endo in his office. The author was surprised by his book collection, which covers a wide variety of disciplines and fields, and includes books from some foreign jurisdictions. In this digital age, many lawyers avoid spending their money on a work-related book collection. This library differentiates Dr. Endo's office from those of other legal practitioners, and demonstrates his unique approach to his work.

Career

Dr. Endo graduated from the Department of Law at the University of Tokyo, the most prestigious national university in Japan. In 1983, he completed an LLM degree at the University of Washington School of Law. Later, in 2001, he earned a doctoral degree from Chuo University—one of the first Japanese universities to establish a Law Department. This distinction is more remarkable as exceedingly few members of the Japanese legal profession hold a doctoral degree in Law. His thesis focused on law reform. His principal ideas to reform the Japanese legal system have been widely published (Endo, 2000, 2002, 2004, 2005, 2008, 2012a, 2012b, 2012c, 2014) and are well regarded by both practitioners and academics.

Dr. Endo's youth in the 1970s was an era of political confrontation, during which period he worked for activists who opposed the Vietnam War and for student activists in the student movement. Working *pro bono* as a defense lawyer with other young lawyers, Dr. Endo represented student activists in numerous cases involving public security issues, such as allegedly obstructing officials in the performance of their duties. In these cases, the key evidence was provided by police witnesses who had observed violations during protest rallies conducted in public places in the city. The defense team had immense difficulty securing a verdict of not guilty for their clients in these cases because it was difficult to access undisclosed evidence—such as testimony of third parties and internal reports of official duties held by the prosecutor. This legal disadvantage left a profound impression on Dr. Endo and later he advocated for changes in pretrial criminal procedure to level the playing field for the defense.

Dr. Endo started his legal career as a solo practitioner at the time of deregulation in the 1980s. His main clients at that time were people with real estate troubles and consumer claims. He also took on many cases involving product liability and losses resulting from business scams in which many consumers were victimized by fraud. However, from this period until the late 1990s, Japan experienced a financial crisis and extended recession known as the "bubble" economy or "the lost decade," and Dr. Endo's clients faced increasing financial hardship. As a consequence, his work became more difficult. He recalls that this was a new and challenging experience.

After retutning to Japan from United States in 1990, Dr. Endo became an independent lawyer, managed his own practice, and discontinued working on difficult criminal cases for indigent clients. The number of claims for damages through environmental litigation and consumer claims in Japan had drastically increased after the 1960s. Dr. Endo researched approaches to these issues in other jurisdictions, such as class action litigation under tort law in the U.S. for victims of industrial diseases such as mesothelioma. On a *pro bono* basis, in civil litigation Dr. Endo represented many victims suffering from industrial diseases such as chromium lung cancer and pneumoconiosis.

Due to the difficulty in obtaining evidence and filing lawsuits for these kinds of cases in Japan, Dr. Endo's *pro bono* work placed a substantial burden on his law firm. The demanding and complex nature of these trials led him to develop a series of strategies for effective practice. One of his practical recommendations about effective lawyering involves using expert opinions in court. Based on his discussions with experts in a certain field, he personally drafts the opinion he is seeking and then gives the draft to the expert to rewrite it and complete it. He explains that his reason for adopting this approach is that often experts are reluctant to contribute their opinions because they are too busy. Dr. Endo believes that his approach makes it easier for the experts to work on his cases. In Japan, collaboration among experts and lawyers to formulate and draft expert opinions is considered ethical. Dr. Endo explained that under the Japanese rules of evidence, an opinion developed through the collaborative work of the expert and the lawyer is admissible and is regarded as reliable.

After the "bubble" economy collapsed in Japan, the directors of many companies faced criminal trials for their company's bad debts. Dr. Endo's dissatisfaction with his experience in litigating over these matters prompted him to undertake a program of doctoral studies in 2011. In his thesis, he submitted that it was not reasonable to pursue company directors' responsibility through the criminal justice system. Instead, he suggested that civil litigation was preferable as a vehicle to apportion this responsibility among company directors and to avoid a verdict of joint liability that lacks the division of responsibility.

In addition to maintain his legal practice, Dr. Endo has contributed to the education of Japanese lawyers by teaching seminars on Corporate Law and Medical Law at Toin University of Yokohama School of Law. In the classroom, he emphasizes that in resolving medical malpractice cases, it is imperative to provide an expeditious solution through civil litigation, rather than to punish medical professionals through reliance on the criminal legal process. Further, Dr. Endo stresses the importance of precautionary measures in order to prevent medical malpractice—as opposed to the traditional approach of pursuing criminal prosecution for doctors' medical negligence. He also encourages students to develop a wide range of knowledge and skills, not only from within the law, but also from medical and other relevant fields.

At present, Dr. Endo is the chair of a law firm that includes 11 young associates and three junior partners. Throughout his career, Dr. Endo has worked extremely diligently and spent a considerable amount of money to develop and expand his law firm. He is kept busy managing the workload. He has practiced as lawyer in both criminal and civil cases with his associates, and has spent his time fulfilling the responsibilities of managing the entire office. He has continued his *pro bono* work as a member of the Japan Civil Liberties Union (http://www.jclu.org/index_e.shtml), committed to advancing human rights in Japanese society. Dr. Endo has also been very active in legal professional associations. Through these activities, he was elected Vice President of the Daini Tokyo Bar Association—one of the three Bar associations in Tokyo.

Philosophy of Legal Advocacy

Alongside his legal practice, Dr. Endo has developed a career as an advocate of legal reform. As the chair of the Tokyo Bar Association Committee with oversight responsibility for legal education, Dr. Endo took the lead in developing a new law school system for Japan. Japan's current law school system was founded in 2004. He argued for the abolition of the Legal Research and Training Institute managed by the Supreme Court and for the reform of the career judge system. His argument partially reflected the principle of judicial reform based on the Final Proposal of the 2001 Justice System Reform Council.

Dr. Endo points to the need to look carefully at practical realities, changes over time and the social context, when considering reform of a legal system within any particular society. He noted that Japan in some respects resembles the United Kingdom, where the members of the legal profession have a unique historical background. For example, in the United Kingdom, the barrister has traditionally been respected as a court practitioner. However, in contemporary British society, legal services provided outside of the courtroom have become increasingly complex and difficult. As a result, the traditional concept that the barrister is superior to the solicitor who works outside of court is no longer valid.

Dr. Endo's insights into limitations of the traditional legal system in Japan that he perceived as outmoded led him to explore innovative ideas in order to reform the Japanese legal system. This state of affairs has motivated him to devote his time to advancing the theory of "Soft Law."

Problems and Successes Experienced

While Dr. Endo was studying law in North America, he was particularly surprised to learn about the concepts of discovery, disclosure, class actions, and punitive damages. He deepened his knowledge of many different legal systems and judicial procedures, which he imported into Japan upon his return. He delivered lectures on these topics to the Japanese public, and to academics interested in law and society.

As a practitioner, Dr. Endo came to believe that Japanese civil and criminal procedure should implement the US style discovery process and disclosure process to reduce the protracted Japanese trial procedures. His practical experience led him to conclude that pretrial disclosure of the evidence in criminal proceedings would assist in preventing wrongful convictions, and that similarly, the process of discovery in a civil trial would be helpful in improving legal services. In a 1988 trial, he applied to the court for an order requiring both parties to exchange documents. Many courts later adopted this innovative idea. He led the development of requests for production of documents as part of the civil procedure law, and this law was ultimately revised in 1996, adopting his idea. Dr. Endo is still advocating further advancements to this idea in civil litigation, arguing that the legislation should give the power of mandatory orders to the court, because he believes that many courts are hesitant to use their discretionary powers to issue discovery orders to the parties.

Recently in Japan, and especially in the years since the Lehman Shock in 2008, the competition between law firms has been very intense, except among very large law firms. Many small law offices have had no option but to reduce the size of their business or the breadth of expertise they offer. Currently, Dr. Endo's firm employs lawyers with diverse types of expertise. For example, one practitioner is both a lawyer and a qualified medical practitioner who graduated from a medical school. Others are tax attorneys and accountants, and lawyers who graduated from technical schools. Although it is not easy to find and recruit lawyers with these specific types of expertise and skills, Dr. Endo carefully considers the type of experts his office needs to recruit, and he personally decides whom to hire. Through these efforts, his office is now thriving among the fierce competition among legal practitioners in Tokyo. They represent clients in criminal cases especially in the category of white-collar crime.

Theory and Practice

Dr. Endo believes that in Japan, people need protection not in a paternalistic top-down fashion according to traditional, authoritative legal theory, but in light of a new bottom-up legal theory. Throughout his legal career, Dr. Endo observed that a legal theory to protect the people of Japan was lacking. He used the following example to make his point. In Japan, if a debtor is bankrupt, even the debtor's house is targeted for compulsory execution. This is not the case in the United States. At a lecture at the University of the Republic of Uzbekistan, he learned that they apply a legal theory similar to that of the United States. Dr. Endo posited that these legal theories had emerged during periods of economic recession, such as the Great Depression. Without a home, a debtor cannot recommence economic activities. He concluded that in Japan, the operant legal theory—offering homeowners no fundamental protection of their livelihood from the government—had emerged in a period of economic inflation. Dr. Endo argues that the protection of fundamental basic life infrastructure should be regarded as inviolate and essential.

These legal deficits prompted Dr. Endo to find a legal philosophy compatible with his ideas. Through this quest, he came up with the idea of "Soft Law," a term appropriated from public international law which Dr. Endo has adopted to increase civilian power and that of local governments to enhance the overall well-being of the community, and to provide a solution to community disputes. In his view, the opposite form of "Hard Law"—which dominates Japanese society—relies only on laws and legal precedents, and in fact precludes civilian participation.

Dr. Endo believes that society should be based on Soft Law, in which the rule of law is oriented to be flexible, relying on preventive administration, and independent self-regulation on the part of the private sector, rather than on "Hard Law," whereby the government takes leadership in devising and implementing reforms and enforces the law by applying strong forms of regulation. Dr. Endo also argues that training on the Soft Law approach should be included in legal education to ensure that lawyers have a wider appreciation and knowledge of the overall legal system, and do not depend exclusively on court precedents and statutes.

According to Dr. Endo's conception of Soft Law, the first stage of rule-making should be conducted jointly by representatives from the administrative and private sectors. At the second stage, the central government should join them in formulating the law. This is what he means by a "bottom-up" approach to legal philosophy. Dr. Endo calls the social values embodied in this methodology a form of Soft Law democracy. Dr. Endo has published many books to disseminate his theory about "Soft Law" to the public. The active implementation of "Soft Law" is his original idea, promoting the rule of law and democracy in society by applying a "bottom-up" approach and rejecting an authoritative "top-down" approach. This activity clearly distinguishes Dr. Endo from other legal practitioners and criminal defense lawyers.

Similar points of argument have emerged elsewhere in the world. For example, in 1978, Nonet and Selznick analyzed the historical development of the rule of law by classifying its developmental stages along a continuum from "repressive law" at one extreme, which relies on criminal sanctions, to "autonomous law," which centers on regulation by civil law, and then to "responsive law" at the other extreme, which represents a strengthening in mutual cooperation by both the administration and the private sectors. Tamanaha suggested that substantive versions or conceptions of the rule of law was important to achieve constitutionally guaranteed freedoms and human rights, as well as the values of democracy and the welfare state. For that reason, he argued that it was more important than "formal legality in the rule of law" (Tamanaha, 2004).

Dr. Endo elaborated on the role of Soft Law and the necessity of using this idea in response to academic theories that originated in other countries. Specifically, in Japan, after the Second World War, the formalistic rule of law and oppressive rule of law needed to be converted first into an "autonomous rule of law" and second into a "responsive rule of law," guaranteeing citizens their human rights and peace. In reality, the emphasis was more on criminal regulation than on the civil resolution, and the statutes enacted by parliament functioned as regulations rather than protections for the people. Dr. Endo points out that the Supreme Court has rarely held that these statutes are unconstitutional, and that surprisingly, in the history of the Supreme Court of Japan, there have only been nine decisions holding that a law or statute was unconstitutional. Dr. Endo evaluates these phenomena as typical examples of a "nonresponsive rule of law." Dr. Endo regards medical malpractice cases and corporate negligence cases as a consequence of the nonresponsive and nonautonomous rule of law in Japan, in which penal sanctions are preferred as solutions. This approach led to the development of the so-called "oppressive legal system" in Japan, and hindered the growth of a healthy "responsive legal system."

Dr. Endo's interest in a bottom-up legal system probably derives from the time when he worked as a lawyer representing progressive doctors using preimplantation genetic diagnosis and their patients as plaintiffs. This was a matter to revoke a quasi-administrative decision depriving a medical doctor of his membership in an authoritative academy to practice because of his contribution to a certain reproductive technique. In the context of these cases, when Dr. Endo observed the nonresponsive and authoritative rule of law, he formed the view that a different approach to implement the rule of law in Japan must be feasible, and started to develop his Soft Law theory.

In reality, the mainstream lawyers' world in Japan is still authoritative, and perpetuates the nonresponsive law system. In legal education, precedents and statutes are emphasized as the most authoritative legal resources. Even in the face of these realities, Dr. Endo never abandoned his beliefs, and has kept developing his legal philosophy.

Dr. Endo criticizes the Japanese criminal justice process as being excessively interventionist in seeking to resolve many social problems. This approach eliminates opportunities to seek solutions through civil trial procedures and via administrative power. Dr. Endo observed that in Japan, there are no opportunities to create a truly "responsive rule of law" based on democracy, such as the bottom-up style. This reality, he believes, shows that Japan is neither a true democratic society nor a country governed by the rule of law.

Transnational Relations

In the Japanese legal reform eras of the late 1990s and the early 2000s, Dr. Endo undertook research trips to the United States as chair of a delegation of the Daini Tokyo Bar Association. Their mission was to observe and gather information about the American law school system and the American judicial system because at that time, in Japan, there was heated debate on two issues. The first was the need to control the growth of the population of the legal profession and determine the optimal size of the lawyer population. A majority of reformers urged the need to increase the number of lawyers to improve access to legal services in Japan. In Japan, there is a taboo in the lawyers' society inhibiting discussion of professional and comprehensive legal service integration among the legal sectors. The second debate centered on the creation of a new system of lay participation in the criminal justice system. Thus, the main research conducted by the delegation was on legal education, legal professionals, and jury service in criminal cases.

Dr. Endo noted that the more research he did, the more he became aware of the scope of differences between the Japanese and U.S. legal systems. For example, in the United States, it is lawyers who dominate the standards applicable to members of the legal profession. In Japan, on the other hand, a variety of qualified legal professionals, including career judges and prosecutors, are influential in establishing standards for comparable legal services.

While the United States has a uniform system of legal education and qualification practice, in Japan, membership of the legal profession is achieved via many different career pathways that lead to different types of legal expertise, qualifications, and approved areas of practice—each overseen by a different professional association. Three main types of legal qualifications are illustrative of these differences, namely (1) administrative scriveners (gyosei-shoshi), (2) judicial scriveners (shihō-shoshi), and (3) certified public tax accountants (zeiri-shi). Each of these groups of lawyers has a distinct role. For instance, administrative scriveners draft government documents, and specialize in immigration matters, wills, and inheritance. Judicial scriveners are qualified to register the ownership of real property, apply for arbitration, and prepare and file articles of incorporation. The certified tax accountants are qualified professionals who deal with issues concerning tax payments and inheritance. In 2014, there were 21,000 certified judicial scriveners, 45,000 administrative procedures specialists, and over 70,000 tax accountants.

He was anxious when he learned that an American-style law school system was to be introduced in Japan, because this ignored the differences in overall licensed legal service providers in a community in the Japanese system. He thought that certain unique features of Japanese legal services and the history of its legal profession should be considered when reforms to legal education and legal profession were discussed. Dr. Endo formed the view that British and Canadian legal education models were better suited as models for Japan to emulate.

Regarding the proposed reform of the legal profession in Japan, he concluded that the population of lawyers may well be smaller than anticipated as the reform proposal was modeled on the status and conditions applicable to North American lawyers, not the situation in Japan. He demonstrated that the total number of law-related professionals for the next 20 years will be decreasing in Japan.

Nowadays, the small audience for his Soft Law theory within the Japanese legal profession society has led Dr. Endo to increasingly present his ideas in international forums. For example, he attended and presented papers on the need for Japan to establish a democratic society based on his theory of Soft Law at the 16th World Congress of the International Society for Criminology (Kobe, 2011), the Annual Conference of the Law and Society Association (Minneapolis, 2014), the 18th World Congress of Sociology (Yokohama, 2014), and the Fourth East Asian Law and Society Conference (Tokyo, 2015).

In his latest paper presented at East Asian Law and Society (Tokyo, 2015), he cited the work of Tamanaha (2014) and argued that in the United States, lawyers have historically relied on both formal legality and substantive legality in their practice, while in Japan, legal professionals rely only on formal legality. He emphasized that, in the future, Japanese lawyers should take up the challenge of establishing substantive legality in society in order to achieve better legal governance in society.

General Assessments

Dr. Endo's uniqueness emerges in his commitment to write a legal essay or article whenever he encounters new legal topics. He recommends his associates to do the same. He explains that writing for publication produces a certain tension in a lawyer's life, because publication of a paper can acquire new readers who used be unfamiliar with the law, and thinking about that challenges the lawyer to write a better paper, and improves the quality of the service for the client.

In general, it is not difficult to find lawyers who are willing to talk about their ideas or their claims in a particular field. However, there are few lawyers like Dr. Endo who are always motivated by philosophical notions, but who are also very practical. As one can tell, the characteristic features of Dr. Endo's professional philosophy and ethos are his passionate efforts to spread his ideas for a better legal system and better jurisprudence, and his objective to achieve greater social well-being. To this end, he is engaged in publishing as many original books as possible to spread these innovative concepts. One of his books is even published in both Japanese and English. His endeavors to circulate his ideas around the world are very unique among members of the legal professional community in Japan.

Generally speaking, most senior attorneys work for the benefit of their clients and for themselves because they are concerned about the financial strength of the law firms in which they work. Some lawyers work *pro bono* for a specific cause in order to pursue their ideals. By contrast, Dr. Endo focuses on educating the next generation of lawyers and on social enlightenment when he works on *pro bono* matters with young associates.

While it may appear to be a diversion to maintain this level of activity, I believe that Dr. Endo's social theory of Soft Law is both viable and reasonable, and that Japanese society needs his idea of a "responsive law" system to achieve democracy and grow away from the traditional "authoritative" social structure. Although two recent criminal justice movements resulted in reforms that were implemented in Japan, these did not contribute much in the way of developing a more autonomous legal system in the bottom-up style. However, a few important changes came about as a result of these reforms. The first is lay citizen participation in the criminal trial process in the "Saiban-in" system, in which six lay judges and three professional judges work together to reach a decision on guilt and sentencing of the accused (Goto, 2014). Lay participation in criminal trials was regarded as the most significant reform by the civil liberty support group, especially since this is a bottom-up legal systemic change (Corey & Hans, 2010; Wilson, 2013). The second is a mandatory recommendation by the prosecutorial review board favoring indictment in specific cases that the prosecutor's office declines to prosecute. The third is victim participation in criminal trials and juvenile proceedings.

If one takes a broad view of the current Japanese situation, few reforms embrace the concept of Soft Law or promote a more responsive rule of law. The heart of the Japanese political decision-making process is locked in a battle for control between politicians and bureaucrats. It is in their mutual interests to protect their economic interests. Since the industrial sector also wishes to expand its influence, the authoritative rule of law remains dominant. As a result, there are few opportunities for citizens and for local governments to accelerate the movement toward a more responsive rule of law.

While the term "decentralization of power" is recited over and over, in the real world, there are many "disappearing villages" in rural areas of Japan because of population crises in these areas. While some democratic reforms may be introduced into the criminal justice system, professional judges continue to dominate trials in civil cases and in administrative litigation. As a result, in most cases brought against large corporations and against government agencies, the judicial decision tends to favor the authorities. A prime example is a lawsuit seeking an injunction against the government and the Tokyo Electric Power Company requiring the shutdown of an atomic power plant after the Great East Japan Earthquake caused the Fukushima nuclear power plant disaster. This incident finally evoked the conscience of the court in that matter. The trial judge expressed his regret that the court did not exercise its supervisory power over the government's decision and decision-making procedures governing the risk assessment that allowed the plant to continue to operate.

Unfortunately, in Japan, there are few opportunities for citizens and NGOs to participate in drafting legislation when they perceive that its adoption could possibly lead to environmental disruption or that a new law might impose limits on human rights. The public hearing and the public comment periods are viewed merely as an opportunity for venting and as posturing by the policy-makers to demonstrate that they are doing their best. In Japan, there are also few mechanisms promoting civilians' commitment to oversee the governance powers. In contrast, in Northern Europe, there is the ombudsman system; in the United Kingdom, an administrative review process and inquiry system; and in the United States, a popular election system for public servants such as the police chief, fire station chief, judge, and local prosecutor. This means that in Japan, there is less momentum to create an autonomous rule of law and the responsive type of legal system that Dr. Endo advocates introducing into society.

If we wish to implement the idea of Soft Law as described by Dr. Endo into the Japanese society, the author believes, at a minimum, that some concrete alternative methodologies and strategies should be introduced. For example, in the criminal justice system, a new alternative philosophy of sentencing, such as the well-known idea of therapeutic jurisprudence (Winick, 2003) is recommended because it draws on the civil power of the community to find solutions for problems affecting the lives of criminals. In the civil justice system, democratic methods of dispute resolution, such as alternative dispute resolution and mediation, should be *integrated* in our society (Cole, 2004; Tezuka & Yajima, 2005/6). However, a comparative study revealed that Japanese citizens have a negative impression of alternative dispute resolution and mediation (Brown, 2012).

Conclusion

A lawyer such as Dr. Endo whose approach to the legal system is so revolutionary is a provocative role model for the younger generation. He has challenged the typical image of a lawyer in the minds of ordinary members of the Japanese community. The author believes that Dr. Endo's ethos and professional style truly exemplify the diversity of the legal profession in Japan.

The key to implementing Dr. Endo's concept of Soft Law in Japanese society is to integrate and expand empowerment in the community as the solution to many social problems, and especially as a solution to legal problems.

Glossary

career judge: in Japan, a judge is generally nominated from the class of students studying at the Legal Research and Training Institute after passing the Bar examination. Directly from law school, they pursue a career inside the court until retirement. Nomination from the bar to judge is quite rare. After nomination, the young judge works as associate judge for 10 years and is reappointed every 10 years by the Supreme Court General Secretariat.

certified administrative procedures specialists (gyosei shoshi): one of the qualifications that legal professionals in Japan can obtain prepares them to give advice on the preparation of documents required by national and local governments, for example, in immigration matters, wills, inheritances, motor vehicle registrations, property development approvals, articles of incorporation, company minutes, registration of the ownership of real estate, and to assist in certifying the residential eligibility of foreign citizens. These legal professionals belong to the Association of Certified Administrative Procedures Legal Specialists.

certified tax accountant (zeiri-shi): a qualified legal professional in Japan who advises and represents clients in tax filing, preparation of tax documents, tax advice, and bookkeeping matters. These legal professionals belong to the Association of Certified Public Tax Accountants.

class action: a type of civil suit against the defendant brought by a representative member of a group of similarly situated victims on behalf of all the members of the group.

disclosure: under U.S. criminal law, since the 1960s, the U.S. Supreme Court has declared that the prosecution has a duty to disclose exculpatory evidence to defense (*Brady v. Maryland*, 1963; *Giglio v. United States,* 1972). Specific evidence, such as an alibi, must be disclosed by the defense to the prosecutor before the defense argues the alibi in court in the course of a criminal trial.

discovery: a formal pretrial procedure under U.S. Rules of Civil Procedure for a party to a civil lawsuit to obtain vital information in the possession or exclusive knowledge of the adverse party that is helpful to the other party's case.

judicial scriveners (shihō-shoshi): a qualified legal professional in Japan who is certified to assist clients in commercial and real estate registration procedures, and in the preparation of documents for litigation, such as inheritance matters, applications for arbitration, and incorporation of a company. They may represent client in the Summary Courts where the amount claimed is less than US$ 10000, and in arbitration and mediation proceedings. These legal professionals belong to the Judicial Scriveners Association.

Lehman shock: a reference to the collapse of the investment bank known as Lehman Brothers, who filed bankruptcy in 2008. The liquidation of this firm was perceived to be symbolic of a wider global financial crisis or recession.

lost decade: the period after the Japanese asset price inflation bubble burst and the Japanese stock market crashed spanning the years 1991–2000. During this time, the strong Japanese economy shrank drastically. The GDP in 1996 was US$ 4706 billion but in 2003, it was 3980.

punitive damages: monetary compensation in excess of actual damages awarded to a plaintiff to be paid by a defendant in a civil lawsuit when the defendant's actions are the result of reckless disregard or malicious and willful violations of reasonable standards of care. In the United States, this compensation is also called exemplary damages as it is intended to punish the wrongdoer by making an example of the wrongdoing and holding the defendant personally liable.

Soft Law: an original idea developed by Dr. Endo described in "The Journal of Soft Law" (2005–2013). This project was conducted by a research group at the University of Tokyo as part of the twenty-first century Centre of Excellence Program supported by the Japanese Society for the Promotion of Science. This idea calls for the strengthening of civil power to find a resolution for social problems. As an advocate of social and legal reform, Dr. Endo has been trying to implement this idea into the judicial system and the legal community in Japan as a key philosophy.

Nepal

DANIELLE CELERMAJER

9

Contents

The Criminal Justice Process of Nepal

Nepal's hybrid legal system draws on Hindu legal traditions but is overlaid with legal influences from a range of sources—primarily British, French, and Indian—thus also combining elements of civil and common law traditions (Urscheler, 2012). Although Nepal was never colonized by a Western imperial power, British common law traditions were introduced into Nepali law principally through the influence of Indian legal education and practice. The French Napoleonic Code was implemented in major reforms introduced in the mid-nineteenth century. At the same time, in a highly linguistically and ethnically diverse society (with over 90 language groups), there remains a patchwork of traditional norms and laws through which different groups of people seek to settle disputes.

To understand the operation of the legal system, one must, however, locate it within broader political developments in Nepal's history. Nepal was unified as the Kingdom of Nepal in 1769 by the Gorkha ruler Prithvi Narayan Shah. From 1909, the country that became known as Nepal (Gellner, Pfaff-Czarnecka, & Whelpton, 1997, p. 5) was ruled by monarchical dynasties until the overthrow of the hereditary Rana (prime ministerial) dynasty in 1951.

In this context, it is important to note that the Ranas were in fact hereditary prime ministers whose family enjoyed political and economic dominance, while the formal position of the King was retained but became purely symbolic, being "eclipsed" by the prime ministerial rule (Shaha, 1978, p. 1). The political marginalization of the monarchy, accompanied by the transfer of dynastic sovereign power to what we might think of as a modern democratic representational political form, is important in understanding the subsequent political dynamics in Nepal and the potential challenge that the royal house could pose at different points in time to the concentration of power elsewhere in the political system. A significant development during the Rana period was the legal codification of caste and ethnicity within the Maluki Ain (legal codification) of 1854 (Gellner et al., 1997).

The 1951 uprising, considered the inauguration of Nepali democracy, formally instated a multiparty political system. It established a constituent assembly to draft a constitution, returned executive power to the King, and set up an independent judiciary. Subsequent reforms introduced in the wake of the 1951 revolution included the formal introduction of the principle of equality before the law (entailing the elimination of caste from the legal system) and the establishment of basic political and judicial institutions such as the Supreme Court (Sarbocha Adlat).

While acknowledging these formal changes, we emphasize that the nominal introduction of democratic principles, the rule of law, and the separation of powers did not equate to their substantive instantiation in a society still infused with caste and gender hierarchies and entrenched concentrations of power. Highly stratified power still remains a feature of the legal and political systems in Nepal today (Bhattachan, Sunar, & Bhattachan, 2009).

Even at a formal level though, this move to multiparty democratic rule lasted until 1960 when King Mahendra dismissed the elected government, introduced a new constitution, and established the Panchayat system, a pyramidic form of government where supreme power was vested in the King, under whom was established a structure of various assemblies, from the national to the village level (Khadka, 1986). Under this system, the principal mechanism adopted for resolving disputes at the village level was the *Parishad*, comprising of "three or more persons who among them knew the Vedas, Vedangas, Itihasas and were versed in logic and vedic interpretation and etymology" (Walker & Allen, 1968, p. 226).

Given the failure of this system to democratize power, in 1991, agitation led to further major political reforms, including the reestablishment of multiparty politics and the first election of parliament in nearly 50 years. However, this reformed system failed to seriously address the entrenched legal, political, social, and economic inequalities. In 1996, the Communist (Maoist) Party of Nepal initiated revolutionary action with a view to introducing a genuine democratic republic and overcoming the structural pathologies that had persisted through various iterations of reform (Lawoti & Pahari, 2009) and explicitly seeking to eliminate marginalization and exclusion based on caste, ethnicity, and gender (Hangen, 2008). The 10 years of civil war that ensued saw Nepal enter into a period characterized by gross and systematic human rights violations, including widespread extrajudicial killings, torture, and enforced disappearances. The scale and severity of violations significantly intensified after the Royal Army entered the conflict in 2002 (Informal Sector Service Centre, 2007) and, within the context of the Western world's "global war on terror," added its significant weight to the violations previously prosecuted by the Nepal Police and Armed Police Force specially established in 2001. The severity of the situation is well represented by the fact that more disappearances in Nepal were reported to the UN's Working Group on Enforced or Involuntary Disappearances than in relation to any other state (Human Rights Watch, 2004). On the basis of his mission to Nepal in 2005, the Special Rapporteur on Torture and Other Cruel, Inhuman or Degrading Treatment or Punishment, Manfred Nowak, unequivocally concluded "that torture and ill-treatment are systematically practised in Nepal by the police, armed police and the RNA [Royal Nepal Army]" (Nowak, 2006, para 17). He also concluded that despite the existence of certain legal provisions, there existed "wide disparities between these formal guarantees and what actually happens in practice" (Nowak, 2006, para 20), with the security forces routinely ignoring such formal legal standards. As recently documented, persistent impunity has left virtually all of these serious violations without legal or other institutional redress (Human Rights Watch and Advocacy Forum [AF] Nepal, 2010; Robins, 2011).

The civil war officially ended with the parties to the conflict signing a Comprehensive Peace Accord in November 2006. In 2007, a new interim constitution replaced the 1990 constitution and a Constituent Assembly (CA) was charged with drafting the permanent constitution. The failure of the first CA to come to an agreement resulted in its dissolution and establishment of a second CA at the beginning of 2014, with a mandate of proposing a permanent constitution. Eventually, in September 2015, the Constitution, Nepal's seventh, was passed. At the same time, the CA declared the Republic of Nepal in May 2008, abolishing the 240-year-old monarchy and establishing a President as the Head of State, a unicameral parliamentary system, a Prime Minister elected by the parliament, and an Executive comprising the Council of Ministers. The interim constitution also established three tiers of the judiciary: the Supreme Court, the Court of Appeals, and the District Courts. Notably, there is no distinction between civil and criminal courts, and although the interim constitution allows for the establishment of several special courts (e.g., the Administrative Court,

Inland Revenue Tribunal), in general, there are no specialized courts, and judges can hear all types of cases.

The Chief Justice of the Supreme Court is appointed by the President on the advice of the Constitutional Council, who in turn and also on the advice of the Constitutional Council appoints the Chief Justice and judges of the Appellate Court and judges of the District Courts. The criteria for qualifying as a lawyer are established by the Nepal Bar Council (a statutory body), which also issues licenses to practice and regulates conduct of lawyers.

Mandira Sharma, Lawyer and Human Rights Activist, Kathmandu

Introduction

Traditionally, the practice and imposition of law in Nepal has represented an exemplary case of law's role in securing and augmenting existing distributions of power (Tushnet, 1986). Such distributions have given rise to substantial social movements and, in the later part of the twentieth century, violent political conflict. During this same period, some legal practitioners began to look to law as a source for challenging the abuse of power and ensuring that the fundamental principles of legal and political equality that had been given nominal recognition were realized in practice. Unsurprisingly, such efforts have faced myriad challenges, in terms of the structures and processes of law enforcement and criminal justice institutions, the education and training of personnel throughout the system, and the culture of the legal profession itself.

Mandira Sharma, the founder of the nongovernmental organization (NGO), Advocacy Forum (AF) Nepal, has been at the forefront of such initiatives to transform law so that it can serve as a tool for human rights, and in particular the protection of the poor and marginalized from the vagaries of power. Her strategies to effect this change have included: seeking to hold Nepali officials to account with respect to Nepal's own constitution as well as to international human rights laws and principles; working at the grassroots level to empower local communities; training young lawyers in a new approach to legal practice that involves ensuring legal defense for those traditionally deprived of it; and through her own practice, performing a different legal culture. In this interview, she discusses how her legal approach and strategies evolved, the obstacles she has faced, and the future path she imagines will need to be forged for her aspirational vision of law to be realized.

Career

The political movement of 1990 (Jana Andolan) turned Mandira Sharma into a human rights activist. Before this time, during the period of absolute monarchy and one party rule, there had been no freedom of assembly. The political changes during the 1990s introduced a new constitutional framework and sharing of power among the parties. The King and those who had been detained for their participation in the movement were released. Some of those who were released were people whom she knew, including her teachers from school and college. Meeting these people again, finding them much changed, and listening to their shocking experiences of torture led her to join the Centre for Victims of Torture (CVICT), a group set up by a team of medical doctors to provide medical treatment to torture survivors. Her first job with CVICT was to document the stories of these survivors.

What was most eye opening for Mandira was coming to understand how torture destroys a person, and not only the individual person but also the whole family. A very bright, articulate lecturer might come back from detention needing to be dependent on his family for the rest of his life. It was witnessing this that made it clear to Mandira that this was an area where she should work.

Mandira stayed with CVICT for 10 years, working in different capacities. She visited more than 40 prisons in different parts of the country, documenting the stories of prisoners. She encountered cases where people had been subjected to all kinds of torture, including sexual torture against women. She witnessed people languishing well beyond their sentences, many not even knowing why they were incarcerated. Women, she found, were particularly vulnerable, because when they were detained, their families disassociated from them. Some mothers had no option than to raise their children in prisons. Others suffered the psychological distress of losing all contact with their children.

These 10 years convinced Mandira that while it was important to assist people once they found themselves in such situations, it was vitally important to prevent their torture before it was, in a sense, too late. To work out how to develop torture prevention strategies, she decided to undertake an LLM in Human Rights at Essex University, and, in 1999, was awarded a British Council Scholarship to do so. The course really opened her horizons. After graduating in 2000, she returned to Nepal and started AF.

Mandira's vision was to create an organization that would visit police detention centers. To do this, she built a team of young lawyers, who worked on a volunteer basis, or with whom she shared the money she earned working as a consultant for international organizations. Detention centers were their initial point of intervention because the people she had interviewed had told her that it was here, where statements and evidence are collected, and where they had no access to lawyers, medical professionals, or family members, that they were most vulnerable. It was also where torture most frequently occurred. Doing this work required breaking the access barrier; no one had previously been permitted to visit police detention centers. Her job in gaining access was not made any easier by her identity as young woman in a very hierarchical society. She decided to use a provision in the constitution specifying that every accused has the right to consult his or her lawyer.

Despite the existence of this provision, there was in fact no general concept or practice of lawyers visiting detention centers. The consensus was that lawyers only came in at the trial stage. To bring the provision to life, Mandira tried to negotiate with the police, maintaining that detainees had constitutional rights to legal consultation, and that if the police did not allow access to a lawyer or permit AF to provide free legal advice, they were violating the constitution. To gain access to higher authorities, she enjoined the support of senior people like retired judges and her former professors. Once they did gain limited access, they worked to gradually expand it. Though their visits, what they discovered and documented was that the legal requirements were routinely violated: people were not taken to court within 24 hours as mandated by the constitution, they had no access to their family members, and they were subjected to torture. AF took this information into confidential meetings where they brought together and presented their findings to judges from the district, police officers, defense lawyers, and public prosecutors with a view to collectively finding ways of improving the situation. At these meetings Mandira would present facts about the number of cases they had documented where different constitutional provisions were violated and would then look to all of the stakeholders to identify the role they could play in preventing these violations. The AF strategy was to expose the stakeholders to the reality of the severity of the problems so as to encourage cooperation, and to address this as a collective problem requiring a coordinated set of solutions.

As the nature of the conflict in Nepal changed, specifically with the entry of the Military into the conflict and the introduction of new "anti-terrorist" strategies and legislation after September 11, 2001, AF had to expand its monitoring and documentation work to a broader range of violations. They started to work on enforced disappearances, extrajudicial killings, sexual violence, and forced recruitment of children, not only by state agents but also by the Maoists. AF soon established itself as one of the leading human rights organizations in Nepal, with four regional offices, 13 district-based offices, and a central office in Kathmandu. During the 10 years that Mandira led AF, they documented more than 8,000 cases of human rights violations, visited thousands of detainees in detention, organized hundreds of meetings, provided legal assistance to thousands of victims, and organized victims groups. She designed an integrated strategy for AF for the prevention of human rights violations by adopting both national and international intervention strategies. The combination of these strategies brought Nepal to the attention of the international community, resulting in a range of responses, including the establishment of an office of the United Nations (UN) High Commissioner for Human Rights in Nepal to investigate human rights violations.

After the Comprehensive Peace Accord of 2006, an important part of AF's work entailed challenging impunity for the violations that had been documented and actively demanding criminal investigation for some of the human rights violations where high-ranking security officials and Maoist leadership were implicated. Because torture and disappearance were not defined as crimes under Nepali law, AF chose to focus on extrajudicial killings. For the first time, there was a demand for criminal investigations of the actions of high-ranking officials. The response from the police was to refuse to register the complaints, because they concerned their own superiors. The AF strategy in the face of this resistance was to bring writs in the Supreme Court. After many years of legal battles, they were able to establish precedents requiring police to initiate investigations of all murders that took place during conflict. The AF helped 128 families and victims across the country to bring such cases. Many are still pending.

One of the impacts of their success in naming and bringing cases against high-level perpetrators was an increase in pressure placed on the advocates. As a counter-strategy, they formed a common platform with other prominent civil rights and human rights activists. The Accountability Watch Committee (AWC), initially coordinated by Mandira, became a collective voice for pursuing some of the cases. Nevertheless, the success of the organization in organizing victims' groups, raising the profile of the problem of impunity, and effecting travel restrictions against high-ranking officials generated a backlash against them. The organization came under enormous pressure not to pursue certain cases, and a media campaign was initiated against key advocates, with Mandira in the firing line. The situation became particularly difficult after AF brought a case for murder against a politician who subsequently became the Minister for Information and Communication and the police officer who became the Chief of the Police. Members of the organization were publicly accused of being agents of western imperialists, dollar-mongers, and "peace spoilers" for taking up conflict era cases.

In the midst of this situation, AF continued to bring cases before national mechanisms and international mechanisms such as the UN committees and instruments and bodies established to monitor the implementation of international human rights obligations. They successfully brought about the repatriation to Nepal of a high-ranking army official and police officer from their UN postings, on the basis of their tainted human rights records. AF also advocated and successfully prevented members of parliament and many other high-ranking officials who had been involved in serious human rights violations from traveling to Europe, the United States, and Australia. These efforts contributed to deepening human rights discourse in Nepal and challenged some of the misconceptions that people held concerning human rights and human rights work in Nepal. This was really the first time that perpetrators experienced the repercussions of their violations. At the same time, it caused a backlash insofar as perpetrators from different sectors—the police, the army, and Maoists—came together to resist the efforts of human rights organizations and to exert pressure on human rights advocates, including AF.

When, as a result of AF's work, a serving Nepali colonel was arrested in the UK under universal jurisdiction for his alleged involvement in torture in Nepal, Mandira was identified by the authorities as the most critical figure advocating for prosecution in the case. To protect the organization, she decided to leave. She now continues to work on some of the cases she initiated earlier, and, drawing on her experience, supports a number of organizations in Nepal and more widely in the region, to strengthen their capacity in documentation, monitoring, and strategic use of information.

Although initially Mandira had not wished to be a lawyer (her first choice was medicine, but this avenue of training was unavailable where she lived), she is very satisfied with her choice to work as a human rights advocate. She sees the potential of law to prevent atrocities and to contribute to social reform more broadly. At the same time, she was surprised by the significant gap between formal standards, with respect to both national and international law and actual practices. Even more shocking was how little others in the justice system seemed to be concerned about this gap.

In light of this combined recognition of law's potential and the reality of the failure for its potential to be realized in many cases, she insists that law is not self-implementing. For it to have this effect requires that lawyers and other actors in the justice system test the limits of law and expand its application.

Philosophy of Legal Advocacy

Mandira's view of the role of legal advocates is consistent with her analysis of the problematic patterns of power distribution in Nepal. In a society where the victims of the abuse of power and authority are mostly poor and come from marginalized communities, she insists that lawyering should be pro-poor. She observes, though, that this has not traditionally been the culture of the legal profession, which has itself been oriented around status. Placing this historical orientation against the social reality, where most of the people with whom lawyers are working come from the lowest part of the social and economic hierarchy, the whole objective of the law and the way it has been interpreted has to be changed. For lawyers to represent these clients, they need to develop a real understanding of their situation from the clients' perspective.

Lawyers, she argued, have a distinctive and critical role in bringing the law to life, but only insofar as they challenge, contest, and work to implement the law. Otherwise, laws remain just an ideal in theory, but not in practice. She quoted a saying in Nepali that law is a punishment for the lower class and leisure for the upper class "*sanalai yen thulalai chain.*" It is the role of lawyers to change this to "everyone is equal before the law." If lawyers tolerate the violations of constitutional rights of ordinary or marginalized people and see it merely as business as usual, other people cannot have faith in the law as a source of justice.

One of the reasons she proposed to explain why the legal profession has failed to provide appropriate support for the marginalized is that lawyers have tended to be reactive and not proactive. They do not actively seek out constituencies who they ought to be defending and who need their assistance, but wait for them to seek help. This was made most evident when AF went out to provide legal advice to detainees and realized that at the very same time as hundreds of people were without legal representation and unable to seek it out (because they were detained), there were many young lawyers without jobs. Because legal education conditions lawyers to work only for those who come to them, this approach is normalized, and legal professionals do not recognize the many barriers that prevent those who are detained or who suffer from human rights violations from seeking their support. Mandira recalled that when AF started to visit detention centers, the reaction was not only one of surprise but also of active resistance. The Bar Association actually challenged and threatened to confiscate their licenses. On the one hand, it condemned her for going out and looking for clients, and on the other, she was challenging them for failing to take up the responsibility to ensure that everyone has access to legal advocates, thereby facilitating illegal detention and allowing torture to continue as routine practice.

The gap between the legal profession and members of marginalized communities is heightened by the fact that in Nepal there is no functioning system of paralegals. Having a community-based paralegal system would in her view provide a bridge between the community and the legal system, and could itself address many of the problems that communities face. Because there were so many victims of enforced disappearances in certain districts, and AF did not have enough lawyers to visit all of the communities with sufficient frequency, they did try to develop a type of paralegal system in the context of human rights violations. They would file cases but could not follow all of them up, so they trained people from the community who then followed up, updated families, and also updated AF, thereby providing a bridge that was also a way of making clients feel better informed and better served. She notes that while there have been some moves by NGOs to put a system of paralegals in place, these efforts have never resulted in systemic change. This is partly because NGO project-based interventions tend not to create longer-term change and, partly because issues such as this are never on the government's political agenda.

Still on the issue of the failure of the legal system to address issues of fundamental justice and the unequal distribution of power, Mandira observed that, in Nepal, historically, those in power have not been held accountable for committing serious crimes and violating human rights, including killing, enforced disappearance, sexual violence, and torture. The notion of equality before law and equal protection of the law have always been very illusive in Nepal and, in her view, the legal profession has not sufficiently questioned and challenged this state of affairs. Part of the role of lawyers in Nepal today must then be to change this—to bring anyone who violates rights before the justice system, so that everyone can have faith in the system and the law as a site of justice, and people believe that the rule of law exists.

This raised questions about how the justice sector can be made more inclusive and accountable. Mandira seeks to consider the practical steps that need to be taken to bring women and people from marginalized communities, for example, into the criminal justice system as active and influential agents. For this to happen, the institutions of the system must provide an environment that is hospitable to members of these groups and in which they can make a real contribution. At present, there is a range of barriers, both informal or cultural and practical.

For example, the Bar Association is the common meeting point for lawyers, physically located next to the court in every district in Nepal. Yet, when Mandira started out as a lawyer, as a woman she felt far from welcomed or at ease there. Things have changed, with some women now present, but even now, it remains a highly masculine space—the men who dominate the space have little awareness of the way in which the types of subjects people discuss, the jokes that they tell, and so on may affect women. The only way this is going to really change in her view is to put measures in place that ensure a substantive proportion of women.

At a more practical level, one of the main barriers to women staying in the legal profession arises from the coincidence of the time of marriage and the time of graduation from law school. Newly admitted lawyers usually get paid nothing at all, but the families of a newly married woman rarely tolerate her working outside the home for almost no pay. So if women are to stay in the profession, these types of factors need to be addressed. This is a good example of the importance of recognizing how embedded the legal system is in other social institutions. If the legal system is to work optimally, you need support change in other institutions.

Similarly, for lawyers to realize their potential in society there needs to be a broadening of the understanding of the role of lawyers. In Nepal, unless you go to court every day you are not thought of as a lawyer. Legal advocates have a critical role to play, however, in other institutions: in labor institutions, human rights institutions, research institutions, corporations, and so on. By lawyers finding spaces for themselves more broadly, these other parts of the system can come to operate in accordance with legal principles and more effectively.

While evidently a number of reforms would be needed to address the problems with the legal system, Mandira identified a few priority areas. One is improving legal education, both at the level of law schools and for legal professionals. In law schools, there is a need to ensure the quality of teachers and to expand the resources that law colleges have available for students. Then for lawyers there needs to be high-quality training. Because of the active presence of the international donor community, there is plenty of training, but no oversight of quality and no institutionalization of the trainings. First, there is a real need for retraining both judges and prosecutors, many of whom are very old and were trained in the old system, which was established to serve particular interests and so they carry the baggage of that past.

Second, the legal system could be much improved through the development of fields of specialization. Currently all lawyers work in all fields and so they have to know a bit about everything. This prevents the development of the kind of rigor that would improve the quality of the system. The same applies to courts, because in Nepal there is generally no specialization in their services—so that both lawyers and judges are responsible for looking into and adjudicating all kinds of cases. Even where there are special jurisdictions courts, for example, for corruption, the judges are not chosen based on their expertise in those areas.

Third, as in other institutions in Nepal, political interference is a major issue in judiciary and other justice institutions. *De facto,* it is political parties that choose the people in these institutions. Unless, political parties are completely removed from the process of hiring, firing, promotion, and transfer of personnel in the justice system, it will remain difficult to professionalize the legal system. She also highlights the need for accountability of justice institutions including the legal profession.

Finally, and continuous with her general analysis, the justice system needs to be made inclusive. Despite the fact that after the political change of 2006, a policy of inclusion stating that there will be proportionate representation in all public institutions has been introduced, this policy has yet to be put in place.

Problems and Successes Experienced

Although Nepal's criminal justice system remains profoundly gendered, there has been some success in terms of the inclusion of women in policing. When the policy of bringing more women into the police force/service was introduced, more cases of violence against women were registered with the police. With the establishment of special Women and Children's service centres, known as "Women's Cells," women have felt more able to report crimes to the police, resulting in an increase in the number of cases of gender-based violence being investigated. This policy and its impacts could also be affected in the judiciary, the prosecutors' office, and the Bar Association.

There has also been some very good progress in the treatment of juveniles in the system. When AF started visiting places of detention, they found that children were frequently detained in the same facilities as adults, and in fact many reported torture and other forms of ill-treatment. Finding this, AF mounted a series of legal challenges and really made this issue a priority in their discussions with stakeholders, building alliances with children's rights organizations. This resulted in establishing precedents for the illegality of certain practices, and eventually the adoption of procedural rules in relation to juvenile justice that prevent the detention of children with adults, and introduce alternatives to custody (diversion) as well as parental custody.

There has also been some movement in relation to defense lawyers' access to documents and periods of remand. In the past, defense lawyers had no access to any of the prosecutors' documents until the charge sheet was filed in court. Similarly, challenges concerning the necessity of the imposed periods of remand have begun to open a debate about the process of imposing a remand period and there is now the prospect of a policy being introduced that will require that both defense and prosecution lawyers having to be satisfied with the reasons for the remand period.

AF successfully challenged the practice of the Chief District Officer (similar to a magistrate) sentencing people to several years of imprisonment for "public offenses" without hearing the defense. This then resulted in amendments to several laws allowing nonjudicial persons like magistrates to exercise judicial power, and mandatory training for them, including training on cases where they were dealing with minor offenses. The amendments do not allow non-judicial bodies to exercise such powers to decide cases resulting in the deprivation of liberty.

An area where success has not been achieved is in relation to the provision of legal aid, once again a reform that would be "pro-poor." There was a Legal Aid Act (1992 and subsequently amended) that provides those who cannot afford to pay a lawyer may apply for legal aid. The problem was that this application process required that you produce a certificate of income—something that most poor people just do not have, and even if someone did have such a certificate, if they were in detention, they could not lodge such an application. Once again, this is an example of policy being built without an eye to the real situation of the people who are supposed to benefit—a policy that does not attend to practical realities of the marginalized.

AF did a review of this policy and provided very practical feedback about why and how it was not working and how it could be amended. The problem was that there was no body driving reform. Although one would expect to look to the Bar Association as the obvious vehicle, it is a highly politicized body in Nepal, and does not see this type of reform as its priority work.

Nepal's criminal justice system faces a range of problems including the need for improved criminal court procedures, the need for a comprehensive criminal code, the absence of a system for plea-bargaining, the absence of any monitoring of the consistency of judgments, and the enormous backlog of cases and the implementation of the courts' decisions. This is largely a product of the lack of accountability of the police, who often fail to implement court decisions. At the same time, if an influential person is facing criminal procedures, they may well receive the protection of political parties, and this has an impact beyond the particular case; it undermines the legitimacy of the judiciary.

Corruption is the other critical issue for Mandira, because it undermines the work of the judiciary and of the whole justice system. Certainly she recognizes that there are individual judges who are not corrupt, but the system as a whole is so corrupt that clean judges are still tainted. The same problem applies to the police and prosecution. Defense lawyers are also accused of playing a role insofar as they provide a bridge between the client and the judges/prosecutors and impede serious investigations of allegations by their clients.

In the face of this range of problems, Mandira considers that the most difficult to address are the entrenched cultures of exclusion, corruption, and impunity. Institutional culture is the reflection of many years of peoples' lived experiences and so changing it takes time. That said, there are interventions that can act as triggers for change, and it is important to remember that change is possible. She points to the efforts of the prior outgoing Chief Justice in relation to corruption. He commissioned a study of the allegations of corruption within the judiciary and took action against some high-profile people, a major step demonstrating the possibility of change. Here, as elsewhere, a critical component of change is real political will.

Theory and Practice

Working in the criminal justice system in Nepal has made evident to Mandira the enormous gap between theories of law and the practice of law. How to mitigate this gap is the challenge, but one important principle she identifies is that theories should be based on the reality of society. In turn, addressing problems on the ground can benefit from certain types of theory.

A clear example concerns the translation of international legal standards into practice. Nepal has ratified a number of key human rights treaties and in fact has a Treaty Act (1990), which stipulates that treaties that have been ratified will serve as national law. So if one attends to the formal protections, they are there theoretically; but when it comes to implementing them, then the problems become apparent: institutions are not prepared, training is absent or unsuitable, legal education does not attend to these principles and practices, there is no system of accountability, and there is no support on the ground.

The implication is that the people who work on building theories should really draw from the experience of practitioners as well. There are so many lessons that can be drawn from practical experience—theory cannot be built in isolation. Practitioners should also be better informed about theories that could help them to understand the logic and rationale behind their work. Certain aspects of feminist theory should, for example, be reflected in the work of the judiciary, but this raises difficult questions about how you really inform members of the judiciary and other actors at this level.

This then points to the need for theory to be contextually informed and sensitive. Certainly there may be a universal principle, but there may be different ways of implementing or realizing it in different contexts. To understand the nature of the institutions, one really has to appreciate the particular culture within which these institutions have developed, and how this shapes the delivery and administration of justice. This requires very context specific research, and it is this that is often missing.

The gap could also be bridged by a greater emphasis on action research—developing and then actually testing hypotheses about reform or practice and then building on the findings to help to develop better interventions. This would certainly require better coordination between academia, where we find the theory builders and those who work in the field—the practitioners. This would benefit all parties and help each achieve their goals. Here, she insists that neither approach is superior; the work of both types of actors is equally important.

Once again, though, there are real practical barriers to achieving this type of integration in a country like Nepal. Most practitioners and even scholars in Nepal do not have access to all of the resources that are available. The Internet has improved the situation, but not all of the information can be found there. Mandira gives the example of her own work on transitional justice and its interplay with accountability. Although she had been working in this field for many years, she never had access to the materials that she can access in the Global North and so was not plugged into the knowledge networks where theories are developed, tested, and contested. Even then, where access can be obtained, the often highly abstract language used can make such work inaccessible to practitioners. This points to the need for those who are working at the more conceptual and theoretical level to ask themselves the same questions about power and access: "Why are these theories being built and for whom?"

Transnational Relations

Translational law and relations have lain at the heart of Mandira's work since she first encountered the UN human rights system in 2001–2002 when she visited Geneva to attend a session of the UN Human Rights Commission. She went fully expecting that they would be discussing the situation in Nepal, given that it was then under a state of emergency, many rights had been suspended and the cases of extrajudicial killings, torture, and forced disappearance were rampant. The constitutional monarch had sacked the elected prime minister and taken power into his own hands and was laying the grounds for a full-fledged coup. At the same time, insurgents were attacking police posts around the country and terrorizing local populations. She was deeply shocked to see how little information was available at the international level; no one had any interest on Nepal because they did not know what was going on in Nepal.

She stayed in Geneva for six weeks and returned aware of the importance of Nepali NGOs' engaging with the UN system in general, and the special procedures in particular. For example, she recognized that if one of the Special Rapporteurs mentioned a particular country in one of their reports, this would be picked up by a number of other actors and could trigger further discussion. She also learned that high-profile international human rights organizations had a real influence on the UN system. Members of country delegations would meet with representatives of organizations such as Amnesty International, the International Commission of Jurists, and Human Rights Watch.

So, upon her return to Nepal she devised a strategy of sending regular communications to different UN bodies responsible for overseeing the implementation of treaties and respect for key human rights principles, as well as to the principal international human rights organizations, both to generate their interest in Nepal and to keep them abreast of what was happening. In practice, AF sent at least 10 cases to different bodies within the UN human rights systems, mostly the special procedures (e.g., Special Rapporteurs and UN Working Groups) every day, and until they had done that, they would not leave the office.

Then in 2004, when the UN Working Group on Enforced Disappearances released a report saying that they had recorded the highest number of new cases of enforced disappearances from Nepal, that changed the landscape. Other special procedures such as UN Special Rapporteur on Torture and Other Cruel, Inhuman or Degrading Treatment or Punishment also mentioned Nepal as a country of concern. At the same time, the major international human rights organizations also started to show an interest in Nepal, holding missions and preparing reports on human rights violations. The systematic application of this strategy eventually also led to the establishment of a monitoring mission of the UN Office of the High Commissioner for Human Rights in Nepal.

Mandira's engagement with international law has also worked the other way around—trying to ensure the implementation of international law at a domestic level. For example, even 10 years after Nepal had ratified the International Covenant on Civil and Political Rights (ICCPR) and its First Optional Protocol (allowing for individual complaints), there had been no complaints. This was largely because there was no knowledge in the country about how these mechanisms might be used. The AF was the first organization to take cases before the Human Rights Committee.

At the same time, activities at the transnational level can have a negative impact on the human rights situation at the domestic level, as Mandira saw in the post-September 11, 2001, context. Formally, Nepal was not involved in the so-called War Against Terror, but there was an impact nevertheless in the sense that the Nepali government used the context to introduce anti-terror legislation in 2001, and to give sweeping powers to the security forces, particularly the military. Prior to this period, the military had not been mobilized in this manner. Even worse, the United States was giving military assistance to Nepal and other countries for countering terrorism, an intervention that made life in the human rights world very difficult, because those responsible for human rights violations were operating under very strong material and legal privilege. More indirectly, when it became known that the United States was using torture in Guantanamo Bay and elsewhere, this provided a certain legitimacy for the use of torture in Nepal. People could justify what they were doing by saying, "Look, powerful countries like the United States are also doing it."

Only when human rights advocates successfully exposed human rights violations, convinced the U.S. Senate to impose conditions on military aid to Nepal, and convinced the United Nations to vet individual officers for peacekeeping missions did the human rights record start to improve. Specifically, the conditions posed on military aid required that the military respect the right to *habeas corpus*, and allowing inspection of detention facilities by the National Human Rights Commission. This was how AF was able to contain some of the violations they were experiencing at that time, and this had a dramatic impact on Nepal. Mandira believes that had this not been done, they would not have been able to reduce the number of enforced disappearances, extrajudicial executions, and the use of torture. Imposing those restrictions saved lives.

General Assessments

Taking a broader view of the changes in the criminal justice system in Nepal over the life of her career, Mandira's conclusions are not positive. While there have been breathtaking changes in some parts of the Nepali justice system, real progress is yet to be seen in the criminal justice system. There are some signs of change. For example, after a lengthy debate, there are now several bills before parliament concerning a separate criminal code, sentencing laws, and a criminal procedural code. Without doubt, significant revisions and amendments will be required, but this remains an important initiative. Also in the area of juvenile justice there are improvements. The new juvenile justice procedural guidelines provide options for diversion, and the release of children in parental custody, among other changes.

Where Mandira sees a need is in the form of support from the international community, particularly in relation to policing practices. Improving systems and practices of investigation, for example, requires specialized services and skills, but police in Nepal largely still lack equipment, knowledge, and skills, leading to their reliance on confessions and hence the use of torture to extract them. For this to change, you need a professional police institution, one free from political interference, and overseen by an independent police commission that can monitor appointment, promotions, transfers, and internal accountability, so that these processes are not at the behest of political masters. External support could assist, but it needs to be of the right type—sustained, and not simply "fly-in, fly-out." What is really required are cooperative endeavors that look at longer-term reform, and that can engage the culture of institutions. Simply reinventing the wheel through a short-term intervention will not assist in shifting the most entrenched causes of injustice.

Given the recency of the passage of the new constitution, it remains unclear how it will effectively contribute to ensuring the check and balance of powers, an independent judiciary, professionalizing the security apparatus, and ensuring people's rights. For Nepal to take this opportunity to correct mistakes that have been made in the past with respect to the legal framework and its capacity to ensure the rule of law, international support can be very helpful. Finally, the inability of justice system to hold those responsible for human rights violations to account is striking in Nepal. If people in power are seen to be above the law and untouched even after committing serious crimes, the result is that inequality, and an atmosphere of fear and violence are perpetuated. As such, addressing impunity for those in power should remain a key priority for those interested in assisting Nepal.

Conclusion

In "The Force of Law," Bourdieu (1987, p.806) sought to illuminate the "internal protocols and assumptions, characteristic behaviors and self-sustaining values—what we might informally term a "legal culture." Often, precisely because lawyers are, as Bourdieu also argues, pulled into this field, its distinctive dynamics remain invisible to them, and they enact (with more or less variation) its internal logic. What is perhaps most striking about Mandira's reflections is her clarity about the components of the dominant legal culture in Nepal, and how they serve to sustain a broader field of power and set of hierarchies and exclusions. This is true both in the narrow sense of the gendering of legal authority and more broadly with regard to how different types of subjects are positioned in relation to the service of the law.

One might then reflect on what it is that provides Mandira with this level of reflexivity or critical distance, a question to which she provides powerful answers. It seems that her ability to discern what is normally transparent has been a function not only of her own different identity (as a woman) but also of the fact that the starting place of her engagement with the legal field was an experience of sharing the perspective of the victims and the excluded. Mandira poignantly describes her early experiences as witness to the destruction of human beings through state sanctioned torture and how she turned to the legal profession as a means for addressing this primary injustice and lived suffering. Thus, even as the assumed truths and meanings of the actual operation of law might have worked to shape her own subjectivity as an actor in this field, she always remained rooted in that other perspective—a perspective that brought into view what was assumed and the values that were perpetuated by the dominant field of legal authority.

Critical Legal Theory (Tushnet, 1986) has provided a theoretical illumination of law's enmeshment in existing fields of power and, more practically, pointed us to the danger that, far from being a rational, ethical or neutral form of regulation, law can implicitly fortify and legitimate existing distributions of power. Mandira's legal practice then illustrates the possibility of using law to deconstruct the dominant organization of power and actively to promote the interests and perspectives of those who are otherwise marginalized and dominated. One might draw an analogy here between the historical deployment of religious texts as a tool for domination and the liberation theologians' use of these same texts (Gutierrez, 1988) as a resource for liberation and resistance. At the same time, her description of the operation of the Nepal Bar Association and the resistances of the security forces and government authorities well illustrates how the different institutions within the field of law will seek to re-establish its existing forms of organization when such resistance emerges. In both this context, and with respect to dimensions of legal culture noted above, her experience renders visible the often-deep contradictions between formal laws and informal norms or the practice of law. It also makes apparent how in practice law is embedded in a broader range of institutional structures (the police, government agencies, the media) and that one cannot achieve legal reform or use the law as a tool of reform without also attending to this broader set of institutions.

Finally, and somewhat contradicting the structural approach of the theorists I have cited, Mandira's narrative shows that agency is not trumped by structure: that individuals, working collectively, can bring about change. Undoubtedly the persistence of human rights violations and the lack of accountability for past violations in Nepal must have a sobering effect on any such conclusions. Nevertheless, the results she recounts of some of the advocacy campaigns (e.g., in relation to the imposition of conditional funding by the United States) demonstrate that where legal advocates combine a sharp vision of justice with well-honed legal, organizational, and political skills and where they work cooperatively with other agents of change, the impact of their work can mean the difference between people being killed, disappeared or tortured and their living dignified lives; in other words, an infinite difference.

Glossary

Accountability Watch Committee: a committee formed in Nepal 2006 to take a coordinated advocacy approach to ensure government action in relation human rights, the rule of law, and transitional justice in Nepal.

Advocacy Forum: a civil society organization based in Nepal established in 2001 by Mandira Sharma to advocate for the protection of human rights and respect for the rule of law.

Amnesty International: an international civil society NGO that conducts research on human rights violations, lobbies and advocates political decision makers for change, and organizes civil society campaigns for action in relation to a range of human rights issues.

Centre for Victims of Torture (CVICT): a civil society organization in Nepal established in 1990 with the primary aims of rehabilitating torture victims and preventing torture.

charge sheet: the formal document that law-enforcement agencies in Nepal prepare and that sets out the content of the accusations against an accused.

chief district officer: an administrative position in Nepal operating under the Ministry of Home Affairs and acting as the highest administrative officer in a district and authorized to carry out certain functions including mobilizing security forces and sitting as a quasi-judicial body.

chief justice: the highest judicial officer in Nepal and chief judge of the Supreme Court (Sarbocha Adlat).

Comprehensive Peace Accord: the agreement signed by the Government of Nepal and the Unified Communist Party of Nepal (Maoist) on November 21, 2006, and formally putting to an end the 10-year armed conflict.

Constituent Assembly: a unicameral body comprising 601 members specifically established to draft and adopt a national constitution and at the same time to serve as the national parliament.

Constitutional Monarch: the monarch who exercises certain powers as established by the constitution. The constitutional monarch acts as a symbol of national unity and may also hold certain formal powers.

Council of Ministers: the highest political executive body, also known in some systems as the cabinet, comprising the prime minister and a set number of senior ministers.

extrajudicial killings: state or government authorized killings that take place without the sanction of a judicial authority, considered under international human rights law to be a gross violation of human rights.

First Optional Protocol to the ICCPR: an additional protocol to the ICCPR, which allows individuals to make complaints directly to the Human Rights Committee, the body overseeing implementation of the ICCPR, where they believe that rights set out under the ICCPR have been violated.

French Napoleonic Code: the civil code of unified law introduced by Napoleon Bonaparte in 1804 to replace the patchwork of feudal laws and privileges that characterized pre-revolutionary France. The code has been widely influential beyond France.

Global North: the distinction Global North and Global South has come to replace the distinction between First, Second, and Third Worlds as a way of mapping global socioeconomic and political divides. The Global North is generally thought to include North America, Western Europe, and parts of East Asia, these being wealthier, more technologically developed countries with more developed social and political infrastructures.

Gorkha: originally a statelet located about 50 miles West of Kathmandu, which was the heart of what became to Kingdom of Nepal. Prior to the creation of what we now know as Nepal, the Gorkha were politically dominant of other "desa" or countries.

Human Rights Watch: an international human rights NGO established in 1978, best known for its fact-finding missions and publication of reports on a range of human rights issues internationally.

International Covenant on Civil and Political Rights (ICCPR): one of the core UN multilateral human rights treaties, and part of the "International Bill of Rights." Along with the International Covenant on Economic Social and Cultural Rights, one of the two key treaties elaborating the UN Declaration on Human Rights.

International Commission of Jurists: an international NGO dedicated to the protection and promotion of human rights and the rule of law established in 1965. It consists of 60 eminent jurists, supported by an international secretariat in Geneva.

Jana Andolan: the "people's movement" that brought together various leftist and other parties to seek a democratic transformation in Nepal in 1990.

Maoists: those associated with the Unified Communist Party of Nepal (CPN) who primarily led the civil war that commenced in 1996 and were involved in a violent armed conflict with the government and security forces until 2006. Following the cessation of the conflict, the Maoists became the ruling government party in 2008.

National Human Rights Commission: the National Human Rights Commission in Nepal is an example of a National Human Rights

Institution (NHRI), an administrative body charged with overseeing the domestic implementation of human rights principles. The Nepal Commission was established as a statutory body under the Human Rights Commission Act 1997 and became a constitutional body under the Interim Constitution of Nepal 2007.

Nepal Bar Association: Bar Associations are formal professional bodies for lawyers. In Nepal, the Bar Association not only issues legal licenses but is also responsible for taking disciplinary action against lawyers for misconduct.

panchayat system: a distinctively South Asian system of political ideals institutionalizing a decentralized form of government that was introduced in Nepal in 1962 and was in effect until 1990.

paralegal: a person who does not have a full qualification to practice as a lawyer, but has received formal or informal education and training to provide some legal services, generally at the community level and under the supervision of a lawyer.

Rana (Prime Ministerial) Dynasty: a hereditary order of rulers initiated when Jang Bahadur Kunwar seized power in 1846 until its overthrow in 1951.

remand period: remand is the pretrial custodial detention and the period of remand refers to this being fixed by a magistrate rather than its being unspecified and so arbitrary.

Republic of Nepal: Nepal was declared a republic with the abolition of the 240-year-old institution of the monarchy in 2008.

Sarbocha Adlat (Supreme Court): the highest court and appellate court in Nepal.

special rapporteurs: a mandate holder under the UN Human Rights Council Special Procedures mechanism, charged with a specific country or thematic focus. Each Rapporteur mandate is specifically established by the Human Rights Council for a set period of time, but can be extended.

Treaty Act 1990: a piece of legislation in Nepal that specifies competence in relation to entering into, suspending, and terminating treaties and the role of parliament in ratification, accession, acceptance, or approval of treaties. The Act also specifies that treaty provisions prevail over the norms of domestic law.

United Nations High Commissioner for Human Rights: the head of the Office of the High Commissioner for Human Rights, established by the UN General Assembly in 1993 to coordinate the human rights activities throughout the UN system and to protect and promote international human rights throughout the world.

United Nations Human Rights Commission: a functional Commission composed of 53 member states established in 1946 under the UN

Charter to examine, monitor, and publicly report on human rights situations in specific countries and major human rights violations globally. The Commission was replaced by the Human Rights Council in 2008.

United Nations Special Procedures: the special procedures of the Human Rights Council are independent human rights experts with mandates to report and advise on human rights from a thematic or country-specific perspective. They fall into four categories: Working Groups, Special Rapporteurs, Special Representatives of the Secretary-General, and Independent Experts. Importantly, they have a universal mandate, meaning that they can examine human rights issues in any member state, even if that state has not ratified the relevant treaty.

United Nations Special Rapporteur on Torture and Other Cruel, Inhuman or Degrading Treatment or Punishment: one of the special rapporteurs under the Human Rights Council Special Procedures with a specific mandate to transmit urgent appeals to states with regard to individuals reported to be at risk of torture and communications on past alleged cases of torture, and to undertake and to report on fact-finding country visits.

United Nations Working Group on Enforced Disappearances: the first special procedure established by the UN Commission on Human Rights in 1980, with its primary mandate to assist the relatives of disappeared persons ascertain their whereabouts. The Working Group undertakes country visits and communicates with governments regarding alleged rights violations, requesting that the state investigate and inform the Working Group of the results.

war against terror: a term first used by U.S. President George W. Bush on September 20, 2001, in the wake of the September 11, 2001, attacks. The war or terror now refers to a widespread military and political operation against organizations and movements that are considered to commit or sponsor terrorist acts. Originally focused on the so-called Islamic terrorism associated with the September 11, 2001, attacks, the term was picked up more broadly to encompass armed and political campaigns against a range of groups in other countries.

New Zealand

10

TARYN GUDMANZ
PATRICIA O'SHAUGHNESSY

Contents

The Criminal Justice Process of New Zealand

Taryn Gudmanz and Patricia O'Shaughnessy

A Crown Colony

New Zealand's most recent indigenous population is Māori. The Māori name for New Zealand is Aotearoa which means the land of the long white cloud. Although there were previous marine expeditions by Abel Tasman and James Cook in and around the land now known as New Zealand (Aotearoa), it was not until after the establishment of the New South Wales penal colony in Australia around 1788 that the gradual interaction between Māori and Europeans, particularly those from Britain, increased steadily. The New South Wales colony gave Māori an opportunity to interact with an impermanent European presence mostly in the form of whalers, traders, and missionaries (King, 2003).

In 1833, the arrival of Mr. James Busby as the first British resident in New Zealand, effectively the representative of British law, symbolized to British settlers the promise of Crown protection. However, the protection that was given was ineffective and resulted in British settlers petitioning the Crown for British intervention. In 1839, attempts were made to establish British sovereignty in New Zealand and Letters Patent were issued that same year, annexing New Zealand to New South Wales. Letters patent are a form of prerogative instrument issued by the monarch under special powers that attach to the Crown and which can be discharged and enforced independently from statute and common law. By extending New South Wales' boundaries, New Zealand became a British possession.

In 1839, with the appointment of the British Colonial Office of Captain William Hobson RN as Her Majesty's Consul in New Zealand, came his instructions to "treat with Aborigines of New Zealand for the recognition of

Her Majesty's authority over the whole or any parts of those Islands" (McIntyre & Gardner, 1971, p. 10). One of the first proclamations made by Hobson was to impose restrictions on land purchases from Māori. His next priority was to enter into negotiation with Māori under the drafting of the Treaty of Waitangi, which was signed in early February 1840. The treaty was later recognized as New Zealand's founding document. It was meant to be a partnership between Māori and the British Crown. Although intended to create unity, different understandings of the treaty and breaches of it have caused conflict. Starting in the mid-1980s, several dozen Acts of Parliament included references to the Treaty of Waitangi. As with the Treaty of Waitangi Act 1975, each of these acts referred (with some variation) to the principles of the treaty. These acts allowed the courts to interpret the extent to which treaty principles are raised in any case covered by legislation. This legal recognition has had significant consequences for government agencies and local government (Orange, 2012, p. 7).

As a colony, New Zealand adopted institutions of government and political practices from England. The Government of the United Kingdom appointed governors to rule New Zealand, who were accountable only to the Colonial Office in London. In 1852, the British Parliament passed the New Zealand Constitution Act providing for an elected House of Representatives and an appointed Legislative Council. The General Assembly (the House and Council) first met in 1854. New Zealand effectively became self-governing in all domestic matters in 1856. However, it was not self-governing in respect of policy matters relating to Māori until the mid-1860s when "native policy" passed to the colonial government.

In 1935, a New Zealand government became responsible for its own foreign relations when the first Labour government explicitly claimed such an onus (Wilson, 2015).

Sources of the Constitution of New Zealand

New Zealand does not have a supreme constitution. Its constitution is unwritten. It is one of the three countries in the world that rely on an "unwritten constitution." The other countries are the United Kingdom and Israel (Palmer, 2006, p. 587). However, New Zealand does have a constitutional framework made up of various acts of parliament (including some entrenched provisions), treaties, Letters Patent, orders-in council, common law (a system of law developed by judges and followed in similar cases). It is supplemented by statute law, and a number of non-legislative conventions.

In December 2010, Deputy Prime Minister Bill English and Minister of Māori Affairs Pita Sharples announced a wide-ranging review of New Zealand's constitutional arrangements. The review, known as the *Consideration of Constitutional Issues,* was part of the supply and confidence agreement reached between the National and Māori parties after the 2008 election and was reaffirmed in their relationship accord of December 2011 (New Zealand Parliament, 2011). To date, the New Zealand constitutional framework remains unchanged.

The New Zealand Legal System

The New Zealand legal system is derived from England and comes from two main sources—statute and common law. New Zealand's Parliament was developed from the Westminster system and is the highest law-making body in New Zealand. It comprises two parts: first, the Head of State of New Zealand (currently, Queen Elizabeth II), who is represented by the Governor-General; and second, the House of Representatives. Legislation passed through the House of Representatives is required to be assented by the Governor-General. As New Zealand's Parliament is not answerable to a higher law (such as an entrenched Bill of Rights or written constitution) and can pass any law it chooses, checks and balances serve to constrain any possible misuse of that power. Instruments such as parliamentary procedure (the process of a bill's passage; use of select committees that scrutinize proposed legislation and standing orders dictating the debating process), public opinion, domestic and ratified international law, and watchdog bodies such as the Ombudsmen all act as constraints on that power.

Despite the existing checks and balances, Parliament as the supreme law-maker has at times exercised its law-making power to benefit the government of the day. For example, in 2003, New Zealand's Court of Appeal overturned the Crown's long-held assumption that it owned the foreshore and seabed. The Court of Appeal opened up the possibility that areas of the foreshore and seabed could be found to be exclusive Māori customary land. In 2004, Parliament, under a Labour government, responded to the court's decision by enacting the Foreshore and Seabed Act 2004, which vested full legal ownership of the foreshore and seabed in the Crown, except for existing privately owned areas. This effectively extinguished any unidentified Māori customary title (indigenous property interests in New Zealand that pre-date Crown sovereignty are acknowledged as customary). In 2011, Parliament, under a National government, enacted the Marine and Coastal Area (Takutai Moana) Act 2011. This Act removed the Crown's ownership of the foreshore and seabed, and replaced it with a "no ownership" regime, restored any Māori interests extinguished by the Foreshore and Seabed Act 2004, and recognized Māori interests in three ways—namely participation rights in conservation processes, customary use rights, and title interests; protection of existing rights and interests including public access, navigation, fishing, development, and mining interests; and development of a new system for reclaiming land including the ability to acquire fee simple title (an interest in land without any limitations or conditions).

New Zealand's Judicial System

In England, the Act of Settlement 1700 was enacted as a protection against royal abuses. The Act put in place some conditions for superior court judges, which could not be reduced during a judge's commission. Under the Act, a resolution of both houses of the British Parliament was required to secure a judge's removal. In New Zealand, as in many other countries, the guarantee of judicial independence is a requirement of judicial office. The guarantees secured under the Act of Settlement 1700 were introduced in New Zealand in 1858 and were re-enacted under the Constitution Act 1986.

New Zealand's first courts were established in 1840. However, these courts did not become entirely independent until 2004, when the New Zealand Supreme Court replaced the judicial committee of the British Privy Council as New Zealand's court of final appeal under the Supreme Court Act 2003. The Judicial Committee of the Privy Council of the House of Lords in England was a committee made up of judges. The Privy Council sat in London, applying New Zealand law. The Privy Council remains the final appellate court for all cases decided prior to December 31, 2003. Some cases are still being decided by the Privy Council; for example, in 2015, it decided an appeal by Teina Pora, quashing his 1994 and 2000 convictions for the murder of Susan Burdett.

A bench of five judges sits on the Supreme Court, and they hear cases by way of leave only. Leave is granted only if it is required by the interests of justice.

The Hierarchy of New Zealand Courts

The Supreme Court and the Court of Appeal are appellate courts, exercising an exclusively appellate jurisdiction. All other courts exercise original jurisdiction. The High Court and the District Court exercise both original and appellate jurisdiction, and all New Zealand courts except the High Court exercise a defined statutory jurisdiction (Figure 10.1).

The High Court has, in addition to its statutory jurisdiction, an "inherent" jurisdiction, giving it general supervisory power to ensure that public administration is conducted according to law under the Judicature Act 1908. Today, New Zealand's High Court remains the superior court of general jurisdiction in New Zealand. It has principal responsibility for maintenance of legality through its supervisory and administrative law jurisdiction. It hears the more serious criminal and civil cases, and it exercises significant supervisory and appellate jurisdiction over lower courts and tribunals (Spiller, Finn, & Boast, 2001).

The Criminal Procedure Act 2011 determines which court (District or High) is the court of first instance in criminal cases. Generally, the court of first instance for criminal offenses is the District Court. There is a District Court in most towns. Each major provincial center houses a High Court, with the frequency of sitting days varying from town to town.

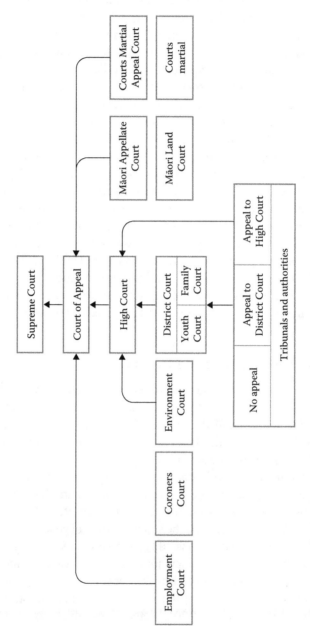

Figure 10.1 Structure of New Zealand Courts.

New Zealand's District Courts have general jurisdiction for jury trials (where the maximum sentence is less than life imprisonment), all summary criminal matters (an offense that does not require a trial by jury), and civil actions up to a value of $200,000. The Family and Youth Courts are divisions of the District Court.

Working in the Legal System

Prosecuting and Defending

The Crown is responsible for prosecuting offenses. Prosecutions for category 3 and 4 offenses under the Criminal Procedure Act 2011 are undertaken by private firms pursuant to a royal warrant on the recommendation of the Attorney-General (a member of Parliament, although the appointment is nonpolitical).

Category 3 offense

An offense

a. that is punishable by imprisonment for life or by imprisonmen for 2 years or more or
b. that, if committed by a body corporate, is punishable by only a fine, but that would be punishable by imprisonment for life or by imprisonment for 2 years or more if committed by an individual.

Category 4 offense

An offense.

If an offense is in a given category, then the following is also an offense in that category:

a. conspiring to commit that offense:
b. attempting to commit that offense, or inciting or procuring or attempting to procure any person to commit an offense of that kind that is not committed:
c. being an accessory after the fact to that offense.

If an offense is punishable by a greater penalty where the defendant has previously been convicted of that offense or of some other offense, the offense is an offense in the category that applies to offenses punishable by that greater penalty only if the charge alleges that the defendant has such a previous conviction.

The royal warrant is issued to a particular individual, who has the position of Crown Solicitor. Warrants are issued to partners practicing within law firms. They are then assisted by their partners and employees. Those firms also carry out civil litigation and commercial legal work, and it is not unusual to see prosecutors undertaking work other than prosecutions (although the other work would not be pursuant to the royal warrant, and they would not undertake defense work). A Crown Solicitor is appointed for each High Court district. The Solicitor-General has overall responsibility for the supervision of the network of Crown solicitors.

Defense lawyers may practice at the independent bar, within firms or with the Public Defense Service. It is not unusual to leave the Crown prosecutor's office and become a defense lawyer.

The defense bar was a private bar only until the government established the Public Defense Service (PDS) in 2004. The PDS operates only in some cities. In those cities, legal aid work is provided by both the PDS and the private bar. A system under which the government funds the defense costs of those who cannot afford it and meet certain criteria. Controversial recent changes have removed the defendant's ability to choose his/her lawyer when charged with an offense carrying a sentence of less than 10 years—the accused has to accept the counsel assigned to him/her.

Legal Aid

The government funds legal defense costs for those who cannot afford it through the Legal Aid System. The availability of legal aid depends on the accused's assets and liabilities, and whether the charge carries a sentence of imprisonment of more than six months or the interests of justice otherwise require that legal aid be granted.

The controversial changes resulting in the establishment of the PDS extended to changing how legal aid is funded and which lawyers may provide legal aid services. For example, fixed fees now apply to steps in the proceedings, irrespective of the actual cost of carrying out those steps.

Criminal Procedure

The Crimes Act 1961 sets out the vast majority of offenses. The Summary Proceedings Act 1957 deals with minor offenses (such as parking infringements). Other statutes do create other criminal offenses—for example, the Resource Management Act 1991 (such as contravening restrictions on the use of land) and the Companies Act 1993 (such as where a director dishonestly fails to prevent an insolvent company from incurring debt).

Criminal procedure was reformed in 2013, with the coming into force of the Criminal Procedure Act 2011. The intention of this reform was to streamline criminal procedure.

Sentencing

Sentencing is governed by the Sentencing Act 2002. The Act sets out the purposes of sentencing. The purposes include holding the offender accountable, promoting in the offender a sense of responsibility, providing for the interests of the victim (including by ordering reparation), denunciation of the offender's conduct, deterrence of both the offender and other persons, protection of the community, and assisting in the offender's rehabilitation and reintegration back into the community. There is no hierarchy of purposes.

The Act also identifies the principles of sentencing. These include the gravity of the offense, the offender's culpability, the maximum penalty prescribed for the offense, the desirability of consistency of sentences for similar offenses, the personal circumstances of the offender (including personal characteristics, which may make a sentence disproportionately severe upon that particular person), and whether any restorative justice agreements have been made.

Court-referred restorative justice programs operate in many parts of the country. They operate only if the victim consents to the process. The defendant must also be willing to take part and must accept responsibility for his/her actions. The intention is that the parties agree about how the offender makes amends for the offense. This may be by way of apology, compensation, or by performance of work or services. The facilitator provides a report to the judge, who must take it into account in determining the sentence.

The Sentencing Act 2002 establishes a hierarchy of sentences. The hierachy (from lowest to highest) is being discharged or ordered to come up for sentence if called on, fine and reparation, community-based sentences of community work and supervision, community-based sentences of intensive supervision and community detention, home detention, and imprisonment.

Judges often require probationary officers to prepare pre-sentence reports to assist in sentencing. These contain information about the offender's personal background and family (whanau) circumstances, and the lifestyle and other factors that are considered to have contributed to them committing the offense. The report also includes recommendations relating to courses of training or treatment (which might assist in the rehabilitation of the offender), an assessment of the risk of further offending, and a recommendation as to the appropriate penalty (including proposed terms and conditions for the offender's supervision, training, and treatment within the community, whether immediately or upon release from prison). Programs include "Straight Thinking" (aimed at promoting life skills needed to avoid further offending) and "STOP" (designed to address the causes of violence).

Judges may also obtain psychiatric and psychological reports before passing a sentence. These are commonly obtained for offenders who have mental health and/or drug- or alcohol-addiction problems. Pursuant to the Victims' Rights Act 2002, judges are also to take into account victim impact statements. These are statements prepared by the victim of an offense to explain to the offender how the offense has impacted the victim. It is considered by the judge at sentencing.

The police also operate a discretionary diversion scheme. This allows certain defendants (usually for first-time minor offenses) to face the consequences of their offending without receiving a criminal conviction. The police may use their discretion if the defendant admits the offense and is willing to complete the diversion program. Once the diversion requirements are satisfactorily completed, the charge is withdrawn and no conviction is entered against the defendant's name.

Becoming a Lawyer

To become a lawyer, a student must obtain a recognized Bachelor of Laws degree, complete the Legal Professional Studies Course, and obtain admission to the Bar. Once the professional course has been completed, the potential candidate must satisfy the New Zealand Law Society that she/he is of fitting character to be admitted to the Bar, which entails obtaining character references.

New lawyers are admitted to the Bar as both barristers (a lawyer who undertakes advocacy work in a court) and solicitors (a lawyer who does not appear in court); the bar is not split as it is in England. Once admitted, a litigator may choose to practice within a firm or at the independent bar (and may subsequently alter his/her choice). Note that any barrister or solicitor who wishes to practice on his/her own account (i.e. not as an employee) must meet certain practicing requirements and complete successfully the New Zealand Law Society's Stepping Up course. Litigators practicing within firms and independent barristers have the same rights of audience. The right of a lawyer to appear and conduct proceedings in court on behalf of his/her client. However, Queen's Counsel are drawn only from the independent bar. A barrister whose seniority and excellence has been recognized by appointment to be "one of Her Majesty's counsel learned in law" is known as Queen's Counsel. It is a recognition of status. The Labour government briefly changed the title to Senior Counsel from 2007 to 2012, and during this time, Senior Counsel could be appointed from firms.

Mark Wilton, Principal Prosecutor, New Zealand, Police Prosecution Service, Police National Headquarters, Wellington

Patricia O'Shaughnessy

Introduction

At seven o'clock on a Monday morning, the commuter train into Wellington City from the leafy Khandallah suburb is typically subdued. Down toward the Wellington harbor, the train rolls past the Westpac Sports Stadium and into the Wellington railway station—the southern terminus of New Zealand's North Island Main Trunk railway, Wairarapa and Johnsonville Line. From there, the journey is by foot past the Old Government Buildings on Lambton Quay, built in 1876, still the largest wooden building in the southern hemisphere, and now part of the Victoria University of Wellington Law School. The commuter continues at a brisk pace into the prevailing north-westerly wind, passing New Zealand's Parliament Buildings, the Wellington High Court, and the Court of Appeal, all within striking distance of the New Zealand Supreme Court. The significance of the walk along the "legal mile" is not lost on the commuter as he contemplates the working week ahead of him and passes his security card through the secure doors into the New Zealand Police National Headquarters.

Mr. Mark Wilton is the Principal Prosecutor at Police National Headquarters in New Zealand Police's Prosecution Service. New Zealand is a small island chain, similar in physical size to Japan or Great Britain but with far fewer inhabitants (4.5 million) (Statistics New Zealand, 2015).

The New Zealand Police is a national organization operating under a single governance structure. The service has nearly 12,000 members, of whom approximately 75% are sworn (New Zealand Police Annual Report, 2012). The organization is divided into 12 geographic districts across New Zealand's north and south islands, and is administered from a national headquarters based in Wellington. The chief executive of the New Zealand Police is known as the Commissioner of Police and is appointed by the representative of Queen Elizabeth II, the Governor-General. The Commissioner of Police is accountable to the New Zealand Minister of Police for the administration of police services, but the organization acts as an independent body in terms of law enforcement decisions.

In New Zealand, the Police Prosecution Service conducts proceedings for most category 1–3 criminal and traffic prosecutions instigated by New Zealand Police, from first appearance to disposal. This process includes case review and trial as required. Where the proceeding is conducted by way of a jury trial, a Crown prosecutor will conduct the prosecution. The Police Prosecution Service also conducts proceedings in Youth Court prosecutions, advocates for New Zealand Police at coronial hearings, and administers the New Zealand Police Adult Diversion Scheme.

This chapter will describe Mr. Wilton's legal career, which includes criminal defense, and prosecutor advocacy and civil litigation in New Zealand and abroad.

Career

Mr. Wilton was born and raised in Masterton, the largest town in Wairarapa. Wairarapa is in New Zealand's North Island, one hour's drive north of the capital city, Wellington. Wairarapa is described in Destination Wairarapa (Welcome to the Wairarapa, n.d.) as "a combination of the Tararua Forest Park, Rimutaka Forest Park and Hurangi Forest Park with the wild stretch of Palliser Bay and Pacific Ocean coast." He studied law and music at Canterbury University in Christchurch in the South Island of New Zealand. After graduating with a Bachelor of Laws and a Bachelor of Arts, he undertook his professional legal studies in Auckland. In 1993, he was admitted as a barrister and solicitor of the High Court of New Zealand. Mr. Wilton worked as a research assistant in the Marlborough District Council's property team for six months, and later travelled to London, where he worked for *Stephenson Harwood* as a paralegal in the litigation department, also qualifying and being admitted as a solicitor of the Supreme Court of England and Wales.

In 1995, Mr. Wilton returned to New Zealand, working briefly in a litigation team in a Christchurch firm before returning to Wairarapa to work in the litigation team for *Wollerman, Cooke and McClure Lawyers* in Carterton. There he acted as a criminal defense barrister, and also conducted civil and employment law litigation. In 2001, Mr. Wilton moved to Wellington to *Tripe, Matthews and Feist Lawyers,* continuing with criminal legal aid work, civil litigation, and an employment law practice.

A move to Southern Taranaki in 2003 was next, where he took a position as a prosecutor with the New Zealand Police Prosecution Service. Mr. Wilton explained that Taranaki was the perfect place to take up a role as a prosecutor not only because it was a beautiful part of New Zealand to live in, but also because he simply did not know anyone there and he had wanted to transition from defense to prosecution work in a place where he had not previously worked as defense counsel.

When asked whether his experience as a defense lawyer was of benefit to him in his role as a prosecutor, Mr. Wilton agreed that it was. He explained that under the adversarial system of criminal trial in New Zealand, the defendant (usually represented by counsel) chooses the evidence he or she will offer in defense of the charges and similarly the prosecutor chooses evidence to offer in support of the charges. The defense and the prosecution have full control over their respective case theories. The judge must ensure the trial is fair but cannot "descend into the arena."

Unlike a judge's role in some civil law countries where a judge assesses the weight and quality of evidence, in New Zealand the admission of evidence occurs in hearings before trial or at trial. It is at trial that the evidence is tested as to its weight and probative value. Mr. Wilton explained that his experience as a lawyer, and specifically as defense counsel, prepared him for the likely challenges opposing counsel might make to the court for the purpose of weakening the prosecution case. Despite the different perspectives and tactics that might be used by defense counsel and a prosecutor to persuade the fact finder of their respective case theories, Mr. Wilton said importantly the rules of evidence and courtroom etiquette remain the same for both. When asked whether prosecuting required any significant shifts in his legal thinking, he remarked that the realization that he represented the party that had the onus of proof upon them was profound. Mr. Wilton remarked this weighed heavily on him in the early part of his prosecutorial career as it underscored to him that he was now acting for the State, not the defendant. In that sense, he was cognizant of the imbalance of power between the State and the defendant, and how the rules of evidence in statute (Evidence Act, 2006) and common law operated to manage that imbalance. Mr. Wilton commented that the onus of proof upon the prosecution to prove the charge being "beyond reasonable doubt" is an appropriately high standard given that the ultimate determination by the tribunal of fact could lead to a custodial sentence under the Sentencing Act 2002.

In 2010, he was transferred to the Police Prosecution Service's Wellington office and then was seconded to the national office at New Zealand Police National Headquarters. While there, Mr. Wilton became involved in training other police prosecutors in advocacy skills and other necessary skills for criminal court work. He still contributes to this learning in his current role by teaching trainee detectives, prosecutors, and other specialist police officers within New Zealand Police at the Royal New Zealand Police College in Porirua.

Current Role

As Principal Prosecutor at Police National Headquarters, Mr. Wilton is a role model for 206 prosecutors spread throughout New Zealand. Of those, 45 prosecutors are civilian lawyers employed by New Zealand Police; the others are police officers that have usually attained the rank of sergeant. Only some of the police sergeants have law degrees, others may appear before the court as prosecutors by virtue of their role and the successful completion of the prosecutors training courses overseen by Mr. Wilton. As Principal Prosecutor, Mr. Wilton stated that his primary purpose is to provide legal advice and advocacy skills for the Police Prosecution Service on complex trials, sentencing submissions, opposition to bail applications, and other court orders. He also provides legal advice at Police National Headquarters on a range of issues including evidential admissibility as it relates to specific hearings and advises frontline police officers on criminal charges that should be laid against a defendant based on the evidence police have obtained. He explained that in circumstances where a prosecution presents particularly complex issues, he will appear in court supported at times by a junior prosecutor.

When asked whether there were particular prosecution cases that he considered more significant than others, Mr. Wilton stated that he preferred not to provide details on matters he had dealt with as either a defense counsel or a prosecutor as he did not consider it appropriate to do so. Moreover, in his view, the details were not the substantial issue when reflecting on his career; the issue for him was that each and every trial had the same components—a complainant (or multiple), a defendant (or multiple), witnesses, and exhibits. Mr. Wilton explained that every trial was important to all parties and the same principles of courtroom conduct and rules of evidence applied regardless of any overt public interest in a matter. He also stated that even in trials that have a particularly high public interest attached to them, it is rare in New Zealand that a prosecutor will make any public comment on the trial outcome. Whereas it is not uncommon for a defense lawyer or police officer in charge of the case to do so. He said he was very comfortable with this general convention.

As a lawyer working within New Zealand's public sector, Mr. Wilton explained that he is an in-house lawyer, which means he provides direct professional legal services to the Police Prosecution Service. Lawyers working in central government and the public sector are the largest legal community in New Zealand, which Mr. Wilton is proud to be part of. A key partnership in his role as Principal Prosecutor is with the Government Legal Network, established in 2014. It consists of lawyers working across the government domestically and encourages them to collaborate with each other when providing legal services to the Crown. Through its combined efforts, the Network delivers legal seminars, and professional development and secondment opportunities to other in-house lawyers as well as networking events and online shared workspaces. Mr. Wilton explained that collaborative partnerships of this type result in a general cross-pollination of legal perspectives across the whole of government within New Zealand and contribute not only to his professional development but to the development of the Police Prosecution Service staff too.

Philosophy of Legal Advocacy

The right of access to justice for all New Zealanders is a topic that Mr. Wilton considers is always at risk of diminishing, as the gap between those who can afford to pay for legal advice and those who cannot increases in New Zealand.

This is not something unique to New Zealand of course. Mr. Wilton points to the fact that the profession is having conversations on the issue is in some measure indicative of a profession that has not lost sight of its role and function. As the interview drew to its end, Mr. Wilton read a passage to me from the former Speaker of the House of Representatives, Professor Margaret Wilson, who wrote: "It is a useful reminder that justice is dependent on institutions and procedures that are fair and accessible. Litigants in the Family Court today may question whether this fundamental objective of the *Magna Carta* has not been forgotten in the interests of financial savings" (Wilson, 2015, p. 14).

Theory and Practice

On the relationship between theory and practice, Mr. Wilton remarked that a criminal lawyer has to know legal theory and findings, and the law. Often it is not until a lawyer becomes a practitioner in court that an appreciation of the gap between the theoretical learning, and the application and practice of the law in that forum is understood. Until that gap is recognized and closed, a "good head on your shoulders" is needed to deal with the dynamic and public environment of the criminal court. Good mentors and advocates should inspire new practitioners to continually improve their advocacy skills and legal knowledge. Mr. Wilton remarked that in his view some of the best criminal lawyers are pragmatists, but pragmatists who have prepared their case theory well.

Transnational Relations

New Zealand's position in the southern Pacific region enables the New Zealand Police to engage with its Pacific neighbors on a range of broad policing interests. This extends to advocacy training and mentorship between lawyers in the Pacific region. Mr. Wilton has regularly travelled to Western Samoa to instruct Western Samoa Police prosecutors and solicitors from the Attorney-General's Office in Western Samoa in prosecution practice and advocacy skills. He is a strong supporter of the Pacific program encouraging and supporting skill exchange between lawyers from Australia and New Zealand, and Western Samoa's Attorney-General's Office.

In Tuvalu, he assisted the Tuvalu Police as it looked at current court process and caseload management with a view to increase efficiency. Mr. Wilton has also recently instructed the Cook Island Police in advocacy and litigation. He points out that though the Cook Islands became self-governing in free association with New Zealand in 1965, the Cook Island Judiciary includes senior members of New Zealand's legal profession and senior or retired members of New Zealand's High Court and Court of Appeal. In that regard, members of New Zealand's legal profession have a special kinship with their Cook Island counterparts (Cook Islands Constitution, 1964).

He readily considers it a privilege to be involved in these types of programs with the Pacific region. Putting aside all of the unique challenges faced by island nations, a prosecutor regardless of where he or she is located is always required to undertake the fundamental analysis of all the available evidence, its evidential sufficiency, and then whether it is in the public interest that a matter that should be brought before the court.

Finishing a further two-year term as Wellington Branch President of the New Zealand Law Society, Mr. Wilton took a National Vice Presidency position for the Society and sat on its Board. He is a current member of the New Zealand Law Society Courthouse Committee. He has made a further contribution to the profession by tackling the issues of courthouse closures around New Zealand due to seismic reasons and the subsequent restructuring of staff in courthouses, all of which have impact on the public's access to justice.

On being asked what he thought was important about the relationship between established legal practitioners and law students, Mr. Wilton explained that the New Zealand Police Prosecution Service has recognized that law students are a valuable future resource and to that end the Service has been running internships throughout New Zealand. While the national oversight of the program sits at its Wellington national headquarters, Mr. Wilton has responsibility for the Victoria University of Wellington internship. He comments that it is important that established members of the profession connect with university law faculties both by lecturing, as he does from time to time, and by providing opportunities in the workplace for law students and exposing the students to potential legal mentors.

Surprises

In response to the question that asked what surprised him as a lawyer, he replied that nothing surprised him. He went on to explain that all lawyers whether in the criminal court or in other areas of litigation practice deal with real people and real-life situations that may involve to a lesser or greater extent some conflict with the law or with other people. Those variables give rise to what might seem to be a measure of human unpredictability, but which an experienced lawyer eventually comes to expect. Mr. Wilton remarked that as a prosecutor, his role is to fairly and dispassionately present evidence to the court for it to determine the extent of a person's criminal liability. He emphasizes the importance of a lawyer knowing his/her role and function.

The importance of role appreciation is demonstrated, he explained, in situations where police prosecutors present criminal prosecutions against police officers or other New Zealand Police employees. Mr. Wilton said the dispassionate and fair application of a lawyer's role and function is key at all times and no more so under circumstances where an enforcement agency is prosecuting one of its employees. When asked whether he thought the public understood the strict roles played by defense and the prosecutor, Mr. Wilton did not think that all members of the public necessarily saw or understood those functions but that a significant number would. In any event, public perception, he remarked, ought not encourage lawyers to forego any aspect of their defined role when facilitating justice.

Importantly, according to Mr. Wilton, each lawyer needs to know his/her exact role and function. In this way, the lawyer can respond fairly and appropriately to the facts in issue. He considers a functioning justice system to be a team effort. He explained that justice cannot be done without everyone fulfilling their individual roles.

Mr. Wilton agreed that at times, public sympathy will rest with the accused. This might arise where the circumstances of the alleged crime involve self-defense or where an accused has through his/her own action or inaction caused the unintentional death of his/her own child. In those circumstances, the public may be highly critical that such a prosecution was brought before the court. However, where there is evidential sufficiency and where the decision to prosecute is consistent with the public interest test in the Solicitor-General's Prosecution Guidelines, 2013, then the prosecution should be instigated, according to Mr. Wilton.

Crown and Police Prosecutors

On the topic of the relationship between Crown prosecutors and police prosecutors, Mr. Wilton explained that under New Zealand's constitutional arrangements, the Attorney-General is responsible through Parliament to New Zealanders for prosecutions carried out by or on behalf of the Crown. In practice, it is the Solicitor-General who, under the Constitution Act 1986, shares all the relevant powers vested in the office of the Attorney-General), and who oversees the conduct of public prosecutions. He explained that these arrangements have been codified under the Criminal Procedure Act 2011, section 185. Most similar jurisdictions have a centralized decision-making agency in relation to prosecution decision; New Zealand does not.

In relation to Crown prosecutions, prosecutions are usually conducted by Crown solicitors, who are private practitioners appointed to prosecute under a warrant issued by the Governor-General. The New Zealand Police and other enforcement agencies, with oversight of a particular regulatory area, conduct other prosecutions.

Alcohol and Other Drug Treatment Court

When asked to what extent New Zealand's justice system could be considered innovative, Mr. Wilton referred to the Alcohol and Other Drug Treatment Court (AODTs) as an example of an alternative justice model, launched on

November 1, 2012, as a five-year program administered by the Ministry of Justice. While he acknowledged that AODTs had been established in other jurisdictions including the United States, the United Kingdom, Canada, and Australia, he explained that evaluative research has come largely from the United States, with scant literature from the Commonwealth jurisdictions. He saw its application within New Zealand as an opportunity for further evaluative research within a New Zealand setting. He also explained that although New Zealand has only recently moved toward addressing offending by adults where alcohol and drug use is a contributing factor, the Christchurch Youth AODT Court has been operational since March 14, 2002. Mr. Wilton explained the New Zealand AODT Court has features unique to New Zealand. For example, the court includes Māori cultural practices operates to meet the needs of Māori participants, and has the ability to require defendants to attend specific drug and/or alcohol support groups. Additionally, the court is a pre-sentence rather than post-sentence initiative (Litmus, 2014).

The AODT sits for one day a week in both the Auckland and Waitakere District Courts and aims to help 100 offenders each year to deal with the underlying addiction issues that arguably have contributed to their offending. The criterion for attendance at the Court is that selected defendants who have pleaded guilty and are facing imprisonment for up to three years have the opportunity to participate in an additional treatment program. Their participation and the overall success of the treatment are taken into account at sentencing (Equal Justice Award, 2015).

Special Circumstances Court

Mr. Wilton also explained that in mid-2010, the Special Circumstances Court, modeled on AODTs, was launched in Auckland. It is now running in Wellington. That particular court includes the mentally ill and homeless who repeatedly come before the court. He stressed that the Special Circumstances Court is rehabilitative in nature and provides, where it is appropriate to do so, therapeutic outcomes ("New Court for Homeless Addicts," 2010).

In response to a question that assumed that most defendants who came before the criminal courts were economically deprived, Mr. Wilton remarked that in many cases this was true and extended to circumstances where a defendant did not have a stable family environment. Often those members regularly experienced violence within the family. He also drew on the Family Violence Courts, where criminal cases relating to family violence are heard as an example of how the Ministry of Justice and judiciary have responded to community concerns about the high rate of domestic violence and domestic homicides in New Zealand.

On the topic of how the criminal legal system in New Zealand should be performing, Mr. Wilton replied that in his observation, the people who are professionals within the criminal justice system have a real commitment, a passion, and a drive to contribute to the law and New Zealand's society. In Mr. Wilton's view, regardless of whether you act as lawyer for the prosecution or defense, the overarching consideration is access to justice. Legal professionals, according to Mr. Wilton, should never stop thinking about that principle as it relates to victims and accused alike—particularly as the 800th year anniversary of *Magna Carta* neared. Today, only clause 29 of *Magna Carta* (as enacted by Edward I in 1297) is directly in force in New Zealand by virtue of the Imperial Laws Application Act 1988, schedule 1. In his view, possibly the foremost constitutional challenge for New Zealand today lies in addressing barriers to access to justice.

Successes and Problems Experienced

On being asked what policies or programs have worked well and which ones have not, Mr. Wilton explained that changes in legal processes brought on by legislation such as the Criminal Procedure Act 2011 have not disturbed the core business done in courts. Shifts in disclosure procedures and obligations on both the prosecutor and defense; doing away with certain pre-trial hearings where oral evidence would regularly be given to establish whether a prima facie case was found; and introducing committal hearings where the standard practice is that no oral evidence is given have all contributed to efficiencies when the facts in issue are known and can be focused on by both parties. Time is precious, remarked Mr. Wilton.

"In a court scenario, however, no matter how great the will of all parties is to deal with a matter in court efficiently, you are dealing with people and different players in the actual courtroom," said Mr. Wilton. "Real life events enter the courtroom and sometimes justice just takes time," he mused. Simply put, Mr. Wilton considers that justice should not only be done, but should be seen to be done.

Mr. Wilton pointed to the New Zealand Police Adult Diversion Scheme as a good policy, which allows for a person who admits guilt to a minor charge and who had not previously been before the court, to avoid a criminal conviction. When the defendant had completed an agreed program set by New Zealand Police (with consideration of the views of the victim of the crime), the prosecutor advises the court of this fact and the charge against the defendant is dismissed.

He also considered the Pre-Charge Warning Scheme implemented by the New Zealand Police as a positive procedure. Under that scheme, evidential sufficiency is still required, and if met, the next consideration is whether there is a public interest in respect of actually instigating a prosecution. Police may invoke that scheme where a person commits a low-end offense such as violating a liquor ban or behaving disorderly. Where police arrest the offender and the test of evidential sufficiency is met but there is no public interest in insti-gating a prosecution, police enter a warning on the arrested person's record held by New Zealand Police. Mr. Wilton considered both schemes as positive alternative resolutions within the New Zealand justice system.

Another positive feature within the New Zealand criminal justice system, which Mr. Wilton drew on, was the Youth Court (TeKootiTaiohi O Aoteroa) and the way in which youth offenders are dealt with. A groundbreaking ele-ment of the New Zealand Youth Justice system is the Family Group Conference, which embodies a shift in modern Western legal systems toward alternative methods of dispute resolution such as mediation. Mr. Wilton explained that in Māori custom and law, tikanga o ngahara, the law of wrongdoing, was based on the notion of collective rather than individual responsibility and that redress for wrongful conduct was due not just to any victim but also to the victim's family. The Family Group Conference enables victims and offend-ers and their respective families to meet with members of police in order to decide on an appropriate penalty.

General Assessments

The interview with Mr. Mark Wilton highlighted the broad range of activities undertaken by him as a Principal Prosecutor for New Zealand Police and also the additional work he undertakes for the benefit of those currently within the profession and those yet to embark on their legal careers. His genuine pride in New Zealand's contribution to reciprocal relationships that New Zealand lawyers and Pacific lawyers have built was evident and is recognizable as a well-placed passion.

Despite New Zealand's geographic isolation, it is a country that has forged its own legal identity with innovative responses to specific areas within the criminal justice system, as can be seen in the area of youth offending and domestic violence offending. Clearly competing resources within the crimi-nal justice system in New Zealand remain an ongoing pressure. However, the view that all parties should respond to those pressures by remaining astute to their respective roles is a personal and professional philosophy of Mr. Wilton and one that has contributed to his professional successes.

Greatest Problems Facing Criminal Courts

On the topic of what are the greatest problems facing the criminal courts in New Zealand currently, Mr. Wilton remarked that adequate resourcing remains a pressure on all professional agencies involved in the criminal justice system. Additionally, the cost of maintaining a robust justice system for any country is daunting when considered against other competing social welfare and the needs of law enforcement agencies. For example, in New Zealand, the justice system deals with people who have allegedly committed crimes. The corollary is that the community expects those people to be put before the courts. Where guilt is found, the community expects them to be punished under a sentence and serve a term of imprisonment for serious offending. A balancing of resources has to be struck where expectations arise, and Mr. Wilton sees this as a challenge for any government.

A Particular Pride

Acknowledgment of te reo Māori (Māori language) is a matter in which Mr. Wilton expressed pride. He explained that by direction of the Chief Justice, the President of the Court of Appeal and the Chief High Court Judge, the opening, adjournment, and closing sessions in all of the higher courts in New Zealand, from October 2013, have been in both te reo Māori and English. Mr. Wilton remarked that the use of the Māori language was already established in the District Courts, courts of special jurisdiction, such as the Māori Land Court and Waitangi Tribunal, and was part of proceedings in the Rangatahi Youth Courts prior to 2013, and so its introduction to the higher courts demonstrates a consistent regard for te reo Māori as an official language of New Zealand.

Conclusion

According to Lord Denning, the law never stands still; it goes at pace and you have to run fast to keep up with it (Denning, 1984, p. vi). The New Zealand criminal justice system seems to be sufficiently agile at least in responding to the dynamism of the law, albeit under inconvenient fiscal constraints. The New Zealand Police holds a particularly privileged position in the race. It not only arrests and charges members of the community who police assert have failed to comply with the criminal law, but also initiates their prosecution through the Police Prosecution Service. The apparent closeness of this legitimate arrangement may seem a constitutional contradiction to some observers.

The principle that everyone is subject to the law, which must be applied equally to all, is a key foundation of New Zealand's constitutional arrangements. Were those foundations to whittle away through police corruption and police prosecutorial bias, then New Zealand Police's current prosecutorial prerogative would likely be challenged. This would be a reasonable response to any untrustworthiness.

As pointed out by Mr. Wilton, competent and accessible legal representation ensures protection of the rights of a citizen at every juncture of the criminal justice system. In that sense, legal practitioners hold a privileged position of trustworthiness, which according to Mr. Wilton legal practitioners should be vigilant to maintain.

Glossary

barrister and solicitor of the High Court of New Zealand: in New Zealand, all lawyers are at first admitted to the roll as both a barrister and a solicitor of the High Court of New Zealand. Once they have sufficient experience, lawyers can choose to practice as a barrister and solicitor or solely as a barrister. Barristers specialize in courtroom advocacy, drafting pleadings and documents, and giving expert legal opinions. Solicitors are in general office-based lawyers.

Category 1 offenses defined by Section 6 of the Criminal Procedure Act (2011) are:
  1. an offense that is not punishable by a term of imprisonment, other than
     a. an infringement offense; or
     b. an offense described in paragraph (b) or (c) of the definition of a category 2 offense; or
     c. an offense described in paragraph (b) of the definition of a category 3 offense.
  2. an infringement offense, if proceedings in relation to that offense are commenced by filing a charging document under section 14, not by the issuing of an infringement notice.

Category 2 offense means:
  1. an offense punishable by a term of imprisonment of less than two years; or
  2. an offense that, if committed by a body corporate, is punishable by only a fine, but that would be punishable by a term of imprisonment of less than two years if committed by an individual; or
  3. an offense punishable by a community-based sentence and not punishable by a term of imprisonment.

Category 3 offense means an offense, other than an offense listed in Schedule 1,
  1. that is punishable by imprisonment for life or by imprisonment for two years or more; or
  2. that, if committed by a body corporate, is punishable by only a fine, but that would be punishable by imprisonment for life or by imprisonment for two years or more if committed by an individual.

Crown prosecutor: crown are private legal practitioners appointed by warrant of the Governor-General on the recommendation of the Attorney-General. Crown solicitors are appointed for a particular geographical area within New Zealand, usually in a High Court center. They are responsible for trials in the High Court and District Court on behalf of the Crown. Crown solicitor warrants are held by partners in private law firms. There are currently 16 Crown solicitor warrants throughout New Zealand. As a Crown solicitor's office, the warranted private firm cannot accept instructions against the Crown, unless an express exemption is obtained from the Solicitor-General, as to do so would effectively mean the Crown accepting instructions against the Crown.

family group conference: means a meeting convened or reconvened by a care and protection coordinator in accordance with Section 20 (Children, Young Persons and Their Families Act, 1989) or in relation to Part 4, means a meeting convened or reconvened by a youth justice coordinator in accordance with section 247 or section 270 or section 281 or section 281B.

Marae: the Māori word for meeting grounds (public spaces) that are the focal point of Māori communities throughout New Zealand.

Rangatahi Youth Court: the use of the marae setting as an alternative to the mainstream courts in dealing with young Māori offenders. The rationale is that taking young Māori offenders back to the marae to be dealt within the youth justice system encourages them to accept their responsibilities and acts to rehabilitate them back into the community.

young person: within the Children, Young Persons and Their Families Act (1989), a young person is a boy or girl of or over the age of 14 years and under the age of 17 years. This does not include any person who is or has been married or in a civil union.

Judith Ablett-Kerr ONZM QC, Criminal
Defense Lawyer, Dunedin

Taryn Gudmanz

Introduction

Judith Ablett-Kerr ONZM QC is one of New Zealand's leading criminal
defense lawyers and is the most-senior-ranked female lawyer in practice in
New Zealand. In 1995, she became only the third woman to be appointed as
Queen's Counsel in New Zealand, and the first female criminal lawyer. She
had been practicing in New Zealand for only 15 years at the time.

Her name is closely associated with the defense of battered women and
the partial defense of provocation. She has acted in some of New Zealand's
best known and most controversial cases. Her advocacy skills were formally
recognized by her election as a Fellow of the International Academy of Trial
Lawyers (IATL) in 2007. Her advocacy skills make her a sought-after barrister,
both in criminal and in civil cases.

She has also been a strong influence in the profession itself and in law
reform. In 2002, Judith was made an Officer of the New Zealand Order of
Merit (ONZM) for services to the legal profession. She has served on various
professional councils, and also on court, Law Commission, and Ministry of
Justice committees. She has chaired various conferences, and written on the
practice of law and access to justice. In addition, she teaches advocacy, in both
New Zealand and Australia. The position of women in the law and female
offenders are issues of interest to her.

Our interview took place not long after she had moved chambers, and
renovation work was still being undertaken in her new chambers. She had
managed to create a calm, organized office in the midst of the turmoil.
Her office was furnished with traditional wood and leather furniture, and
retained that time-honored feeling of English chambers while still giving
glimpses of her personality, with photographs of her family and "Team A-K"
caps on the wall.

We began by discussing what drew Judith to the law. It was apparent that
this motivation strongly influenced the development of her career, including
how she has run cases and become involved in the legal profession and legal
reform, and her views on legal theory. She is not a practitioner who studied
jurisprudence and relegated it to the back of her mind—she appears to practice
within a theoretical framework.

Career

Judith was born and educated in Wales. She has been practicing for over 45 years, in England, Wales, and New Zealand, in both civil and criminal law (although predominantly in the latter). She is not someone who chose to go to the bar because it seemed like a good job; it was (and is) a vocation.

Wanting to help those whom she believed were being wronged was what brought Judith to the law. She comes from a family with a strong sense of social justice. Her father was a lay preacher (he viewed this as not incompatible with his day job as a wine importer). One of her ancestors was Noah Ablett, a leading proponent of independent working-class education and the main author of the 1912 work *The Miner's Next Step*, a treatise that demanded a minimum wage for miners, a six-day working week, and a ban on working down the coal mines by children under the age of 10.

It was within this context that her own social conscience developed. Judith has always bothered herself with sticking up for the downtrodden and has a strong desire to contribute to putting things right. She remembers bringing home impoverished children for her mother to feed. She realized that the law was the way for her to "put things right" when she was about 12. She remembers reading an article in the Sunday newspaper about a review of the Derek Bentley case. Bentley was a 19-year-old youth who was executed in January 1953 for his part in the death of a police officer. Bentley was of low intelligence and had been rejected for national military service as "mentally substandard." He and a 16-year-old accomplice, Christopher Craig, were undertaking a burglary when they were interrupted by the police. Craig pulled a gun on a police officer and when the officer demanded the gun, Bentley said, "Let him have it, Chris." Craig shot the officer. It was argued for Bentley that his words meant "Give him the gun, Chris" rather than "Shoot him, Chris." Both were convicted, but only Bentley was sentenced to death. He was executed within four months of the commission of the crime. Bentley eventually received a posthumous pardon in 1998 (*R v. Derek William Bentley (Deceased)*, 1998). Judith was incensed with the injustice suffered and wanted to be part of stopping this sort of thing. From then on, she knew that she wanted to be a barrister.

While she is currently one of New Zealand's leading defense counsel, Judith in fact began her career in the United Kingdom in the early 1970s. She has been a trailblazer for her gender in both jurisdictions.

She obtained an Honours degree in law from Queen Mary College, University of London. She was one of only four women studying law in her year, one of whom left without completing her degree. Having completed her degree successfully, Judith had to undertake the task of obtaining admission to the bar.

This required, first, student membership of one of the Inns of Court, and then obtaining a pupilage from one of the chambers. Obtaining student membership at Middle Temple was fairly simple, relatively speaking. Students needed to be sponsored, which required either knowing someone or knowing someone who knew someone. This could be achieved with a little effort. However, getting a seat in chambers was a huge hurdle. Judith approached three sets of chambers at home in Wales before she obtained a seat. The first turned her away with little explanation. She believes that they simply did not want a female barrister. She obtained an introduction to the second set of chambers through her father-in-law, but they turned her away, saying "we already have a woman." She was successful with the third chambers. Even so, the head of chambers attempted to dissuade her from the path she had chosen to follow, suggesting that she might be better doing family law and becoming a solicitor. But Judith had always been clear that she wanted to be a barrister and so commenced her pupilage. She, thus, became the second of only two female barristers in Wales.

Her pupilage provided Judith with exposure to a healthy mixture of significant criminal and civil work (the latter including personal injury cases for the British Iron and Steel Federation). It was here that she was introduced to the ultimate interpersonal violence, murder trials. She juniored on several brutal trials where questions of insanity arose.

Once her pupilage ended, she had to start building her own practice with minor briefs. Judith was just starting to establish her practice when it became apparent to her that the impending birth of her first son was incompatible with remaining in chambers. And so she moved to the Welsh Chief Prosecuting Solicitor's Office (now the Crown Prosecution Service). She progressed up the ranks over nine years, prosecuting offenses such as assaults, grievous bodily harm, riots, and robberies. She became the chief prosecutor for alcohol licensing, which involved a crossover with civil work. She was in charge of submissions on closing down premises and attending to planning permissions for new premises, which she found an enjoyable mix. However, she was not convinced that this was a position for life.

In the early 1980s, she visited her brother in Dunedin, New Zealand, for a holiday following a difficult breakup of her marriage. Her brother was eager for her and her two sons to join him and his family in New Zealand on a more permanent basis. Being informed that she could not immigrate to New Zealand because there was no skills shortage for lawyers fired her fighting spirit, and Judith soon found herself a resident of New Zealand. She could not prosecute in New Zealand, as prosecutions are carried out by firms of lawyers acting as both barristers and solicitors owing to the Crown warrant system, and Judith had no desire to take on the solicitor's role.

Accordingly, in 1982, she hung out her shingle as defense counsel once more and began the task of building her professional reputation in New Zealand. That reputation proved to be formidable. She went for 22 months (July 1992–May

1994) without losing a jury trial. In 1995, she became the third woman and first female criminal lawyer to be appointed as Queen's Counsel in New Zealand (the first two were Dame Sian Elias GNZM PC QC, now the Chief Justice, and Dame Lowell Goddard DNZM QC, now a High Court judge, recent head of the Independent Inquiry into Child Sexual Abuse in England and Wales).

Judith's name is associated with some of New Zealand's best-known cases. Her best-known cases often seem to be those that are most repugnant to some New Zealanders—illustrative perhaps of how seriously she takes her obligation to accept instructions (known as the cab-rank rule in both the United Kingdom and New Zealand) and her dedication to speaking for those who need it.

One of the first cases to bring her to prominence in the public's mind was the defense of Dr. Vicky Calder, also known as the "poisoned professor" case. Dr. Calder was a microbiologist accused of poisoning her former partner, internationally respected plant scientist Professor David Lloyd, who had left her for another woman. Professor Lloyd was left blind and severely disabled after being struck down by a mystery illness. Dr. Calder was tried for attempted murder or alternatively poisoning with intent to murder. The alleged weapon was acrylamide monomer, an obscure but readily traceable poison. The case is still regarded as the most forensically complex criminal case in New Zealand history. More than 20 expert scientific witnesses, mostly from overseas, gave evidence in the trials. The first trial ended sensationally with a hung jury and the second with an acquittal. This case was one of the first in New Zealand where media cameras were permitted in court to film the proceedings.

Judith is often associated with the use of the partial defense of provocation by those who have allegedly been in abusive relationships. The defense requires that something was said or done which was sufficient to deprive the accused of self-control (where he/she had the self-control of an ordinary person). Successful application of the defense could reduce a charge of murder to one of manslaughter. The defense was available until 2009.

In 1992, June Gordon was convicted of the murder of her husband after a jury found that she had hired a third party to shoot him. The Court of Appeal rejected Gordon's appeal but acknowledged that had the defense of diminished responsibility been available in New Zealand, then Gordon may well have qualified. Judith began representing Gordon following her unsuccessful appeal and succeeded in obtaining Gordon's early release from prison on parole on the basis that she suffered from what was then described as "Battered Women's Syndrome." Gordon was released from prison three years earlier than her minimum period of imprisonment. This laid the foundation for a later application for the early release of Gay Oakes.

Gay Oakes was convicted of the 1993 murder of her former partner, after poisoning him and then burying him in her garden. Her defenses were provocation or self-defense, on the basis that she suffered from battered women's syndrome. The defenses failed and she was sentenced to life imprisonment.

Mrs. Ablett-Kerr began to act for Gay Oakes after her appeal to the Court of Appeal failed, and Judith took an unsuccessful appeal to the Privy Council. However, the foundation was laid for Oakes to later obtain early parole on the basis that she had suffered from battered women's syndrome. Oakes obtained parole two years before her minimum sentence had been served.

Judith subsequently wrote and spoke widely on the subject of battered women's syndrome and the effects of post-traumatic stress disorder, and the appropriate way for the courts to deal with those in such a situation (Ablett-Kerr, 1997). In 2005, she successfully persuaded a jury to accept the provocation defense to reduce charges against Christine King from murder to manslaughter. King fed her partner sleeping pills and then buried him in the garden. She said that she and her daughters had suffered years of physical and mental abuse.

By far the most controversial case in which Judith argued the provocation defense was the Weatherston case (2009). Clayton Weatherston was a university economics lecturer who had a romantic but turbulent relationship with one of his students, Sophie Elliott. Weatherston stabbed Elliott 216 times with a knife and a pair of scissors. Elliott suffered clusters of stab wounds to both eyes, her genitals, her breasts, her left cheek, temple and ear, and the left side of her neck, as well as 45 wounds to the front of her throat. Her ears and the tip of her nose were cut off and several pieces of her hair were also cut. The pathologist concluded that these wounds were intended to disfigure her. Elliott also suffered seven blunt force injuries. Elliott was killed at home, while her mother was downstairs.

Weatherston told police that he had killed Elliott because of the emotional pain that she had caused him. He said he was provoked by Elliott, who attacked him with a pair of scissors, and lost control. The defense case was that he was provoked by Elliott's attack with the scissors that morning against the background of the emotional pain of a torrid and tumultuous relationship with Elliott, which he was psychologically ill-equipped to deal with. This necessitated evidence of both Weatherston's and Elliott's personalities, and the tumultuous relationship between the two. Two psychiatrists also gave evidence that Weatherston suffered from narcissistic personality disorder. The defense was rejected, and Weatherston was convicted of murder. Media coverage was unprecedented and intense. Public reaction was extreme, and Judith suffered extreme abuse herself. It was one of Judith's most harrowing cases.

The Peter Ellis case is another example of Judith standing up for those for whom justice has seemingly miscarried. Ellis was a childcare worker in Christchurch who in June 1993 was found guilty on 16 counts of sexual offenses involving children. At the trial, he had faced 28 charges involving 13 children. The evidence included allegations of ritual satanic abuse. His conviction has been one of the most controversial in New Zealand, with concerns centering on how the children's testimonies were obtained and presented to the jury.

Judith became involved in 1997 after the Court of Appeal had rejected Ellis's appeal (although it did quash three convictions) and Ellis's application for legal aid to appeal to the Privy Council had been rejected. She pursued other avenues to overturn his conviction, variously seeking that the Governor-General invoke the royal prerogative of mercy and seeking a Royal Commission of Inquiry into the whole case. She succeeded in obtaining a limited rehearing, which was unsuccessful. In 2000, Ellis was released after serving the mandatory two-thirds of his sentence. Efforts to clear his name continued after his release, but all have been unsuccessful to date.

Criminal law is not, however, the extent of her practice. Judith finds that her courtroom skills are in demand for complex civil proceedings. She finds this aspect of her practice interesting and rewarding, but ensures that it is confined to only one case at a time, where she can be assured of thorough instruction and support from her instructing solicitors, in the English style.

She has been involved with her professional body throughout her practice. She served the profession itself through membership with the Otago District Law Society Council, as well as several of its sub-committees, the New Zealand Law Society (NZLS) Criminal Law Committee (including three years as Convener) and the New Zealand Bar Association (NZBA) Council. She has contributed to the continuing development of criminal and civil trial advocacy skills through being a faculty member for many years with the NZLS Litigation Skills and Advanced Litigation Skills programs. She has also been an advocacy coach for both the NZBA and the Australian Bar Association (ABA).

Judith has been extensively involved with law reform. She has been a member of the Chief Justice's Criminal Practice Committee for the last 20 years. In this capacity, she has provided input into the guidelines for practice in the criminal courts and the implications of law reform in that area. She was the coordinator of the 2010 subcommittee that drafted the current Guidelines for Defense Counsel in dealing with the media. Judith also served on various Law Commission and Ministry of Justice ad hoc committees, including the Law Commission Core Advisory Group on Juries and committees dealing with the prosecution of sexual abuse cases, sentencing indications and case-flow management. She has chaired various conferences, including the Legal Research Foundation's Auckland conferences on Miscarriages of Justice, and is the author of numerous papers and articles to do with the practice of law and access to justice. Judith was elected a Fellow of the IATL in 2007.

In 1985, Judith was a founding member of the Otago Women Lawyers Society. She has contributed in case law, publications, and presentations on issues pertaining to women who offend. She was made an ONZM for services to the legal profession in 2002.

Philosophy of Legal Advocacy

Judith considers that all prospective advocates should understand that this is a very difficult career, requiring its practitioners to be strong of mind and to have a strong moral code. The law challenges its practitioners and they must be dedicated to the law. To her mind, the law is one of the most important professions in the society. This is because justice is the cornerstone of a civilized society. While everyone else—electricians, doctors, architects, teachers, and so forth—are also needed for the society, there must be a justice system that allows people to live in harmony with one another (harmony being a society that is fair and just). She has little time for those who come to the law as advocates because it is something to do or because they are fulfilling someone else's expectations—the law and the society deserve something more than that.

This belief means that the rule of law is paramount. While New Zealand appears to be acknowledged as sixth in the world for adherence to the rule of law (World Justice Project, 2015), Judith's experience in the criminal law leads her to believe that there are several major red flags that are hindering the performance of New Zealand's criminal legal system.

The first is access to justice, which Judith believes is being significantly challenged by recent changes to the Legal Aid system. Judith considers that in the late twentieth century, New Zealand had made great strides in providing funding that allowed defendants, who could not otherwise obtain such representation, to be represented by counsel of their own choice. It was not a perfect system; the level of funding for defense lawyers was always set as less than that of Crown lawyers and bore no relation to the free market. However, with assistance of the Legal Aid Review Authority, there were enough skilled practitioners willing to carry out the work. While the fee level did put some senior practitioners off doing "legal aid work," there was still a good body of skilled senior practitioners with social consciences who were prepared to participate in the Legal Aid scheme.

However, the changes to legal aid in the second decade of this century appear to have decreased in the pool of appropriately skilled lawyers. Funding has increasingly become unrealistic (with "fixed fees" applying to most trials, including rape), and the ability to access adequate resources such as expert evidence is constrained. The defendant's ability to choose his/her counsel has been removed where the defendant is accused of an offense that carries a sentence of less than 10 years imprisonment. The argument that the new system has actually improved the quality of representation just does not stand up to close scrutiny. Judith's opinion is that quality representation cannot be guaranteed simply by establishing the lawyer's skill level by reference to "time served," attending courses which provide the requisite number of Continuing Professional Development points, and having appeared as a junior in two or three trials. Accordingly, she is concerned that the interests of justice are not being served.

The second red flag relates to the trial process. Judith has made many speeches to juries that include the words "New Zealand has a First World justice system as is to be expected in a first world democratic society…." However, she finds that this view is being challenged by the changes made to the trial process over the last six years, especially since the introduction of the Criminal Procedure Act 2011 and the Criminal Procedure Rules 2012. The rationale behind the changes was to "simplify" and "speed up" the criminal justice system. Judith, however, considers that the changes have been counterproductive in many ways.

The changes did away with the deposition process. Depositions identified the evidence that the Crown intended to lead at a relatively early stage, and gave defense lawyers the opportunity to assess the strength of that evidence early on and advise their clients appropriately. This process now takes place much closer to trial, requires judicial intervention, and can result in significant delays—contrary to the original intention. This is both stressful and difficult to understand for the defendants and the witnesses, and no doubt frustrates the Court when it is obliged to re-schedule its trial list. Judith believes that confidence in the justice system is affected when it appears to participants, who often have their lives put on hold during the remand period, that trials which are scheduled to start are in fact not ready to do so.

Other issues that Judith is concerned about include:

- Unrealistic short time frames and expectations for each step in the process.
- Over-generalization of the content and form of the "Formal Statement" procedure. This over-generalization means that formal statements may merely be a handwritten document sometimes difficult to read and with generous amounts of irrelevant and inadmissible material, making it difficult and time consuming to identify exactly which parts of the document the Crown intends to lead.
- The requirement that the defense should declare its defense before it knows the full case that the Crown intends to place before the court.

The new system appears to be driven by paper (physical or electronic), which means that there are fewer attendances in court for defendants. There is thus less human interaction, fewer opportunities for meaningful dialogue between parties, and fewer opportunities for resolving issues in a constructive and just way. Judith notes that it is possible in the case of a trial by jury for the defendant to make only one court appearance between arrest and trial. In one instance recently, there was no appearance by the defendant before trial on a charge of murder. While there may have been good reason for that situation, it does highlight a potentially dangerous path.

Judith does not intend to advocate pointless appearances. However, she sees it as essential that a defendant is fully aware of the processes and is part of what is taking place. Most defendants come from lower socio-economic backgrounds, have limited education, and have limited insight into the decision making that is taking place in relation to their own case. It is essential that they not only are assisted in understand what is happening, but also take part in what is occurring. This is of particular concern in relation to the Maori, who are overrepresented in New Zealand's prison population.

How then do we ensure that procedural legislation, like the Criminal Procedure Act 2011, is able to promote the achievement of justice? Judith considers that in a democratic society, the answer must lie in genuine consultation between government agencies and those who actually participate in the trial process, including both defense and Crown counsel.

Problems and Successes Experienced

Our discussion took us to the challenges faced by Judith during her career, rather than her successes. My research directed me toward the public highlights of Judith's career, which are outlined in the Career section above. The challenges she has faced during her career give an invaluable insight into the personal toll that practicing law can take and the challenges that can be faced in defense of justice.

The Weatherston case was the most discomforting episode of Judith's career, really challenging her faith in the society. Her car was burnt with acid, and she received letters where the text comprised letters cut out from magazines that spelled out death threats. She could not walk down the street in Christchurch without being yelled at or tooted at. People yelled abuses at her across the atrium in Crowne Plaza hotel (a high-end hotel). She needed to be escorted when making her way to the court house bathroom to protect her from the hissing and the spitting. The press climbed the fence at her home in attempts to get photographs of her and her home. The level of abuse was such that the President of the NZLS made public statements in her defense (*Otago Daily Times*, 2009).

At the time, Judith kept silent on the matter, considering that she should not engage with the press on the issue. However, it was privately devastating to have to deal with these things. As she puts it, she was subjected to this abuse simply because she fulfilled her obligation as a barrister and as one of Her Majesty's counsel. The public failed to understand that Judith was obliged to accept the instructions and that providing defense to a person is not necessarily a justification of their actions. Clayton Weatherston was entitled to the best defense that Mrs. Ablett-Kerr could provide, and he received that—it was for the jury to assess his culpability, which it did.

While clearly hurt by the level of vitriol directed toward her, it was the reaction of those in positions of some power and influence who Judith considered should have known better that appalled her. One such person gave, on her count, eight media interviews during the course of the trial about the need to get rid of the partial defense of provocation. Judith believes that this showed no respect for the trial process. She is appalled that this could occur in a first-world country that upholds ideals of democracy and civil justice.

Judith's greatest failure, in her opinion, was that she was unable to assist Greg King in dealing with his troubled state of mind in the last days of his life. Greg King was a rising star at the defense bar—already successful and highly accomplished—who committed suicide in 2012. King left a note in which he described himself as *"exhausted, unwell, disillusioned, depressed and haunted"* and *"totally burnt out"* (Backhouse, 2013). Four months prior to this untimely death, he had finished defending Ewan MacDonald in his high-profile trial for the murder of his brother-in-law and best man, Scott Guy. Guy was found shot to death at the gate to the family farm, which he and MacDonald managed. The trial attracted intense media speculation given allegations that Guy was killed over a battle for control of the farm. MacDonald was acquitted. Media scrutiny only increased after the trial when MacDonald was convicted of other offenses, including burning down a house on Guy's property and vandalizing a house that Guy was building. The jury had been aware of these allegations—it had not been aware that he had already pleaded guilty to three other charges, including killing 19 calves by beating them over the head (Garrett-Walker, 2012). Coverage was sensationalist, with some unable to understand how King could have defended MacDonald, again demonstrating the public's failure to understand an advocate's obligation to accept instructions.

King was Judith's mentee. He was employed by Judith for three years soon after his admission to the Bar and worked with her on many complex criminal trials during that time. Even after moving to Wellington, King continued to work with Judith on high-profile cases—including those of Ellis and Weatherston. They had a close working relationship, and Judith respected his quick mind and his passion for the law and his clients.

Judith believes that King gave hugely of himself to his profession and his clients. She gave an example of King driving to the Rimutaka prison each day to transport a client to the Wellington High Court for his trial so that the client would be spared the ride in the prison van. King also gave of his time to provide continuing legal education for the profession and had significant involvement with the NZLS law reform groups. He presented *The Court Reporter* for, now defunct television channel, TVNZ7, which aimed to make the justice system more accessible to the public. He also made himself available to the press for interviews, not just to provide brief comments on cases but to engage in in-depth discussions. Judith believes that he simply gave too much of himself—particularly to the press, which can be fickle and demanding, and he took criticisms to heart. She carries the fear that had she recognized King's need, she may have been able to say something to help him. Depression and stress are acknowledged problems for the profession in New Zealand, and current and intending practitioners need to take care of themselves. Notably, the NZLS provides the Practising Well initiative, a collection of resources to enhance the health and wellbeing of the legal community.

Theory and Practice

One of the attractions of this project for Judith was the opportunity to discuss matters of theory, but ultimately our conversation took us more to practical matters than to theoretical matters. We attempted to return to theory, but given that Judith's opinion is that the relationship between theory and practice in legal advocacy is a complex one unless you are of the Legal Positivism School, a proper discussion required more time than Judith's workload allowed. Accordingly, theory is touched on only lightly.

At a superficial level, Judith considers that theory and practice should inform and respect each other. Practitioners should be familiar with theory, as it will make them more persuasive and more complete advocates. Theory builders need to consult practitioners so that theories can be of relevance to the administration of justice and address practical issues. Theories developed without relevance to process are unlikely to provide satisfactory solutions.

Judith's opinion is that currently in New Zealand, there is generally an imbalance in the relationship between theory and practice. This is demonstrated by the recent changes to criminal procedure, which many legal practitioners consider have challenged the fair-trial process.

On the more positive side, Judith accepts that the theory of therapeutic jurisprudence (Winick, 2003) can be seen as a successful interaction between theory builders and practitioners. This model attempts to ensure the needs and rights of the parties have been accommodated in a legal process. Judith considers that one might argue that such an important result has come about because of positive interaction and dialogue, and the creation of a process by which a positive outcome can be achieved.

Judith believes that in New Zealand, there are two fundamental tenets essential to the justice system which should not be minimized by any other jurisprudential theory. They are:

- everyone is entitled to a fair trial; and
- only the guilty should be convicted.

Of course, what amounts to fair trial is a constant debate. Provided one reads both fundamental tenets together, Judith suggests that what is a fair trial will be informed by the objective that only the guilty should be convicted.

Transnational Relations

As New Zealand's legal system is based on the English system, moving between jurisdictions is possible. But the lawyer moving must obtain admission to the Bar in the new jurisdiction. Requirements for admission differ depending on the experience that the lawyer has had, and some examinations may have to be sat. The process may take up to two years.

Aside from legal requirements, Judith also had to deal with more subtle differences in practice between the two jurisdictions. In England and Wales, barristers practice together in chambers, which are run by clerks. Particularly in smaller centers in New Zealand, barristers will practice alone. Clerks are unheard of. As a barrister in Wales, Judith would have received full briefings from her instructing solicitors. In New Zealand, the approach to briefing can be more casual. In England, a barrister requires an instructing solicitor in all cases. In New Zealand, no instructing solicitor is required for criminal legal aid cases. Judith would even have observed some barristers engaging in "reverse briefs"—where the client approaches the barrister directly, and the barrister (at the one permitted meeting with the client) may advise the client to seek out a solicitor to instruct the barrister. (The operation of this rule was changed by the NZLS from July 1, 2015). One can imagine that these practices might have seemed unusual to Judith when she first arrived.

Nevertheless, she clearly thrived in the New Zealand environment. She has not been confined by her physical location, near the bottom of the South Island. As noted earlier, the trial of Dr. Vicky Calder for poisoning her former lover involved overseas expert scientific witnesses. Both the New Zealand forensic scientist and a UK expert had analyzed hair samples taken from Professor Lloyd. The hair results were said to show levels of "CEC," a chemical compound, about 50 times higher than the average level found in control samples. CEC is a compound formed by the bonding of acrylamide with cysteine, part of hemoglobin.

The Crown alleged that the results of the hair analysis, together with the clinical symptoms exhibited by Professor Lloyd, proved that he was poisoned by acrylamide. Judith unsuccessfully challenged the admissibility of this evidence on the basis that the hair analysis was novel scientific evidence (*R v. Calder*, 1995). During the course of the two trials, Judith had found two overseas experts who had actually dealt with acrylamide poisoning cases. Preparation for the trials required travel to the United Kingdom to brief expert witnesses in Manchester, Leicester, and London (University of Otago, 2013). Calder was ultimately acquitted. Had she confined the experts to those who were New Zealand based, it is questionable that Judith would have achieved the same result.

Another example of her use of overseas experts is the Peter Ellis case, in which she engaged experts in the interviewing of children from both the United States and the United Kingdom. Only last year, she engaged one of the world's leading scientific experts in the analysis of blood/alcohol in order to address a novel argument the Crown had sought to raise in a rape case. The expert, who was based in Sweden, gave evidence for several hours via satellite, resulting in the Crown withdrawing their scientific evidence and, ultimately, not resisting the dismissal of the case.

Judith maintained her link with the United Kingdom by retaining a doorstep tenancy in London chambers for many years after moving to New Zealand. From time to time, she has returned to conduct the occasional case in the United Kingdom and has also appeared before the Privy Council.

Her transnational practice is also reflected in her involvement with the ABA and IATL. While I was corresponding with Judith over this chapter, she was involved in acting as an advocacy coach for the ABA. The advocacy courses are residential, which is intense for both students and coaches. The similarity in the legal systems and styles of advocacy makes such involvement simpler. One can only imagine how rewarding it is for Judith to be able to engage with peers in Australia, as well as other faculty members from further afield and talented individuals coming through the programs. It also fits with her ethos of giving back to the profession. It is interesting that she chooses to give back in Australia as well as in New Zealand. This perhaps indicates the international reach this high-level practice has.

The IATL is a grouping of trial lawyers, with membership by invitation only. Membership is limited to 500 fellows from the United States, with additional international fellows permitted. Judith was elected a fellow in 2007. She is one of eight New Zealand fellows, five of whom are judges and three of whom are QCs. The Academy's aims include facilitating the administration of justice, promoting the rule of law internationally, and elevating the standards of integrity, honor, and courtesy in the profession. These were certainly themes that emerged from my discussions with Judith.

Judith has not limited her practice to New Zealand. This does not mean that she appears in overseas courts, but rather that she utilizes international resources to benefit of her clients and also engages with advocates, and contributes to advocacy skills, in other jurisdictions.

General Assessments

Developments in the criminal justice system over the last 10 years have been deeply concerning to Judith. As discussed in further detail above, changes in the legal aid system have the potential to affect the quality of legal aid providers, and hence challenge the administration of justice. Certain changes to criminal procedure in the name of efficiency have been counterproductive and have in some ways estranged defendants from the process that they are going through.

One of the saddest things that Judith has seen in her 45 years of practice is the enormous diminishment of the public's regard for lawyers. She considers that the profession needs to understand how this has come about—is it because of poor-quality practitioners? Because it is fashionable? Is it media-driven? Are practitioners simply not doing a good-enough job? She suspects that it is likely a combination of these factors. However, the profession needs to understand what is behind this and then address it. If the public simply sees barristers as "guns for hire," then they cannot understand barristers' obligations to accept instructions or their duty to the court. If they do not understand that, then they will inevitably lose faith in the justice system, as demonstrated by the public's reactions to the Weatherston and MacDonald cases.

Judith harbors deep concerns about the role of the press in the administration in justice. The media's involvement with court cases looms very large on how justice is administered in New Zealand. She continues to find disturbing the role that the media played in Weatherston's case and in the subsequent removal of the partial defense of provocation.

Judith considers that the improvement of legal advocacy and the justice system must start at the beginning—with law students and then junior barristers. As noted earlier, Judith considers that the law is best served by those who come to it because of a dedication to the law and to justice. She believes that taking a jurisprudence paper at university (i.e. studying the philosophy of the law) is essential, as it provides a theoretical framework for all that follows. For those who wish to be advocates, an evidence paper is also essential. With this foundation, practitioners can engage with theory builders and legislators, and build up and defend a principled criminal justice system.

Once barristers begin their careers, the pupilage system provided to young barristers in England and Wales is an excellent model. It provides the pupil with the advantage of being involved in high-level cases without being responsible for them; the pupil's only role is to assist. In doing so, it is important for the pupil to keep in mind that he/she does not know the answer—he/she is there to learn from the pupil master. While New Zealand has made some steps in this direction, imposing in 2012 a requirement that barristers must be employed for three years before commencing practice on their own account, Judith considers that junior barristers would benefit from a proper pupilage experience. There would likely be more quality control in this process than under the current legal aid assessment process.

Judith believes that students must come to the law with a firm understanding that they will continue to learn throughout their careers. Too often, junior barristers who are enthused with the new knowledge provided by their universities fail to understand the importance of guidance (from skilled senior practitioners) on how to use this knowledge. At the same time, senior barristers can be reinvigorated by the enthusiasm of juniors and learn from their new ideas and new perspectives. Judith feels privileged to have enjoyed such a relationship with Greg King. Barristers at all levels can and should learn from each other, whether acting on the same side or against each other. Professional support is one of the things that makes a profession special.

Judith also remains concerned about the status of female lawyers. While the profession is publicly presenting a positive view of women in the profession, she is not convinced that attitudes have changed overwhelmingly in private. Only a wide pool of talented lawyers can benefit the justice system. If lawyers came to the law for the right reasons, understand its special place in the society, and continue to learn throughout their careers, this can only be positive for legal advocacy and the justice system.

Conclusion

I found my interview with Judith fascinating. She was generous with her time and honest in her reflections, and I did genuinely feel privileged by the experience. As a practitioner, you are always aware when you come up against a leading practitioner, but when that practitioner is on the other side, you do not get the insight into what is actually going through his/her minds. I did genuinely feel invigorated and more positive about the law following our interview.

Judith's concern with the rule of law and issues of access to justice were genuine. She has not used her privileged position simply to set herself up for retirement. Her concern with justice and fairness was evident from a young age, and did not seem to have become blighted with the cynicism of experience. Some of the cases that she has been involved in must have taken a personal toll. The pressure she has been under has been immense. Personally, I do not believe that anyone could have come away from that unscarred. Yet Judith was still clear that the accused has the right to a defense. Her only sign of disappointment was due to the lack of understanding exhibited by some sections of the population.

I consider that to be effective as a criminal lawyer, one must maintain a sense of humanity. A desire for justice is essential also, but perhaps for some, there is a danger that this can become an academic exercise. For Judith, that humanity was particularly evident in her identification of the loss of Greg King as her greatest failure—rather than the loss of a particular case, which might be about the legal arguments, the evidentiary points. It can be easy for the public to demonize defense lawyers, but real people remain underneath. And, as the loss of Greg King demonstrates, the profession also needs to look after its people.

As a woman in the law, Judith's experiences were always going to be of interest to me. I consider that there is always a strain between identifying as a woman in the law and simply as a lawyer. Some of Judith's experiences indicate that being a woman was an issue. To have been at the forefront of gender bias issues in two countries is a unique experience. In some ways, things have changed a lot since Judith was a young practitioner. Yet in other ways, they have not changed nearly enough. Recent data from the New Zealand Law Society indicate that despite women having been admitted to the profession in equal numbers since 1995, they make up only 22% of partnerships with 20 or more partners, 17% of Queens' counsel, and 30% of the judiciary (New Zealand Law Society, 2015, 2016). Why is that, one might ask? To what extent are the changes that have emerged since Judith's time as a junior practitioner merely superficial?

As was evident from what Judith said, to do justice to this job requires dedication, which is not a desire for money or status, but a love of the law and a willingness to uphold it.

Glossary

battered women's syndrome: a physical and psychological condition suffered by a person who has been subjected to (usually persistent and continuous) abuse by another.

brief: instructions to a barrister to undertake legal work.

cab-rank rule: the obligation upon a barrister to accept any instructions within his/her area of competence. A barrister cannot turn down instructions that are distasteful or unprofitable.

chambers: a room or set of rooms used by a barrister or shared by a group of barristers. Barristers cannot join in partnership, but may share administrative costs.

common law: a system of law developed by judges and followed in similar cases. It is supplemented by statute law.

Crown warrant: an authorization issued by the Crown to a solicitor in a particular district to undertake the conduct of certain criminal trials within that district on behalf of the Crown. The solicitor holding the warrant (the Crown solicitor) is assisted by colleagues within his/her firm, as they are within the Crown solicitor's supervision.

deposition: a type of preliminary hearing that establishes whether there is sufficient evidence to commit the defendant to a trial.

diminished responsibility: a term applied to any type of defense that involves a plea by the defendant that while he/she committed the act in question, he/she should not be held criminally liable for his/her actions as his/her mental functions were "diminished" or impaired.

doorstep tenancy: membership of barristers' chambers while not physically practicing from the chambers' premises.

formal statement procedure: a document required to be filed under the Criminal Procedure Act 2011. These are formal statements of the evidence that the prosecutor considers sufficient to justify the trial.

hang out one's shingle: an idiom, to establish a professional practice, especially in law.

Inns of Court: the professional association for barristers in England and Wales.

International Academy of Trial Lawyers (IATL): a fellowship of trial lawyers, whose membership is by invitation only following a vetting process. Fellowship is limited to 500 American trial lawyers, with additional international fellows.

Law Commission: an independent Crown entity, whose role is to review the law and make recommendations for improvement, and to advise the Minister and government agencies on ways in which the law of New Zealand can be made as understandable and accessible as is practicable. The government considers the recommendations and determines what, if any, amendments are to be made to the law.

legal aid: a system under which the government funds the defense costs of those who cannot afford it and meet certain criteria.

legal positivism: a school of thought that "in any legal system, whether a given norm is legally valid, and hence whether it forms part of the law of that system, depends on its sources, not its merits" (Gardner, 2001).

Middle Temple: one of the Inns of Court in England and Wales.

narcissistic personality disorder: a personality disorder in which the person has an inflated sense of self-worth and a lack of empathy for others.

New Zealand Order of Merit (ONZM): an order of chivalry in New Zealand's Honours System, awarded by Her Majesty the Queen to those who, in any field of endeavor, have rendered meritorious service to the Crown and the nation or who have become distinguished by their eminence, talents, contributions, or other merits.

paralegal: a person who is not a qualified lawyer and is employed by a lawyer to undertake legally related tasks under the lawyer's supervision.

post-traumatic stress disorder: a condition of continuing mental and emotional stress suffered by a person as a consequence of an injury or severe psychological shock.

Privy Council: the Judicial Committee of the Privy Council of the House of Lords in England, being a committee made up of judges. It was New Zealand's highest court of appeal for all cases heard until December 31, 2003.

provocation: formerly a partial defense to a murder charge, which, argued successfully, reduced the charge from murder to manslaughter. The defense would be successful if something was done or said which, in the circumstances, was sufficient to deprive a person (having the self-control of an ordinary person, but otherwise having the characteristics of the offender) of self-control, and did in fact deprive the offender of self-control and induce him/her to commit the act of homicide.

pupilage: the final stage of training to be a barrister in England and Wales, requiring the student barrister (the pupil) to work in a barrister's chambers.

Queen's Counsel: a barrister whose seniority and excellence has been recognized by appointment to be "one of Her Majesty's counsel learned in law." It is a recognition of status.

Senior Counsel: a term used instead of Queen's counsel between 2007 and 2012, and still used by some of those appointed to the rank during that period.

solicitor: a lawyer who does not appear in court. In England and Wales, solicitors do not have rights of audience in court, whereas in New Zealand, they do, although many solicitors choose not to exercise this right. Solicitors hold trust accounts to deal with clients' money, whereas barristers do not hold funds for clients.

therapeutic jurisprudence: the study of how legal systems affect people's mental health, emotions, and behaviors.

South Africa

11

DON PINNOCK

Contents

The Criminal Justice Process of South Africa

The democratic elections in South Africa in 1994 marked the end of legal apartheid and stimulated intense and exciting debate on the legislative structures that needed to be put in place. Many repugnant racist laws, such as the Immorality Act (1927), Prohibition of Mixed Marriages Act (1949), Group Areas Act (1950), Bantu Authorities Act (1951), Suppression of Communism Act (1950), were struck down and offensive sections of retained laws amended.

Central to the renovation and reconstruction of the legal framework was the development of a Constitution and Bill of Rights as the supreme law that binds all legislative, executive, and judicial organs of the state at all levels of government. Defense of the Constitution was vested in a Constitutional Court, which is required to declare any law or conduct that is inconsistent with the Constitution of the Republic of South Africa (1996) to be invalid, and develop common law that is consistent with the values of the Constitution and the spirit and purpose of the Bill of Rights. This court, together with the Supreme Court of Appeal and the high courts, is an important source of law. No person or organ of state may interfere with the functioning of the courts, and an order or decision of a court binds all organs of state and people to whom it applies.

Today South African law is a combination of different legal systems, with its origin in Europe and in Great Britain. Its foundation lies in Roman–Dutch law, which is itself a blend of indigenous Dutch customary law and Roman law. As with any other country, the common law has been augmented by statutory law, and many of the cases before the court are now concerned with their interpretation and application. Because of the unique heritage of South African law, and the constitutional imperative to regard comparative law, foreign law is frequently consulted, not as binding but as persuasive authority.

The legal profession that supports this is divided into two branches—advocates and attorneys—who are subject to strict ethical codes. Advocates are organized into Bar associations or societies, one each at the seat of the various divisions of the High Court.

There are voluntary associations of advocates such as the General Council of the Bar of South Africa and other formations of independent bars. For attorneys, there are four regional societies, each made up of a number of provinces. A practicing attorney is *ipso jure* a member of at least one of these societies, which seek to promote the interests of the profession. The Law Society of South Africa is a voluntary association established to coordinate the various regional societies.

Advocates can appear in any court, whereas attorneys may be heard in all of the country's lower courts and can also acquire the right of appearance in the superior courts. All attorneys who hold an LLB or equivalent degree, or who have at least three years' experience, may acquire the right of audience in the High Court.

State law advisers give legal advice to ministers, government departments, provincial administrations, and a number of statutory bodies. In addition, they draft Bills and assist the Minister concerned with the passage of Bills through Parliament. They also assist in criminal and constitutional matters.

On the eve of the country's first democratic elections, the entire judiciary was predominantly white and male, with three black males and one white female. By 2013, under an intense program of transformation, 239 judges (61%) were African, as were 974 magistrates. As of that year, there were 76 female judges and 1,841 advocates as well as 7,477 female attorneys (Tibane & Vermeulen, 2015). The court system they administer is structured as shown in Figure 11.1.

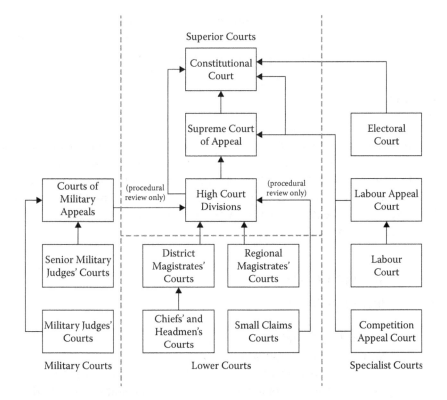

Figure 11.1 Courts of South Africa.

Constitutional Court

This court is the highest court in all constitutional matters. It is the only court that may adjudicate disputes between organs of state in the national or provincial sphere concerning the constitutional status, powers or functions of any of those organs of state, or that may decide on the constitutionality of any amendment to the Constitution or any parliamentary or provincial Bill.

The Constitutional Court makes the final decision on whether an act of parliament, a provincial act or the conduct of the President is constitutional. It consists of the Chief Justice of South Africa, the Deputy Chief Justice, and nine Constitutional Court judges.

Supreme Court of Appeal

This is the highest court in respect of all matters other than constitutional ones. It consists of the President and Deputy President of the Supreme Court of Appeal and 23 other judges of appeal. The Supreme Court of Appeal has jurisdiction to hear and determine an appeal against any decision of a high court.

Decisions of the Supreme Court of Appeal are binding on all courts of a lower order and the decisions of high courts are binding on magistrates' courts within the respective areas of jurisdiction of the divisions.

High Courts

A high court has jurisdiction in its own area over all persons residing or present in that area. These courts hear matters that are of such a serious nature that the lower courts would not be competent to make an appropriate judgment or to impose a penalty. Except where a minimum or maximum sentence is prescribed by law, their penal jurisdiction is unlimited and includes handing down a sentence of life imprisonment in certain specified cases. There are 13 high courts.

Specialist High Courts

These include the following:

- The Labor Court and Labor Appeal that adjudicate over labor disputes and hear labor appeals, respectively
- The Land Claims Court that hears matters on the restitution of land rights that African people lost after 1913 as a result of racially discriminatory land laws

- The Competition Appeal Court that deals with appeals from the Competition Tribunal
- The Electoral Court that sits mainly during elections to deal with associated disputes
- The Tax Court that deals with tax-related matters, including non-compliance with tax obligations

Circuit Local Divisions

These are itinerant courts, presided over by a judge of the provincial division, who conducts hearings at remote areas outside the seat of the High Court with a view to enhancing access to justice.

Regional Courts

Regional courts are established largely in accordance with provincial boundaries with a regional court division for each province to hear matters within their jurisdiction. There are nine regional court presidents and 351 regional court magistrates. These courts adjudicate civil disputes. In 2010, divorce courts were subsumed under the regional-court divisions in order to address the challenges in terms of which litigants have to travel to remote courts to get legal redress.

Magistrates' Courts

Magistrates' courts are where most ordinary people come into contact with the justice system. For this reason, the bulk of the department's budget and resources are concentrated here. Magistrates' courts include special backlog courts. All magistrates in South Africa fall outside the ambit of the Public Service, the aim being to strengthen the independence of the judiciary. In addition, full jurisdiction was conferred to courts in rural areas and former black townships that formerly exercised limited jurisdiction.

Small Claims Courts

These courts were established to adjudicate small civil claims and eliminate time-consuming adversary procedures before and during the trial of these claims. The limit of cases involving civil claims in these courts is R12,000. By June 2013, there were 277 small claims courts. Most of these courts and places of sitting are in rural areas.

The Small Claims Court model is an effective dispute resolution mechanism that contributes toward the realization of the department's mandate to ensure access to justice for all.

Equality Courts

These courts aim to prevent and prohibit unfair discrimination and harassment, promote equality, eliminate unfair discrimination, and prevent and prohibit hate speech.

Traditional Courts

These are traditional courts in community areas in rural villages.

Community Courts

These courts focus on restorative justice processes, such as diverting young offenders into suitable programs. They also seek to assist the country's case backlog. Community courts are normal district magistrates' courts that assist in dealing with matters in partnership with the local community and businesses.

Courts for Income Tax Offenders

These courts deal only with cases concerning failure to submit tax returns or to provide information requested by Revenue Service officials. They do not deal with bigger cases such as tax fraud.

Sexual Offenses Courts

These courts feature specially trained officials, procedures, and equipment to reduce the chance of secondary trauma for victims. There is a screening process to identify cases that fall within the sexual offenses category, a special room where victims testify, a private waiting room for adult witnesses, and a private waiting room for child witnesses and victim support services.

Maintenance Courts

The main objective of these courts is to facilitate the securing of maintenance money from parents and/or other people able to maintain maintenance beneficiaries, mainly children, who have a right to maintenance.

Criminal Jurisdiction of the Respective Courts

- The *High Court* may try all offenses.
- A *magistrate's court* has jurisdiction over all offenses except treason, murder, and rape.
- A *regional court* can impose a sentence of not more than 15 years' imprisonment or a fine not exceeding R300,000. They have jurisdiction over all offenses except treason.
- Apart from specific provisions of the Magistrates' Courts Act 1944 or any other Act, jurisdiction regarding sentences imposed by *district courts* is limited to imprisonment of not more than three years or a fine not exceeding R60,000.

Depending on the gravity of the offense and the circumstances pertaining to the offender, the Director of Public Prosecutions decides in which court a matter will be heard and may even decide on a summary trial in the High Court.

The sentencing of petty offenders to do community service as a condition of suspension, correctional supervision or postponement in appropriate circumstances, has become part of an alternative sentence to imprisonment.

Antoinette Ferreira, Senior State Advocate, National Prosecuting Authority, Bloemfontein

Introduction

Senior State Advocate Antoinette Ferreira is one of South Africa's most experienced legal authorities on environmental crime. Advocate Ferreira is stationed at the Office of The Director of Public Prosecutions for the National Prosecuting Authority (NPA) in Bloemfontein, the country's judicial capital. She has served in a prosecutorial role in courts throughout the country. She was given the Award of Excellence in 2008 for her outstanding contribution to the prosecution of environmental crimes. In 2012, she received the Rhino Conservation Award in the category of Best Judicial Systems and Policing. She is a founding member of the Free State Environmental Crime Working Group and a member of its national body. She has received five additional merit awards from the NPA.

Advocate Ferreira is also a specialist in organized crime and obtained the first authorization in the country in a racketeering case in terms of the newly promulgated Prevention of Organized Crime Act (POCA) of 1998. The case involved an abalone poaching syndicate that was illegally stripping shellfish from areas of the country's West Coast for sale to Chinese syndicates. Advocate Ferreira has also successfully prosecuted gang members in the Free State Province where she is based. Her expertise and knowledge in these diverse areas—environmental crime, organized crime, and gang-related crime—has earned her wide recognition. She acts as adviser to a number of government departments and to the South African Police Services.

Career

Advocate Ferreira grew up and was schooled in the Free State mining town of Welkom. She studied for a bachelor of law at the University of Potchefstroom, and completed her LLB and LLM qualifications at the University of South Africa.

The country's transition to democracy in 1994 required extensive transformation of political, social, and legal structures and a welter of new laws, including a Constitution and Bill of Rights. Part of this process was the formation of the NPA. After a spell of volunteer work on Kibbutz Palmahim in Israel, Ferreira returned to join the NPA at its inception. She worked as both district and regional court prosecutor in the Cape and Free State provinces before being appointed as senior state advocate at the Director of Public Prosecutions in Bloemfontein.

I never planned to be a prosecutor. We all watched *LA Law* and were mis-informed about what happens when you hit the real world. When you're a prosecutor, you become everybody's skivvy,* and get the blame for any-thing, and everything that goes wrong. It makes you quite thick-skinned at the end of the day. You work under a lot of pressure. Each magistrate's court is assigned one or more prosecutors, depending on its size. Their duties are extensive.

As a prosecutor you run the court. You're responsible for the witnesses, for the court personnel—interpreters, police officers—and the accused being on time. The magistrate expects the prosecutor to keep everything running smoothly and that involves quite a lot of people. It sometimes feels like the whole world's responsibilities are on your shoulders. It's particularly hard in South Africa with so many cases.

Most decisions on criminal cases are taken by prosecutors in the lower courts, after securing the written authority to prosecute from the Director of Public Prosecutions.

Prosecutors are the gatekeepers of the criminal law. We represent the public interest in the criminal justice process. Our mandate is to make a decision about whether or not to institute prosecution in a criminal case. We are the people's lawyer.
Before prosecutors can act, they must take an oath of office:
A prosecutor has to adhere to the highest ethical and professional stan-dards in prosecuting crime and we need to conduct ourselves in a manner that will maintain, promote and defend the interests of justice. This includes prosecuting without fear, favor or prejudice.
When there's a victim, you're the person who goes to court for them. That can be difficult, particularly with environmental crime, because the environ-ment doesn't speak. It's very different to, say, a robbery case where you have a victim who can go on record and you can protect them from an attorney asking unfair questions. What people often don't understand is that we're not there to get their money back. Of course there are procedures to get compen-sation. But that's not our focus. We're there to balance the scales.

There are many days, she says, when people thank her for what she did for them. They feel as if the whole world has abandoned them, and she helps them through the system and gives them some sort of resolve. Often the cases are tough, and take years to finalize. But at the end of the day, she says, you feel like you really made a difference. These days, Advocate Ferreira can't see herself doing anything else. "The work is extremely rewarding," she says, "and for her there's no other job."

---

* Servant or person at the bottom of the social order.

But after 13 years, nothing surprises her anymore. These days, in the higher courts, she says, the stresses are different because the stakes are so high. There is media presence and everyone is watching. She is less busy, but never has an empty desk, with lots of backlog cases that keep her awake at night. In each province, the Offices of the Directors of Public Prosecutions review, among other cases, all those involving murder, and all cases where police officers are accused.

> I have at least 50 cases on my desk right now, some of which consist of maybe 20 ring binders a case. Boxes and boxes of ring binders. Environmental cases have really big files with a lot of expert witnesses involved. Almost every day I'll come across something that requires research before I can make an informed decision.

When asked whether she would ever like to be a criminal defense attorney, she responded:

> Absolutely not! Even though a prosecutor deals with a small component of the law, being the criminal law, if I look at what defense attorneys have to do for a living … I know I can go to bed at night with a clear conscience from trying to help people in society. For me, there's no other job.

At the moment, she says, some defense attorneys are clawing at the door to get into state practice especially since working circumstances in the state system have improved substantially:

> When you're in the lower courts and inundated with work and no light at the end of the tunnel, that's where you see prosecutors leaving to become attorneys. But being a private attorney is not easy. You have to be available for your clients 24/7. You have to go to prison and bail out clients. For me there's no temptation to go private and that's true for 99% of my colleagues. We're happy doing what we're doing. It's certainly not greener on the other side. Our work circumstances are very good. We can't complain.

For younger prosecutors, she can understand the lure of private practice:

> In the lower courts there are so many cases and you go through them like a sausage machine. I am presently in a managerial role, working with 38 other advocates in our directorate, I have more time to consult with witnesses or embark on an undercover operation. We work with more experienced police officers; I can plan and build a case. Maybe I have three months to prepare. In a lower court you're just inundated and you can't focus sufficiently on witnesses or victims. A district court prosecutor receives the court roll the day

before and must make time to consult with witnesses on the same day that they have to testify—and they must do this whilst running the court roll without losing too many court hours. It's quite a juggling act at times.

Philosophy of Legal Advocacy

Advocacy means representing the interests of a client in the best manner possible, an art in which lawyers are trained. South Africa has a unique accusatorial system, opposed to an inquisitorial system, as for example in Germany. In the German legal system, judges are actively involved in investigating the facts of the case, whereas in an adversarial system, the role of the judge is primarily that of an impartial referee between the prosecutor and accused. "Your case might not be too strong," says Advocate Ferreira, "but when you get the opportunity to cross-examine the accused, you can quite easily use his or her own version and other objective evidence to show the person is lying. It's a harsh but effective justice system."

Advocate Ferreira added that, guided by the Constitution (1996), the NPA's vision is to achieve justice in society, so people can live in freedom and security.

> Integrity is paramount to a prosecutor, and it's their task to ensure that justice is done and seen to be done: All decisions must be made keeping in mind fairness and reasonableness. One must never become a persecutor instead of a prosecutor. My mentor taught me never to look at a case in the light of "winning" or "losing." Truth and justice must prevail at all costs. Integrity, accountability, service excellence, professionalism, and credibility are the values of the NPA and are values we live by every day. It's our duty to place all relevant facts on record so a presiding officer can come to a just decision, whether those facts are in favor of your case or not.

Working as a prosecutor in Cape Town's juvenile courts taught Advocate Ferreira the importance of empathy. Many of the youngsters, she found, were committing crime out of need, which required her to put on a different cap:

> There's a huge difference between someone who stole bread because he was hungry and someone who stole a rhino horn to make a lot of money. I've seen such dire poverty and it requires a sense of humanity rather than a need to prosecute. When clients are too poor to afford a lawyer, you have to be very careful to see true justice done. It's easy to become blasé in the lower courts when you're just milling through cases. Not all prosecutors have the same levels of empathy and patience.

Advocate Ferreira observed that atmosphere and processes in the lower courts were alienating as officials are overloaded and lack empathy:

> From the beginning, I promised myself I would treat every single person with respect. And it worked in my favor and helped me advance in my profession. When you're rude, people talk and it gets out. If you care for people it makes a big difference to procedure. Officials like having you in their court and witnesses don't feel intimidated.

Problems and Successes Experienced

> My first organized crime case was in 2004 and I'm quite proud of it. I was the first person to request the National Director's authorization to institute a racketeering prosecution, which was related to abalone in Ventersburg. I noticed certain patterns from the cell phone records and pulled out the newly promulgated Organized Crime Act, and learned about it. From that case I began working on organized crime, gaining information and expertise.

That knowledge led to work on gang-related matters because of obvious connections. High-profile cases she was involved in included a satanic gang called the Triple Sixes (State v. *Lehasa*, 2013), and the Born To Kill gangsters, whose leader she put in prison for 23 years. Organized crime is particularly implicated in the illegal wildlife trade, which is one of the top four illicit economies in the world. It is a huge problem in South Africa, which has abundant plant, animal and avian diversity, good transport and banking systems, and a criminal justice system barely managing to cope with high levels of general crime.

After apartheid ended in 1994, international syndicates from Russia, Italy, Colombia, Nigeria, and China, among others, entered the country in search of opportunities. This is a common phenomenon in unstable or transitioning economies where new administrations are still reorganizing and power structures are in flux. The rise of the Russian mafia is an example of this. Advocate Ferreira says:

> South Africa is a haven for syndicates. Everyone's focusing on rhino poaching, but there's so much going on that we don't know about, or haven't had time to focus on—like reptiles and birds. Right now the Chinese 14K gang are (sic) well entrenched in our country in this trade, and I'm working with informers to get a better picture of how they operate. The 14K here appear[s] to have held hands with the Russian and Bulgarian mafias, and deal in drugs, rhino horns, human trafficking and weapons.
>
> Our Constitution has, ironically, given criminals a lot of rights. I'm not against it of course—we need a Bill of Rights—but it's being used against us in courts of law. One criminal kingpin, who is wanted in his home country

for tax fraud and was tried in South Africa for attempted murder, told a policeman he specifically chose South Africa when he had to flee his country because of our Bill of Rights. He said he looked at various countries and saw that, in a court, our constitution was more in his favor than in any other country.

The Constitution also poses problems for policing and many cases are being lost over accusations of brutality during arrest. Advocate Ferreira cites a case in Harrismith where the police tactical response team arrested five gang members on double murder and rape charges following a housebreaking, in the course of which a kettle, a cellular phone, and a hotplate stove were stolen. Two of the gang members were juveniles, aged 16 years, and the oldest gang member was 19 years of age. In the course of the arrest, one gang member's arm was broken. He admitted complicity to the murder in a statement, but in court he withdrew it, claiming his arm was broken while being coerced to confess. A time-consuming trial-within-a-trial ensued to decide if his rights were infringed in terms of the Constitution.

The case was particularly evocative for Advocate Ferreira as the two victims, a mother and her daughter, were exactly the same age as she and her own daughter at that time. The victims' bodies were discovered by the woman who was their mother and grandmother, devastating her and robbing her of her will to live. The loss of this minor child at 11 years of age was particularly tragic for her father, as all of his other children were deceased. Ultimately, a conviction was secured against three of the offenders, and a life imprisonment sentence imposed on the adult offender (*State v. Nhlapo and two others*, 2015). Advocate Ferreira commented that no sentence imposed could ever return the deceased to the loved one and family members left behind.

Given the police reputation for heavy-handedness, she says an accused person very often says they were beaten up. She noted that if she wanted to take a case to trial and saw evidence of police brutality during the arrest that would change her decision.

We also have quite a few cases that go on appeal because the accused claims they didn't have a fair trial—for instance, where the judge or magistrate comes down into the arena and doesn't give the accused a proper chance to cross-examine the witness or the court didn't assist the accused to affect their proper rights within the trial. But rights are mostly infringed in the pretrial process. It's also often a problem that the police don't know their own rights, or what their powers are. Some of them simply don't know the law too well. Such lack of knowledge often shoots us in the foot. And it's also not a secret that too many of our police officers are easily corruptible.

A simple solution to the problem of policing could be to film arrests with a head-mounted camera:

> It's not that costly, and this way, officers would cover themselves. It's a little bit of technology that would have a big outcome. There are cops in whose hands I'd put my life—I know they would never assault someone they're interviewing. But they still get accused of that. It's demoralizing for them.

Little Things That Would Make a Big Difference

Higher courts run more smoothly than lower courts, but the biggest challenge in South Africa is the amount of work. Advocate Ferreira says she would like to deal with just environmental crime, but it's not possible as she has to "do all and sundry in between." This cuts down on research time of specialist prosecutors who are called on to fill gaps.

> I would love to be able to focus on an area. Every time we get a new offense, you have to do research and it takes time. The problem is a lack of resources. There are only about 2,000–3,000 prosecutors in the whole country—very few to deal with the levels of crime we have here. You can count the number of environmental prosecutors in this country on one hand, but none of us are lucky enough to deal exclusively with our specialty.
>
> For a start, in lower courts, we should have two prosecutors per session. If you're alone in a court, you have to run around, consult and manage the court. With two prosecutors you could utilize court time so much better if one could run the court and the other prepare the next case.

Main Interest and Focus

In terms of conservation (if not until recently in law), environmental crime is hundreds of years old in South Africa. Starting from European colonization in the seventeenth century, huge herds of game that roamed the country were decimated by hunters who shot for pleasure (the term "game" is indicative). Later, countless elephants were killed for their ivory and predators for their skins, leading to the elimination of species in many areas of their natural habitat. The famous Kruger National Park was originally preserved as a resource area for hunters. When the park was proclaimed in 1903, most of the lions were shot as they were said to be a threat to game animals.

The most prominent environmental issues in the first three centuries of South African law dealt with control of drinking water, pollution, and conservation of wild animals. In the mid-twentieth century, a number of new environmental laws were passed, but issues were generally dealt with in an ad hoc manner, and were not very effective. A shift came after the democratic elections in 1994. Section 24 of the new Constitution (1996) imposed a duty on the State to protect the environment and "to secure ecologically sustainable development and use of natural resources while promoting justifiable economic and social development." The full clause reads:

Everyone has the right—

1. to an environment that is not harmful to their health or well-being; and
2. to have the environment protected, for the benefit of present and future generations, through reasonable legislative and other measures that—
   a. prevent pollution and ecological degradation;
   b. promote conservation; and
   c. secure ecologically sustainable development and use of natural resources while promoting justifiable economic and social development.

Embedding these rights in the Constitution means that contraventions of environmental laws may also be infringements of fundamental Constitutional rights and are consequently treated more seriously by the courts. These clauses were bolstered in 1998 through the promulgation of the National Environmental Act (NEMA, 1998). This legislation defines "environment" as the surroundings within which humans exist. The definition includes the built environment and intangible aspects such as aesthetic and cultural properties. This definition is now used in many other environmental laws including the Air Quality Act (2004), the Integrated Coastal Management Act (2008), and the Waste Act (2008).

In the late 1990s, South Africa also ratified several international conventions and treaties relating to the environment. These were incorporated into South African law in three ways: by incorporation of the provisions of the treaty into an Act of Parliament, by including the treaty as a schedule of a statute, and by bringing the treaty into effect by proclamation in the *Government Gazette*.

As can be imagined, Section 24 definitions in the Constitution have come under intense scrutiny and contested interpretation. An example is the term "well-being." Its ambit, it has been argued, is potentially limitless and relative to the nature and personality of the person seeking to assert this right. The arguments on this point continue.

In preventing pollution and ecological degradation, it has been asked what degree of pollution should be tolerated? Is what holds true in a First World country applicable to a developing country like South Africa? A hotly contested term is "sustainable development," a fundamental building block around which environmental legal norms have been fashioned. It has stimulated fierce argument within both legal and NGO circles. Although some entrepreneurs—for example, rhino farmers—have argued for sustainability in financial terms only, opposing arguments have been that pure economic principles cannot, in an unbridled fashion, determine whether a development is acceptable. Development that may be regarded as economically and financially sound, it is argued by environmental activists, has to be balanced by its environmental impact. A key issue is the principle of intergenerational equity and sustainable resource use over time. How do you arrive at an integrated management of the environment, sustainable development and address socioeconomic concerns in the present that will have an impact in the future? More radical arguments have been to point out that sustainability is adjudged solely from a human perspective, and that it is unlikely that a species, such as lion, elephant, and rhino, would deem hunting quotas acceptable in terms of their rights.

Reasons for administrative decision making in the environmental context have also been under the spotlight, and were highlighted in a case *Minister of Environmental Affairs and Tourism v. Phambili Fisheries* (2003). The first respondent, a fishing company, feeling aggrieved by the inadequacy of the fishing quota it was allocated, contended that inadequate reasons had been given regarding the historical baseline used to allocate current quotas. The court dismissed the argument, quoting, interestingly, from *Ansett Transport Industries (Operations) Pty Ltd v. Wraith* (1983), an Australian decision in which it was held:

> [The Australian] Judicial Review Act requires the decision maker to explain his decision in a way that will enable a person aggrieved to say, in effect: "Even though I may not agree with it, I now understand why the decision went against me. I am now in a position to decide whether that decision has involved an unwarranted finding of fact, or an error of law, which is worth challenging." This requires that the decision maker should set out his understanding of the relevant law, any findings a fact on which his conclusions depend (especially if those facts have been in dispute), and the reasoning processes that led him to those conclusions. He should do so in clear and unambiguous language, not in vague generalities or the formal language of legislation.

The NEMA framework also requires State officials to become proactive in their protection of the environment through the appointment of Environmental Management Inspectors whose specific mandate is to monitor and enforce compliance with environmental laws and to investigate potential offenses and breaches of them.

For inspectors, the legal system, police, and prosecutors, the rhino poaching crisis has been a severe testing ground. In the 1970s, the demand for ivory and rhino horn in the East shifted to Africa as numbers of these animals fell in Asia, forcing suppliers to look further afield. Environmentalists, alarmed by increased poaching, convinced the Convention on International Trade in

Endangered Species (1973) to list these animals as endangered, forbidding international trade in products derived from them.

Poaching dropped dramatically, but high prices and huge demand from China and Vietnam caused it to rise again. In 2008, around 80 rhinos were poached in South Africa, but by 2014 the number has risen to 1,215, and extinction of the species in the wild became a possibility. Asian demand was also putting strain on elephants. In Africa, in 2013, it was estimated that five elephants were being killed by poachers every hour (Vira & Ewing, 2014). These issues are of particular concern to Advocate Ferreira.

> Environmental crime is a huge problem here, and it involves so many fields and areas. We're losing rhinos at a shocking rate. It's totally unsustainable. There's also illegal hunting, or should I say "illegalities in legitimate hunting" around things like licensing and quotas.
>
> I would like to see a minimum sentence attached to environmental crimes. It would make the cost of crime clear. The law as it stands only prescribes a maximum sentence. But for a crime like rhino poaching we need a minimum. It's a much better way to put off criminals. Now they know if they have money they just pay a fine and walk away. If there was a minimum sentence there'd be no arguments and no option of a fine.
>
> Although rhino poaching is a big issue in South Africa right now, there are not many rhinos in the province under my jurisdiction. So I also deal with a lot of issues around water pollution and things like medical waste. I'm awaiting judgment in a big water pollution case that's important to me because it will be against eight municipal managers in charge of the water works but who neglected their jobs and endangered the public.

Environmental crime is posing particular problems for the courts because South Africa has 11 official languages and the accused are entitled to conduct their defense in their home language. This puts pressure on the courts to locate reliable translators. In addition, poaching and trafficking is increasingly being carried out by foreigners such as Chinese and Mozambicans. "There are so many Chinese dialects," she says, "and we only have a single Chinese interpreter in my province. Does she know the right dialect? Can we trust her?"

Another issue is how environmental crime is defined. If it were deemed a serious crime, bail could be refused. Under the present definition, however, bail is almost a matter of course. "If you're from Mozambique and you're caught poaching," says Advocate Ferreira, "you pay bail and we never see you again. The case cannot be finalized. We really need to renovate the bail laws—though of course it would overcrowd the prisons."

Pollution cases, she says, are much harder to deal with because, instead of an accused standing, you are faced with top lawyers hired by corporations. Their job is to frustrate the system on behalf of their clients:

You have to be sharp or they'll walk all over you. But if you have 50 files on your desk it's hard to focus on a big case. Ideally you want to sit with that case alone for a year and see it through from start to finish. But we don't have that sort of luxury. Every day a new crisis pops up. We have to prioritize.

Theory and Practice

On the question of the relationship between theory and practice, Advocate Ferreira said:

> Particularly in environmental law you really have to know what you're talking about. Theory is super important. The more I studied, the easier it became in court. The more you empower yourself with the letter of the law, the easier your job becomes. After doing a master's, I felt much more confident before the bench. It made a big difference in my life. In environmental matters, especially, you really have to stay up to speed because it changes every week. New regulations come up.
>
> I remember the first year as prosecutor it was harsh. I think I cried every day. You feel so stupid. Those days there wasn't training. They just popped you into a court and said: "There you go." These days we put prosecutors through a theoretical program that lasts six months. The NPA also requires you to go on a Justice College course each year. This way you strengthen your skill in different fields. There's a beginner-prosecutors course, trial advocacy and an advanced prosecutors' course. The guys who teach it really know their subjects. It's empowering. Without a theoretical understanding it's hard times in court. Especially when you're a new prosecutor dealing with more advanced lawyers—older guys with experience and strong on their legal principles. Then you're a fish out of water.

Transnational Relations

Environmental and organized crimes know no borders. For this reason, transnational connections are an essential component of judicial functioning. South African prosecutors have been trained in environmental law by both the United States and British Departments of Justice. "They've been focusing on it for much longer than we have," says Advocate Ferreira. "But in a country with such a shortage of skills, training means opportunity, of the initial 18 prosecutors that were trained, only two of us remain in the NPA. The rest went across to the private sector or have since retired. That's a problem."

An area of transnational cooperation becoming increasingly important is the connection between terrorism and poaching. In South Africa, this began during the bush war in the 1980s between the SA Defense Force and Angolan troops. Much of the action was in wilderness areas and national parks. Widespread elephant poaching took place, and ivory was sold to secure arms in a conflict that lasted for more than a decade (Vira & Ewing,

2014). Today, in many parts of Africa, forces attempting to destabilize governments and seize power have found ready markets for the continent's raw materials and wildlife. "Terrorists are definitely still getting money through poaching," says Advocate Ferreira. "Ivory is a high value commodity that you can purchase with a single bullet and sell for weapons."

General Assessments

Advocate Ferreira noted that:

> In a country that acknowledges it has a big crime problem, the justice system is, in general, under-resourced. Take police salaries. They're really low. I'm not surprised if officers are corruptible. In small towns you can get a cop to look in the other direction for a quart of beer. Because of this, naturally, the police get a bad reputation and the public don't report crime to them. Corruption hits the poor hardest because they can't pay when bribes are asked, and in many cases they just give up hope in the justice system. They don't see the value of going all the way to the police station and then being treated with disrespect. We need an overhaul of policing ethics.

The massive adjustments needed to transform judicial processes from a race-based to rights-based system in South Africa have required a major relearning process at all levels of governance and control. Advocate Ferreira acknowledges that this needs time for officials to adjust, but says new legislation is taking too long to take effect. The Organized Crime Act was promulgated in 1999 but the first case was only in 2004. There have been similar rollout problems with the Child Justice Act (2008) and Child Protection Act (2005).

> It takes quite a few years for an Act to get traction, but we really need key legislation up and running by now. So the problems are not with promulgation but with implementation. For instance legal training around POCA legislation only started 10 years after the law was promulgated. It's all very well to promulgate wonderful laws, but if you don't give proper training, you're going to get lost between the writer and the implementer.

Advocate Ferreira identified a number of other problems that impair the smooth running of the justice system:

"There are certain things that would make our lives easier," she says:

> We need to arm prosecutors with more electronic equipment. It would work wonders. For example, each court needs to have a laptop computer with all the Acts and Statutes accessible at your fingertips. You can't carry all those legal books to court. We also need to get dockets off of paper and into an electronic system so they don't get lost or stolen. These are simple things but they're not happening.

Video-conferencing between prisons and courts is in the process of being implemented. Advocate Ferreira noted that it will speed things up, make trucking to and from courts unnecessary and provide an instant record. This would also serve to reduce escapes by prisoners from court.

Prison crowding is another concern mentioned by Advocate Ferreira:

> We're filling jails with petty offenders. Something like cannabis shouldn't land you in prison. Then there's the guy who stole bread but he can't be released because he doesn't have a fixed address. So these people sit in prison. But a syndicate of car thieves can afford to bring a fancy lawyer to court and get bail. And if they don't secure bail, they take it on appeal and the judge gives bail.

Her general assessment was that:

> We have good laws in place. But that doesn't mean it's all working well. In fact I am seeing systems breakdown. Last week I was in court and we couldn't continue because of electricity load shedding—Eskom turned off the lights! That's not a failure of legal procedure but a breakdown of the systems required for justice to function.

Conclusion

South Africa has a high crime rate and a judicial system under severe strain. Its per capita murder and assault statistics are among the highest in the world and steadily rising. But because the structural heritage of apartheid cannot be swept aside overnight, most crime is confined to racial ghettos and hits the news only when it breaks into middle-class suburbs or city centers. Despite more than two decades of democracy, there are still huge deficits regarding education, health care, and the economy.

Advocate Ferreira says:

> The root of the problem in our country is socioeconomic. In a sense we're over-legislated, under-resourced and dealing with widespread poverty. The average person doesn't know anything about all the laws and regulations and we have to explain them to people before we can get on with a case. So many people are just struggling to get by. As prosecutors, we must never forget this.

Glossary

14K: organized triad crime gang based in Hong Kong and mainland China that engages in illegal gambling, human trafficking, drug trafficking, counterfeiting, weapons trafficking, prostitution, kidnapping, money laundering, loan sharking, vehicle trafficking, extortion, robbery, and murder.

Constitution of the Republic of South Africa: the supreme law of South Africa. It provides the legal foundation for the existence of the Republic, sets out the rights and duties of its citizens, and defines the structure of the government. It was drawn up by the Parliament elected in 1994 in the first nonracial elections. It was promulgated by President Nelson Mandela on December 10, 1996, and came into effect on February 4, 1997.

Convention on International Trade in Endangered Species of Wild Fauna and Flora: a multilateral treaty to protect endangered plants and animals. It was drafted as a result of a resolution adopted in 1963 at a meeting of members of the International Union for Conservation of Nature. The Convention entered into force on July 1, 1975. Its aim is to ensure that international trade in specimens of wild animals and plants does not threaten the survival of the species in the wild and it accords varying degrees of protection.

Director of Public Prosecutions: the office or official charged with the prosecution of criminal offenses in several criminal jurisdictions both in South Africa and around the world. The title is used mainly in jurisdictions that are or have been members of the Commonwealth.

Free State Province: one of South Africa's nine provinces. Its capital is Bloemfontein, which is also South Africa's judicial capital.

Kruger National Park: a large game preserve on the northeast border of South Africa with an area of approximately 20,000 km^2 that contains more than 10,000 elephants and more than 90% of the world population of Black and White rhinos. In recent years, as many as 500 rhinos per year have been poached for rhino horns.

National Prosecuting Authority (NPA): this agency was created under the Constitution of the Republic of South Africa (Act No. 108 of 1996) and is governed by the National Prosecuting Authority Act (Act No. 32 of 1998). The Constitution, read with this Act, provides the NPA with the power to institute criminal proceedings on behalf of the State, to carry out any necessary functions incidental to institution of criminal proceedings, and to discontinue criminal proceedings. It is accountable to the Minister of Justice and Correctional Services.

Prevention of Organized Crime Act (No. 121 of 1998) (POCA): this legislation introduced measures to allow South African prosecutors to combat organized crime, money laundering, and gang activity. It also prohibits certain types of racketeering activities. It abolished money laundering and established an obligation for people to report it.

Sri Lanka

12

SHANTI NANDANA WIJESINGHE
MENAKA LECAMWASAM

Contents

The Criminal Justice Process of Sri Lanka

The Sri Lankan legal system is a confluence of Roman–Dutch law, English Law, and the personal and territorial laws operative in the country, namely Kandyan Law, Tesawalamai Law, and the Muslim Law. Personal laws generally operate in the spheres of property rights, matrimonial matters, and inheritance. Since its independence in 1948, Sri Lanka's legal system has evolved quite freely, responding to contemporary issues and challenges and learning from other jurisdictions.

Sri Lanka's system of administration of justice is based primarily on the British judicial system modified to suit the country's needs. After independence from the British Empire, the judicial system was reformed to a greater degree by the First Republican Constitution of 1972, the Administration of Justice Law of 1973, and later by the 1978 Second Republican Constitution. The constitution provides that the judicial power of the people of Sri Lanka shall be exercised by parliament through courts, tribunals, and institutions created and established, or recognized by the constitution or created and established by law.

The Hierarchy of Courts

Article 105(1) of the constitution stipulates that the institutions for the administration of justice shall be the Supreme Court of Sri Lanka, the Court of Appeal of Sri Lanka, the High Court of Sri Lanka, and such other courts of first instance created by parliament.

Section 2 of the Judicature Act No.2 of 1978 enumerates the courts of first instance for the administration of justice as the High Court of Sri Lanka, the District Courts, the Family Courts, the Magistrates Courts, and the Primary Courts. The 13th Amendment to the Constitution in 1987 introduced another court of significant importance, namely the High Court of the Provinces (Figure 12.1).

The Supreme Court

The Supreme Court is the highest and final superior court of record in the republic. Subject to the provisions of the constitution, the court exercises *inter alia* jurisdiction with regard to constitutional matters, original jurisdiction in applications challenging the alleged infringement or imminent infringement of fundamental rights, final appellate jurisdiction in both civil and criminal matters, consultative jurisdiction, jurisdiction in election petitions challenging the lawfulness of presidential elections, and jurisdiction in respect of the breach of the privileges. The court also regulates the entry of

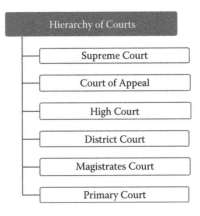

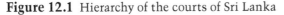

Figure 12.1 Hierarchy of the courts of Sri Lanka

persons to the bar as attorneys-at-law and possesses disciplinary control over all attorneys.

The Court of Appeal

As the second highest and final superior court of record, the Court of Appeal exercises appellate jurisdiction over the courts of first instance and tribunals. It also has the powers to impose punishment for contempt of court and most importantly exercises writ jurisdiction by issuing writs in the nature of *Certiorari*, *Procedendo*, *Mandamus*, and *Quo warranto*.

High Court

The High Court of the Provinces is the highest court of first instance and exercises both civil and criminal jurisdiction in addition to exercising appellate and revisionary jurisdiction in respect of certain lower courts and tribunals.

The High Court of Civil Appeal, which is a division of the High Court of the Provinces, was established through the High Court of the Provinces (Special Provisions) Amendment Act No. 54 of 2006 to expedite civil appeals emanating from the District Courts. This court has also been conferred with jurisdiction to take cognizance of matters over which indictments are filed by the Attorney-General and the Commission to Investigate Allegations of Bribery or Corruption.

The Commercial High Court, which is yet another manifestation of the High Court of the Provinces, has jurisdiction over disputes involving commercial transactions beyond a certain monetary value, as well as jurisdiction over the matters arising in terms of the Intellectual Property Act No. 36 of 2003 and the Companies Act No. 07 of 2007.

District Court

The District Court is the principal civil court of first instance. It has jurisdiction over all civil matters not expressly assigned to the Primary Court or the Magistrates Court, including disputes relating to land and other property, recovery of debts in excess of a particular monetary value, claims for compensation in excess of a particular monetary value for injuries suffered due to negligence and any other delict, and matrimonial disputes.

Magistrates Court

The jurisdiction of the Magistrates Court is primarily of two types: summary procedure and nonsummary procedure. In summary procedure, the Magistrates Court tries and determines cases arising within its jurisdiction in respect of all offenses and matters assigned to it under the Code of Criminal Procedure Act No. 15 of 1979 or any other law. In the absence of any special procedure being prescribed by law, summary trial in the Magistrates Court follows the procedure set out in Chapter 17 of the Code of Criminal Procedure Act. In the nonsummary procedure, the Magistrate's Court is required to conduct a preliminary inquiry in order to ascertain whether there is sufficient evidence to commit the accused to stand trial in the High Court on indictment. Nonsummary proceedings are generally conducted in cases of murder, attempted murder, and rape.

Primary Court

The Primary Court is the lowest court of first instance. Subject to the monetary bar of One Thousand Five Hundred Rupees (Rs. 1,500/=), the Primary Court has limited jurisdiction with regard to criminal and civil matters and powers to impose sentences of imprisonment and of fines.

The Attorney-General

The Attorney-General is the chief legal advisor to the state, and, in that capacity, advises the Head of State, cabinet ministers, government ministries and departments, statutory boards, and public corporations on all legal issues. The Attorney-General is also empowered to institute criminal proceedings in the High Court by forwarding indictments against persons accused of serious criminal offenses. His officers conduct criminal prosecutions, and appear on behalf of state agencies and public servants. The Attorney-General is a mandatory party to all fundamental rights applications. Article 126 of the Constitution of Sri Lanka provides that when there is a violation or imminent violation of a fundamental right through executive or administrative action, the affected party may invoke the fundamental rights jurisdiction of the Supreme Court. As the state is the alleged violator of rights, the Attorney-General, as the legal representative of the state, is required to be made a party to the action.

Administrative Tribunals

In addition to the hierarchy of courts enumerated above, the legal system in Sri Lanka includes several administrative tribunals performing functions of a quasi-judicial nature. Labor Tribunals, provided for by the Industrial Disputes (Amendment) Act No. 62 of 1957, seek to provide a remedy to a workman aggrieved by his termination of employment by recourse to the tribunal. Further instances of such bodies are the Rent Board of Review established pursuant to Section 40 of the Rent Act No. 07 of 1972, Land Acquisition Board of Review established in terms of Section 19 of the Land Acquisition Act No. 09 of 1950, and Boards of Quazis appointed pursuant to the provisions contained in the Marriage & Divorce (Muslim) Act No. 13 of 1951 to entertain matters in relation to marriage and divorce within the Muslim community. Appeals and, in some instances, applications for revision lie to appellate courts from these bodies.

Alternative Dispute Resolution (ADR)

Apart from the judicial and quasi-judicial fora for dispute resolution, there are several ADR mechanisms available in Sri Lanka. The Mediation Boards Act No. 72 of 1988 established mediation boards in various geographic areas within the country, which are empowered to mediate on certain criminal and civil matters. The boards entertain any dispute in relation to movable or immovable property, debt, damage, or demand the value of which does not exceed Rs.500,000 as provided for by a 2016 amendment to the said Act. No court of first instance could entertain any action in relation to a dispute within the said monetary bar without a certificate of nonsettlement issued by a mediation board when it fails to bring about an amicable settlement.

The Arbitration Act No. 11 of 1995 provides for the resolution of both domestic and international commercial disputes through arbitration. The law was enacted to give effect to Sri Lanka's international obligations incurred under the New York Convention on the Recognition and Enforcement of Foreign Arbitral Awards of 1958. In terms of the Act, the jurisdiction of any court of law cannot be invoked by parties to an arbitration agreement, unless arbitration proceedings have failed or parties only request interim orders pending arbitration proceedings.

Yasantha Kodagoda, President's Counsel, Additional Solicitor General, Attorney-General's Department, Colombo

Introduction

Mr. Yasantha Kodagoda, President's Counsel, is an outstanding prosecutor in Sri Lanka. Having taken silk in March 2015, he currently serves as an Additional Solicitor General of the Attorney-General's Department of Sri Lanka. Amid his myriad professional commitments, for purposes of this chapter, Mr. Kodagoda generously spent a morning with us one Friday that would otherwise have been a relatively stress-free day for him. The course of our discussion was interrupted many times by people who sought his counsel on various issues, the occasional respite from which gave us glimpses into a personality that had many interesting facets.

This chapter maps Mr. Kodagoda's career as a prosecutor, tracing the time spanning a few decades from a junior State Counsel to an Additional Solicitor General admitted recently to the Inner Bar of the Supreme Court of Sri Lanka. It also contains an overview of his supplementary professional assignments bearing special significance, including his involvement in proceedings of landmark judicial decisions in the history of the Sri Lankan legal system. Through his participation in many national and international endeavors in the sphere of criminal law and counter-terrorism activities, as well as representing Sri Lanka before numerous UN bodies, Mr. Kodagoda has put his indelible stamp on the political and legal course of the country. Counting among his many strengths is the distinction of being a prolific lecturer, a successful trainer, and an effective communicator. His vision for advanced legal education in Sri Lanka equipped to produce intelligent, capable, insightful, and ethical practitioners and judicial officers is enlightening.

Career

Mr. Yasantha Kodagoda, PC, was born in Colombo, Sri Lanka, in 1965, and attended Ananda College, Colombo, for his primary and secondary education. He had begun his secondary education with the intention of joining the medical profession. However, as fate would have it, he missed his opportunity to join a state-sponsored medical college. His father, Professor Nandadasa Kodagoda, a brilliant forensic medical specialist cum pathologist, did not have the financial means to invest in a foreign medical education for his son. Young Kodagoda did not want to join the only private medical college in the country, as his late father and he were then ideologically opposed to the establishment of private medical colleges in the country. He is still proud of the fact that despite trying circumstances and irresistible temptation, he did not betray their ideology. After a brief foray into studying accountancy on the prompting of his brother, he decided to sit for the entrance examination to the Sri Lanka Law College when his father saw an advertisement calling for applications to the Law College in the paper and encouraged him to apply. Having no previous exposure to the legal profession, he saw it as making a Hobson's choice. He applied himself very seriously to the entrance examination, and received a Mahapola Scholarship for the duration of his studentship as a result of passing the entrance examination with a high aggregate of marks. By his own admission, he had not been an academically inclined student of the law. However, he had been active in student politics and had even contested and won election to the students' union of the Sri Lanka Law College.

After apprenticing in the chamber of a former Director of Public Prosecutions Ranjit Abeysuriya, PC, he joined the Bar in October 1988 and commenced practicing both civil and criminal law under B. J. Fernando, PC, and R.I. Obeyesekera, PC, respectively. In early 1989, Mr. Kodagoda left a gradually developing private Bar practice to join the Attorney-General's Department of Sri Lanka. He recalls that he would not have had the opportunity to join the Attorney-General's Department if not for the generosity of an otherwise dour-faced chief clerk at the department who accepted his application for the position of State Counsel 24 h past the deadline.

Mr. Kodagoda was appointed Acting State Counsel in February 1989 and rose through the ranks of the department to the position of a State Counsel in 1991, Senior State Counsel in 1999, Deputy Solicitor General in 2005, and Additional Solicitor General in January 2015. His entire career has been centered in the criminal division of the Attorney-General's Department. His primary role had been to conduct prosecutions in high courts and appear in criminal appeals in the Court of Appeal. Since 2000, he has supervised junior colleagues, and presently is in charge of both civil and criminal cases handled by State Counsel in the Central Province. In addition to his core-career positions, he was the Director of the Advanced Legal Studies Unit of the Sri Lanka Law College from 2005 to 2009 and the Director of the Institute of Advanced Legal Studies from 2009 to 2011. Mr. Kodagoda was a visiting lecturer for the Conflict Resolution Program of the Bandaranaike Centre for International Studies from 2004 to 2009. Currently he is a visiting lecturer in Security Law for the LLM program of the Kotalawala Defense University, and a visiting lecturer at the Postgraduate Institute of Medicine of the University of Colombo. Of course, quite frequently he is invited by the Police Department to deliver lectures on numerous topics. Since of late, he has been teaching investigation officers and lawyers of the Commission to Investigate Allegations of Bribery or Corruption.

He considers his extra-departmental activities to be as rewarding as those of his core-career and they afford him immeasurable stimulation. His duties as the Director of the Advanced Legal Studies Unit and the Institute of Advanced Legal Studies of the Sri Lanka Law College provided a positive experience from a productivity perspective. The unit was established to provide postgraduate study opportunities for attorneys who were interested in postgraduate studies but unable to pursue overseas educational options. Under Mr. Kodagoda's direction, the unit delivered well-tailored, effective study programs to attorneys-at-law in Sri Lanka in fields such as Banking and Insurance Laws and Corporate Law. He was instrumental in developing syllabi and other course material, as well as delivering lectures on subjects such as criminal justice, criminology, conflict resolution and dispute resolution methodologies, human rights, and international human rights mechanisms.

His appointment as the Project Coordinator of the Attorney-General's Department for the UNICEF-funded project for the expeditious processing and passage of cases of child abuse through the criminal justice system and for the prevention of secondary victimization of victims of child abuse gave him intrinsic satisfaction. The project was developed to expedite the various phases of the criminal justice process in relation to victims of child abuse and to prevent secondary victimization of such victims through their participation in the criminal justice system. He recounted with delight a recent development in which a civil society social service organization of repute had pledged to fund a special children's unit of the Police Department of Sri Lanka following a presentation he had made to the membership of the club.

In 1999, during the height of domestic terrorism and the ensuing armed conflict, Mr. Kodagoda was appointed head of the multidisciplinary team of forensic and criminal investigators appointed by the Attorney-General to investigate the alleged existence of a mass grave in Chemmani, in the Jaffna Peninsula. The government agreed to carry out a local investigation in accordance with internationally recognized standards with international observers at a time when international pressure was mounting on the state to engage international investigators to launch an investigation into the matter. Mr. Kodagoda undertook this onerous task that culminated in him making 48 visits to the Jaffna Peninsula in military aircraft, since there was no other viable access route to the peninsula. He recalls, how during that period, a couple of Sri Lanka Air Force aircraft crashed due to missile attacks launched by the Liberation Tigers of Tamil Eelam (LTTE), killing all passengers and crew. The team of investigators, including forensic pathologists, concluded its investigation to the satisfaction of the international community having exhumed 15 human skeletal remains from seven multiple graves. The original allegation that 400 persons had been murdered and surreptitiously buried was proven to be a gross exaggeration. He noted that the Chemmani assignment was one which none of his colleagues were willing to undertake, for quite understandable reasons.

The antiterrorism investigations that Mr. Kodagoda undertook are noteworthy as these investigations contributed significantly to the successful termination of the armed conflict in Sri Lanka in 2009. He had the opportunity to work with foreign law enforcement and intelligence agencies in the course of these investigations. Mr. Kodagoda was the head of the Sri Lankan team of investigators and prosecutors appointed by the government of Sri Lanka to extend cooperation to the Metropolitan Police of the United Kingdom and the Anti-terrorism Task Force of the Australian Federal Police. These investigations and corresponding prosecutions were related to LTTE fundraising and arms procurement activities in foreign countries. He was the chief witness in judicial proceedings instituted in the Supreme Court of Victoria in Australia against three LTTE activists, in which it became imperative to establish that the LTTE was an international terrorist organization, and not a liberation front, or a humanitarian organization. This case of *Commonwealth Director of Public Prosecutions v. Aruran Vinayagamoorthy, Sivarajah Yathavan, & Arumugam Rajaveen* (2010) was also the first instance and in his knowledge the only time in Sri Lanka where testimony was transmitted from Sri Lanka via a contemporaneous audiovisual link. Through their testimony, the witnesses were able to convince the Australian court that the LTTE was in fact a terrorist organization. However, as a result, Mr. Kodagoda became the only nonpolitical civilian on a list of assassination targets of the LTTE, and during this period had to avail himself of a detailed security outfit for the remaining duration of the armed conflict. Mr. Kodagoda further noted that the Commercial High Court in Sri Lanka has received evidence into the country via a contemporaneous audiovisual link from New York on a particular occasion. Unfortunately he could not recall the details of the particular case. He is confident that the recently introduced Assistance to and Protection of Victims of Crime and Witnesses Act No. 4 (2015) that provides for the transmission of audiovisual evidence from remote locations within the country could be a useful tool to introduce modern technology to the court room and thereby assist the speedy dispensation of justice.

Sharing his thoughts on what surprised him most during his career, he said that he is surprised that he is where he is today, tolerated by the state, holding office despite the fact that he is unorthodox and progressive in his thinking and approach to personal and professional life. He has taken many risks in his professional life by being an outspoken individual. He also commented that he had never dreamt, either while still a law student or even after joining the Attorney-General's Department, of being appointed a President's Counsel.

Mr. Kodagoda further professed that the unpredictability of the outcome of litigation is a constant source of amazement to him. He has lost many cases in which he was reasonably convinced that he could secure a conviction, but at the same time he had won other cases in which his chances of success originally seemed quite slim. He uses these anecdotes to advise possible litigants of the counter-productivity of litigation in certain instances, and the desirability of pursuing alternate means of dispute resolution.

While he had seriously contemplated returning to the private bar on certain occasions due to professional setbacks experienced through no fault of his own, he had persevered in his public office. He considers his professional life as rewarding and does not regret a single day of it. His mantra is to take the bad with the good, deliver to the best of his ability. He holds fidelity to duty in very high regard. He also believes in continuing to strive hard to achieve a high degree of professionalism and eminence.

Philosophy of Legal Advocacy

Role of the Prosecutor

From a generic global perspective, the role of a criminal prosecutor commences upon the completion of the conduct of investigations and primarily has three phases: (a) consideration of investigative material and the institution of criminal proceedings, (b) conducting the prosecution, and (c) defending the judgment during the appellate stage. These duties are quite distinct from those of a criminal investigator. Although the prosecutor bases his case on the investigative findings, he has a duty to detach himself from the investigation and view the investigative material objectively. He is situated in a unique position with access to material that the judge and defense counsel never see. He also exercises considerable discretion in the selection of witnesses, presentation of evidence, and maneuvering witnesses. This combination requires a prosecutor to act in an honest and forthright manner to facilitate a fair trial for the accused, resulting in conviction of only the guilty and in acquittal of the innocent. He regrets the trauma that ensues when perpetrators of crime are sometimes acquitted despite dedicated prosecutors. This can leave agonizing scars even on experienced prosecutors.

Against this backdrop, Mr. Kodagoda views the role of a prosecutor as quasi-judicial in nature. In his opinion, it is erroneous to expect a prosecutor to present evidence in court both against and in favor of the accused. Presenting evidence favorable to accused is the duty of the defense attorney. If the prosecutor is reasonably convinced of the veracity of the evidence favoring the prosecution, he ought to press hard toward securing a conviction. That requires the prosecutor to accurately assess the investigative material and to reassess the material and the unfolding evidence throughout the prosecution. At some stage, if a doubt arises as to the culpability of the accused, the prosecutor must appraise court of that fact and facilitate an acquittal. A prosecutor should not strive to win every case he handles. Overall, a prosecutor, unlike a defense counsel, is expected to strategize, assess, and exercise a great degree of enthusiasm throughout what can be protracted trials.

From a purely Sri Lankan perspective, the role of a prosecutor has some unique duties. He does not participate in criminal investigations, unlike, for example, a district attorney in the United States. He cannot direct investigations or even facets of investigations. He may, however, advise the police who conduct the investigation. This advice differs from that of a routine advisor. Whereas a routine advisor gives advice only when it is sought, a prosecutor of the Attorney-General's Department is empowered to advice investigators either when advice is sought by them or on his own volition, if and when he feels it necessary. Most unfortunately, by and large the Sri Lanka police system does not have the required degree of professionalism and sophistication to conduct complex criminal investigations of crimes perpetrated after careful and meticulous planning and organization, crimes in which direct eyewitness evidence is unavailable, in matters of corporate and other white-collar crime. Therefore, it is imperative that the investigators are advised by prosecutors on how investigations ought to be carried out. Mr. Kodagoda views this as a very important duty of state prosecutors in the contemporary era which assists in improving the quality of prosecutions.

He goes a step further and urges the Attorney-General's Department to reconsider some of its work ethics. An especially problematic aspect is the prohibition on consultations by prosecutors with lay witnesses, including victims, either before or during the trial. This affects the ability of a prosecutor to plan an effective prosecution because notes taken during the investigation may not fully reflect the entirety of what had happened, and without details of the prevailing circumstances at that time, changes cannot be detected when the matter comes up for the institution of proceedings and at the time of the trial. Mr. Kodagoda commented that some senior officials of the department are mooting the need to revisit the prohibition, and that discussions are underway to develop a set of guidelines to direct and ethically regulate consultations with victims of crime.

Mr. Kodagoda also discussed the importance of streamlining the solid but informal relationship the Attorney-General's Department has with the Police Department and other law enforcement agencies. He suggested formalizing the relationship with the police in all parts of the country in line with the recommendations proposed by the Lessons Learnt and Reconciliation Commission and facilitating regular meetings between prosecutors and police officers in order to ensure expeditious and accurate investigations into reported crimes.

On Victims of Crime

He said he certainly does not find any difficulty in empathizing with victims of crime. "We have sufficient empathy, in particular with more vulnerable victims of crime, such as victims of child abuse and sexual abuse." However, he is of the opinion that at times empathy alone is insufficient, particularly in the face of the distance between a prosecutor and the victim because of the prohibition on direct communication with the victim. The situation is further exacerbated by what he terms "the huge system overload" in the High Court that has led to inordinate delays in trials. This in turn has undermined the efficacy of the criminal justice response to crime.

To illustrate his point, he selected two case briefs randomly from the sizable stack of files he was working on, two appeals pending in the Court of Appeal and the Supreme Court, respectively. The matter before the Court of Appeal was one where the accused–appellant had been convicted and sentenced of having committed grave sexual abuse. The incident had taken place in September 2004. The accused had been indicted by the Attorney-General in December 2008, but the trial had not commenced until June 2011. The High Court delivered the judgment convicting the accused in November 2011, and at the time of the interview it was at the stage of criminal appeal against the conviction and sentence. He said that he could not predict when the hearing on the appeal would conclude. The second matter was an appeal recently concluded in the Supreme Court, about an incident that had taken place in August 2003. The charge was committing rape against an 11-year-old girl. The accused had been indicted in August 2006 and had pleaded guilty to the charge that had curbed a protracted trial. But he was not sentenced until October 2008. The Court of Appeal had affirmed the sentence at the stage of appeal and delivered its judgment in July 2012, from which another appeal had been referred to the Supreme Court. The Supreme Court delivered its judgment in March 2015. Mr. Kodagoda was frustrated by the delay in the dispensation of justice, especially within the criminal justice system of Sri Lanka, and believes that these delays could be addressed if judicial administrators took cognizance of the issue and persevered in providing additional courts to handle the workload.

Some Reflections on the Functioning of the Criminal Justice System

On the topic of how the criminal justice system ought to be functioning, Mr. Kodagoda noted that contrary to popular opinion, the entirety of the criminal justice system consists of a wider range of areas beyond litigation. To ensure an effective criminal justice response to crime, he suggested improvements in many arms of the system, including the police, the prosecutors, as well as the judiciary. He is of the view that the Sri Lankan police system ought to be more effective in crime prevention. Mr. Kodagoda suggests enhancing the capacity of police investigators, especially by adopting stringent criteria at the stage of recruitment including intelligence testing, which he opines ought to go a long way in remedying the situation. Further suggestions in this regard are investing in more methodical and in-depth training of police investigators, facilitating the development of specialties such as in criminal investigations and crime prevention soon after recruitment, and retaining trained police officers within their realms of competencies. Further, the issue of inadequate staffing across the board in most institutions ought to be addressed. He says that, as at present, there is a telling dearth of officers at the Attorney-General's Department. This pervasive problem has created considerable delay in criminal investigations, institution of criminal proceedings, and in completions of trials.

In terms of the priorities in the criminal justice system, Mr. Kodagoda focused on adopting a Japanese style mechanism for suspending the institution of proceedings in appropriate cases, if the accused tenders an unqualified admission of guilt and pledges to perform an act of restorative justice and undertakes to be of good behavior. He emphasized that an all important factor in this regard is protecting the best interests of the victim of crime and safeguard the interests of the society. He also advocates for mandatory pretrial conferences as a means to ensure timely commencement and conclusion of trials. In a pretrial conference, contentious portions of evidence versus portions that are not in dispute can be discussed and noncontentious areas of evidence admitted. Pretrial conferences facilitate time management and optimal use of in-court time. Further, considering the current mode of presenting testimony to court, Mr. Kodagoda strongly believes in reducing the amount of testimony presented in-person to court and favors evidence by way of affidavits, especially where the demeanor and deportment of witnesses, such as official witnesses and forensic experts, is not an issue. Accepting that in-person appearances of witnesses are necessary for cross-examination, he noted that affidavit evidence could be used in lieu of the examination-in-chief. He also thinks criminal trials ought to be heard on consecutive days similar to trials by jury.

Mr. Kodagoda considers alternative dispute resolution as the way forward for the Sri Lankan criminal justice system. He suggests expanding the schedule of offenses before the Magistrates Court where mediation for the possible resolution of the dispute between the victim and the offender is a condition precedent to the institution of criminal proceedings. Victim–offender mediation is one of the great successes of ADR in Sri Lanka. The country records a success rate of 65% in mediations of this kind, and it could be mobilized at the community level with minimum expense to the state.

With respect to sentencing policy, he rejected the trend to hand out suspended terms of imprisonment, citing the minimum deterrence impact and the frustration it brings to the victim as major drawbacks. While not an advocate of the death penalty, he strongly suggests not remitting a sentence for imprisonment for life to anything less than the entire life of the convicted prisoner. The famous Father Mathew Pieris double murder case, also known as the Vicarage Murders, in Sri Lanka, involved "an A grade premeditated murderer" who was out of prison as a free citizen after 12½years due to various remissions available in the prison system. He pointed out that the national conviction rate in the High Court was 75% (both due to pleading guilty to the indictment as well as after trial) that is a good conviction rate even by international standards. Sri Lankan courts and prosecutors are performing well despite the scarcity of resources. As a final point he noted that there is serious reason to revisit the penal sanctions management system in the country because penal sanctions do not seem to be achieving their objectives. He was dismayed by the prevalence of corruption within penal institutions.

Problems and Successes Experienced

Mr. Kodagoda is skeptical about the extent to which the objective of "rehabilitation" is achieved by sending a person to a penal institution. The objective of deterrence is achieved by publicizing sentences imposed on convicted accused and keeping the wrongdoers away from society. However, the environment of Sri Lanka's penitentiaries, where corruption is rampant and health facilities are abused by affluent prisoners, raises serious concerns as to whether the convicted are in fact rehabilitated and suffer due to punishments imposed.

Surprisingly, Mr. Kodagoda is a strong advocate of mandatory minimum sentences. Unlike the popular discourse on the subject that tends to disfavor mandatory minimum sentences over the exercise of judicial discretion, he advocated a closer examination of the reasons behind the legislature's decision to impose mandatory minimum sentences and narrow the discretion of the judiciary. He reasoned that this is necessary in the face of the blatant abuse of sentencing options, especially handing down suspended sentences and various available remissions. Mandatory minimum sentences reflect the gravity the legislature perceives of the commission of certain crimes, and courts are duty-bound to comply with the policy adopted by the legislature. He grappled with the question of whether the Sri Lankan criminal justice system in fact achieves its objective of convicting the guilty and acquitting the innocent through lawful and fair law enforcement and judicial processes, particularly when there is need to scrutinize whether courts expect prosecutors to prove cases with mathematical accuracy and the available penal sanctions are lawful, appropriate, and proportionate to the crime committed?

As a prosecutor, Mr. Kodagoda finds judicial ego very difficult to deal with. He mentioned with deadpan humor that it is a manifestation of a broader disease that affects certain judges called "judge-itis"! Most often the judges forget or are oblivious to the fact that they themselves are attorneys-at-law and that they are only called upon to perform a judicial function in their capacity by resolving disputes presented by litigants through the adjudicative method of dispute resolution. "Unlike in civil law countries, we do not breed a separate species called 'judges.' We breed only 'lawyers' who later on take the mantle of prosecutor, practicing lawyer, judge, etc." Mr. Kodagoda observed that many judges do not appreciate this fact and become blind to difficulties that lawyers encounter. Then again there are judges who join the judiciary when there is still a lot of advocacy left in them. In the ensuing years, they fail to appreciate the role of a judge in an adversarial system, within which the judge is required to act as a passive umpire. Judges should not enter into the arena of debate and advocacy, unless absolutely necessary to administer justice. The inability of counsel to respond to the bench on equal terms is frustrating to encounter on a daily basis. Similarly, he is frustrated when an impatient judge denies an opportunity to present the case on behalf of the state and a silent, hapless victim, or a client accused of committing an offense.

The capacity of judges to understand, appreciate, and assess complex legal issues, intricate facts, and possible ground situations has sometimes created problems. Such inability is often reflected in the poor quality of the judgments. Mr. Kodagoda hopes for the formulation and adoption of a recruitment process and conditions of employment, which will attract the cream of the bar to the judiciary. He recommends providing better emoluments, better work conditions, and making provision to continue the same salary that sitting judges receive during postretirement, in order to attract more capable individuals to the judiciary, and as a means of ensuring independence of the judiciary. Referring to some of the drawbacks of a judicial career in Sri Lanka, he points to the lack of appropriate and comfortable work conditions for judges in the provinces, frequent transfers, and career blocks in terms of delayed promotions. He recommends enhancements to the quality of the overall environment within which judges are called to perform their duties. He also strongly recommends, in the same vein as for investigators, intelligence testing at the time of recruitment, as in his opinion no amount of further training will remedy subpar intelligence. Of course, continuing legal education is a must for judicial officers. Mr. Kodagoda called for an "independent, capable and ethical judiciary." He stressed that the judiciary should be independent of not only the politico-executive but also from the possible influence from all quarters of society. They should be competent to handle complex questions of law and facts. Above all, they should adhere to an ethical lifestyle in both their official and personal lives.

Another problem he has experienced and which permeates the entire criminal justice system is the enormous backlog of cases littering the High Court. The inordinate amount of time spent on pre- and post-trial matters is a waste of valuable resources and energy. Mr. Kodagoda suggested appointing, on an interim basis, High Court Commissioners to flush out the backlog of cases, such as very old cases in which there was no prospect of a conviction because documents were missing, and witnesses were no longer alive. As he sees it, the existing infrastructure could unburden the overloaded system. Policymakers must spearhead such reform following careful and inclusive consultations among stakeholders. He pointed to the 1989 amendment to the Judicature Act of Sri Lanka that provided for the appointment of Court-Recorders and Court Masters to attend to pre- and post-trial matters in chambers so that time in court could be spent on trials and proper inquiries. This amendment was not operative due to other concerns. However, Mr. Kodagoda suggested that the same amendment could be modified to address certain concerns the scheme had previously given rise to and thereafter be implemented to address this ubiquitous situation.

Theory and Practice

On the topic of the correlation, if any, between legal theory and practice, Mr. Kodagoda was of the view that legal practice depends to a great extent on legal theory. Whether in chambers or in open court, the process is that of converting legal theory to practice. Therefore, legal theory does play an important role. As to the extent of this role in Sri Lankan courts, he said that the theoretical input of a practitioner is very minimal, either because they have not received a university education or they are not interested in learning the theoretical underpinnings and principles of the law. The system of legal education at the Sri Lanka Law College, which is the only body awarding professional qualifications to attorneys-at-law, does not enable an ordinary law student to properly learn the foundations and theoretical basis of various streams of law. Therefore, in the case of a routine practitioner these sorts of considerations are sadly minimal.

As a remedy, he advocated a scheme that moves away from the current practice in Sri Lanka of issuing an attorney a license to practice for life in all areas of the law. Emphasizing the importance of post-attorney legal education, he recommends the adoption of a scheme of points allocated for continuing professional development as a prerequisite to renew the license to practice. He also recommends the adoption of a licensing scheme, which recognizes specialization to practice in certain areas of the law. Continuing legal education will give practitioners an opportunity to engage in academic pursuits.

Mr. Kodagoda sees an unfortunate divide between legal academics and practitioners in Sri Lanka that needs to be bridged. A symbiotic relationship between legal academia and practitioners needs to be developed to remedy the situation. However, he questions whether, unlike in tertiary legal educational institutes in other countries, legal academics in Sri Lanka are sufficiently versed in the practicalities of the law to impart knowledge on those matters to their students? He is keen to see more legal academics spend time in courts, either as litigators or in organizations as advisors, in order for them to familiarize themselves with the practical aspects of the application of law. He recalled his time as a postgraduate student at University College London where he obtained his LLM in Public International Law, lectured to by Professor Philippe Sands, QC. While Professor Sands had been teaching law and policy relating to International Courts and Tribunals, he devoted his mornings to appear before the House of Lords on behalf of an intervening party presenting submissions on Augusto Pinochet's universal jurisdiction case. Mr. Kodagoda envisions a "fine blend between theory and practice" by Sri Lankan legal academics. He visualizes the engagement of academics in practice as an encouragement for their full time practicing counterparts to start using legal theory to make arguments in court. The one factor holding back collaboration between the two could be a protectionist mentality on both parts, as each is apprehensive of the other entering their domain. Taking an example from his teaching assignments, Mr. Kodagoda designed the Security Law course module for the LLM program at the Kotalawala Defense University of Sri Lanka, where he tried to achieve a fine blend between theory and its application, as well as the final practical elements needed in court.

Lamenting the fact that the recent jurisprudence in the country woefully lacks substance and fails to predicate reasoning on legal theory, Mr. Kodagoda suggests devising methods to get judges more interested and involved in legal theory, and to urge them to base their reasoning in legal theory that would enrich the jurisprudence of the country. The lack of theoretical underpinnings in judicial reasoning has severe repercussions for a legal system based on judicial precedent. It leads to chaotic judicial decisions and creates uncertainties in the law that ultimately dilutes the essence of the law within a country.

The heavy caseloads of legal practitioners usually do not allow them sufficient time to reflect and learn legal theory in a formal, systematic manner. Therefore, much of the research that goes into advocacy is ad hoc in nature and is dependent on the type of legal issues they encounter in arguing cases. However, Mr. Kodagoda emphasized the importance of in-depth research for legal practitioners. He is currently engaged in academic research on criminal justice responses in Sri Lanka to child abuse. The project involves analyzing 450 cases drawn from all 25 districts in Sri Lanka. At the time of the interview, he was in the process of collating the information gathered in the course of the research.

Transnational Relations

Being a prosecutor who has had vast exposure to and interactions with international elements, Mr. Kodagoda does not view transnational relations as harmful. On the contrary, his experiences were decidedly positive and led to considerable personal development. Since 1999, he had been representing the Government of Sri Lanka at multilateral levels at the UN Human Rights Commission that was subsequently replaced by the UN Human Rights Council, as well as the UN Working Group on Enforced Disappearances, and the UN Security Council's Working Group on Children in Armed Conflict. He has also engaged in bi-lateral negotiations on Human Rights and governance-related issues with western and European governments, both in their capitals and in Colombo. These opportunities had widened his horizons and had given him a keen appreciation of and hands-on experience with the linkages between human rights, criminal justice, law enforcement, national security, and international politics. Exposure to the theory, practice and politics of International Human Rights and International Humanitarian Law mechanisms and general foreign relations, international politics, and international criminal justice mechanisms, gave him the unique ability to devise nuanced approaches to his work in the field.

Commenting on the direct impact of these relations on Sri Lanka, he said that the concept of national sovereignty needs to be redefined, taking into consideration contemporary international politics and the prevailing world order. In the past six years, Sri Lanka seems to have misunderstood the ground realities of the international rule of law and the impact of international politics. A better understanding of the prevailing situation would have enabled Sri Lanka to move away from the situation it faced with the UN Human Rights Council that mandated an international investigation into matters preceding the final stages of the armed conflict in 2009. In a positive move, the present government is reassessing Sri Lanka's isolation from crucial international relations that the country may not have been able to withstand for long. He says that, Sri Lanka, while protecting its sovereignty and other national interests, must freely interact with other players in the international scene, of course while maintaining its policy of non-alignment. He does, however, caution the need not to swing the pendulum to the other end, and thereby expose Sri Lanka to exploitation and attack by certain harmful elements. Coincidentally, he appeared and argued for the Attorney-General in the case of *Nallaratnam Singarasa v. Attorney General* (2006) in which the Supreme Court questioned the constitutionality of Sri Lanka's accession to the 1st Optional Protocol of the International Covenant on Civil and Political Rights (ICCPR) in 1997. This judgment is under serious debate and was castigated by the human rights community within and outside Sri Lanka. He steadfastly maintains that the rationale contained in the judgment regarding the relationship between International Law and national or municipal law is sound, particularly in light of the context of Sri Lanka with a dualist legal regime.

His exposure to transnational relations Mr. Kodagoda believes would be of immense use in his newly assigned capacity as a member of the Presidential Task Force for the recovery of proceeds of crime located overseas. The task force is mandated to identify proceeds of corruption, fraud, money laundering, terrorist funding, and tax evasion, located outside the territory of Sri Lanka, to work with law enforcement and judicial authorities of those territories in which assets are located, to cause seizure and subsequent confiscation of the assets and work with those foreign authorities to ensure the value of those proceeds are returned to Sri Lanka to be vested in the general treasury. While thrilled by this turn of events, he understands it will be a herculean task and a long, drawn-out process. However, he is confident that the objectives are achievable if there is continuous political commitment to it.

General Assessments

From a general overall standpoint, Mr. Kodagoda reflected that in the field of substantive criminal law, Sri Lanka is performing well. However, in the field of white-collar crime he suggests that Sri Lanka may need to move away from the existing archaic definition of offenses of criminal breach of trust, cheating and criminal misappropriation of property, and substitute them with an overarching offense such as "fraud." He also advocates revisiting the statutory definition of the offense of corruption. At the same time, it is important to review the Prevention of Terrorism Act and go in for a broader piece of legislation in the nature of a new National Security Act, which will make domestic laws compatible with international human rights norms, and equally importantly respond efficaciously to future threats and attacks on national security, particularly in the sphere of unconventional forms of attack, such as cyber terrorism.

In commenting on criminal procedure, he opined that many aspects of criminal procedure need to be revisited. Firstly, he suggests moving away from the conduct of nonsummary inquiries in the Magistrates Courts into offenses as it is a waste of time and resources. He recommends leaving pre-indictment material in the hands of the Attorney-General alone, or in the alternative, to have a paper committal process by magistrates, as opposed to the present scheme of an oral inquiry.

The question of whether sufficient safeguards are provided in the law for a safe trial for the accused is no longer a tangible issue because there are sufficient measures to ensure a safe trial. But the question is whether the accused could unfairly benefit from such safeguards? Mr. Kodagoda noted that due to the paucity of professionalism among defense counsel who is retained by accused persons who do not have sufficient finances, the accused may not be able to effectively avail themselves of the existing safeguards. He recommended conversion of the system of "assigned counsel" into a public defender system in which accused persons from economically and socially disadvantaged backgrounds have access to better quality defense lawyers.

Another suggestion was to begin enforcing the provisions of the Assistance to and Protection of Victims of Crime and Witnesses Act No. 4 (2015) that was enacted by the parliament unanimously. Mr. Kodagoda devoted his time and expertise to the drafting process since 2006, and defended two versions of the Bill in 2008 and 2014, and considers the Act sufficient recompense for nine years of arduous work. He is excited about the enforcement phase of the new law, which he expects will finely balance protection of the interests of victims and witnesses with the legitimate right of the accused to a fair and impartial trial.

Commenting on the prevalent political situation in the country that has legal and constitutional connotations, Mr. Kodagoda noted that a positive trend toward constitutionalism is visible, which is in direct contrast to the authoritarian bend of the previous government. He views the recent enactment of the 19th Amendment to the Constitution and the creation of the Constitutional Council as the first step toward improving the rule of law, establishing good governance, and improving the justice system of Sri Lanka. The Constitutional Council is mandated to recommend to the president persons to be appointed to certain commissions and other offices, including the appointment of judges to the superior courts. The president cannot make any appointments without taking cognizance of the recommendations of the council. Therefore, there is a reasonable prospect in the future of nonpolitical appointments to the judiciary, which are needed to ensure an independent judiciary.

Reiterating the need, not only for an independent judiciary but also for a competent and ethical judiciary, Mr. Kodagoda recommends capacity-building through continuous training and postgraduate legal education for judges. He emphasizes the importance of training prosecutors as well. While the judiciary needs to be strengthened and protected, the prosecutorial system, too, ought to be made independent within the realm of public service and from the political machinery, as the exercise of prosecutorial discretion can be influenced by persons or entities attempting to use the criminal justice system for collateral purposes. He wonders whether it may be necessary to re-establish a Director of Public Prosecutions (DPP) by carving out the functions of the Attorney-General associated with the criminal justice system and conferring those functions on the DPP, while of course ensuring that the DPP is constitutionally protected from influence and pressures.

Mr. Kodagoda emphasized the importance of professional development particularly in the legal profession. Reminiscing about his formative years in the profession, he said that he began his career as a prosecutor during an era where there was no focus at all on professional training. It was a case of being thrown into the deep end of the swimming pool, either to swim or sink depending on personal ability. He himself has never been formally trained in the art of prosecution, which he mastered through observation and by participating in trials with senior counsel who led him. He considers this a wholly inappropriate way forward, and firmly espouses the need to focus and invest in further legal education and training. It is the duty of the state to provide educational opportunities to breed competent prosecutors. Mr. Kodagoda agreed that members of the unofficial bar, too, ought to have access to better training and continuing legal education opportunities.

On a concluding note, commenting on the issue of professional legal ethics, Mr. Kodagoda was of the opinion that professional ethics among lawyers in Sri Lanka need to be stringently enforced. Oversight ought to be effectively provided by the Supreme Court and the Bar Association of Sri Lanka. He expressed his concern over the lack of emphasis placed on professional ethics in legal education, which he believes led to ethics being disregarded by most practitioners and to a gradual decline in standards. This situation is exacerbated by the undue and misplaced conviction of legal practitioners that the overall goal of a practitioner is to prosper financially while winning litigation at any cost. He concluded by conceding that this may not be a unique issue to Sri Lanka, but emphasized the need to revisit many aspects of the criminal justice system in an adversarial environment.

Conclusion

This candid interview with Mr. Yasantha Kodagoda was both introspective on his part and enlightening for the reader. We were afforded a glimpse into the routine of a public prosecutor as well as the opportunity to discuss myriad facets of his fascinating work, which oftentimes go unnoticed. The prosecutor is an essential individual in the criminal justice process. The efficacy of the system is jeopardized without his contribution. While his practical skills are indispensable to the criminal justice process, a sound legal education with strong theoretical underpinnings is mandatory for an effective prosecutor. It is such theoretical training that gives gravitas to arguments in court, safely grounding the prosecutor's case in sound reasoning, which a court of law would take cognizance of. In addition, an empathetic personality, strong fidelity to ethics, an avid curiosity to explore novel concepts, technology and practices, and the willingness to incorporate these into his professional activities together are the hallmark of a thriving prosecutor. These characteristics were evident in both the personal and the professional conduct of

Mr. Kodagoda, which illustrate his success as a prosecutor. The anecdotal evidence he kindly shared with us further cemented our positive notion of his accomplishments as a prosecutor.

Sharing his concerns about the criminal justice system in Sri Lanka, Mr. Kodagoda especially noted how the quality of criminal investigators has a bearing on investigations, the delays inherent in the criminal justice response to crime, measures that need to be taken to streamline the criminal justice system in order to expedite prosecutions, the necessity to revisit the system of penal sanctions in order to achieve effective and sustainable offender rehabilitation, the value of continuing legal education for practitioners, and the need to enhance the quality of the judiciary. At the same time, he reflected on some of the successes of the Sri Lankan legal system such as alternative dispute resolution mechanisms, the content of substantive criminal law, and enactment of laws to protect victims and witnesses of crime.

A constitutionalist at heart, he believes steadfastly in the rule of law and human rights for a state to prosper. Mr. Kodagoda also is an advocate of fostering international relations both from a legal and a political perspective for the growth of the legal system. He does not hesitate to draw best practices from comparative jurisdictions for the enhancement of the legal system of Sri Lanka. His contribution to the law in Sri Lanka is reflected both in his capacity of a prosecutor and in his extraprosecutorial endeavors in the law reform process, as a representative of Sri Lanka in international fora and as an educator of law.

Glossary

attorney-at-law: the official name for a lawyer in Sri Lanka.

certiorari: a writ issued by a superior court confining the activities of an inferior court, tribunal, or other administrative body to within its jurisdiction.

Kandyan Law: a personal law applicable to Kandyan Sinhalese residents within the Kandyan provinces of Sri Lanka.

Kotalawala Defense University: a Sri Lankan University established through an act of parliament to offer bachelors and postgraduate degrees in defense studies for officers of the armed forces. It now offers degrees in engineering, law, management, social sciences, and information technology to civilians.

LTTE: Liberation Tigers of Tamil Eelam was a secessionist militant organization in Sri Lanka now proscribed as a terrorist organization.

Mahapola scholarship: a higher education scholarship granted by the Mahapola trust fund to students in publicly funded higher education institutions in Sri Lanka on the basis of merit or financial need to continue their undergraduate education.

mandamus: a writ issued by a superior court compelling an inferior court, tribunal, or administrative body to perform a public or statutory duty which such inferior tribunal is obliged under the law to perform.

Muslim Law: the portion of Islamic civil law that is applied to Sri Lankan Muslims as a personal law.

President's Counsel: a senior attorney-at-law who is conferred the title of President's Counsel by the president of Sri Lanka taking into account his/her eminence in the profession and high standards of conduct and professional integrity.

procedendo: a writ issued by a superior court ordering an inferior court to proceed to judgment.

quo warranto: a writ issued by court requiring the person or authority to which it is directed to show whether it has authority to exercise a particular right or power.

Sri Lanka Law College: the sole institution in Sri Lanka that administers legal education, leading to the professional qualification (attorney-at-law) necessary for admission to the bar.

Tesawalamai Law: the personal law applicable to the Tamil inhabitants of the Jaffna Peninsula in Northern Sri Lanka. It also applies as a territorial law to land within the peninsula irrespective of the residence or ethnicity of the owner.

University of Colombo: a publicly funded tertiary education institution in Sri Lanka located in Colombo offering bachelors and postgraduate degrees in a variety of disciplines.

Thailand

SARAH BISHOP
MARK NOLAN

13

Contents

The Criminal Justice Process of Thailand

The modern Thai legal system owes its origins to reforms undertaken between 1892 and 1935 in a context where Siam (as Thailand was then known) was facing incursions on its sovereignty caused by foreign powers asserting extraterritorial jurisdiction and by the threat of possible colonization (Hooker, 1988). Foreign transnational elites and foreign legal models played a prominent role in the reform process, and the legal system that emerged had more in common with Western and colonial systems than the former Siamese system (Harding, 2008; Loos, 2006, pp. 29–71; Petchsiri, 1987). However, the Siamese elite were nevertheless able to influence which parts of foreign law were adopted and to partially preserve elements of the former system including elements of hierarchy and the position of the monarch as giver and final arbiter of justice (Engel, 1975; Kittayapong, 1990; Loos, 1998). As a result, the system developed was not a close replica of any single foreign system but rather an "amalgam" of elements of civil and common law traditions and, to a lesser extent, the former Siamese tradition (Darling, 1970, p. 197). In the period that has followed, new reforms and changing attitudes of core personnel have affected the balance between the elements, but all have retained some influence.

The Court System

The current Thai court system, shown in Figure 13.1, consists of four parallel court systems. While the Courts of Justice and Military Court systems have existed in some form since 1908, the Constitutional Court was created only in 1998 (and then again in 2007 after being briefly replaced by a Tribunal in 2006) and the Administrative Courts only in 2001. The four parallel court systems are almost fully independent of each other: there are no avenues of appeal between them and each has its own administrative body and its own rules regarding court procedure and judicial qualifications, appointments, and removal. There is, however, a committee that is able to solve jurisdictional disputes between the multicourt systems and there are some links between the Constitutional Court and other systems with all constitutions that have recognized the Constitutional Court requiring other courts to refer some issues to it. All four systems play some role in the criminal justice process.

Courts of Justice

The Courts of Justice have the most prominent role in the criminal justice process. Within the Courts of Justice the Criminal Courts, Provincial Courts, Kwaeng Courts (courts of limited jurisdiction with jurisdiction over

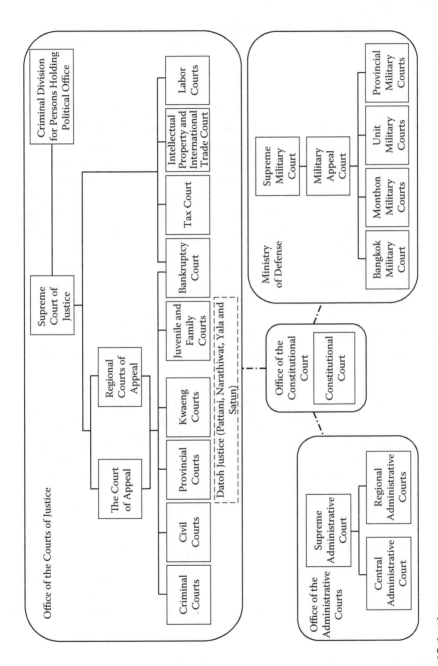

Figure 13.1 Thai court system.

minor civil and criminal matters), Juvenile and Family Courts, Bankruptcy Court, Intellectual Property and International Trade Court, and Supreme Court Criminal Division for Persons Holding Political Office have some jurisdiction over criminal cases. In 2013, courts of first instance in this system received 637,715 new criminal cases and finalized 635,868 criminal cases (Office of the Courts of Justice, 2014, p. 67).

Military Courts

The Military Courts have the second most prominent role in the criminal justice process. Ordinarily, the Military Courts have jurisdiction only in cases that involve military personnel, civilians in military service, or persons lawfully detained by or in the custody of the military. However, in "abnormal times"—legislatively defined as times of fighting, war or when martial law is declared—Military Courts can be given power to try cases involving civilians. This has happened on a number of occasions, most recently on May 25, 2014, in the aftermath of the 2014 coup. Although on April 1, 2015, nationwide martial law was lifted, the National Council for Peace and Order relied on exceptional powers granted by Article 44 of the *Constitution of the Kingdom of Thailand (Interim) B.E. 2557*(2014) to extend this jurisdiction. As the Military Courts do not release statistics, it is difficult to know how many cases they receive. However, on May 11, 2015, the International Commission of Jurists reported that since the 2014 coup more than 700 civilians had been tried in Military Courts.

Unlike other courts in the Thai justice system, the Military Courts do not have their own independent administrative body but rather come under the Ministry of Defense. Also, unlike other Thai courts, the Military Courts are not staffed primarily by a career judiciary. Instead, the majority of the bench in all Military Courts, except the Supreme Military Court, is composed of commissioned military officers who are rotated through that post as part of their regular rotation and who often do not hold any legal qualifications.

There are also differences in protection of defendants' rights. Most significantly, in "abnormal times," decisions of Military Courts of first instance are final and cannot be appealed. Lawyers have also reported that since the 2014 coup, in the Military Courts as compared to in the Courts of Justice: it has been harder for defendants to access information on charges; processes have been slower and afforded parties less chance to identify flaws in the taking of evidence; trials have more often been held in camera; and bail conditions and sentences have been less favorable than those in otherwise comparable cases ("2014 Situation Summary Report 2/5," 2015; Thai Lawyers for Human Rights, 2015, pp. 4–7).

Administrative and Constitutional Courts

The role of the Administrative and Constitutional Courts in the criminal justice process is limited. Neither is able to determine criminal guilt. However, the Administrative Courts have accepted jurisdiction in some cases concerning actions of law enforcement officials, and the Constitutional Court has decided on the constitutionality of criminal laws.

The Criminal Law

The criminal law in Thailand is primarily stipulated in two codes: the *Criminal Code* and the *Criminal Procedure Code*. There are also many laws that create offenses, confer law enforcement powers, and modify criminal procedure. In some periods, constitutional provisions have also been relevant. This was particularly so when the *Constitution of the Kingdom of Thailand B.E. 2540* (1997) and *Constitution of the Kingdom of Thailand B.E. 2550*(2007) were in force as they contained provisions that qualified provisions of the *Criminal Procedure Code* and expanded rights of victims and defendants.

Investigation of criminal cases in Thailand is primarily the responsibility of police and administrative officials. Prosecutors have little ability to be involved. Exceptions apply for cases tried in the Military Courts and for cases investigated by the Department of Special Investigations where prosecutors can sometimes have investigative powers. Protections of a suspect's rights during investigation generally include: limitations on powers of officials to conduct searches, and arrest and detain persons; rights when arrested to inform another person of the arrest and to be informed of charges and of the rights to remain silent and to consult a lawyer; rights in some types of case to have a lawyer provided during inquiries; and a right when detained to seek provisional release. However, the scope of these protections has often been narrowly interpreted. They are also often avoided by application of security focused laws such as the *Martial Law Act B.E. 2457*(1914), *Emergency Decree on Public Administration in Emergency Situations B.E. 2548*(2005), and *Internal Security Act B.E. 2551*(2008). These laws have been particularly significant in the three southern border provinces where ongoing conflict has led to their long-term use (Haberkorn, 2011).

Criminal cases in both the Courts of Justice and the Military Courts are usually prosecuted by state prosecutors. However, there is also a limited right to private prosecution by victims. This right does not apply in the Military Courts in "abnormal times" or when the victim is a civilian. Another option open to victims whose cases are tried in the Courts of Justice is to request that the court order that the defendant pay compensation. Where a victim is indigent, the court may appoint a lawyer to assist with this compensation request.

Court procedure in criminal cases is generally adversarial with strict rules of evidence and with all cases decided by judges. However, courts do have power to take evidence on their own motion, and in some specialist courts and divisions rules are modified such that powers of the court to conduct their own inquiries and to rely on ordinarily inadmissible evidence are expanded. Also, in the Military Courts, not all judges are career judges or legally trained, and, in some specialist courts, Associate Judges who are not necessarily legally trained are appointed for limited terms to participate alongside career judges in deciding cases.

Defendants in all criminal cases are entitled to appoint a lawyer, and defendants who are minors or face charges that may lead to the death penalty or imprisonment have a right to a state provided lawyer. Methods for appointment are not stipulated, but in practice, courts tend to appoint lawyers on a rotating basis from a court-specific list of lawyers who have expressed willingness to take on the role, only sometimes considering expertise.

There are two main ways criminal cases can be settled. Where offenses are minor, cases can sometimes be settled by voluntary payment of a fine. Alternatively, in cases where offenses are expressly defined to be offenses against the individual or as able to be settled between parties, cases can be settled at any time by the victim and defendant. Controversially, offense currently in this latter group include some rape offenses.

A defendant who is convicted has the right to petition the monarch for a full pardon or commutation of their sentence. Pardons are granted fairly frequently, especially in cases involving *lèse-majesté* or white-collar crime, and the possibility of receiving a pardon can often compel defendants to confess rather than risk the consequences of contesting their case that can often include detention during trial ("Requesting a Royal Pardon," 2013).

The Legal Profession

The legal profession in Thailand consists of professionals who fall into three main categories: judges, prosecutors, and lawyers. Two professional bodies regulate these professions: the Thai Bar Association and the Lawyers Council of Thailand. Membership of the Thai Bar Association is required to be a career judge in the Military Courts or Courts of Justice, a public or military prosecutor, and a lawyer. However, only career judges in the Courts of Justice and public prosecutors are required to pass the Bar examination. In contrast, membership of the Lawyers Council of Thailand is limited to lawyers. It is responsible for registering and deregistering lawyers and handling ethical complaints. It also has an official duty to support provision of and provide legal assistance, legal advice, and legal education to the people.

As is common in civil law systems, judges and prosecutors are civil servants. Unlike in some civil law systems, however, judges and prosecutors are not able to readily move from one position to the other. Most judges and prosecutors are recruited early career by way of competitive examination, and promotions are based on seniority and merit. This system affords senior judges considerable power over the future advancement of junior and mid-ranking judges, and has been shown in other countries to foster a conservative culture (Ramseyer & Rasmusen, 2003).

In contrast, lawyers are independent professionals. Although exceptions apply in some courts, registration as a lawyer is usually necessary to appear before a court or to prepare a plaint, motion, petition, or appeal for a court on behalf of another. Registration is open only to Thai citizens and is subject to good character requirements.

At present, there is no strong culture of *pro bono* or public interest lawyering within the Thai legal profession, and taking on controversial or public interest causes can place lawyers at risk of harm from both the state and private actors. The best-known case is that of Somchai Neelapaijit, a lawyer who represented defendants in terrorism cases in the three southern border provinces, who is widely understood to have been forcibly disappeared and likely murdered by state authorities in 2004, soon after publicly accusing police of torture (Kummetha, 2014). While instances as extreme as this are rare, lesser forms of intimidation are common. Despite this, there are a number of legal assistance and public interest law initiatives, and a dedicated core of lawyers who devote themselves to *pro bono* and public interest causes (Munger, 2009, 2011, 2012; Pichaikul & Klein, 2005).

Yaowalak Anuphan, Thai Lawyers for Human Rights, Bangkok

Introduction

On May 20, 2014, nationwide martial law was declared in Thailand. Two days later, the military-led National Council for Peace and Order (NCPO) staged a coup and repealed the *Constitution of the Kingdom of Thailand B.E. 2550*(2007) (2007 Constitution). Immediately after, the NCPO began issuing announcements and orders suppressing freedom of speech; criminalizing public meetings and shows of opposition; requiring individuals perceived to have subversive views to present for what the NCPO called "attitude adjustment;" and transferring some criminal cases involving civilians to the Military Courts (for a partial list of announcements, see "ThaiCoup: All NCPO Announcements in One Place," 2014). In the first 12 months since the coup, over 71 public events were canceled, over 751 individuals were required to present for attitude adjustment, and over 700 civilians were tried in Military Courts (Thai Lawyers for Human Rights, 2015, pp. 1–2). The NCPO also relied on exceptional powers granted to them by Article 44 of the *Constitution of the Kingdom of Thailand (Interim) B.E. 2557*(2014) to initiate criminal forest encroachment cases against many villagers living in forest areas and to replace an existing committee investigating criminal cases related to the dispersal by the military and law enforcement authorities of political protests in 2010 with a new committee that included military officials as committee members (Thai Lawyers for Human Rights, 2015, pp. 9–13, 16–17).

Three weeks before the interview was conducted nationwide martial law was lifted. However, the NCPO continued to issue a large number of orders and announcements. Among these was an order that gave military personnel powers to arrest and detain similar to those which they had had under martial law, and ensured that new cases involving civilians could continue to be initiated and tried in military courts (*Order of the Head of the National Council for Peace and Order No. 3/2558*, 2015). On the day of the interview, the National Reform Council set up after the coup was reviewing the first draft of what was intended to be a new permanent constitution before returning it to the drafting committee for final amendment. The draft contained many provisions antithetical to democracy and weakened protections of rights. Overall, a quick return to democracy and rule of law appeared unlikely. Due to these conditions, the authors were unsure what level of frankness could be expected.

It was, however, Yaowalak Anuphan's actions in the aftermath of the coup that first brought her to the authors' attention. On May 24, two days after the coup and before the consequences could be fully calculated, she had joined with other lawyers to found Thai Lawyers for Human Rights to offer legal assistance to those impacted by the coup. In the first 12 months since the coup, they offered advice on 122 occasions and provided representation to 60 defendants in 38 cases (Thai Lawyers for Human Rights, 2015, p. 2). They also played a prominent role in publicizing rights violations. Given this background, it is, perhaps, unsurprising that on the day of the interview Yaowalak was forthcoming. She declared at the outset that "nothing is closed, everything is open" and, while at times choosing her words carefully, she never avoided answering a question.

The interview was conducted in Thai by Sarah Bishop on April 24, 2015, and lasted about 90 minutes. Questions were not disclosed beforehand. It was later translated by Sarah Bishop. The approach taken to translation was firstly to attempt to retain the emphasis, connotations, and ambiguities of responses and only secondly to maintain naturalness of expression. The final version of this chapter has been seen and approved for publication by Yaowalak. Any flaws in translation remain the responsibility of Sarah Bishop.

Career

Yaowalak has worked for 24 years, 22 of which as a full-time lawyer. Like most Thai lawyers, she has had a diverse career working across civil, criminal, and public law matters. She sees the common thread that has bound her work as being that she has "always worked on human rights issues." Throughout her career, she has been recognized on multiple occasions for her contributions to human rights advocacy. In 2004, she received an award on International Women's Day from civil society groups for her role in advocating for women's rights in the justice process. In 2014, she received an honorable mention from the Somchai Neelapaijit Memorial Fund for her work in cases involving violence against women, the situation in the three southern border provinces of Thailand, community rights, refugee issues, and political crimes. In 2014, Thai Lawyers for Human Rights, which she cofounded, received an award from the French Embassy for their post-coup work.

Yaowalak grew up in Narathiwat—one of the three southern border provinces of Thailand that have been affected by long-running ethnic and religious conflict and periodic violence and insurgency. When asked whether growing up in these conditions had impacted her choice of career, she initially denied that it had, identifying involvement in university student activities as more instrumental:

> I think actually the turning point probably came more from studying at Ramkhamhaeng. I was an active student: I studied at university; I went on camps; I was involved in political activities; I studied Thai history—the events of 14 October 73, 6 October 76; I was involved in student activities; we

assembled. Things like that… When I was a child, I was well-mannered. My parents were also normal. It was at Ramkhamhaeng that I think I got ideas that had an influence. I worked on social issues and I felt it was enjoyable. It was me. It was right for my disposition. It was more that. It was probably not associated with where I came from.

Upon further reflection, however, she thought her childhood may have had some impact:

A moment, actually, at home—my father was a policeman—I may have been influenced by that, on issues of injustice, or things like that. My older sister also worked in law. I therefore felt, whatever happened, I had to go and study law. It probably, it might have, had some [influence]. Because there are many people who have studied law, been involved in [student] activities but who have felt, have gone back to, live a normal life.

As to what led her to become an active student, Yaowalak suggested that it had happened largely by chance:

I wanted to join a camp. I was from the South. But I wanted to go on a camp in the North. Really, that was it. It turned out I went on the camp in the North and by chance ended up with a club that was involved in society-oriented activities. Once we went, the older students had books for us to read and told us about 14 October 73, 6 October 76. And I felt: *Huh*, why had I never known about this before? And I was interested.

In the early years of her career, Yaowalak worked mostly on women's issues. She started out in 1990 as a coordinator for a legal education program, run by the Chiang Mai University Faculty of Social Sciences, which taught northern women leaders about the law. In 1991, she then moved to a semilegal role with the Friends of Women Foundation in their Centre for Protection of Women's Rights. In 1993, she left to become a full-time lawyer. Between 1993 and 1997, she worked with law firms that focused on public interest litigation; between 1998 and 2001 with the Friends of Women Foundation as a lawyer; and from 2002 as an independent lawyer. In 2000, she was approached by the Office of the United Nations High Commissioner for Refugees (UNHCR) to take on a case involving a refugee who had been raped by soldiers. This led her to become involved in other cases with that office and with refugees and migrants. Describing cases she worked on in this period, she said:

The cases were related to gender and sexual violence: sexual harassment, gang rape, women murdering their husbands, domestic violence, rape and cases like that. I also worked on human trafficking cases, migrant worker cases and cases for the UNHCR with Burmese refugees. If it was human trafficking, these were the Rohingya.

From 1999, the types of cases Yaowalak worked on began to expand beyond those involving women's issues. In 1999, she became a member of the Human Rights Committee of the Lawyers Council of Thailand (Lawyers Council) leading to involvement in cases concerning land rights and forest encroachment. Then, in 2003, she became a member of a National Human Rights Commission of Thailand subcommittee investigating extrajudicial killings associated with the government's much criticized "war on drugs."

In 2006, following a military coup, Yaowalak became dissatisfied with the political position taken by the Lawyers Council and disengaged from that body. A large part of her work in the subsequent period, especially between 2007 and 2012, has involved working on cases related to the three southern border provinces of Thailand, initially as an advisor to the Cross Cultural Foundation, then as a director of the American Bar Association Rule of Law Initiative. Describing this latter work, she said:

> We did what they called a case audit. We took 100 cases concerning terrorism in the three southern border provinces to check each process, each mechanism, each law—to see whether it was in accordance with the law, in accordance with the rights of the accused. For instance, in the three southern border provinces they have the issue of being detained under the *Martial Law* [Act B.E. 2457(1914), s. 15 Tawi] for seven days, and under the *Emergency Decree* [*on Public Administration in Emergency Situations B.E. 2548* (2005), s. 12] for 30 days, and there are issues under the *Criminal Procedure Code*. Therefore we would check whether under martial law when soldiers arrested people, were their rights under law respected, were they beaten?… In addition we organized training on law for young lawyers in the three southern border provinces… and organised seminars and shared knowledge on forensic psychology, as it was a new issue.

From 2008, Yaowalak has also headed her own law firm, remained involved in women's rights and human trafficking issues, and begun to represent defendants facing *lèse-majesté* charges and victims in cases related to use of force in the dispersal of 2010 political protests. From 2010 to 2013, she also held a position as a board member of the Human Rights and Development Foundation. From 2012, she has been a member of a committee of the Law Reform Commission of Thailand considering gender equality-related law reforms. From 2013, she has been a board member and treasurer of the Human Rights Lawyers Association. Since 2014, she has headed Thai Lawyers for Human Rights.

Personal Advocacy Philosophy

When asked about lawyers' duties and responsibilities, Yaowalak responded quickly and confidently. On issues of limitations she was more hesitant, asking for examples and explaining that sometimes the fact that she did a lot meant that she might not be aware of what was not her responsibility. When examples were given, she responded directly to those examples.

When first asked about duties, her answer focused on provision of legal advice and the importance of client agency:

> Give legal assistance. Give legal assistance to the people. Our role, it is as if we explain the law for them. Explain the advantages and disadvantages. And, have them *choose*, do you see what I mean, have them *choose* whether they will contest the case. We have to explain what the effects will be. Because if we don't, assume before they contest a public case, that is a case which may have the impact that they will go to jail, we have to explain and let them *choose*, *choose* what path to take, whether to contest the case or not. For example, cases where villagers have claimed land, we must explain the way we would contest the case, and ask if the villagers agree with us.

These elements were also emphasized in several other responses. For example, in response to a suggestion that perhaps some duties should be those of the courts, she made it clear that she saw that lawyers had a duty to be proactive legal representatives:

> The Thai court system is an adversarial system. Therefore, in my view, we have to present evidence for the court to see. Courts, Thai courts, say they will not interfere by conducting their own inquiries. Thai courts will position themselves as neutral. Thai Courts will not see anything [for themselves]. They must have the parties present it. I therefore think I must, that is I try to, push every issue. I say I am a lawyer: I am not passive, I am active. Therefore I must open the way, work proactively. I feel the duty of a rights lawyer is that they must work proactively. There will never be a day when Thai courts will see anything for themselves if we do not present it.

Yaowalak saw that this duty to be proactive could sometimes extend to filling gaps left by other agencies. She saw this was often necessary in cases involving state officials accused of beating villagers. Describing what victims' lawyers could do, she said:

> Our power is less than that of prosecutors and the police. We have to raise the issue. Put it in a letter. Appeal for justice. And sometimes we go and find additional witnesses for the police to conduct further examinations. We will send a letter appealing for justice to the prosecutors stating that this case has special characteristics. For example, where villagers are beaten, where they are beaten and die, but it turns out that the doctor's certificate records that they died because of a traffic accident. We have to say: Was it is like this? There were people who saw that they were beaten. Things like that. We have to raise the issue, report it to the prosecutors, have them go and conduct a new investigation.

However, she emphasized that it was also important for lawyers to know when to hold back:

> In criminal cases, there are victims and defendants. Under law the prosecutor has a duty to establish the facts. The prosecutor must have the duty to present the facts. If we represent the victim and the prosecutor does not do their duty adequately, we have to present evidence for the victim to prove the guilt [of the perpetrator]. But if we represent the defendant, our defendant did not do wrong. Therefore, if it turns out the prosecutor has few facts, we will not present our facts because we know that if this is all that the prosecutor has, the court will have to dismiss the case against our defendant. We therefore have to look at it on a case by case basis.

Other responses indicated a broader nonlegal role and wider nonclient focused considerations. For example, when asked whether defense lawyers have special duties, Yaowalak's answer incorporated a responsibility to provide nonlegal assistance:

> Yes. It is as if, for defendants in criminal cases, it has an impact on their rights and freedoms. We have to work, if you asked do. Therefore we have to work harder, actually I work hard on every case. I don't discriminate. But I feel that in criminal cases , it must be special. They have special characteristics. We have to commit fully. Do you see what I mean? From bail onwards. And the villagers whom we help are poor. When they are poor, it is not only explaining the law and conducting the case, we have to empower the villagers. For example, assume a bail application and villagers are poor and don't have money, we have to try to liaise to see if there is an organisation that will sponsor bail for the villagers. It starts from there.

And, in a response to a question on who defense lawyers owe responsibilities to, it became clear that while Yaowalak viewed a client-focus as important it was not her sole focus:

> We have to accept responsibility for everything. When we work on human rights cases, we have to say those cases will send reverberations. They will provide a norm for society. Firstly, of course we must be responsible to the defendant. And I think these cases can, I want to lead them to be able to, be a norm for society.

This dual focus also came across in Yaowalak's response to a suggestion there may be ethical limits to a lawyer's actions, such as when they know a client is guilty:

> Assume in a criminal case. Villagers have gone and seized land. We have to look at the reason why the villagers seized the land. We see the villagers did wrong. Right? That they seized the land. But the villagers will say that they seized the

land because title to the land was issued illegally. That is, there was a motive. Therefore, I consider the villagers did not do wrong. Thailand has its problematic systems. Therefore, when villagers go and seize land, I will contest the case like this. But if there was a case where I felt villagers genuinely did wrong, which in human rights cases I mostly never see, but in regular cases—such as property offenses, I would have to say, "You did wrong. You have to confess." I am not the type of lawyer who uses technicalities. I look first. If I am working on a rights case, for example, if villagers go and injure someone—there was a case in Prachuap Khiri Khan like this. Villagers went and caused damage to people associated with a company which was going to build a power plant. The villagers were wrong. They had no right to do this. We said to them, "You had no right to do this." But the villagers said the reason they caused damage was because a group of oil companies had released oil and it was going to cause dolphins to die. They had a reason, and they argued this reason of protection.*

How this dual focus influenced Yaowalak's litigation strategy was further elaborated in response to a question on the importance of human rights to her work:

When I am a lawyer who says I am a human rights lawyer, I have to take principles of human rights, that is international law principles, and apply them. Set them up as rules in contesting [cases]. I use international law, I use constitutional law and I also use domestic implementing laws in contesting cases. If I was not a rights lawyer, I would contest cases in a basic way. Contest issues of evidence. Argue it is not shown by the evidence. Things like that. For example, if it was a villagers' case, I would say we will argue based on the constitution and that we have freedom to assemble. Similarly, in three southern border province cases, for example with issues of beatings and torture, I would say the state has a duty not to beat as it is a party to international law—to the CAT [Convention Against Torture and Other Cruel, Inhuman or Degrading Treatment or Punishment], and also under the '07 Constitution Article 32 that prohibits beatings and torture. When I contest [a case], I have to take these laws and use them as tools in contesting [the case] as well.

---

* Five villagers involved in opposition to construction of a power plant at Bo Nok were accused of depriving three officials of the Gulf Power Generation Co Ltd of their liberty and of assaulting them causing grievous bodily harm on October 13, 2002. One of the villagers, Charoen Wataksorn, was subsequently murdered with evidence strongly suggesting his murder was connected to his opposition to the power plant and other local development projects. On August 17, 2005, the court of first instance decided the case against the four remaining defendants, dismissing the case against one, finding two guilty of assault, and finding one guilty of depriving another person of their liberty. All three who were found guilty were given jail sentences, but the sentences were suspended in part on grounds that their actions were an expression of concern for the environment and as a result they deserved an opportunity to reform their behavior. On September 17, 2010, the Appeal Court upheld the decision of the lower court with respect to the two defendants found guilty of assault, and dismissed the case against the defendant found guilty of depriving another person of their liberty.

A tendency to prioritize principle also came through in Yaowalak's response to a question on whether she had ever been threatened or felt unsafe because of her work:

> Last year Thai Lawyers [for Human Rights] were going to organise an event for the 100 day mark. We were going to present on violations of human rights in the 100 days since the coup. The military phoned, said we could not hold it. The military threatened that if we held it, they would prosecute [us]. We said we were not afraid and were prepared to go to jail. We spoke in that manner. But if you asked—we did feel unsafe, but we had to insist, insist that we had a right under law to hold it.

The event was not held. Unsurprisingly, speakers were unprepared to speak. Still, Yaowalak thought it was important to make a stand and issued a press release. In June 2015, after the interview, there was a similar incident when the group sought to report on the situation one year after the coup. Despite the ban, Yaowalak went ahead and made a public statement ("Thai Junta Rejects Allegation of Denying Free Speech," 2015).

Problems and Successes Experienced

Legal System

Yaowalak had a very pessimistic view of the Thai legal system. This first became clear in her response to a question on what the goals of the system should be:

> ...the Thai system, it is as if it aims at retribution. In truth it should be designed for prevention, rehabilitation, and remediation in order to prevent offenders coming back and reoffending. But I have not yet experienced this. The Thai justice process has not yet achieved this standard. At the moment, for example with [Section] 112 [the provision of the *Criminal Code* which creates the offense of *lèse-majesté*] where people are jailed again and again, I feel it is not even retribution. What is it? I feel the Thai justice system has been damaged. The system is broken. The legal system has collapsed.

Asked whether she had always perceived the legal system as damaged in this way, she responded:

> Actually, from the time I started working I have seen that the justice system has not yet been up to standard. There was discrimination. There were issues of rich people and poor people. Poor people had little access to justice and found access to justice harder than rich people or people with money. I began to see this from the beginning. Then, once I started to work on cases involving groups of people with this I could see it from the start. Women's issues were

a matter of attitude. Refugee or human trafficking issues became a matter of attitude and of state security—there was discrimination based on ethnicity and other things like that. Once I came to work on three southern border provinces issues, this caused me to see that they were a matter of security and of the attitudes of state officials, in the same manner. Once I came to work on [Section] 112, with this I could see matters of attitude and of values and, what do they call it, security. These attitudes, values, security, which damage the Thai rule of law system and prevent the law being up to standard.

While Yaowalak has never perceived the legal system as up to standard, pre-2006, she perceived it to be gradually improving. She saw the adoption of the *Constitution of the Kingdom of Thailand B.E. 2540*(1997)(1997 Constitution) as an important driver of this change:

> ...in '97, once Thailand had a [new] constitution, the law was amended to give more rights to both victims and the accused. Many laws emerged to support those rights... The constitution caused implementing laws to be developed. People could use them. They had various mechanisms and rights which they could use in a holistic manner.

In contrast, she perceived the post-2006 period as one of breakdown and collapse. She saw this collapse as having been driven by political crisis, by the monarchy being drawn into the crisis and by political groups having used the law selectively to aid their own causes. She considered that events of the period had led the law to "become a political tool to be used to strike at each other" and to develop "double standards."

While Yaowalak drew a sharp distinction between the pre- and post-2006 periods, when she was asked to identify the most important positive developments in criminal justice during her career she identified developments from both periods. The first development she identified was the reduction by Article 237 of the 1997 Constitution of the maximum period for which an arrested person could be detained without a court order, from seven days to 48 hours. She believed this had led police to work faster. The second was recognition of Article 32 of the 2007 Constitution of the right of persons to seek compensation for damages suffered when wrongly deprived of their rights to life or liberty. While she acknowledged that this right had rarely been successfully invoked in court, she considered that efforts by lawyers working in the three southern border provinces to raise it had led the courts to recognize the extent of abuses of power and to develop guidelines which required judges to more actively check actions of state officials. Other positive developments mentioned during the interview were the enactment of the *Act on Compensation for Victims and Compensation and Expenses for Defendants in Criminal Cases B.E. 2544*(2001), and the creation in 2006 of a Justice Fund to help parties meet the costs of civil, criminal, and administrative litigation.

In contrast, when asked if the justice system retained any strengths post-2014, Yaowalak responded:

Not at all. Since the coup I have not yet seen anything. I have not yet seen anything! It looks as if, at the moment the people lodging complaints are military officials. And it has become such that the military apply the law as a tool to bring people to face proceedings. I will give a simple example: people who staged a rally to commemorate, and call for, elections on 14 February [2015]. This was [exercise of] freedom of expression at a very basic level. But it turned out military officials lodged a complaint and brought proceedings. And the police were not neutral: they followed military orders, rushed to create a file. Actually, this case should not have been a case. There are many cases which should not have been cases, but which have become cases. Therefore, in summary, it is that the law has been applied as a tool.

And when asked whether there remained any recognition of defendants' rights, she responded:

Recognition of the right to a lawyer. There is no need to speak of [detention under] martial law. The *Martial Law* does not allow lawyers to visit. But they can have a lawyer once they have been sent to jail. I see they are still allowing them to meet a lawyer. But there are limitations. The right is not realised 100 percent... Actually, the accused should be given bail. But in [Section] 112 cases bail has not been granted... And lawyers, if they have a lawyer, the lawyer can ask to meet them. But there are problems and obstacles in many cases. Lawyers cannot request documents. Things like that.

While Yaowalak saw these restrictions as most serious in the Military Courts, she saw them as also applying to some extent in the Courts of Justice:

In the Courts of Justice, if it is requesting documents, you can do it. If it is jails, they are required to allow visits. But everything has changed. Once NCPO orders emerged, the jails changed. They have limited rights of visitors. Things like that... If it is [Section] 112, it has become policy not to grant bail. And court orders have tended not to give legal reasons. It has become an issue of sentiment... Court orders, for example if we request bail, the court will disallow the request because the conduct was serious and impacts sentiment... If I am to put it in words, the reasons for the judgements do not contain legal reasoning; they are subjective, not objective.

In follow-up questions, Yaowalak clarified that in nonpolitical cases ordinary mechanisms were still being used and that performance was more acceptable.

Although Yaowalak reserved her strongest criticism for the post-2014 period, when asked to identify the greatest flaw in the system, she took a longer term view returning to the issue of attitudes of personnel which she had previously identified as a major flaw:

Having litigated cases for a long time, I feel it depends on each judge. It becomes an issue of judges' attitudes. How should I say it? If it is [Section] 112, it is an issue of attitudes of personnel in the justice process— the lack of bravery, of courage, in using the law of judges and prosecutors. Do I see this as atrocious? It is the direct failure to do their duty of people who hold the law. Suppose, is the law good? Assuming the law is good, where does the problem arise? The problem arises from each official in the justice process. The police are not courageous in doing their duty. The police do not dare order not to prosecute. They send it to the prosecutor. The prosecutor is not brave. The prosecutor says it is a policy case—[Section] 112 [cases] are policy cases—no matter what, even if there is no evidence, they must be prosecuted. They send it to the judge. The judge, I feel it is based on beliefs, they judge in accordance with their attitudes. Therefore the atrocity is the failure to act in accordance with the law of people—of the people in the justice process.

In follow-up questions, it was established that not all judges and prosecutors lacked courage to act and that acting often had significant consequences. Two examples were given. One involved the Chief Justice of the Criminal Court who in 2014 gave a dissenting opinion in a case in which the majority held that the court lacked jurisdiction to hear a murder charge brought against the former prime minister and deputy prime minister for ordering the dispersal of political protests in 2010 (*Criminal Court Black Case Or 4552/2556*, 2013).*

The second case involved a young judge who issued a suspended sentence in a [Section] 112 case in which there was a confession (see "Man Found Guilty of Lèse-Majesté for Uploading Clips," 2014). In both cases, Yaowalak had heard that the judges had since been transferred from their posts, and in the latter case also subjected to a disciplinary committee investigation.

The barrier posed by incumbent officials also featured in Yaowalak's assessment of future prospects for the system:

At the moment it looks as if there is no hope. I feel the legal system has been destroyed. The orders and announcements of the NCPO are still

---

* The case was brought by the prosecutor and families of the victims. The majority dismissed the case on grounds it related to misuse of power and so fell within jurisdiction of the Supreme Court Criminal Division for Political Office Holders not the Criminal Court. The Chief Justice rejected this reasoning primarily on grounds that the charge was premeditated murder not misuse of power, and that if proven this charge would carry a higher penalty than misuse of power. He also reasoned that dismissing the case at that stage, when the body with power to bring misuse of power charges, the National Anti-Corruption Commission (NACC) had not yet decided whether to do so, would result in the NACC being given power to act as a court and would unjustly limit the rights of families.

there. There is not yet a future. How is Thailand to go on? You ask if it [the legal system] will develop. As someone who works in the area, I have not yet seen [any indication]. Suppose the law is good, but the officials are not good. I think that you will have to ask the law reformers in the Law Reform Commission [of Thailand] what they think when they are reforming the law every day but NCPO orders also come out every day.

When asked how she would most like to see the legal system develop, it was another earlier theme, unequal access and lack of affordability, which she emphasized:

I want to see it give justice—for people to have the opportunity to access and use the services of the law, no, the services of justice, faster and more easily. But at the moment it is as if the justice process has a high price. Do you see what I mean? For example, poor people do not have a right to bail if they don't have money. What can be done to reduce the security for bail, reduce costs? Start with this. Then the justice process which is slow—what can be done to make it faster?

Legal Profession

Yaowalak's assessment of the legal profession was as pessimistic as that of the legal system. Overall, she felt the quality of lawyering in criminal cases was often low:

It seems that the quality of lawyers in criminal cases is still lower than that in civil cases. When I meet lawyers in civil cases, [lawyers] who are involved in business, it seems they are of better quality than lawyers in criminal cases... In civil cases lawyers get more money. But in criminal cases, if the defendant has money then they might get a quality lawyer. But if it is a villager's case, or a case like that, it seems that the clients don't really get quality... [The lawyers] don't work to their full ability. Also their knowledge is still low and they are not skilful.

Yaowalak considered that in recent years politicization, internal division, and lack of state support and job security had also impacted the performance of the legal profession:

At present, if we talk of rights lawyers, there are lawyers who work on each problem issue—for example the environment, migrant workers, refugees. There are more lawyers who are specializing full time. Do they [lawyers] work together? Thailand has had a political crisis. There has been division into [political] colours. Red cases they do not work on. They work on yellow cases. There have been instances like this. [The political crisis] has caused lawyers to come to choose sides, choose the work they do. In truth, we shouldn't choose. For example with [Section] 112, some people won't work on it at all. And groups of lawyers have demanded that the Lawyers Council deals with people who violate [Section] 112.* Everything is in crisis. Like with the emergence of Thai Lawyers [for Human Rights], we don't have enough lawyers. I feel we have few lawyers, very few, such that it impacts us personally. There are some who do not come and help at all... Lawyers may be very individualistic. There are many problems. The State does not assist lawyers. Being a lawyer may be seen as insecure. There are many factors.

Since 2006, the Lawyers Council has issued many announcements on contentious political issues. Specific instances mentioned in the interview included announcements issued: between 2006 and 2014 in which the council supported claims of political protestors that Article 7 of the 1997 and 2007 constitutions could be used as a basis for royal political intervention; in 2010 in which the council indicated it would provide assistance to members of one political faction accused of political crimes but not the other; in 2011 in which the council criticized reform proposals put forward by *Nitirat*, a group of politically active academic lawyers; and in 2014 in which the council supported the coup. Yaowalak was critical of all of these announcements, seeing that by issuing them the Lawyers Council had "led the institution [Lawyers Council] to join political rallies." However, she reserved her strongest criticism for the announcements that supported the 2014 coup, addressing her comments to the Lawyers Council and stating:

> You are an institution which gives direct legal assistance to the people, but you have chosen to show a political stance which does not respect the law. You are legal professionals, but you have gone and supported a coup. This is already wrong! And you go and issue announcements supporting it. And choose to say that this is the Thai way. You can't do that!

She was also critical of the role of other legal professionals in the aftermath of the 2014 coup. In response to a direct question on the issue, she stated:

> I am disappointed. If I speak directly, it is the Lawyers Council, the professional organisation for lawyers in Thailand, which has gone and supported the coup and not come out and made demands on issues of the rights of people who have been arrested by military officials and brought before Military Courts. The Lawyers Council has not come out and demanded anything at all. It is extremely disappointing. And there are laws that the NCPO has issued, orders, where the penalty is disproportionate. But legal professionals are all silent. Legal academics, legal professionals, the Lawyers Council—they have

---

* On at least one occasion, the Lawyers Council of Thailand responded to the demand issuing announcements pressing the state to act (Lawyers Council of Thailand Announcements Nos. 4/2554, and 5/2554, 2011).

not come out and said anything and have left the NCPO to issue laws and set penalties which are very high. Thai society—I don't know why it is like this. I don't know. Including human rights lawyers as well—that have supported the coup. Including legal professionals involved in society-oriented work or NGOs who have come out and supported the coup. So many of them! Therefore, I feel that Thai society is experiencing a major crisis.

Asked what may have driven even human rights lawyers to act in this manner, Yaowalak suggested relevant factors may have included: personal benefits, including ability to access power under each regime; political attitudes, especially opposition to particular political parties; and, for the older generation, having become accustomed to coups and thinking only in terms of human rights not also in terms of democracy or the rule of law.

In response to specific questioning, Yaowalak acknowledged that non-political attitudes could also affect the quality of the assistance lawyers were able to provide:

> If understanding is lacking, even if they have a lawyer, they can't do anything. It's like in forest cases, if the lawyer doesn't understand, they say, "You encroached. You must confess." There are many cases like this. They don't contest the case for them.

The importance of attitude and understanding also came through in responses to questions on lawyering in human trafficking cases. In such cases Yaowalak saw that the quality of lawyering was often better than in other cases as there were nongovernment organizations which assisted in finding and paying for lawyers. Even in these cases, however, she saw that lack of sufficient lawyers, issues of lawyers' attitude and limitations in lawyers' understanding could be obstacles to justice. On attitude and understanding, she said:

> It depends on the person. Some may not work to their full ability. It depends on the person… When I was with the Lawyers Council we organised workshops on human trafficking for lawyers to create understanding. But later, this completely disappeared. It became such that lawyers had to do their own research. If the attitude is not good, it is not possible to read the law and to advocate. It must come from understanding.

When it came to addressing issues of availability of lawyers and of attitude and understanding, Yaowalak considered it the responsibility of the Lawyers Council to lead:

> In truth, the Lawyers Council, the direct organisation for lawyers, should work in a more proactive manner. It should strengthen the capacity of lawyers—organise training or things like that. But the Lawyers Council is very static. It is a defensive organisation. This causes there to be few lawyers who go and assist disadvantaged

groups. Even among women lawyers—strengthening understanding on issues of gender and of things like that are still at a low level. There is a shortage—lawyers who understand rights are still few, and are in short supply.

While emphasizing the role of the Lawyers Council, Yaowalak did not absolve lawyers of individual responsibility. When asked what she would most like to see lawyers change, she responded:

Firstly, they must constantly search for additional knowledge, and must develop their capabilities. Lawyers must develop their own capabilities. I have seen many people, it is as if they do not do any research, do not learn anything additional or new. And lawyers, those doing society-orientated work, there are still very few. [Lawyers] focus on working to collect money, on establishing themselves. It is up to them, I suppose.

Practice and Theory

When asked about the importance of academic work to lawyers, Yaowalak initially spoke of the importance of academic work as evidence and of academics as expert witnesses. When asked how she identified academic work to use in her work, she said she mostly used personal networks and asked academics whom she knew to come and discuss issues and sometimes to be witnesses. Overall she felt it was usually hardest to get cooperation from doctors and forensic experts, especially in torture cases.

When questioned on other interactions between academics and lawyers and on what each could learn from the other, Yaowalak considered that the main thing academics should learn from lawyers was the importance of going into the field and experiencing events, and that the main thing lawyers could gain from academics was the benefit of their deeper analysis of judgments and of causation. She saw face-to-face meetings as one of the best ways to facilitate these exchanges.

Transnational Relations

Transnational influences have had a strong impact on Yaowalak's career. Yaowalak describes herself as a human rights lawyer and has worked with and received support from foreign and international organizations. When she explains her approach to her work, human rights standards are given a central place. When she offers assessments of the Thai legal system, not meeting international standards and not recognizing human rights are given as core examples of failures, and concepts of the rule of law and democracy also feature.

One transnational experience, however, stood out as having had a particularly strong impact on her philosophy and career. Describing an internship served with the Hong Kong based Asian Human Rights Commission in early 2007, she explained:

It enabled me to learn about broader issues. I saw experiences from other countries. And it caused me to understand the principle of the rule of law at an international level. If we stay in our country, we will be immersed only in our country in Thainess. But once I went abroad, I could see absolutely and immediately that international principles, international law, they offer guarantees for and reach everyone. It caused my perspective to change, my way of thinking to change.

And on another occasion, when asked to reflect on an earlier stage of her career:

At that time I felt it was enjoyable. The work of the Lawyers Council varied. I met many groups of villagers. The issues and problems were many. Almost every type of case came to the Lawyers Council. I enjoyed my work. With the Lawyers Council, with case work in Thailand, it was enjoyable engaging with the facts, solving problems. But before I went to Hong Kong, it [going to Hong Kong] caused me to get new notions, new ways of thinking and theory on consistency with international standards. Once I returned and looked back on society, on Thailand, when Thailand did not act in accordance with the law, discriminated. I could see Thailand was in disorder.

While Yaowalak stated that seeing experiences of other countries had been informative, when asked whether she had relied on foreign law in her work she said that she had not yet done so. Also, while she referred extensively to international standards, she did not refer to regional standards.

When asked about transnational influences on the Thai legal system more broadly, the first issue Yaowalak turned to was the lifting of martial law which she saw as a direct result of foreign pressure. While this did not end the role of the Military Courts in civilian cases, it meant that for cases involving offenses committed after martial law was lifted there would be rights of appeal. Yaowalak considered even this limited improvement significant. Other examples of positive influence mentioned were Thailand becoming a party to international conventions leading to adoption of domestic laws, and foreign pressure leading to enactment of the *Act on Prevention and Suppression of Trafficking in Persons B.E. (2551)(2008)*.

When asked specifically about impacts of the global terrorism response, Yaowalak responded:

It led Thailand to get a developed anti-terrorism law. And the security forces, it's as if they both had a conception, and adopted practical measures, which lacked understanding—which saw Muslim people as terrorists and saw that the problem must be fixed by use of military measures. And there were more terrorism cases initiated, but it turned out they did not have evidence and this caused the courts to dismiss the cases. That is to say: there was a terrorism law, more cases were brought against Muslim people on terrorism charges; but in the cases it turned out there was no evidence and they were dismissed.

Overall, Yaowalak saw transnational influences as positive and terrorism as an exception:

> Mostly the impact has been good, because the international system is the standard. But if you ask about terrorism [laws], this is something which is special, which suddenly surfaced. Is it essential to have it? It is not essential because there are already other laws. It is as if, perhaps, America forced it to be adopted.

General Assessments

As can be seen from the foregoing discussion, Yaowalak's assessment of the Thai criminal justice system was strongly negative. She saw it as heavily affected by conservative attitudes, and as generally failing to meet international standards. Words like "collapse" and "crisis" featured prominently, and she saw no clear way forward.

Conclusion

Yaowalak is not a typical Thai lawyer. She takes risks and makes sacrifices that many others do not. Her career narrative, in particular the place in it of university experiences and awareness of the events of 1973 and 1976, is closely reflected in career narratives of other Thai "cause lawyers" (Munger, 2009). Her critique of the legal system and profession, in particular the centrality to it of *lèse-majesté*, is also widely reflected in contemporary Thai discourse.

While many of the issues Yaowalak has worked on have been strongly shaped by local political and social particularities, it is clear that transnational influences have strongly influenced her philosophy and her approach. Yaowalak's responses in the interview, and her actions more broadly, show a clear desire for legal professionals in Thailand to apply criminal procedure and to respect individuals in a way that resonates with internationally recognized norms of justice, human rights, and protection of economically, socially, and politically vulnerable people including during periods of political crisis. As her responses in this interview show, there are presently many obstacles to fulfillment of this desire.

Glossary

14 October 73: is the date that student-led popular uprisings led to the resignation of the military government led by Field Marshal Thanom

Kittikajorn. Student protests commenced in Bangkok on October 9 following the arrests over the previous three days of 13 activists who had been advocating for early promulgation of a new constitution. Over the following days numbers swelled, and satellite protests emerged in the provinces. Early on October 14, violence broke out between protestors and state forces in Bangkok. That evening the King announced that the military government had agreed to resign, and that a new civilian prime minister had been appointed. Violence continued into the next day, with at least 77 people killed and 856 wounded in the incident. Despite these deaths, the incident is commonly remembered as a high point for Thai democracy and Thai civil society.

6 October 76: is the date that right-wing militia and border patrol police attacked student activists and protestors who were opposing the return to Thailand of former military dictator Field Marshal Thanom Kittikajorn who had been ousted on October 14, 1973, following a popular uprising. The students and protestors were treated brutally, and at least 46 were killed. Following the incident, the military staged a coup. None of the perpetrators have been brought to account, and many now hold important positions in Thai society. The incident remains extremely sensitive and is treated briefly, if at all, in official Thai histories.

Section 112: is the provision of the *Criminal Code* that creates the offense of *lèse majesté*. It provides: "Whoever defames, insults or threatens the King, Queen, Heir-Apparent or Regent shall be punished with imprisonment of three to 15 years."

Article 44 of the *Constitution of the Kingdom of Thailand (Interim) B.E. 2557*(2014): provides:

In the case where the Head of the National Council for Peace and Order considers it necessary for the benefit of reform in various fields; to promote the unity and harmony of the people in the nation; or to prevent, stop or suppress any act which subverts national peace and order, national security, the throne, the country's economy or state affairs, whether the act occurs inside or outside the Kingdom, the Head of the National Council for Peace and Order with the approval of the National Council for Peace and Order shall have the power to order the action stopped or to take any action regardless of whether it will have legislative, executive, or judicial effect, and it is to be considered that that order or action, including implementation of that order, are orders, actions, or implementations that are legal, constitutional, and final. When this has been done, it shall be promptly reported to the President of the National Legislative Assembly and the Prime Minister. (Author's own translation)

Justice Fund: it is able to provide funding to cover costs associated with litigation in cases where funding is required to protect the rights and freedoms of the applicant or the public interest. Provision of funding is discretionary. In 2014, the fund provided 46,315,185 baht in funding, 78.56% of which went toward assisting defendants to make bail payments.

Lèse majesté: see [Section] 112.

Nitirat: is the name used since 2010 by a group of politically active academic lawyers based at Thammasat University. While the group's name is transcribed into English in the same way as one of the common Thai terms for rule of law, the Thai term is not the same term.

Ramkhamhaeng: is a public open-admission university with its main campus in Bangkok. It was among the first Thai universities to offer a law degree, having done so since 1971.

red cases: since 2005 Thailand has been affected by ongoing political crisis, with political groups and activists becoming polarized into groups popularly known as "red" and "yellow" shirts. Many understand the red shirts to be rural and uneducated and to support controversial former Prime Minister Thaksin Shinawatra. In practice, the composition of the group is more varied, and it is heavily factionalized. The reference to red cases is to cases related to actions of the red shirt movement or persons associated directly or indirectly with its causes.

Rohingya: the name used by a group of Muslim people living mainly in western Myanmar. They are not recognized as citizens by Myanmar and are consequently stateless. Attempts by members of the community to emigrate to Bangladesh and Southeast Asian states are common. The migrants claim to be refugees fleeing persecution, but recipient states tend to claim that they are economic migrants. At the time of the interview, mass graves of Rohingya human trafficking victims had recently been discovered in Thailand and Malaysia.

rule of law: in Thai, two terms denote rule of law concepts: *nitirat* and *nititham.* Some academics suggest *nitirat* refers to the concept of the *Rechtsstaat* or *État de Droit* and *nititham* to the concept of rule of law as theorized by A.V. Dicey. There are also other differences in nuance and historical association, including a greater historical and linguistic association of the term *nititham* with royalist and Buddhist discourses. In practice, however, the terms are often used interchangeably with no distinction made. In this interview, the term used by Yaowalak was *nitirat.* She confirmed she wanted it to be translated as rule of law.

war on drugs: the name given by the Thaksin Shinawatra government to a strict antidrugs policy pursued between February and December 2003. It is estimated that in the first few months of the program over 2000 people were killed.

yellow cases: since 2005 Thailand has been affected by ongoing political crisis, with political groups and activists becoming polarized into groups popularly known as "red" and "yellow" shirts. The yellow shirts are generally understood to be a loose grouping of royalists, ultranationalists, and the urban middle class and to oppose former Prime Minister Thaksin Shinawatra. The reference to yellow cases is to cases related to actions of the yellow shirt movement or persons associated directly or indirectly with its causes.

United States of America 14

MICHAEL W. GENDLER

Contents

The Criminal Justice Process of the United States

The American judiciary is a separate and independent branch of government established by Article III of the U.S. Constitution adopted in 1789. Congress (a Senate in which each state has two Senators and a House of Representatives in which representation is based on each state's population) is the legislative branch that enacts the laws.

The President leads the executive branch that carries out the laws, and the judiciary interprets the laws in decisions on controversies including criminal trials and appeals. Federal courts preside over civil and criminal cases. Some states have separate civil and criminal trial courts. The United States follows the United Kingdom common law system, in which judicial interpretations of the law follow the precedents of prior cases. The fundamental rights of defendants charged with a crime are set forth in the Bill of Rights, which were adopted in 1791 as the first 10 amendments to the 1789 Constitution. The Bill of Rights protects citizens against most searches and seizures without a judicial warrant (Fourth Amendment), prohibits compulsory self-incrimination, prohibits being tried twice for the same offense ("double jeopardy"), and provides for due process (Fifth Amendment), and provides a right to a speedy trial, to be informed of the nature of the charges, to confront witnesses and have compulsory process to call witnesses for the defense, to be tried by a jury of peers and to be represented by counsel (Sixth Amendment). The Eighth Amendment prohibits excessive bail and fines and cruel and unusual punishment. The Fourteenth Amendment was adopted in 1868 after the American Civil War. It prohibits the states from denying due process of law and equal protection of the laws (as well as securing citizenship to then recently freed slaves born in the United States). The Fourteenth Amendment has generally been interpreted as applying the Bill of Rights to the states. The states have their own constitutions. Many state courts have ruled that differences in language addressing the same right as in the Bill of Rights (such as privacy against government searches) result in greater protection for that state's citizens than under the Bill of Rights. But the states are not free to provide less protection than required by the Bill of Rights and the Fourteenth Amendment.

Each of the 50 states has its own judiciary, with jurisdiction over state law crimes and appeals. The great majority of criminal cases are adjudicated in state courts. The states typically prosecute state law felony trials in county courts. Felonies are crimes punishable by more than one year of imprisonment as set by state statute. Most states have intermediate appellate courts that have jurisdiction to decide appeals from the county courts, and a high court that is the state's court of last resort. In most states, the high court is a discretionary appellate court that can grant or deny review, and usually limits its docket to cases of great public importance, and cases that offer the opportunity to set a precedent for future cases. Nomenclature of the state courts varies. In many states, the county trial court is called the "Superior Court," and the high court is the "Supreme Court." But in New York, to take one example, the trial court is the "Supreme Court," and the high court is the "Court of Appeal."

Counties and cities usually have courts of limited jurisdiction that hear misdemeanor charges that typically are crimes with sentences punishable by fine or imprisonment up to a year, such as traffic violations and petty theft. Many states also have courts with specialized jurisdictions, such as drug courts, juvenile courts, and domestic violence. States usually have separate juvenile detention facilities for convicted juvenile offenders.

The federal judiciary has jurisdiction over crimes established by Acts of Congress and crimes committed on federal lands (military bases, national parks, national forests, Indian reservations, and the high seas). Federal judges are appointed by the President, subject to confirmation by a simple majority vote of the Senate. Federal judges have lifetime terms, subject only to "impeachment" by Congress for criminal conduct. The intent of lifetime terms is to ensure the independence of the federal judiciary.

There are 94 federal judicial districts. Each has a district court that has trial court jurisdiction. District judges preside over trials, decide what evidence the jury can see and hear, instruct the jury orally and in writing on the law governing the case, and how to conduct their deliberations, and decide sentences if a jury returns a guilty verdict, or if the defendant pleads guilty. District judges decide guilt or innocence in cases where the right to a jury trial has been waived. Sentences are established by Congress (and by state legislatures for the state courts). Sentencing statutes often prescribe a range of prison time (e.g., 5–10 years); whether there is a mandatory minimum prison time, and whether (and for what reasons) the sentencing judge can "enhance" the sentence upward or "depart" downward from the statutory minimum.

Federal criminal jury verdicts must be unanimous. The jury typically consists of 12 persons. The parties can stipulate to a smaller jury. If a jury cannot reach a verdict (a hung jury), the court will declare a mistrial. The government can retry the defendant after a mistrial without violating the Fifth Amendment rule against double jeopardy, because no verdict had been reached. Almost all of the states require unanimous verdicts in criminal cases; Louisiana and Oregon allow a verdict by a 10-2 majority.

Appeals can be filed to the "circuit" Courts of Appeals, so named because judges used to travel ("ride circuit") to hear appeals in remote places. There are 12 geographic circuits, and a federal circuit that hears appeals of patent cases and of monetary claims against the federal government. There is also a Court of Appeals for the Arms Forces, which has jurisdiction to hear court martial appeals. The 12 circuit courts are uneven in size. The Ninth Circuit is the largest in both territory and population, covering the U.S. west coast, and has the most judges of any federal circuit. The number of judges in each circuit is set by Congress (28 U.S.C. Section 44).

Appeals are argued and decided on the record made before the trial (district) court. No new evidence is allowed. Appeals can be filed only after final decisions by the trial court, with limited exceptions. Appellate courts in both federal and state judiciaries primarily decide issues of law, for example, whether evidence was properly admitted or excluded, or whether a police search or seizure violated the defendant's constitutional rights. Appellate review of fact issues typically is limited to whether there was substantial evidence to support a jury verdict. Appellate courts can affirm or reverse a trial court decision, or remand the case for a new trial if, for example, an evidentiary error was committed.

The U.S. Supreme Court has discretionary jurisdiction over appeals from the circuit courts, and grants review (also called *certiorari*) to about 75–80 petitions per year out of about 10,000 seeking review. The Supreme Court also has discretionary jurisdiction over cases decided by the states' high courts if the appeal presents an issue of federal law, such as cases presenting constitutional issues regarding search and seizure, the validity of confessions, and whether a state court's death penalty verdict meets federal constitutional requirements. The Supreme Court has nine members.

There is a second path for a state law criminal defendant to obtain federal judicial review of state criminal proceedings. A convicted state court criminal defendant can file a petition for a writ of *habeas corpus* (Latin for "you have the body"). Petitioners can file such actions in federal district court only after exhausting all of their state court remedies including appeals. The claim must arise under federal law. District court decisions can be appealed to the circuit Court of Appeals, and *certiorari* can be sought in the Supreme Court. Courts and Congress have adopted rules limiting *habeas corpus* actions in a variety of ways, including prohibitions against repetitious actions or asserting claims that could have been brought earlier.

The states employ a variety of schemes for selecting judges. Many states elect judges, by county election for trial judges and state-wide election for their high courts. Some states have a retention system where a state governor initially appoints judges, who then have to stand for re-election after a designated term. Another variation is that some states have a recall process, through which citizens can file a petition to obtain a vote on whether the judge should remain in office. The recall process varies among the states as to matters such as the number of signatures required to obtain a vote and whether there must be malfeasance or other wrongful conduct alleged. Until about the 1980s, incumbency typically worked strongly in favor of a sitting judge, and incumbents often ran unopposed. From that decade on, judicial races often have been hotly contested, much more expensive, and politicized. Recall elections have targeted judges who wrote opinions or sided with the majority in cases on high profile issues such as death penalty, gun rights, abortion, and regulation of land development.

Native American (a.k.a. Indian) tribes often have their own judiciaries, with power to try tribal members for offenses committed on the tribe's reservation. Tribal court jurisdiction sometimes overlaps with state court jurisdiction, often with conflict between the courts. There also can be conflict over whether tribes have jurisdiction over non-Indians on the reservation, or over the use of property within the reservation not owned by the tribe or a tribal member. Some smaller tribes join with others to fund courts to hear cases from all tribes in the group. The federally recognized tribes have sovereign immunity and cannot be sued in any court.

Tom Hillier, Federal Public Defender 1982–2014, Western District of Washington, Seattle

Introduction

"My work as a public defender informed my vision of the law."

Tom Hillier devoted four decades to unrelenting advocacy for the rights and dignity of indigent criminal defendants that challenged prosecutors and jurists alike. He developed an incipient Seattle Federal Public Defenders' office into an entity that earned the respect of the same prosecutors and jurists, along with other policymakers, in efforts to reform a judicial system attempting to deal with the high costs and unanticipated consequences of laws that have caused an alarming rate of mass incarceration and racial disparity throughout the United States. The systemic policy issues on which Tom has worked for years while running his office and representing clients have jumped to the forefront of American public attention, accelerating in prominence and hopes for reform in the brief time since our interview. Tom was appointed head of the Seattle Federal Public Defenders' office by the judges of the Western District of Washington in 1982, and reappointed seven more times until his retirement in 2014. Tom's career has seen the expansion of federal criminal law as Congress "federalized" more and more crimes. Tom currently works as Senior Counsel at *Perkins Coie* (one of Seattle's largest law firms) developing the firm's *pro bono* criminal defense practice representing indigent federal defendants. Tom graciously came to my house for our interview, to accommodate my limited mobility. He arrived by city bus, eager to contribute his views of the U.S. judicial system and radiating the relative tranquility of working part-time in a supervisory, programmatic capacity after decades of high stress litigation constantly as a heavy underdog. I asked if he wanted anything to eat or drink, he asked only for water. About four hours later, I suddenly realized that I had neglected even that minimal request. I think Tom could have continued talking for several hours more about his passion for his clients and their rights to the best possible defense.

Career

Thomas W. Hillier II grew up in Spokane, Washington, the largest city in the more rural half of Washington State, east of the Cascade Mountains. Tom was inspired to law by the uncle for whom he was named, and another uncle, Harold Petrie ("Uncle Pete"), an appellate judge in the Washington state court system. Tom graduated from St. Martin's College, a small Benedictine school in Olympia, Washington, where he learned to "read more, write better, and think critically." He then attended Gonzaga University Law School, enrolling in 1969 in its four-year night program so that he could work day jobs (two exhausting years in labor jobs and two years in law related clerkships) to support himself through school. Tom portrays his decision to practice criminal defense as an accident of history and circumstance lacking altruism, but it is better seen as his initiative to seize the opportunity to pursue a career that matched his ideals. In 1963, the U.S. Supreme Court decided in *Gideon v. Wainwright* that criminal defendants in state courts who could not afford a lawyer were entitled to appointment of a lawyer at public expense. The right of indigent federal defendants to a court-appointed lawyer was decided 25 years earlier (*Johnson v. Zerbst*, 1938) but did not include funding to pay lawyers appointed to represent indigent federal defendants, which Congress approved in the Criminal Justice Act (1964). In 1972 in *Argersinger v. Hamblin*, the Court held that the right to counsel applied to any case that threatened a defendant's loss of liberty, including misdemeanor charges (generally crimes with maximum sentences of less than one year; see *McInturf v. Horton*, 1975). These rulings greatly expanded the need for lawyers to defend indigent criminal defendants. In his last year of law school in 1972–1973, Tom and two classmates went "knocking on the door" of the Spokane County public defender and told him, "You need us." They became that office's first interns.

The student interns were "cold and inexperienced—we had no supervision, [were] given files, pointed toward the courtroom." Tom had his first jury trial as a legal intern, a marijuana case, with no lawyer sitting next to him. Tom was inspired rather than intimidated, "We cut our teeth basically on the liberty of others. Just lit my fuse big time. It was obvious to me that I wanted to be a public defender or at least a criminal defense lawyer as long as I could." What was obvious to Tom Hillier was not so obvious to very many lawyers entering practice in the 1970s. Public defense work was well regarded for giving new practitioners extensive courtroom experience, but generally seen as a stepping stone to more prestigious and well-paying work. But for Tom, "I just really enjoyed working with the people, figuring out what their story *was*, why they were there. And even more, I enjoyed pushing back against a system that I thought even then was unbalanced and weighted in favor of law enforcement and prosecution. So it was a way of trying to even the playing field a little bit."

Upon graduating from law school in 1973, Tom was hired by the Spokane County Public Defenders' Office as a staff lawyer to represent indigent defendants in the Washington state court system. Each of Washington's 39 counties has trial court jurisdiction over state law criminal and civil cases arising in that county. Washington State has two federal jurisdictions: the Western District and the Eastern District. In 1975, the Seattle Federal Public

Defenders' office was created in Seattle to provide attorneys to represent indigent defendants in Washington's Western District. Tom applied to head the office, which he described as "ambitious to say the least," but figuring that applying would get him "on the radar screen" and indeed he was hired as one of three assistants to the lawyer chosen to head the new office.

Until the 1960s federal courts relied on "panels" of lawyers in private practice to represent indigent defendants. The panels initially were created *ad hoc*, and they became officially established in the 1968 Criminal Justice Act. Even after that, Tom described their implementation nationally as "hodgepodge," crediting the Western District of Washington with trying to find panel lawyers suitable for the cases, "at least the serious ones." Typically judges would call law firms to "send a warm body over here," counting on the federal courts' prestige to conscript lawyers. Panel lawyers did not take on indigent federal criminal clients for love of money. Tom told of one well-known criminal defense lawyer who told Tom that he would accept such appointments for $10 per hour "if you could get that."

The 1964 Criminal Justice Act gave federal judicial districts (there are 94 nationally; including the two in Washington State) the option of establishing a defender office. Federal defender offices began as "pilots" in some larger cities (Chicago, Phoenix, San Francisco), and expanded as judges saw the improvements in quality of representation and efficiency provided by the pilot defender offices. Seattle was approximately 17th to establish a defender office. The judges quickly came to appreciate that high-quality defense made their jobs a lot easier. Federal Public Defender Offices now enjoy a prestige that did not exist 40 years ago. Results of a survey of federal judges by the well-known federal appeal judge Richard Posner of Chicago revealed that lawyers in Federal Public Defenders' Offices provide higher quality representation than retained counsel, appointed private counsel, and even federal prosecutors (Posner & Yoon, 2010). One federal judge described federal defender offices as "the gold standard" (*Wilbur v. City of Mount Vernon*, 2013).

In 1978, Tom left his federal defender job for private practice of criminal defense law in Seattle. In late 1981, the Seattle Federal Public Defender position became open. Tom applied, and on March 1, 1982 was appointed to the position by the federal judges of the Ninth Circuit Court of Appeals. On his first day on the job, the office was assigned a high seas murder case. A huge commercial vessel had "unloaded a dead body and done some minimal investigation," then left for Japan and returned to Seattle three months later. When it returned, Tom got a friend who happened to be the head of the pilot's union that guides commercial vessels into Puget Sound, to arrange for him to board the vessel at night, climbing a rope ladder three to four stories in height up the side of the moving cargo ship, a "white knuckle" experience. Tom interviewed everyone on board. When the ship docked, he walked off past FBI agents waiting to board and interviewed the crew. "Had a fairly major jump on the facts of the case for a change! And [my client] was found not guilty. A fun case." Getting such a major case on his first day on the job allowed Tom to "avoid the administrative chores that were awaiting my attention." There were only two lawyers when he began his tenure, as his predecessor had stopped hiring in his last few months. In 2014, the office had about 20 lawyers. In contrast to the start of Tom's career when public defenders were inexperienced new lawyers on their way to more lucrative and higher prestige positions, in 2015 an advertisement for an attorney opening in the Seattle office required five years of trial and significant appellate experience and offered a salary range of $96,142 to $146,617 (Federal Public Defender, 2015a, 2015b).

In about 1985, the Chief Judge of the Alaska Federal District Court asked Tom to start a Federal Public Defender's Office in Alaska as an adjunct to the Seattle office, an option provided to less populous federal judicial districts as alternatives to establishing their own defender's office or panels. Tom did that, overseeing the Alaska adjunct for about five years until it became large enough to operate independently. He served on the Advisory Committee on the Federal Rules of Evidence from 2000 to 2006 by appointment by then Chief Justice of the United States Supreme Court, William H. Rehnquist. Tom also serves on the King County Public Defense Advisory Board (King County Public Defenders represent indigent defendants in that County's state courts, which include Seattle), and has gone to Thailand and Iraq as part of the federal government's rule of law program to teach about human trafficking, developing the evidence to build a case, and public defense.

The quality and commitment to clients of Tom's work has been recognized repeatedly. He received the Federal Bar Association Outstanding Service Award in 1990. In 1993, his work was honored by awards from the Washington Association of Criminal Defense Lawyers and the Washington Bar Association for extraordinary courage and dedication to his work. In 1996 Tom was inducted as a Fellow by the American College of Trial Lawyers, and that year the American Civil Liberties Union (ACLU) of Washington presented Tom with its highest honor, the William O. Douglas Award. In 1998 Gonzaga University awarded Tom the Gonzaga Law Medal recognizing lifelong commitment to the service of others. The Seattle-King County Bar Association recognized Tom with its 2005 Outstanding Lawyer Award. In 2010 University of Washington Law School faculty inducted Tom as an honorary member of the *Order of the Coif.* In 2014 The Association of Federal Public Defenders presented Tom its highest honor, the Terence F. MacCarthy Award for excellence in a career dedicated to representing the poor.

Tom argued two cases before the U.S. Supreme Court. In *United States v. Bagley* (1985), the Court clarified the standards for obtaining reversal that apply when prosecutors withhold potentially exculpatory evidence that has been requested by the defense. Although the Court adopted a less favorable standard than Tom had sought, his client's conviction was reversed and the Court later relied primarily on *Bagley* to overturn a death penalty verdict (*Kyles v. Whitley*, 1995).

> The effect of [*Bagley*] has been fairly far-reaching in the death penalty community. I'm very proud of that, because even though it wasn't what the case started out to be, it had an impact in an area of the law that is near and dear to me. I don't think there should be a death penalty. One of the reasons I do what I do is that I am trying to see it abolished before I die.

In 2005, Tom argued a terrorism case before the Supreme Court, *United States v. Ressam* (2008). Ressam tried to enter the United States on a ferry from Canada to Washington, with explosives he intended to use to bomb the Los Angeles airport. He made false statements on his customs declaration about his name and citizenship. When the explosives were discovered during the border search, Ressam was charged with carrying explosives "during" the commission of a felony (making false statements on a customs declaration), a charge with a 10-year mandatory minimum sentence. The issue was whether the word "during" as used in the statute required more than a temporal relationship. The Court held that it did not. The case became far better known publicly when the Government twice successfully appealed a 22-year sentence as too lenient. The sentencing judge gave substantial weight to Ressam's change of heart after trial to cooperate with the Government that helped prevent other planned terrorist plots, which Tom thinks "occurred because he felt respected and treated fairly by his defense team."

Tom highlighted a case about 20 years ago where he represented a Pakistani schoolteacher charged with smuggling arms to Afghani freedom fighters, now known as the Taliban, but then supported by the United States because they were fighting the Russians. Tom presented a rule of law defense, that the Government knew of and approved what his client was doing. After a hard-fought legal battle, the defense was able to get access to classified information and secure a decision that such a defense can be valid under an "estoppel" theory. That line of law is becoming more significant with the increasing amount of classified information coming out.

On the subject of significant cases, Tom said:

> You measure significance by the impact on the person. ... It's the impact of good representation on keeping somebody home with their family that makes us go. In that respect, in the office as a group, we work very, very hard on sentencing issues, and trying to be creative, so that we can give judges information and reasons to impose fair sentences.

Tom explained why this was especially important between 1987 and 2005 when judges were required to sentence according to guidelines that were then mandatory "except in rare instances and we really expanded the notion of what is a rare instance in this district and had a downward departure rate from the guideline recommendations of more than 50 percent, ... leading the nation many, many years in that."

Achieving such results required hard work:

> Effort and a willingness by lawyers to go back in front of a judge again and again and again, say the same thing again and again and again even though they shot you down again and again and again, even when you are right, until the judge starts making incremental positive change.

When asked about failures, Tom responded:

> Every time I don't get a result I like, I consider it a failure, even if my clients think it's pretty good. I left court almost in tears once because I didn't think the guy should have gotten jail, and he said, "Tom, shake it off dude—18 months! I was thinking I was getting four years. I'm ecstatic!" The guy came by my office before I [retired] and said, "I wanted to drop in and say thanks. I got a job. I'm supporting my kids. I haven't used drugs since you started representing me, and prison was a breeze, and thank you very much." So even the failures sometimes have a measure of hope and measure of success or happiness anyway.

In reflecting on the surprises in his career, Tom commented that one surprise in all of this is that public defense became a career:

> Early on when we were becoming lawyers, you didn't stay in the public defender's office or prosecutor's office for long. You got your chops, your experience, and moved on. And public defense has become the criminal justice system, and in most jurisdictions that are well-resourced, it's a good job. You can make a living, and it's very exciting. Criminal law is very real, very human. It's dirty as it can get, it's just on the ground, and so it's a real, decent career if you're interested in action as a lawyer.

After leaving the Seattle Federal Public Defender's office, Tom has undertaken a new project working part-time as Senior Counsel to the Seattle law firm *Perkins Coie* to develop the firm's practice for representation of indigent accused persons in federal court. He credits George Kendall, a lawyer who became prominent because of his criminal defense work with a nonprofit, and then joined a major New York law firm, with an endowment from one of the firm's founders to establish a *pro bono* major impact criminal defense litigation program, who encouraged Tom to pursue a similar undertaking in Seattle. Tom chose *Perkins Coie* because he knew and admired lawyers in the firm who volunteered representation in a Guantanamo Bay terrorism case ultimately decided by the Supreme Court (*Hamdan v. Rumsfeld*, 2006), and because of the firm's commitment to championing *pro bono* criminal defense (including death penalty work) and backing that commitment strongly with the firm's resources.

Tom envisions that the firm's lawyers will accept appointments in "conflict cases" (where multiple persons may be charged, which would prevent the federal defender's office from representing one or more persons who would then need representation), and in cases where the firm's abilities and resources justify "harnessing that energy," such as cases involving specialized legal skills or large databases). Tom is already thinking ahead to expand the program to others of the firm's 19 offices in the United States. The firm does not benefit directly financially from this program. Indeed its lawyers will work *pro bono*. The firm benefits through getting courtroom experience for newer associate lawyers and from the inducement to junior lawyers who crave courtroom experience and representing the poor to stay at the firm, although Tom wants a mix that includes experienced attorneys, and is pleased that several firm partners have expressed interest.

Changes Observed during Mr. Hillier's Career, 1973–Present

In Tom's initial years as a federal public defender, federal criminal practice was limited primarily to federal statutory crimes such as bank robbery and fraud, gun running, mail theft, and crimes involving interstate commerce. There also are a "a fun array" of crimes to defend that ordinarily would be in state court (e.g., murder, assault, and burglary) but are prosecuted federally because the alleged crime occurred on federal lands or the high seas. Since there is a lot of federal presence in Washington State (national parks and forests, military bases, Native American reserved lands), water, and the international border with Canada giving rise to smuggling cases, Seattle provided "a pretty fun practice in federal court compared to most, I think." However, beginning in the late 1970s, a "get tough on crime" mood spread through the American public, with decreasing acceptance of alternatives to incarceration. Congress became amenable to "federalizing" (i.e., enacting a new criminal law covering the same conduct as existing state laws) what Tom called the "crime du jour," listing carjacking, child pornography, and human trafficking as examples of the priorities a new president had brought to Congress. Republicans focused on drugs, guns, and immigration, Democrats on bank fraud and human trafficking. In 1986, Congress began enacting laws requiring lengthy mandatory minimum sentences for drug crimes. At one point nearly half of federal prisoners were serving time for drug crimes.

The effect of these changes is that the federal jurisdiction and its caseload are always expanding. This has been compounded by an explosion of immigration cases in the last 10–15 years. Such cases now constitute about 30% of the federal criminal law caseload. Immigration violations typically are charged if the person has a prior record. There are "powerfully harsh" penalties for re-entry into the United States after a felony conviction, much more severe than, for example, defrauding a bank of millions of dollars.

As Congress enacted lengthy mandatory minimum sentences, so did about two thirds of the 50 states. About 90% of the U.S. prison population is in the state systems, although the fastest growth since the late 1970s has been in the federal prison population. In 1978, there were 30,000 prisoners in the federal system and 277,000 in state prisons; in 2013, there were 216,000 federal prisoners and 1.36 million in state systems. There has been increasing attention to the disparity in imprisonment between the United States and other countries. The United States has 5% of the world's population, yet 25% of the world's prison population (Patton, 2013). In the mid-twentieth century, the United States incarcerated 170 out of 100,000, on par with European nations; now, the United States incarcerates 750 per 100,000, "by far the highest rate of any Western nation" (Steinhauer, 2015).

After seeing the pendulum swing so much further in one direction than any public defender might have imagined starting a legal career in 1973, Tom now sees it finally start to swing back. There has been sentencing reform to roll back some of the lengthy mandatory minimums, although not retroactively, and therefore not achieving a quick reduction in prison populations, nor relief for those still serving lengthy sentences. Tom brought up a Clemency Project just started by President Obama and Attorney General Eric Holder to identify nonviolent offenders who are serving extremely long sentences imposed under prior mandatory minimum sentencing laws who would have completed their sentences under current sentencing laws, so that the President can use his executive authority to commute those sentences. Just over a month after our interview, President Obama became the first sitting U.S. President to visit a federal penitentiary, using the occasion to highlight the societal costs of mass incarceration under harsh sentencing laws and to explain the Clemency Project. The President cited his own youth as a casual drug user who could have been caught up in those laws, "but for the grace of God" (Baker, 2015). The President commuted 46 sentences and will have the opportunity to commute many more.

However, Tom points out that there are tens of thousands of these cases, and federal defenders are the only institution with the ability to identify who they are and advocate for their commutations. Unfortunately, federal judges decided that working with the Department of Justice to identify prisoners eligible for commutation was not a function for federal public defenders because it is an executive initiative, not a judicial one. Because of Tom's belief that the judges "crimped view" of the defenders' function is "really to the detriment of what this effort to restore some justice in the lives of these people is all about," he made himself "a bit unpopular in the federal judiciary" with speeches he gave to judges about "opening their hearts and mind and pockets" to allow "our independence in letting us do what we do for our clients, assuming we are doing it in a fiscally and responsible way." Tom is frustrated that the independence of public defense is compromised by resource limits, "so the ability to do a larger menu of things that seem logically to fall to the public defenders is difficult to accomplish because of those fiscal constraints."

Unlike some state court systems, the explosion of federal criminal law has not caused severe stress regarding individual attorney caseloads for federal defenders, because federal indigent defense costs are funded as part of congressional funding of the judiciary, which has been "generally enough for what we do." Still, Tom acknowledges resources as a major problem exacerbated by "sequestration," the name given overall budget constraints recently imposed by the U.S. Congress in 2013 that required Tom to reduce the staff in his last year. Historically, federal judges overseeing the budgets of defender offices have allowed leeway to the offices. As budget constraints have tightened, judges have become concerned about the scope of defender office activities. Tom identified training programs, death penalty resource counsel, and sentencing resource counsel as programs that have been criticized as outside the proper role of the defender offices, but have so far been allowed to continue. Sentencing resource counsel are groups of federal defender lawyers that work exclusively on sentencing issues, and go to different offices to help in a particular case or to conduct training.

Notwithstanding his frustration over the inability to participate actively in the President's clemency project, Tom applauds the Judiciary's support of defender legislative committees, sentencing guideline committees, and committees who prepare position papers and information to educate Congress. Tom characterized the effort overall as not proactive, but "pretty successful in stopping an expansion of harsher penalties."

Philosophy of Legal Advocacy

Tom saw the question whether public defenders have a role in addition to representing their clients as a "very hot topic," with sequestration tugging in one direction and the services needed to deal with our country's high rate of incarceration pulling the other way. That has "opened eyes to what a broader sort of public defense can do, and many offices ... have for a long time taken a broad view of the need to collaborate with politicians and leaders and law enforcement and prosecutors to identify areas that contribute to commission of crime and develop front-end, preventative programs. Clients also need back-end help to avoid future contact with the criminal justice system.

Many offices are expanding staff to include social workers and people who are expert at helping clients get relicensed in medical fields, or just a driver's license, so they can go about getting a job or getting from their home to school. Many essentials, like a driver's license, go away when you get caught up in the criminal justice system, especially if you go to jail for a while." Tom also mentioned having health experts in many defender offices, and federal defender attorneys going to state court to address problems that impact the present situation of their federal clients. "I always took the view that if something is happening elsewhere that influences how we can best handle a case, then get after it and I will endorse it. And I've always felt using that institutional muscle was important." Tom brought up criticisms that a defender's function should be limited to representing the client, and that

> If you start trading horses with politicians on stuff, you may be compromising somebody. For example, I had a policy in my office that we didn't waive appeals as part of a plea agreement unless the Government agreed to a deal that we didn't think we needed to appeal. Appeal waivers are rampant in the system and they really undercut the development of law but also operate to hurt clients who get a sentence they weren't anticipating. So when I preached no waivers, public defenders would yell at me saying, you can't do that because your client may need that waiver in order to get a deal. And so, well, they can fire me and get a panel lawyer and that's fine by me, but my office ain't doing it.

While admitting that he finally got "beat down" on waiver of appeals, Tom continues to believe in "flexing the muscle of the office" regarding policies affecting their clients' rights. "So I think there's a huge role in public defense, in both trying to shape the law but also in how we can help our client in a more holistic way than simply representing them in court." Tom identified several noncourtroom functions that are handled by public defenders, including drug courts, dependency cases, and juvenile truancy cases, as examples of "programs that are designed to make people less vulnerable to getting swept up into the criminal justice system."

Asked how difficult it is for defense counsel to develop the empathy needed to counsel clients of different economic strata and backgrounds, Tom answered forcefully that such empathy is at the very core of his philosophy regarding public defense. A defender may not be able to control the substantive outcome of a case, but can control his or her relationship with the client: "My passion is my client, and my federal public defender's office, if I can be immodest for a minute, is a good office, and the reason it is it a good office is because of our philosophy. And the philosophy at that office is agape (a term of Greek origin meaning 'brotherly love, charity,' subsequently used in a similar manner in Christianity, pronounced with the accent on the last syllable.) It's about a form of love that's pillared by compassion and forgiveness and showing people respect. When you can step up and forgive somebody and be compassionate, it makes you a better person and it really has a potential of making the person that you're dignifying a better person. For years, we were successful in this push back." To combat the wearying impacts of so many clients being over-punished,

> I prop up the troops by saying we can't necessarily change the system, we can't always get the results we want but we can influence our client's opinion of how we represented them and it's important to me as a priority in this office that everybody leaves this office feeling that they have been treated fairly, with respect, with love, with compassion, with mercy, that they're dignified by the experience they've had, and the hope is that as a result of that they're going to be better because of it and less inclined to come back in the system.

Tom believes providing such representation promotes public safety, helping alleviate the bitterness inevitable of a typical young defendant receiving a 20-year mandatory minimum sentence for dealing a small drug quantity from a judge telling the defendant that the sentence is unfair but the judge has no choice. ("Judges have said this more often than you can imagine.") Tom believes strongly in proximity, "getting close to your clients." He rejects the notions of not touching clients, shaking hands, or getting to know them. He described making sentencing videos taken in the home with children, and on the jobs.

> In the process of that, the judge gets closer to the client, but more importantly we do, and we learn a little bit more about how it is that they're there. We don't ask questions like, "How could you have done that?" because who are we to ask that question? We're not where they are, broke but trying to feed a family or victims of childhood abuse, or any of the things that might have influenced the behavior.

Yet Tom emphasized that agape did not mean that his office

> ...was all about touchy-feely stuff. Having our clients feel they were treated fairly is huge, but it's really gratifying that the system allows, requires tough legal representation and really relentless effort from the lawyers and all the staff. Everybody does it willingly, and I think because of the relationships that we formed with our clients.

Tom explained that sentencing videos are especially important in plea bargain cases where the judge sees the person whose life the judge's pronouncement will control so greatly for the first and only time at sentencing. Defense lawyers have expressed concern that the greater ability of defendants with resources to produce such a video is a further divide between criminal defendants of different economic standing. Tom's telling of his office's first sentencing video captured his innovation, compassion for his clients, and his belief that the defender needs to get to know the client to represent them. In contrast to the slick, costly productions described recently in the New York Times (Clifford, 2015), no one in the office was expert in filming. Tom went to a community college video class, talked with the professor, and "conscripted" the class to do a sentencing video. The client, Jerome, is:

> About 250 pounds, six foot five, had 11 felony convictions, 19 misdemeanor convictions, was in for drugs and guns again, and my God it's a 15 to life possibility. And I just loved him. He is the nicest, softest person I've ever met. But there's no way I'm going to be able to tell that story to a judge.

So they talked to people in the neighborhood and interviewed his kids, wife, and mom.

> We videotaped all of that, and it was very compelling. We played it in the courtroom at sentencing. All the people that were in the film were in the courtroom. All we needed was popcorn. They were in there yelling, just laughing and clapping. When Jerome's mom said, "I've been clean for nine months," everybody started clapping. "And the judge had a smile on his face. And the people left feeling, "Wow, this was good. I didn't know this happened."

Tom did not mention the sentence, but the experience inspired his office that now has a video team. They are not done in every case, but the office has developed sufficient expertise to teach at training conferences for other defender offices.

Tom describes his philosophy based on agape as "one of those Tom Hillier things that happens whenever I'm at the podium," and cites its therapeutic effect on defenders as well as its benefits in guiding the defenders' work, "It's a way to beat back the sadness that goes with public defense and getting results that aren't fair. And when you have that client say 'Thank you' and at the end of the day, their mom says you're 'a guardian angel,' or whatever it might be, it is kindness returned and it helps."

Problems and Successes Experienced

The harsh results of lengthy mandatory sentences, racial imbalance in the administration of criminal justice, and mass incarceration that Tom has been fighting throughout his career have become some of the hottest topics of national attention in the last year, and especially in the weeks just before and after our interview. Over just three days in late July, 2015, the New York Times gave prominence to bipartisan efforts to reform sentencing laws, the comedian/political commentator John Oliver devoted a 15 minute segment on his weekly show to mandatory minimums, and

National Public Radio talk show host/commentator John Hockenberry raised the question as to why even violent offenders sentenced under harsh sentencing laws no longer in effect should not receive consideration for commutations (Steinhauer, 2015). Oliver's segment featured an interview with a federal judge who had sentenced a minor drug dealer to a mandatory 55 years because he had no choice. The judge compared it with sentences for terrorism (20 years), hijacking an airplane (24 years), and for child rape (11 years), calling to mind Tom's recollection of the countless times that federal judges told his clients how unfair were the mandatory sentences they were about to pronounce upon them. The common thread that Tom sees in these issues is the imbalance of power in the federal judiciary, such that prosecutors have greater power even than federal judges let alone defense lawyers.

This is because prosecutors can threaten charges with lengthy mandatory minimum sentences:

> to beat pleas out of people who shouldn't be pleading guilty, that should be testing the proof and putting it through the crucible of process. What happens when you're not exercising your rights is that they atrophy. So these rights to jury trials and proof beyond a reasonable doubt are diminished, and the truth seeking function is compromised too. You don't know if the cop is lying or not, but when a prosecutor threatens if you contest this you're going to prison for 20 years, you don't have that chance.

True to form, Tom illustrated this imbalance with a compelling case example that turned out well anyway. His office had a client "who was a bad guy, a lot of drugs and guns." His potential sentence was 15 years to life, and after difficult negotiations the prosecutor grudgingly offered a 12-year sentence for a guilty plea. But the client rejected that deal, "because the cop is lying." The prosecutor's response was to reindict him and add additional gun charges carrying a 60-year mandatory minimum. "So he gets a 48-year penalty for exercising his right to trial. Most everybody is going to capitulate to that kind of a threat." Except, of course, this defendant. He chose to fight, and the court granted his motion to suppress evidence and ordered the government to initiate a perjury investigation regarding the officer's testimony. Tom used this case in a paper he wrote to Attorney General Holder urging new policies on charging and plea negotiation.

But as Tom points out,

> So how many times does that happen? Having the courage to fight despite such risk is rare. Having a police officer not telling the truth isn't. And that corrupting imbalance is created by the penalty structure that we suffer and the authority that's vested in the prosecutor, which is basically unreviewed, whereas what the judge does happens in open court and is subject to review.

So [prosecutorial charging authority] has had a real corrosive effect on the confidence that the public has in the system and certainly had a huge effect on the prison population.

Diversionary programs such as drug courts have expanded in the state systems and are now being used in federal courts as one means of reducing prison populations. There has been some success in initiating "front end" drug programs that allow a defendant to enter the program without having to plead to the charge. Such efforts have had to overcome Department of Justice policies that discourage allowing diversion without a guilty plea. Attorney General Holder has amended those policies to allow diversion for defendants with not more than two nonviolent felony convictions. Diversion is not limited to drug crime charges, if the behavior was influenced by drugs or alcohol. The Western Washington District was one of the first three federal judicial districts to adopt such a program, called "Dream." Every month each of the participants comes to court, with District Judge Martinez, the prosecutor, the federal defender and the probation officer, "and a lot of courtroom personnel because it's inspiring, and they talk about what they've been doing that month, ups and downs and people are weeping and hugging and joyful and sad, it's just an extraordinary process." Tom cites the Dream program (and also "back end" drug and alcohol counseling programs) as the means of tracking results on the local level. Tom commented on "a real cottage industry of scholarship on alternatives" to what prison do, which "emphatically shows" the correlation between diversion programs and lower recidivism. Further, this scholarship has produced "really good information that you can then give to the judge" to mitigate a sentence even if the client is not getting a diversion. The national federal defenders' website provides a breadth of resources including a "mitigation websites" column which links to studies that can be cited to support mitigation arguments under categories such as impact of incarceration, alternatives to incarceration, childhood health/victimization, mental health disorders, medical diseases, racial and ethnic disparity, and more (Federal Public Defender, 2015b).

While acknowledging the "great effort" of the clemency project to rectify some of the racial and sentencing imbalances at the "back end," Tom urges that "the change has to come at the front end, repealing laws that so empower the prosecutors," and "convincing judges and prosecutors not to think lengthy terms of imprisonment should be the norm. And that attitudinal shift is going to take time. But more and more relevant information is becoming available."

Asked about networking efforts, Tom pointed out that there were not many public defender offices until almost the 1970s, "so it's a fairly new baby." As the federal caseload expanded and defender offices were established, networking organizations such as the National Association of Criminal Defense

Lawyers and National Legal Aid and Defender Association were created. The American Civil Liberties Union (ACLU) historically has been involved in criminal justice issues, in many years appearing before the U.S. Supreme Court more than any entity other than the federal government. These groups became institutions that shared information and initiated collaborations to protect and advance defendants' rights.

Tom cited the American Bar Association (ABA) and state Bar associations as influential to public defense. The ABA (2002) created the 10 Principles of Defense that have been used to convince governments at all levels of the need to fund defenders sufficiently to meet constitutional requirements. The principles include adequate funding, independence, parity with the prosecution, and training. The King County Public Defense Advisory Board (on which Tom serves) has convinced King County to adopt the ABA's 10 Principles "as part of the underlying structure of what public defense is all about." Tom gives this example of a federal defender working with defenders, prosecutors, and the judiciary in the state judicial system to illustrate his assessment that the work of public defenders now is "highly collaborative." "It would be very unusual not to see a federal public defender or state or County public defender presence" on committees involved in shaping policy at the national or state level, "and that collaboration has been very significant in raising our profile."

The ABA's 10 Principles influenced Washington State's standards for indigent defense, which recently were the "keystone" of a strong federal court decision holding that the City of Mount Vernon (a smaller city of about 33,000 population about 60 miles north of Seattle) was failing to meet constitutional requirements for public defenders in its municipal court system (limited to misdemeanor cases with maximum sentences of less than a year), largely due to inadequate funding and defenders burdened with excessive caseloads that precluded adequate defense (*Wilbur v. City of Mount Vernon*, 2013). Tom described the City's defense that misdemeanor defendants were getting "sweetheart deals" with no jail time because the system was so flawed, contrasting that with the federal system where "we've got all sorts of process, but the end result of substance is so horrible you'd think that they didn't have it so bad in Mount Vernon." But the ACLU argued that there has to be a real attorney–client relationship, not clients meeting their lawyers for the first time at trial as was going on in Mount Vernon. Still, Tom sees "an interesting dichotomy" with the federal system where representation has better financial support, but its defendants tend to receive worse substantive outcomes.

When asked what may be the easiest problems to change, Tom answered that nothing really is easy. Addressing internal problems, as an office leader he had the authority to set the tone and standards, and "try to hire people that are engaged with the mission. I don't hire people that are brilliant but think the death penalty is okay." Recognizing that not all public defenders are good leaders, Tom cited the growth of organizations that network as enabling better monitoring of leadership. Addressing external problems, Tom emphasized how the literature has generated more community support, but "getting people to understand what the problems really are and to be active enough to push their policymakers and fiscal managers to do the right thing is just inordinately difficult."

Theory and Practice

Tom focused on research addressing the United States' highly disproportionate rate of imprisoning people, and that the impacts fall just as disproportionately on people of minority communities. The impact on minorities has spawned "some very serious scholarship and literature in the last 10 years." Tom cites a book by Georgetown University law professor Paul Butler (2010), an African-American former prosecutor who was prosecuted by the very office for which he worked on an unfounded complaint on which he was quickly acquitted. The event changed his career and his focus. Butler points out that there are more African-Americans in prison now than were slaves in 1850 or are in college right now. Tom also cites Ohio State University law professor Michelle Alexander's book, *The New Jim Crow: Mass Incarceration in the Age of Colorblindness* (2010), as a mainstream bestseller that has brought attention to the marginalization of people of color. Alexander describes the fallout of imprisonment, explaining the difficulties of getting a job, a driver's license, and housing. These and other studies are gaining the attention of policymakers. Tom cited an example in Washington State, of the defense lawyer associations working with the state legislature that has enacted a law sealing juvenile records to try to limit the lifelong damage that a criminal record can carry. Tom sees a growing awareness of the societal problems of overpunishment and overincarceration emerging from such research and writing.

Tom traces his own understanding of the theory of punishment in criminal justice centuries back to the Reformation, citing Montesquieu, Bentham, and Beccaria among those who asserted that a government that overpunishes its citizens commits "tyranny." The statutory code that embraces federal sentencing law captures this philosophy, directing that punishment should be "sufficient, but not greater than necessary," (Crimes and Criminal Procedure Act, 2010). Tom persisted in supporting his sentencing arguments with this Code language and Reformation philosophers who viewed overpunishment as a form of tyranny, arguments that "I am sure judges were not really amused by. But I think hearing the word tyranny in a sentencing argument had an impact."

Asked what theory builders can learn from legal advocates, Tom encouraged scholars to integrate into their work the compelling human stories that illustrate the data that comes out of their research. He cited University of Washington professor of sociology and law Katherine Beckett, whose work focuses on the consequences of penal practices (Beckett & Herbert, 2010). Professor Beckett described a program where students teach and tutor "lifer" prisoners, using a film of the students describing the impact of the project that carried a forcefulness that the data alone cannot achieve. "The way you do that is to go to prison and go into the homes of our clients. So I think scholars would do well to have more of the sort of clinical experiences where they're actually in the community getting their hands dirty, learning." Tom also credits Bryan Stevenson for using compelling individual stories to illustrate racial injustice (Stevenson 2014). Tom acknowledged that research conclusions must be data driven, but complains that a lot of the published research is inaccessibly dense to practitioners and lacking in reference to particular cases.

As to what holds back greater collaboration, Tom believes the adversarial system that underlies American justice has been carried to the extreme. When it comes to policy, prosecutors and defense lawyers need to use the political approach of compromise to reach a set goal. Tom believes that could be accomplished regarding the goal of remedying overpunishment, but lacks confidence in Congress to do anything (a belief about Congress currently shared by an overwhelming majority of Americans regarding all topics). When asked in follow-up correspondence about the extraordinary public attention that occurred after our interview, Tom was enthusiastic but still dubious about Congress despite even reports of strong bipartisan support for sentencing reform. Tom brought discussion of theory and practice back to why Americans are "so infatuated with such long sentences." But when asked what research practitioners would find most useful, Tom responded that most of the research "showing the correlations between poverty, unemployment, broken families, abuse and crime" has been done, "but there seems to be no willingness to fix that." Notwithstanding the growing public momentum for sentencing reform, Tom anticipates controversy and resistance, including lobbying from the "prison industry," referring to employment in state and federal penitentiaries as well as the privatization of the American prison system that followed the enactment of harsh penalty laws as the prisoner population grew faster than states could build prisons.

Transnational Relations

Tom brought up one of his cases that taught him the views of some outside the United States toward our justice system. He represented the wife of a prominent developer charged with bankruptcy fraud, then fled the United States taking large jewels and bank accounts. The developer was in his 80s and in poor health when the couple was arrested in France. When the United States sought extradition, Tom informed French officials that if extradited the couple would end up in prison notwithstanding their age and poor health. Tom rebutted unfounded U.S. government contentions that prosecutors could not guarantee judicial approval of a plea deal with no prison time, "Here's the rule, gives the judge the authority to preapprove the deal for no jail. It's all in the code." The French authorities decided not to allow extradition because they viewed imprisonment of an elderly couple for bankruptcy fraud as "barbaric." International relations and law were important to Tom's best known terrorism case, his representation of Ahmed Ressam, the man caught with explosives at the United States–Canadian border. Tom compared terrorism sentences throughout the world, finding that the sentences Ressam was facing "were exponentially larger." The government nevertheless successfully appealed the district court's 22-year sentence as too lenient.

Tom addressed how the September 11, 2001, attack on the United States affected justice more broadly. He has found terrorism cases to be very difficult because of the amount of resources the government devotes to them, its "unforgiving" stance regarding plea bargains, and its very aggressive litigation tactics. Terrorism cases are rare, but have led to bad law (for the defense) on constitutional issues under the Fourth Amendment (search and seizure, arrest, privacy), Fifth Amendment (self-incrimination), and Sixth Amendment (attorney–client privilege, right to counsel). However, the Supreme Court has become more concerned about Fourth Amendment privacy issues as technology affecting privacy evolves, such as multifunction cell phones, GPS tracking, and camera surveillance.

Tom has seen a lot of cases charged as "terrorist" cases, such as being charged for materially assisting a terrorist by sending money to parents in Somalia. Many of those cases have been dismissed, victories for the defense lawyers but not necessarily members of the large Somali communities in Seattle. After September 11, 2001, the FBI started questioning Somalis and threatening deportation for noncooperation. One of the federal defenders had led an immigration project and became aware of this practice. Tom's office took their concerns to the U.S. Attorney in Seattle who agreed to stop the practice.

General Assessments

Tom is optimistic but not satisfied about developments in criminal law and procedure over his career. Despite the extreme difficulty of correcting the harms caused by "the war on crimes and drugs," Tom is "very proud to be a part of our system." He sees the procedural foundation of our system as "very solid," broadly citing the right to counsel, the right to proof beyond a reasonable doubt, and all of the core Bill of Rights. "I'm an optimist by nature" who sees ahead an evolution in American criminal justice with a younger generation that is open and smart and can bring a lot of positive change through the political system. Tom's colleague, New York Federal Defender David Patton, wrote an essay asking whether federal criminal defendants receive fairer process now than in 1963, when *Gideon* was decided. Patton concluded that in many ways defendants receive far worse, citing the severity of sentences and the prosecutor's control of sentencing. As does Tom, Patton emphasized the systemic harm of these factors to the adversary process. Tom's career and philosophies illustrate the best of the ways in which the adversary process promotes justice in the American system. He led an office that litigated vigorously while retaining the ability to work cooperatively when it advanced the causes of his clients. Where would we be without people who pushed back so tirelessly against the criminal justice politics that defenders like Tom were dealt throughout their careers?

Glossary

attorney general: the chief law officer of the federal government or of each state. With respect to the USA federal judicial system, the Attorney General is the head of the U.S. Department of Justice.

Bill of Rights: the first 10 amendments to the U.S. Constitution, which guarantee fundamental rights and privileges of individuals, including freedom of religion, speech, press, and assembly; guarantee of a lawyer and a speedy jury trial in criminal cases; and protection against excessive bail and cruel and unusual punishment.

district court: constitutional trial courts which have territorial jurisdiction over federal cases arising in a state or part of it. Both civil and criminal cases are heard in district court. There are 94 U.S. district courts.

habeas corpus: Latin for "you have the body," a writ sought by a confined individual requesting a court to determine the legality of an individual's custody. The term typically refers to a postconviction challenge brought in district court claiming constitutional error in the state court conviction.

U.S. attorney: a lawyer who, under the direction of the Attorney General, enforces civil and criminal laws within his or her federal judicial district and represents the federal government within that district.

Conclusion: Closing the Gap between Law in Action and Research

15

JANE GOODMAN-DELAHUNTY
DILIP K. DAS

Contents

Introduction

Legal advocates make many critical decisions in the course of prosecuting and defending cases (Goodman-Delahunty et al., 2010). Accordingly, more scholarship on their decisions and their role in the justice process is overdue (Kiser, 2010, 2011). However, practicing lawyers are an elusive group to study, primarily because they are time-poor, creating a dearth of studies on this group. This is especially true of prosecutors and public defenders working in the public sector, both of whom carry a caseload that has at times been acknowledged as capable of overworking them to a point of ineptitude, with detrimental outcomes for justice (e.g., Gershowitz & Killinger 2011; Kleinman & Lee, 2010). The interview methodology applied in this book facilitated access to legal practitioners because its flexibility was well-suited to the time constraints of this busy group of professionals. The resulting book is a form of collective biography investigating features of a group of six prosecutors and eight criminal defense lawyers working in public and private practice, from a total of 13 different countries and jurisdictions.

Interviews and Legal Life Writing

Empirical studies of lawyers have typically focused on their views about a specific issue, such as eyewitnesses, drugs, plea bargaining, and so on, and are not self-reflective in terms of their personal careers or roles within a legal system. In contrast, the chapters in this book provide an insider's perspective as well as information on how those professionals are engaged in their careers within the legal system.

The methodology selected for studying prosecutors and defense lawyers can influence the research outcomes. For instance, observational studies of lawyers in action may reveal their public advocacy skills, but the private thoughts and perspectives of lawyers are more difficult to access. A strength of the book in presenting outcomes of structured interviews with multiple professionals across international and jurisdictional boundaries is that their reflections on their activities and decisions provide an autobiographical exposition and insider view. Using an in-person interview methodology, the interviews outlined in the foregoing chapters made visible a group of 14 outstanding prosecutors, public defenders, and criminal defense lawyers in their respective communities, and shed light on factors that motivated them to become legal advocates, as well as the challenges that they faced in their careers.

The purpose of open-ended interviewing, the method used in the interviews conducted for this book, is not to put ideas into someone's mind, but to access the perspective of the person interviewed (Hannabus, 1996). Interview responses gathered in this way can challenge long-held assumptions and recast ineffective public policies (Rubin & Rubin, 2013, p. 3). Thus, the observations and opinions of this group of leading advocates are a rich and important source of information about each legal system, the evolution of the case law and legislation within that system, and the respective legal cultures (Nelken, 2014) within which the lawyers practice their craft.

The term "life writing" has been applied to scholarly works that use life stories as a primary source for the study of history and culture (Mulcahy & Sugarman, 2015a, 2015b). Through life writing, untold stories and unheard voices can be accessed, and new perspectives shared. The collaborating academics and legal practitioners who conducted these interviews uncovered unique perspectives and insights about this group of legal practitioners. Collectively, the scholarly and scientific approach applied to these biographies qualify them as an example of prosopographical research (Stone, 1971; Sugarman, 2015, p. 94), as the chapters explore the common characteristics of the group, and how its members operate within and upon the social, political, legal, economic, and intellectual institutions of their time. Legal life writing has been described as "a heterogeneous field that offers new ways of advancing legal history and socio-legal scholarship, and of encouraging interdisciplinary dialogue, both between them and also with other fields and audiences" (Sugarman, 2015, p. 32). Together, these interview reports demonstrate several valuable features of legal scholarship in the form of legal biographies or life writing (Parry, 2010). This series of interviews is an ideal way to introduce students and professionals to scientific empirical methods of scholarship through life writing.

Comparative Methods and Commonalities

Since criminals operate across national borders, and often exploit the differences between laws that exist in different countries, members of the legal profession, like police, are often engaged in cross-national work. Within an expanding global regime of international cooperation in criminal matters, the value of comparative studies across jurisdictions is enhanced (Dandurand, 2007).

The interviews explore features that the group members have in common, and others that distinguish them by examining their lives and careers in law, their training and chosen profession, their social role, and their engagement with the criminal justice process. While the details of day-to-day practice of lawyers may seem mundane, and at times even trivial and repetitious, when the practitioners' reflections in response to parallel questions are aggregated into a book such as the present volume, the underlying structures or tendencies become visible and more salient (Sugarman, 2015, p.12). Additionally, because the interview questions remain constant across interviews, readers can directly compare the legal philosophy, challenges, theory, and practice underpinning different legal settings.

Common sources of frustration included addressing corruption and the lack of available resources. More positive common experiences were their flexibility in employing technological changes to advantage and their successes in replacing outmoded theories and policies, such as those on deterrence and mandatory sentencing, with contemporary, evidence-based practices. Few described motivators other than their commitment to "do the right thing" (Joy & McMunigal, 2011).

Contribution to Transnational Law

Existing publications have not posed similar questions to interviewees across transnational boundaries. Accordingly, the outcomes of the interviews in this book make a valuable contribution to the growing body of research on transnational lawyering, documenting common approaches and shared values within legal cultures that transcend jurisdictional boundaries. In some respects, cross-institutional commonalities in the roles and experiences of the prosecutors and criminal defense lawyers may be stronger than their cross-national features. For example, a number of interviewees discussed how rights were constructed, reconstructed, and defended.

In the interviews, the lawyers shared their insights on internal and external constraints that affected their work and decisions, causes and effects of prosecutorial diversity, and their subsequent effect on the character and nature of local law.

Several of the countries in which interviews were conducted had recently experienced or were still experiencing periods of intense social and political transition, such as the shifts toward democracy in China, Nepal, South Africa, and Thailand. Thus, these chapters have historical significance within the jurisdictions within which these lawyers are situated and interact. The American Bar Association Prosecution Rule of Law Initiative led to the development of the *Prosecutorial Reform Index (PRI)*, one of a series of assessment tools developed by experts in criminal law reform to provide an empirical basis to evaluate the role of prosecutors and the environment in which they work in transitioning states throughout the globe. The chapter in this book on transitioning states may inspire future comparisons using those tools.

Innovation and Law in Action

Other books in the field about either prosecutors (e.g., Harris, 2010) or defense lawyers (e.g., Wice, 2005) are mostly descriptive of the role (e.g., Jacoby, 1980; Williams & Hsiao, 2010) or specific to a single jurisdiction (Davis, 2007; Wice, 2005). A key feature distinguishing the chapters in this book is that they provide rarely available perspectives by the legal advocates of how they view their roles in the criminal justice systems within which they work.

The role of the prosecutor in many legal systems has been described as the most powerful position in the criminal justice system, and current knowledge about legal practitioners has emphasized the perspectives of prosecutors (Luna & Wade, 2012; Tonry, 2013) and their experiences within a single jurisdiction or country. Thus, consideration of the counterbalance offered by members of the criminal defense bar, such leading federal public defender, as Tim Hillier in the United States (Chapter 14), is most instructive. This chapter is supplemented by the perspectives of defense advocates in seven other countries who were interviewed for this book.

Through practice in applying legislation and in representing the public interest and individual or corporate defendants, legal counsel in criminal cases have the opportunity to innovate. The content of the interviews demonstrated that the roles of prosecutors and defense counsel were far less passive and impersonal (McCann, 2013) than those of many presiding judges, who are estopped from initiating matters and restrained from intensive activism. While judges are clearly duty-bound to interpret and apply existing law, legal advocates can argue for new interpretations. Their innovations at a local level often reflected their abilities to incorporate global trends. Some legal advocates used the existing structure and system, and innovated by bringing fresh matters under these laws. For example, Chapter 9 outlined how Mandira Sharma has used international law to address domestic Nepalese legal issues. Along similar lines, in Tokyo, through the Fairness Law Form, Naoya Endo has advocated to implement changes into the existing legal system of Japan to make it more responsive to people's legal needs by incorporating the flexible "soft law" concepts drawn from public international law (Chapter 8). In Sri Lanka, the shift toward more widespread adoption of alternate dispute resolution in criminal cases was the mechanism favored by Mr. Kodagoda, President's Counsel, Additional Solicitor General, Attorney-General's Department (Chapter 12). A further example was provided by Antoinette Ferreira who used existing conspiracy law in a fresh way to prosecute rhino poachers and put a stop to the traders of rhino horns (Chapter 11).

The foregoing examples underscored that the lawyers' interview responses in describing their roles in their respective jurisdictions and contexts illuminated the interrelationship between law and politics, especially in times of social upheaval and change (Worrall, 2008). Thus, the themes of legal work in combat widespread or systemic corruption were most prominent in the interviews conducted with legal counsel in China (Chapter 6) and South Africa (Chapter 11).

Professional Practice Role Models

Prelaw students contemplating a career in law, and law graduates about to enter legal practice, will find guidance and inspiration in the book from the personal career stories of successful legal leaders. Each chapter in the book is a rigorous and comprehensive qualitative case study that can be used to teach students in a university setting. These contributions by the chapter authors in collaboration with the legal professionals, whom they interviewed, fill a gap in the literature on the professional identity of members of the legal profession (Cownie, 2004) and on legal career guidance. Although "the bulk of legal biographies have focused on the lives of the elite, most often white, male, higher court judges" (Sugarman, 2015, p. 13), this book departs from that model in that all of the biographies are about lawyers, not judges, and only one-third of the group are white males.

Although the gendered power of the legal profession (McCann, 2013) did not comprise an explicit focus in questions to the practitioners, interviews with three prominent women defense lawyers, Mandira Sharma in Nepal (Chapter 9), Judith Ablett-Kerr in New Zealand (Chapter 10), and Yaowalak Anuphan in Thailand (Chapter 13), shed some light on this topic. The roles and extraordinary nature of the professional work undertaken by these women as agents of change through their focus on human rights advocacy, the rights of women in a legal system in transition, and the trafficking of women and battered women defense in criminal cases, reflected this aspect of their experience. The gendered nature of the legal profession may also have been a factor leading some of the women lawyers to make career transitions from one side of the bar table to the other. For instance, criminal defense barrister Judith Ablett-Kerr commenced her career in law practicing as a prosecutor, in Wales (Chapter 10), while Maria Teresa Rivero Gutierrez in Bolivia took the opposite path, starting out as a public defender, and then progressed to the position of a magistrate, and then prosecutor of appeals, before she was appointed President of the Supreme Court (Chapter 4). The career paths of the male prosecutors and defense lawyers described in this book did not reflect similar transitions.

Prosecutors, public defenders, and judges are institutionally separated within their criminal justice system (Levenson, 2013), but researchers have demonstrated that the day-to-day work in courts is often conducted by small groups of these individuals who share a common understanding and expectations of the procedures, and efficiently process large numbers of cases together (Lutze, 2014). Thus, the apparent boundaries between prosecutors, defense lawyers, and judges may be more permeable within functionally close-knit court "workgroups" (Wandall, 2008). This permeability can be increased by the participation in these working groups of professionals who have filled different roles in criminal justice system in the course of their careers.

The Place of Research in Contemporary Legal Practice

A singular contribution of this book is the exploration of the place of research in contemporary legal practice and the manner in which research is used or valued by leading global prosecutors and defense counsels. Practitioners on both sides of the bar table underscored the need for accurate information on local and national crime trends, and on social issues that bear on crime trends, such as racial factors and drug and alcohol consumption. A related concern was the need for research evaluations of the extent to which criminal justice policies that have been implemented are effective. A number of the advocates specified that that future research on the effectiveness of penological theories that underpin the criminal law was desirable. For this reason, institutions such as law reform agencies that aggregate relevant research findings to inform the development of legal policies were valued. The recommendation was made that law reform agencies would be even more valuable if they undertook empirical tests of proposed reforms before these were adopted. One prosecutor suggested that the access that members of the legal profession have to cases at the trial level should be exploited, and more in-depth research conducted using records of litigated cases, that are otherwise inaccessible to academics and researchers. Successes of legal psychological research on criminal investigation and interrogation methods were cited as particularly useful and influential examples to emulate in future.

The foregoing comments reflected a keen appreciation by the legal advocates of the value of evidence-based practice. One defense practitioner observed that future research needed to go beyond merely demonstrating the predictors and causes of crime to undertake interventions to remedy the problems identified. Further suggestions for future research included more research collaboration by practitioners and academics. However, practitioners also noted that much relevant research remains somewhat inaccessible to members of the legal profession. In sum, if practitioners and researchers jointly engaged in transdisciplinary research that extends beyond documenting the shared problems, they might devise and test innovations. Perhaps if legal practitioners had more direct engagement in research, the findings might also be more directly applicable and available to members of their profession.

Summary

This book is well-suited for use in teaching in multiple disciplines, including law, criminology, justice studies, psychology, policing, public policy, and sociology. It is appropriate for undergraduate upper level courses, postgraduate level courses, and for use in continuing education courses for practicing professionals. The book will inform the public, students and established scholars, and criminal justice practitioners of the actual workings of legal proceedings in diverse jurisdictions and regions. These interviews also have popular appeal to nonacademics, and will foster their engagement with public issues, global trends, and public history.

References

2014 *Situation summary report 2/5: Lèse majesté cases: One step forward, three steps backward.* (2015, July 21). [Web log post]. Retrieved from http://freedom. ilaw.or.th/en/report/2014-situation-summary-report-25-l%C3%A8se-majest%C3%A9-cases-one-step-forward-three-steps-backward.

2015 Equal Justice Award: A profile of the alcohol and other drug treatment courts [Web log post] (2015). Retrieved from http://equaljusticeproject.co.nz/2015/03/the-2015-equal-justice-award-a-profile-of-the-alcohol-and-other-drug-treatment-courts/.

Ablett, N. (1912). *The miners' next step* [Pamphlet]. Tonypandy: Robert Davies and Co General Printers.

Ablett-Kerr, J. (1997). A licence to kill or an overdue reform? The case of diminished responsibility. *Otago Law Review, 9*(1), 1–13.

Abuse of Ablett-Kerr "unacceptable." (2009, August 12). *Otago Daily Times*. Retrieved from http://www.odt.co.nz/news/dunedin/69398/abuse-ablett-kerr-039unacceptable039.

Act on Compensation for Victims and Compensation and Expenses for Defendants in Criminal Cases B.E. 2544 (2001).

Act on Prevention and Suppression of Trafficking in Persons B.E. (2551) (2008) [in Thai].

Act of Settlement 1700, c.2 12 and13 Will 3 [Eng.] (1700). Retrieved from http://www.bailii.org/uk/legis/num_act/1700/1565208.html.

Air Quality Act, South Africa, No. 39 (2004). Retrieved from https://www.environment.gov.za/sites/default/files/gazetted_notices/nemaqa_listofactivities_g33064gon248.pdf.

Alexander, M. (2010). *The new Jim Crow: Mass incarceration in the age of color blindness*. New York: The New Press.

Alister, P. (1997). *Bombs, bliss and baba*. Maleny, Queensland, Australia: Better World Books.

Amendment (IX) to the Criminal Law of the People's Republic of China, 37 P.R.C.C. (2015).

Amerasinghe, A. R. B. (1986). *The Supreme Court of Sri Lanka: The first 185 years*. Ratmalana, Sri Lanka: Sarvodaya Book Publishing Services.

American Bar Association. (2002). Ten principles of a public defense delivery system. Chicago, IL: Author. Retrieved from http://www.americanbar.org/content/dam/aba/administrative/legal_aid_indigent_defendants/ls_sclaid_def_tenprinciplesbooklet.authcheckdam.pdf.

American Bar Association Rule of Law Initiative. (2016). Chicago, IL: American Bar Association. Retrieved from http://www.americanbar.org/advocacy/rule_of_law.html.

Anderson, T. G. (1985). *Free Alister Dunn and Anderson: The Ananda Marga conspiracy case—The true story of the Hilton Hotel bombing*. Sydney, Australia: Wild & Woolley.

Anderson, T. (1992). *Take two: The criminal justice system revisited.* Sydney, Australia: Bantam Books.

Anil Sharma and others v. S. N. Marwah and another, 30 DRJ 566 Delhi High Court (1994).

Ansett Transport Industries (Operations) Pty Ltd v. Wraith, 48 ALR 500 (1983).

Argersinger v. Hamblin, 407 U.S. 25 (1972).

Backhouse, M. (2013, October 17). *Greg King suffered "massive breakdown"- coroner.* New Zealand Herald. Retrieved from http://www.nzherald.co.nz/nz/news/article.cfm?c_id=1&objectid=11141626.

Baker, P. (2015, July 16). *Obama, in Oklahoma, takes reform message to the prison cell.* *The New York Times.* Retrieved from http://www.nytimes.com/2015/07/17/us/obama-el-reno-oklahoma-prison.html?_r=1.

Bantu Authorities Act (Act No. 68 of 1951). Retrieved from www.aluka.org/stable/10.5555/AL.SFF.DOCUMENT.leg19510615.028.020.068.

Barry, Y., Cano, C., & Chambers, A. (n.d.). *Judicial reform of criminal justice in Latin America.* Unpublished manuscript, Office of the Legal Adviser, US Department of State, Washington, D.C. Retrieved from www.oas.org/legal/english/osla/judicial_reform.doc.

Basu, D. D. (2015). *Introduction to the Constitution of India* (22nd ed.). New Delhi, India: Lexis Nexis.

Beccaria-Bonessana, C. (2015). *An essay on crimes and punishments.* The Perfect Library.

Beckett, K., & Herbert, S. (2010). *Banished: The new social control in urban America.* New York: Oxford University Press.

Benns, M. (2003). *When the bough breaks: The true story of child killer Kathleen Folbigg.* Sydney, Australia: Bantam Books.

Bentham, J. (1775). *Rationale of punishment.* London: Robert Heward.

Bhattachan, K. B., Sunar, T. B., & Bhattachan, Y. K. (2009). *Caste-based* discrimination *in Nepal* (Volume III, Number 8). New Delhi: Indian Institute of Dalit Studies.

Bilger, P. (2003). *Un avocat général s'est échappé* (avec la collaboration de Stéphane Durand-Souffland). Paris: Éditions du Seuil.

Bourdieu, P. (1984/2003). *Distinction: A Social Critique of the Judgment of Taste.* London: Routledge.

Bourdieu, P. (1987). The force of law: Toward a sociology of the juridical field. *Hastings Law Journal, 38*(5), 805–853.

Brinkmann, S. & Kvale, S. (2015). *Interviews: Learning the Craft of Qualitative Research Interviewing* (3d ed.). London: Sage Publications.

Brown, R. C. (2012). Comparative alternative dispute resolution for individual labor disputes in Japan, China, and the United States: Lessons from Asia? *St. John's Law Review, 86,* 543–577. Retrieved from http://www.upf.edu/gredtiss/_pdf/2013-LLRNConf_Brown.pdf.

Butler, P. (2010). *Let's get free: A hip-hop theory of justice.* New York: The New Press.

Carmon, I., & Kniznhnik, S. (2015). *Notorious RBG: The Life and Times of Ruth Bader Ginsburg.* New York: Harper Collins Publishers.

CES and Anor ACES v. Superclinics Australia Pty Ltd ORS (1995). 38 NSWLR 47. Chamberlain v. The Queen (No. 2), 153 CLR 521 (1984).

Chen, J. (2016). Chinese law: Context and transformation: Revised and expanded edition. Leiden: Brill Nijhoff.

Chen, R. (2000). The theoretical foundation of procedural justice: A review of Mathew's "concept of dignity." *Chinese Law, 3*(95), 145–153.

Chen, Y. Y., & Wang, X. Q. (2013). *Evidence science institutions of higher learning in the 21st century jurisprudence series of fine arts colleges teaching materials* (5th ed.). Beijing: China Renmin University Press.

Child Justice Act, South Africa, No 75 (2008). Retrieved from http://www.justice.gov.za/legislation/acts/2008-075_childjustice.pdf.

Child Protection Act, South Africa, No. 38 (2005). Retrieved from http://www.justice.gov.za/legislation/acts/2005-038%20childrensact.pdf.

Children, Young Persons and Their Families Act (New Zealand) (1989). Public Act No. 24. Retrieved from http://www.legislation.govt.nz/act/public/1989/0024/latest/DLM147088.html.

China. (1983). *The Constitution of the People's Republic of China: (adopted on December 4, 1982 by the Fifth National People's Congress of the People's Republic of China at its fifth session).* Oxford: Pergamon Press.

China Internet Information Center. (n.d.). *China's judiciary.* Retrieved from http://www.china.org.cn/features/judiciary/node_1025025.htm.

Civil Procedure Law of the People's Republic of China (Revised in 2012). Order of the President of the People's Republic of China No.59.

Clifford, S. (2015, May 24). A flattering biographical video as the last exhibit for the defense. *The New York Times.* Retrieved from http://www.nytimes.com/2015/05/25/nyregion/defendants-using-biographical-videos-to-show-judges-another-side-at-sentencing.html?src=relcon&moduleDetail=lda-articles-1&action=click&contentCollection=Opinion%C2%AEion=Footer&module=MoreInSection&version=WhatsNext&contentID=WhatsNext&configSection=article&isLoggedIn=true&pgtype=article&_r=1.

Code of Criminal Procedure of India 1973. (Act No. 2 of 1974).

Cole, T. (2004). Commercial arbitration in Japan: Contributions to the debate on Japaneses non-litigousness, *International Law and Politics, 40,* 28–114.

Cole, T. (2007). Commercial arbitration in Japan: Contributions to the debate on "Japanese non-litigiousness". *New York University Journal of International Law and Politics, 40,* 29–114.

Companies Act (New Zealand) (1993). Public Act No 105. Retrieved from http://www.legislation.govt.nz/act/public/1993/0105/latest/DLM319570.html.

The Constitution Act (1982). Schedule B to the Canada Act 1982 (UK), 1982, c 11. Retrieved from http://canlii.ca/t/ldsx.

Constitution Act (New Zealand) (1986). Public Act No 114. Retrieved from http://www.legislation.govt.nz/act/public/1986/0114/latest/DLM94204.html.

Constitution of the Kingdom of Thailand B.E. 2540 (1997) [in Thai]. Unofficial translation. Retrieved from http://www.asianlii.org/th/legis/const/1997/1.htm.

Constitution of the Kingdom of Thailand B.E. 2550 (2007) [in Thai]. Unofficial translation. Retrieved from http://library2.parliament.go.th/giventake/content_cons50/cons2550e-kd.pdf.

Constitution of the Kingdom of Thailand (Interim) B.E. 2557 (2014) [in Thai]. Unofficial translation. Retrieved from http://library2.parliament.go.th/giventake/content_give/cons_temp2557E.pdf.

Constitution of the Republic of South Africa (1996). Retrieved from http://www.gov.za/sites/www.gov.za/files/images/a108-96.pdf.

Convention Against Torture and Other Cruel, Inhuman or Degrading Treatment or Punishment, (1984, December 10), 1465 U.N.T.S. 85.

Convention on International Trade in Endangered Species of Wild Fauna and Flora (1973), 27 UST 1087; TIAS 8249; 993 UNTS 243.

Cook Islands Constitution Act (New Zealand) (1964). Public Act No 69. Retrieved from http://www.legislation.co.nz/act/public/1964/0069/latest/DLM354282.html.

Cooray, L. J. M. (1987). *An introduction to the legal system of Sri Lanka* (2nd ed.). Pannipitiya, Sri Lanka: Lake House Investments.

Corey, Z., & Hans, V. P. (2010). Japan's new lay judge system: Deliberative democracy in action? *Asian-Pacific Law Policy Journal, 12,* 72–94.

Cownie, F. (2004). *Legal academics: Culture and identities.* Oxford: Hart Publishing.

Cownie, F. (2009). *A great and noble occupation: The history of the Society of Legal Scholars.* Oxford: Hart Publishing.

Crimes Act (New Zealand). (1961). Public Act No 43. Retrieved from http://www.legislation.govt.nz/act/public/1961/0043/latest/DLM327382.html.

Crimes Act New South Wales Sections 82, 83, 84 (1900). Retrieved from http://www.austlii.edu.au/au/legis/nsw/consol_act/ca190082/.

Crimes and Criminal Procedure Act (United States), 18 U.S.C. Section 3553(a) (2010).

Criminal Code [in Thai].

Criminal Justice Act of 1964 (United States), Pub. L. No. 88-455, 62 Stat. 684 (codified as amended at 18 U.S.C. § 3006A (2006)).

Criminal Procedure Legislation (Amendment) Act No 74, New South Wales Schedule 1 (1990). Retrieved from http://www.austlii.edu.au/au/legis/nsw/num_act/cpla1990n74407.pdf.

Criminal Law of the People's Republic of China (1979). National People's Congress.

Criminal Law of the People's Republic of China (97 Revision) (1997).

Criminal Law of the People's Republic of China Amendment (9) (2015).

Criminal Procedure Act (New Zealand) (2011). Public Act No 81. Retrieved from http://www.legislation.govt.nz/act/public/2011/0081/61.0/DLM3359962.html.

Criminal Procedure Code [in Thai].

Criminal Procedure Law of the People's Republic of China Amendment (2012).

Criminal Procedure Rules (New Zealand) (2012). SR 2012/415. Retrieved from http://www.legislation.govt.nz/regulation/public/2012/0415/latest/whole.html#DLM4914717.

Criminal Procedure Act 1986 (NSW). Retrieved from http://www.austlii.edu.au/au/legis/nsw/consol_act/cpa1986188/.

Crown Law Solicitor-General's Prosecution Guidelines (New Zealand) (2013). Retrieved from http://www.crownlaw.govt.nz/uploads/prosecution_guidelines_2013.pdf.

Cunliffe, E. (2011). *Murder, medicine, and motherhood.* Oxford: Hart Publishing.

Dandurand, Y. (2007). The role of prosecutors in promoting and strengthening the rule of law. *Crime, Law and Social Change, 47* (4/5), 247–259.

Darling, F. C. (1970). The evolution of law in Thailand. *The Review of Politics, 32*(2), 197–218.

Davis, K. (2007). *Defending the damned. Inside Chicago's Cook County Public Defender's Office.* New York: Avenue of the Americas.

De Ruyver, B., & Van Impe, K. (2000). De minnelijke schikking en Bemiddeling in strafzaken. [Amicable settlement and negotiation in criminal cases.] *Rechtskundig Weekblad*, 64(11), 445–463.

Dhanda, A. (2000). *Legal Order and Mental Disorder*. London: Sage Publications.

Dietrich v. R, 177 CLR 292 (1992).

Director of Public Prosecutions Act New South Wales (1986). Retrieved from http://www5.austlii.edu.au/au/legis/nsw/consol_act/doppa1986343/.

Dodek, A.M. & Jutras, D. (Eds.) (2009). *The Sacred Fire: The Legacy of Antonio Lamer. Markham*, Ontario, Canada: LexisNexis.

Domingo, P., & Sieder, R. (2001). *Rule of law in Latin America: The international promotion of judicial reform*. London: University of London.

Dressler, J., & Michaels, A. C. (2014). *Understanding criminal procedure* (5th ed., Vol. 1). Providence, NJ: LexisNexis Co.

Eades, D. (2010). *Sociolinguistics and the legal process*. Bristol: Multilingual Matters.

Eades, D. (2013). *Aboriginal ways of using English*. Canberra, Australia: Aboriginal Studies Press.

Emergency Decree on Public Administration in Emergency Situations B.E. 2548 (2005) [in Thai]. unofficial translation. Retrieved from http://www.lawreform.go.th/lawreform/images/th/legis/en/act/2005/2354.pdf.

Endo, N. (2000). *Rō sukuuru kyōiku ron – atarashii bengo gijustu to soshō unei [Philosophy of law school education: new advocacy skills and trial management]*. Tokyo: Shinzansha.

Endo, N. (2002). *The theory of divided responsibility for directors: Reforms to the Commercial Code of 2001 and the theory of shareholder derivative lawsuits*. Tokyo: Shinzan-sha.

Endo, N. (2004). *Kiki ni aru seisho iryō e no teigen — jendaa barietii girukazenshindan seishi ranshi teikyō dairi shussan [Proposal for reproductive medicine in crisis: Gender diversity, preimplantation genetic diagnosis, sperm and egg donation, and surrogacy]*. Tokyo: Kindai Bungeisha.

Endo, N. (2008). *Itsumo yatō ni tōhyō shiyō! - Kurikaesu seiken kōtai* [Always elect the opposition - keep political power changing hands!]. Tokyo: Makino Shuppan.

Endo, N. (2012a). *Sofuto rō ni yoru shakai kaikaku* [Social reform via soft law]. Tokyo: Gentōsha.

Endo, N. (2012b). *Sofuto rō ni yoru iryō kaikaku* [Health care reform via soft law]. Tokyo: Gentōsha.

Endo, N. (2012c). *Atarashii hō shakai o tsukuru no wa anata desu? "Softo rō" to "bunkaku sekinin ron" no katsuyō* [Using the shared responsibility theory of soft law to build a new social order]. Tokyo: Art Days.

Endo, N. (2014). *Sofuto rō demokurashii ni yoru hō kaikaku* [The reform of Japanese law via soft law democracy] Bilingual edition (Japanese & English). Tokyo: Art Days.

Engel, D. M. (1975). Law and kingship in Thailand during the reign of King Chulalongkorn. Ann Arbor: Center for South and Southeast Asian Studies, University of Michigan.

Engel and Others v The Netherlands (1); ECHR 8 June 1976.

Evidence Act NZ (2006). Public Act 2006 No 69.

Evidence Act New South Wales (1995). Retrieved from http://www5.austlii.edu.au/au/legis/nsw/consol_act/ea199580/.

Fang, C. (2009). The urbanization and urban development in China after the reform and opening-up. *Economic Geography, 29*(1), 19–25.

Faundez, J. (2011). Legal pluralism and international development agencies: State building or legal reform? *Hague Journal on the Rule of Law, 3*, 18–38.

Federal Public Defender. (2015a). *Assistant Federal Public Defender*. Retrieved from http://waw.fd.org/employment/150605_AFPD_Seattle.pdf.

Federal Public Defender. (2015b). *Mitigation*. Retrieved from http://www.fd.org/navigation/select-topics-in-criminal-defense/sentencing-resources/subsections/mitigation-websites.

Federation of Law Societies of Canada. (2015). *Our Members*. Retrieved from http://flsc.ca/about-us/our-members-canadas-law-societies/.

Feiberg, J. (1984). *The moral limits of criminal law volume 1: Harm to others*. Oxford: Oxford University Press.

Fiske, Jr., R. B. (2014). *Prosecutor Defender Counselor: The Memoirs of Robert B. Fiske, Jr.* Brooklin, ME: Seapoint Books and Music.

Foreshore and Seabed Act 2004 (NZ), Public Act 2004 No 93.[repealed April 2011].

Gardner, J. (2001). Legal positivism: 5 ½ myths. *American Journal of Jurisprudence, 46*, 199–227.

Garrett-Walker, H. (2012, September 14). Ewen MacDonald sentenced to five years. *New Zealand Herald*. Retrieved from http://www.nzherald.co.nz/nz/news/article.cfm?c_id=1&objectid=10834002.

Gellner, D. N., Pfaff-Czarnecka J., & Whelpton, J (Eds.) (1997). *Nationalism and ethnicity in a Hindu kingdom: The politics of culture in contemporary Nepal*. Abingdon: Routledge.

Genn, H., Partington, M., & Wheeler, S. (2006). *Law in the real world: Improving our understanding of how law works*. London: Nuffield Foundation.

Gershowitz, A. M., & Killinger, L.R. (2011). The state (never) rests: How excessive prosecutor caseloads harm criminal defendants. *Northwestern University Law Review, 105* (1), 261–301.

Gideon v. Wainwright, 372 U.S. 335 (1963).

Gillerion, G. (2014). *Public Prosecutors in the United States and Europe: A Comparative Analysis with Special Focus on Switzerland, France, and Germany*. Switzerland: Springer.

Gluckstein, D. (2011). *The Paris commune: A revolution in democracy*. Chicago, IL: Haymarket Books.

Gonzales v. R, NSWCCA 321 (2007).

Goodman-Delahunty, J., Granhag, P. A., Hartwig, M., & Loftus, E. F. (2010). Insightful or wishful: Lawyers' ability to predict case outcomes. *Psychology, Public Policy, and Law, 16*, 133–157.

Goto, A. (2014). Citizen participation in criminal trials in Japan. *International Journal of Law, Crime and Justice, 42*(2), 117–129. doi:10.1016/j.ijlcj.2013.07.001.

Government of the Northern Territory. (1987). *Royal Commission of Inquiry into Chamberlain convictions, Report of the Commissioner the Hon. Mr. Justice T. R. Morling*. Darwin, Australia: Government Printer.

Grabosky, P. N. (1989). *Wayward governance: Illegality and its control in the public sector*. Canberra: Australian Institute of Criminology.

Greenspan, B. (1987). Towards a distinctively Canadian jurisprudence: The Charter's impact upon the criminal law. In F. E. McArdle (Ed.), *The Cambridge lectures 1987. Selected papers based upon lectures delivered at the conference of the Canadian Institute for Advanced Legal Studies, 1987, held at Cambridge University, England* (pp. 349–365). Montreal, Québec, Canada: Canadian Institute for Advanced Legal Studies.

Group Areas Act 1950 (Act No. 41 of 1950). Retrieved from www.aluka.org/stable/10.5555/al.sff.document.leg19500707.028.020.041.

Gutierrez, G. (1988). *A theology of liberation: History, politics, and salvation.* Maryknoll, NY: Orbis Books.

Haberkorn, T. (2011). Dispossessing law: Arbitrary detention in Southern Thailand. In S. Feldman, C. Geisler, & G. A. Menon (Eds.), *Accumulating insecurity: Violence and dispossession in the making of everyday life* (pp. 122–137). London: University of Georgia Press.

Hall, J. (1947). *General principles of criminal law.* Indianapolis, IN: Bob Merrill Company.

Hamdan v. Rumsfeld, 548 U.S. 557 (2006).

Hangen, S. (2008). *Creating a "new Nepal": The ethnic dimension.* Washington DC: East-West Center.

Hannabus, S. (1996). Research interviews. *New Library World, 97*(5), 22–30.

Harding, A. (2008). The eclipse of the astrologers: King Mongkut, his successors, and the reformation of law in Thailand. In P. P. Nicholson, & S. Biddulph (Eds.), *Examining practice, interrogating theory: Comparative legal studies in Asia* (pp. 307–341). Leiden, the Netherlands: Martinus Nijhoff.

Harris, K. D. (2010). *Smart on crime: A career prosecutor's plan to make us safer.* San Francisco, CA: Chronicle Books LLC.

Hart, H. M. (1958). The aims of criminal law. *Law and Contemporary Problems, 23,* 401–441.

Hausegger, L., Hennigar, M., & Riddel, T. (2015). *Canadian courts.* Toronto, Canada: Oxford University Press.

He, B. (1999). *Prevention and punishment of duty crime.* Beijing: China Fangzheng Press.

Hocking, J. (1993). *Beyond terrorism—The development of the Australian security state.* Sydney, Australia: Allen and Unwin.

Hooker, M. B. (1988). The "Europeanization" of Siam's law 1855–1908. In M. B. Hooker (Ed.), *Laws of South-East Asia: European Laws in South-East Asia* (Vol. 2, pp. 531–607). Singapore: Butterworths.

Human Rights Watch. (2004). *Between a rock and a hard place: Civilians struggle to survive in Nepal's civil war.* New York: Human Rights Watch.

Human Rights Watch and Advocacy Forum Nepal. (2010). *Indifference to duty: Impunity for crimes committed in Nepal.* New York: Human Rights Watch.

Immorality Act 1927 (Act No. 5 of 1927). Retrieved from www.aluka.org/stable/10.5555/al.sff.document.leg19500512.028.020.021.

Imperial Laws Application Act (1988), schedule 1.

Indian Evidence Act. (1872).

Indian Penal Code. (1860).

Informal Sector Service Centre (INSEC). (2007). *Human rights yearbook 2007.* Kathmandu, Nepal: INSEC. Retrieved from http://www.insec.org.np/pics/report/1242904095.pdf.

Integrated Coastal Management Act, South Africa, No 24 (2008). Retrieved from http://www.gov.za/sites/www.gov.za/files/38171_3110_Act36of2014Integrated CoastalManagem_a.pdf.

Internal Security Act B.E. 2551 (2008) [in Thai].

International Commission of Jurists. (2015). *The International Commission of Jurists' submission to the UN Committee on Economic, Social and Cultural Rights in advance of the examination of Thailand's initial and second periodic reports under Articles 16 and 17 of the International Covenant on Economic, Social and Cultural Rights*. Retrieved from http://tbinternet.ohchr.org/Treaties/CESCR/Shared%20 Documents/THA/INT_CESCR_CSS_THA_20446_E.pdf.

Japan Today (2016, Sep 24). Japan's bar federation targets abolishing death penalty for 1st time. https://www.japantoday.com/category/crime/view/ japans- bar-federation-targets-abolishing-death-penalty-for-1st-time.

Jenkins, M. (Director). (1995). *Blue Murder [Television Miniseries]*. Sydney, Australia: Australian Broadcasting Corporation.

Jiang, J. H. (2010). *Events Chronicle of Anti-Corruption in China* (1978–2010). Beijing: China Fangzheng Press.

Jianming, C. (2014). *Report of the Supreme People's Procuratorate*. Retrieved from http:// news.cntv.cn/2014/03/10/ARTI1394445208837407.shtml (unofficial translation).

Jiggens, J. (1991). *The incredible exploding man: Evan Pederick & the Trial of Tim Anderson*. Brisbane, Australia: Samizdat Press.

Jinhua, J. (2010). *A chronicle of events in anti-corruption in China (1978–2010)*. Beijing: China Fangzheng Press.

Jocoby, J. E. (1980). *The American prosecutor: A search for identity*. Lexington, MA: Lexington Books.

Johnson v. Zerbst, 304 U.S. 458 (1938).

Joy, P. A. (2004–2005). Prosecution clinics: Dealing with professional role. *Mississippi Law Journal, 74*, 955–981.

Joy, P. A., & McMunigal, K. C. (2011, Fall). Contingent rewards for prosecutors. *Criminal Justice, 26*, 55–58. Retrieved from http://ssm.com/abstract/2067674.

Judicature Act 1908, (NZ), Public Act 1908 No 89.

Jury Amendment Act No 78, New South Wales (2007). Retrieved from http://www5. austlii.edu.au/au/legis/nsw/num_act/jaa2007n58198.pdf.

Jury Amendment (Verdicts) Act New South Wales (2006). Retrieved from http:// www5.austlii.edu.au/au/legis/nsw/repealed_act/jaa2006263/.

Jury Amendment Act New South Wales (1977). Retrieved from http://www5.austlii. edu.au/au/legis/nsw/consol_act/ja197791/.

Jury Amendment Act New South Wales (1997).

Kennedy, L., & Whittaker, M. (1998). *Sins of the brother*. Sydney, Australia: Pan McMillan Australia.

Khadka, N. (1986). Crisis in Nepal's partyless Panchayat system: The case for more democracy. *Pacific Affairs, 59*(3), 429–454.

King, M. (2003). *The Penguin history of New Zealand*. Auckland, New Zealand: Penguin Press.

Kiser, R. (2011). *How leading lawyers think: Expert insights into judgment and advocacy*. New York: Springer Science+Business Media.

Kiser, R. (2010). *Beyond right and wrong: The power of effective decision making for attorneys and clients*. New York: Springer Science+Business Media.

Kittayapong, R. (1990). *The origins of Thailand's Ministry of Justice and its early development*. Unpublished doctoral dissertation. University of Bristol.

Kleinman, M., & Lee, C. (2010). *North Carolina Assistant District Attorney/Victim Witness Legal Assistant Workload Assessment: Final Report*. Williamsburg, VA: National Center for State Courts.

Kummetha, T. (2014, March 25). Crime of the state: Enforced disappearance, killings and impunity. *Prachatai*. Retrieved from http://prachatai.org/english/node/3904.

Kyles v. Whitley, 514 U.S. 419 (1995).

Lal, B. V. (2006). *Islands of turmoil: Elections and politics in Fiji*. Canberra, Australia: ANU EPress and Asia Pacific Press.

Law of the People's Republic of China on the Organization of the People's Courts (2006). Retrieved from http://www.lawinfochina.com/display.aspx?lib=law&id=5623&CGid=.

Lawoti, M., & Pahari, A. K. (Eds.) (2009). *The Maoist insurgency in Nepal: Revolution in the twenty-first century*. London: Routledge.

Lawyers Council of Thailand Announcement No. 4/2554 (2011) [in Thai]. Reproduced in: (2011). *Thanaikhwan Magazine, 1*(3), 16.

Lawyers Council of Thailand Announcement No. 5/2554 (2011) [in Thai]. Reproduced in: (2011). *Thanaikhwan Magazine, 1*(3), 17.

Levenson, L. (2013). Discovery from the trenches: The future of Brady. *UCLA Law Review. Discovery, 60*, 74–90.

Li, L., & Tian, H. (Eds.) (2014). *Blue book of rule of law: Annual report on China's rule of law No. 12*. Beijing, China: Social Sciences Academic Press.

Li, Y. (2014). The judicial system and reform in post-Mao China: Stumbling towards justice. Aldershot, UK: Ashgate Publishing.

Litmus. (2014). *Formative evaluation for the alcohol and other drug treatment court pilot*. Retrieved from http://www.justice.govt.nz/publications/global-publications/f/formative-evaluation-for-the-alcohol-and-other-drug-treatment-court-pilot.

Lord Denning, Rt. Hon. (1984). *Landmarks in the law*. New York: Oxford University Press.

Loos, T. (1998). Issaraphap: Limits of individual liberty in Thai jurisprudence. *Crossroads: An Interdisciplinary Journal of Southeast Asian Studies, 12*(1), 35–75.

Loos, T. (2006). *Subject Siam: Family, law and colonial modernity in Thailand*. Ithaca, NY: Cornell University Press.

Luna, E., & Wade, M. (2012). *The prosecutor in transnational perspective*. New York: Oxford University Press.

Lutze, F. E. (2014). Professional Lives of Community Corrections Officers: The Invisible Side of Re-entry. Thousand Oaks, CA: Sage Publications.

Man Found Guilty of Lèse-Majesté for Uploading Clips. (2014, September 1). *Prachatai*. Retrieved from http://www.prachatai.com/english/node/4312.

Marine and Coastal Area (Takutai Moana) Act (2011).

Martial Law Act B.E. 2457 (1914) [in Thai]. Unofficial translation. Retrieved from http://www.thailawforum.com/laws/Martial%20Law.pdf.

Maslin, S. (Producer) & Dellora, D. (Writer/Director). (1995, February 19). *Conspiracy* [Television documentary broadcast]. Sydney, Australia: Film Art Doco.

McCann, M. (2013). The personal is political: On twentieth century activist lawyers in the United States. *Tulsa Law Review, 49*, 485–500.

McEwan, J. (1992). *Evidence and the adversarial process*. Oxford: Blackwell Publishers.

McInturf v. Horton, 85 Wn.2d 704 (1975).

McIntyre, W. D., & Gardner, W. J. (Eds.) (1971). *Instructions from Lord Normandy to Captain*. In W. D. McIntyre & W. J. Gardner (Eds.), Speeches and documents from New Zealand history. Oxford: Clarendon Press.

McLean, G. (Director). (2005). *Wolf Creek* [Motion picture]. Australia: Tus Australian Film Finance Corporation, the South Australian Film Corporation.

Minister of Environmental Affairs and Tourism v. Phambili Fisheries (Pty) Ltd, All SA 616 (SCA) (2003).

Ministry of Justice. (2012). *The registered intermediary procedural guidance manual*. Version 2.0. London: Author.

Molomby, T. (1986). *Spies, bombs and the path of bliss*. Sydney, Australia: Potoroo Press.

Montesquieu, C. (1742). *De l'esprit des lois* [*The spirit of the laws*]. Cambridge: Cambridge University Press.

Morris, A. (2015). *A Practical Introduction to In-Depth Interviewing*. London: Sage Publications.

Mulcahy, L., & Sugarman, D. (2015a). Legal life writing: Marginalised subjects and sources. Chichester: Wiley-Blackwell.

Mulcahy, L., & Sugarman, D. (2015b). Introduction: Legal life writing and marginalized subjects and sources. *Journal of Law and Society, 1*, 1–6.

Munger, F. (2009). Globalization, investing in law, and the careers of lawyers for social causes: Taking on rights in Thailand. *New York Law School Law Review, 53*(4), 745–802.

Munger, F. (2011). Cause lawyers and other signs of progress—three Thai narratives. In S. Cummings (Ed.), *The paradox of professionalism: Lawyers and the possibility of justice* (pp. 243–273). Cambridge: Cambridge University Press.

Munger, F. (2012). Constructing law from development: Cause lawyers, generational narratives, and the rule of law in Thailand. In J. Gillespie, & P. Nicholson (Eds.), *Law and development and the global discourses of legal transfers* (pp. 237–276). Cambridge: Cambridge University Press.

Nallaratnam Singarasa v. Attorney General (Unreported) (Supreme Court Special (Leave to Appeal) No. 182/99) (2006).

Narcotics Drugs and Psychotropic Substances Act (1985), (India), Act No 61 of 1985.

National Bureau of Statistics of China. (2014a). *Annual resident population by province*. Beijing, China: State Council of the People's Republic of China. Retrieved from http://www.stats.gov.cn/english/.

National Bureau of Statistics of China. (2014b). *Annual gross domestic product by province*. Beijing, China: State Council of the People's Republic of China. Retrieved from http://www.stats.gov.cn/english/.

National Environmental Management Act, South Africa, No. 107 (1998). Retrieved from https://www.environment.gov.za/sites/default/files/legislations/nema_amendment_act107.pdf.

National Environmental Management Waste Act, South Africa, No. 59 (2008). Retrieved from http://sawic.environment.gov.za/documents/384.pdf.

National Prosecuting Authority Act 1998 (South Africa) (Act No. 32 of 1998). [www.npa.gov.za].

Nelken, D. (2014). Thinking about legal culture. *Asian Journal of Law and Society, 1*(2), 255–274.

Nepal Treaty Act, 1990, 9 November 1990. Retrieved from http://www.refworld.org/docid/3ae6b51724.html.

New Court for Homeless Addicts. (2010, July 25). Stuff.co.nz. Retrieved from http://www.stuff.co.nz/national/crime/3955558/New-court-for-homeless-addicts.

New Zealand Constitution Act (1852), 15 and 16 Victoria, Cap. 72, sec.71. Retrieved from https://archive.org/stream/constitutionofne00grea/constitutionofne00grea_djvu.txt.

New Zealand Law Society. (2014). *Snapshot of the profession at 01 February 2014.* Retrieved from https://www.lawsociety.org.nz/__data/assets/pdf_file/0003/76332/LawTalk-836-WEB.pdf.

New Zealand Parliament. (2011). *Consideration of constitutional issues.* Retrieved from http://www.parliament.nz/en-nz/parl-support/research-papers/00PlibCIP081/consideration-of-constitutional-issues.

New Zealand Police Annual Report. (2012). Retrieved from http://www.police.govt.nz/about-us/publication/annual-report-2012.

Nonet, P., & Selznick, P. (2001). *Law and society in transition: Toward responsive law.* Somerset, NJ: Transaction Publishers.

Notice of the Supreme People's Procuratorate on Issuing the Provisions on the Management of Property Involved in Criminal Proceedings by People's Procuratorates (2005).

Notice of the Supreme People's Procuratorate on Issuing Several Provisions of the Supreme People's Procuratorate on Preventing and Redressing the Extended Custody in Procuratorial Work (2003).

Notice of the Supreme People's Procuratorate on Issuing the Eight Prohibitions of the Supreme People's Procuratorate on Duty-related Crime Investigations (2015), 47 P.R.C.C. Chapter 3 (2015).

Nowak, M. (2006). *Report by the special rapporteur on torture and other cruel, inhuman or degrading treatment or punishment: Mission to Nepal.* E/CN.4/2006/6/Add.5.

Office of the Courts of Justice. (2014). *Annual judicial statistics, Thailand 2013* [in Thai]. Retrieved from http://www.oppb.coj.go.th/userfiles/file/Statistic/stiti_2556.pdf.

Orange, C. (2012). *Treaty of Waitangi—Creating the treaty of Waitangi* (p. 7). Wellington: Bridget Williams Books. Retrieved from http://www.teara.govt.nz/en/treaty-of-waitangi/page-1.

Order of the Head of the National Council for Peace and Order No. 3/2558 (2015), issued April 1 2015 [in Thai]. Unofficial translation. Retrieved from http://www.prachatai.com/english/node/4933.

Organic Law of the People's Procuratorates of the People's Republic of China, (1979), art 2.

Otani, T., & Endo, N. (2005). *Initiating Preimplantation Genetic Diagnosis: Infertility Treatment to Prevent Repeated Miscarriages.* Tokyo, Hara Shobou.

Ottavio Quattrocchi v. CBI, 75 DLT 97 High Court of Delhi (1998).

Palmer, M. S. R. (2006). Using constitutional realism to identify the *complete* constitution: Lessons from an unwritten constitution. *American Journal of Comparative Law, 54*(3), 587–636.

Parry, R. G. (2010). Is legal biography really legal scholarship? *Legal Studies, 30*(2), 208–229.

Patton, D. E. (2013). Federal public defense in an age of inquisition. *Yale Law Journal*, 122, 100–124.

Penney, S., Rondinelli, V. & Stribopoulos, J. (2011). *Criminal Procedure in Canada*. Markham, Ontario, Canada: LexisNexis.

People's Procuratorate of Henan Province. (2015). *Report of the People's Procuratorate of Henan Province*.

Petchsiri, A. (1987). *Eastern importation of western criminal law: Thailand as a case study*. Littleton, CO: FB Rothman.

Pichaikul, R., & Klein, J. R. (2005). *Legal literacy for supporting governance*. Bangkok, Thailand: The Asia Foundation.

Pillai, K. N. C. (Ed.) (2014). *R. V. Kelkar's criminal procedure* (6th ed.). Lucknow, India: Eastern Book Company.

Pinch, D. (2007, November 16). *Inquest into the death of Brian Raymond Peters (one of the Balibo 5)* (Coroner's Finding). Retrieved from http://www.coroners.justice. nsw.gov.au/Documents/brian%20peters%201975%20(balibo)%20-%20find-ing%20and%20recommendations.pdf.

Platt, J. (2001). The history of the interview. In J. F. Gubrium & J. A. Holstein (Eds.), Handbook of interview research: Context and methods (pp. 33–54). Thousand Oaks, CA: Sage.

Plotnikoff, J., & Woolfson, R. (2007). *The "go-between": Evaluation of intermediary pathfinder projects*. London: Ministry of Justice.

Plurinational State of Bolivia. (n.d.). Criminal Procedure Code (promulgated by Law No. 1970 of March 25, 1999). Retrieved from http://www.wipo.int/wipolex/en/ details.jsp?id=6828.

Posner, R. A., & Yoon, A. H. (2010). What judges think of the quality of legal representation. *Stanford Law Review*, 63, 325–327.

Powell, M., Bowden P., & Mattison, M. (2014). Stakeholders' perceptions of the benefit of introducing an Australian intermediary system for vulnerable witnesses. *Australian & New Zealand Journal of Criminology*, 48(4), 498–512. doi: 10.1177/0004865814543391.

Praveen Malhotra v. State through Delhi Administration, 41 DLT 418 (1990). Criminal Miscellaneous 161/90 decided on 22nd March 1990 Delhi High Court. Retrieved from http//www.scconline.com.

Prevention of Corruption Act (1988). (India), Act No. 49 of 1988.

Prevention of Organized Crime Act, South Africa, No. 121 (1998). Retrieved from http://www.gov.za/sites/www.gov.za/files/a121-98.pdf.

Prohibition of Mixed Marriages Act of 1949. Retrieved from www.aluka.org/ stable/10.5555/al.sff.document.leg19490708.028.020.055.

Provisions of the Supreme People's Court, the Supreme People's Procuratorate, the Ministry of Public Security, the Ministry of State Security, the Ministry of Justice, and the Legislative Affairs Commission of the Standing Committee of the National People's Congress on Several Issues concerning the Implementation of the Criminal Procedure Law (2012).

Public Prosecution Service of Canada. (2015). *About the public prosecution service of Canada*. Ottawa, ONT: Author. Retrieved from http://www.ppsc-sppc.gc.ca/ eng/bas/index.html#intro.

R v. Anderson, 53 A Crim R 421 (1991).

R v. Armour Pharmaceutical Co. (2007).

R v. Calder. T154/94, HC Christchurch, Tipping J (1995, April 12).

R v. Derek Bentley (Deceased) EWCA Crim 2516 (1998, July 30).

R v. Dodd, 2015 ONCA 286, O.J. No. 2129 (Canada) (2015).

R v. Drabisky and Gottlieb (2009).

R v. Gittany, NSWSC 1503 (2013).

R v. Gonzales, NSWSC 822 (2004, September 17).

R v. Ngo, NSWSC 1021 (2001, November 14).

R v. Ryan, S.C.R. 14, 2013 S.C.C. 3 (Canada) (2013).

R v. Shirley Justins, NSWSC 1194 (2008, November 12).

R v. Sood, NSWSC 1141 (2006, October 31).

R v. Stinchcombe, 3 S.C.R. 326 (Canada) (1991).

R v. Wald, 3 DCR (NSW) 25 (1971).

R v. Wood, NSWCCA 21 (2012).

R v. Wood, NSWSC 1273 (2008, December 4).

Raj Kumar Khanna v. State, 95 DLT 147 (Delhi High Court 2002).

Rajepakse, R. (2006). *An introduction to law in Sri Lanka*. Pannipitiya, Sri Lanka: Stamford Lake.

Rama Narang v. Ramesh Narang, 2 SCC 513 (Supreme Court of India 1995).

Ramseyer, J. M., & Rasmusen, E. B. (2003). *Measuring Judicial Independence: The Political Economy of Judging in Japan*. Chicago, IL: University of Chicago Press.

Requesting a royal pardon: The gap on the path to freedom. (2013, October 9). [Web log post]. [in Thai]. Retrieved from http://freedom.ilaw.or.th/RoyalPardon2013.

Resource Management Act (New Zealand). (1991). Public Act No 69. Retrieved from http://www.legislation.govt.nz/act/public/1991/0069/latest/whole.html#DLM230265.

Roberts, P., & Saunders, C. (2010). Piloting PTWI: A sociolegal window on prosecutors' assessments of evidence and witness credibility. *Oxford Journal of Legal Studies, 30*(1), 101–141. doi: 10.1093/ojls/gqq004.

Robins, S. (2011). Towards victim-centred transitional justice: Understanding the needs of families of the disappeared in postconflict Nepal. *International Journal of Transitional Justice, 5*, 75–98.\

Rubin, H. J., & Rubin, I. S. (2012). *Qualitative Interviewing: The Art of Hearing Data* (3d ed.). Thousand Oaks, CA: Sage Publications.

S. M. Malik and Others v. State and Another, 1919 Delhi High Court (1990).

SADF's poaching industry exposed. (n.d.). *The free library.* (2014). Retrieved from http://www.thefreelibrary.com/SADF%27s+poaching+industry+exposed.-a018307790.

Sanjeev Nanda v. CBI, Bail Application of 749/2008 High Court of Delhi 29.4. (2008).

Sato, M. (2015). Vox populi, vox dei? A closer look at the 'public opinion' argument for retention. In: I. Šimonovic (Ed.), *Moving Away From the Death Penalty: Arguments, Trends, and Perspectives* (pp. 250–258). New York: UN Office of the High Commissioner for Human Rights.

Sato, M. (2016). 世論という神話─望むのは「死刑」ですか？ *(Public opinion myth: Is 'death' what we really want?)*, 世界 (Sekai), 879, 183–191.

Schmidt, P. (2002). *Capital Punishment in Japan*. Leiden, the Netherlands: Brill.

Sentencing Act (New Zealand) (2002). Public Act No 9. Retrieved from http://www.legislation.govt.nz/act/public/2002/0009/latest/whole.html#DLM135342.

Shaha, R. (1978). *Nepali politics: Retrospect and prospect*. Delhi, India: Oxford University Press.

Shanti Behal v. State, 51 DLT 354 (Delhi High Court 1993).

Sharpe, R. J., & Roach, K. (2013). *The charter of rights and freedoms* (5th ed). Toronto, Canada: Irwin Law.

Shibhu Soren v. CBI, 97 DRJ 629 (High Court of Delhi 2007).

Shine Australia (Production Company). (2015, May) *Catching Milat* [Television Series]. Australia: Channel 7.

Shirk, S. (1993). *The political logic of economic reform in China*. Berkeley, CA: University of California Press.

Simester, A. P., & Hirsch, A. V. (2011). *Crimes, harms, and wrongs: On the principles of criminalization*. Oxford: Hart Publishing.

Smith, A. (2012). Are prosecutors born or made? *Georgetown Journal of Legal Studies, 25*, 943–960. Retrieved from http://scholarship.law.georgetown.edu/facpub/1215.

Smith, A., & Noble, T. (2005). *Neddy: The life and crimes of Arthur Stanley Smith. Sydney, Australia:* Noble House.

Spiller, P., Finn, J., & Boast, R. (2001). *A New Zealand legal history*. Wellington, New Zealand: Thomson Reuters.

State Compensation Law of the People's Republic of China. (1994).

State v. Lehasa, Case No. 17/57/2013, Bloemfornetin Regional Court, July 10 2013, Magistrate Daya.

State v. Nhlapo and 2 others, Case No. 86/14, Harrismith High Court (Oct 28 2015).

Statistics New Zealand (2015). *Resident population of New Zealand at 31 March 2015.* Retrieved from http://www.stats.govt.nz.

Steelman, D.C, Goerdt, J.A., & McMillan, J.E. (2000). *Caseflow management: The heart of court management in the new millennium*. Williamsburg, VA: National Center for State Courts.

Steinhauer, J. (2015, July 28). Bipartisan push builds to relax sentencing laws. *The New York Times*. Retrieved from http://www.nytimes.com/2015/07/29/us/push-to-scale-back-sentencing-laws-gains-momentum.html?_r=0 (accessed July 28, 2015).

Stevenson, B. (2014). *Just Mercy: A Story of Justice and Redemption*. London: Spiegel & Grau.

Stone, L. (1971). Prosopography. *Daedalus, 100,* 46–79.

Sugarman, D. (2015). From legal biography to legal life writing: Broadening conceptions of legal history and socio-legal scholarship. *Journal of Law and Society, 1,* 7–33.

Summary Proceedings Act 1957 New Zealand.

Suppression of Communism Act of 1950. Retrieved from www.aluka.org/stable/10.5555/al.sff.document.leg19500717.028.020.044.

Supreme Court Act (New Zealand) (2003). Public Act No 53. Retrieved from http://www.legislation.govt.nz/act/public/2003/0053/latest/whole.html#DLM214028.

Tamanaha, B. Z. (2004). *On the rule of law history, politics, theory*. New York: Cambridge University Press.

Tezuka, H., & Yajima, M. (2005/2006). *Country Q & A Japan*. Retrieved from https://www.jurists.co.jp/ja/publication/tractate/docs/0504_ht.pdf.

Thai Junta Rejects Allegation of Denying Free Speech. (2015, June 5). *Prachatai*. Retrieved from http://www.prachatai.com/english/node/5140.

Thai Lawyers for Human Rights. (2015). *Human rights one year after the 2014 Coup: A judicial process in camouflage under the National Council for Peace and Order*. Retrieved from https://tlhr2014.files.wordpress.com/2015/06/20150604_tlhr-report-human-rights-one-year-after-the-2014-coup.pdf.

ThaiCoup: All NCPO Announcements in One Place. (2014, June 15). [Web log post]. Retrieved from https://thaicoup2014.wordpress.com/2014/06/15/thaicoup-all-ncpo-announcements-in-one-place/.

Tibane, E., & Vermeulen, A. (Eds.) (2015). *South Africa yearbook 2013/2014*. Pretoria: Government Communications. Retrieved from http://www.gcis.gov.za/content/resourcecentre/sa-info/yearbook2013-14.

Tonry, M. (Ed.) (2013). *Crime and justice volume 41: Prosecutors and politics: A comparative perspective*. Chicago, IL: Chicago University Press.

Treaty of Waitangi Act (New Zealand) (1975). Public Act No 114. Retrieved from http://www.legislation.govt.nz/act/public/1975/0114/latest/whole.html#DLM435368.

Tushnet, M. (1986). Critical legal studies: An introduction to its origins and underpinnings. *Journal of Legal Education, 36*, 505–517.

United Nations Office on Drugs and Crime. (2011). *2011 Global study on homicide: Trends, context, data*. Vienna, Austria: United Nations Office on Drugs and Crime.

United States v. Bagley, 473 U.S. 667 (1985).

United States v. Ressam, 553 U.S. 272 (2008).

University of Otago. (2013, November 5). A life remembered [Online Bulletin Board]. Retrieved from http://www.otago.ac.nz/otagobulletin/news/otago058541.html.

Urscheler, L. H. (2012). Innovation in a hybrid system: The example of Nepal. *PER: Potchefstroomse Elektroniese Regsblad, 15*, 98–119.

Van den Wyngaert, C. (2014). *Strafrecht en strafprocesrecht in hoofdlijnen* [Criminal law and criminal procedure law]. Antwerp: Maklu Uitgevers.

Victims' Rights Act (New Zealand) (2002). Public Act No 39. Retrieved from http://www.legislation.govt.nz/act/public/2002/0039/latest/whole.html#DLM157813.

Vira, V., & Ewing, T. (2014). *Ivory's curse: The militarization and professionalization of poaching in Africa*. Washington, DC: Born Free USA.

Vowles, E. (Presenter). (2010, August 17). *The Chamberlain case: The lessons learned* in *The Law Report*. Melbourne, Australia: ABC Radio. Retrieved from http://www.abc.net.au/rn/lawreport/stories/2010/2983998.htm.

Walker, B., & Allen, G. (1968). *Hindu world: An encyclopedic survey of Hinduism* (Vol. II). London: George Allen & Unwin Limited.

Waluchow, W. J. (2007). *A common law theory of judicial review: The living tree*. New York: Cambridge University Press.

Wandall, R. (2008). *Decisions to imprison: Court decision-making inside and outside the law*. Burlington, VA: Ashgate Publishing Co.

Welcome to the Wairarapa. (n.d.). Retrieved from http://www.wairarapanz.co.

Wice, P. B. (2005). *Public defenders and the American justice system*. Westpost, CT: Praeger Publishers.

Wilbur v. City of Mount Vernon, Memorandum Decision 23 (W.D. Wa. Dec. 4, 2013).

Williams, L. D., & Hsiao, I. (2010). *Sizing up the prosecution: A quick guide to local prosecution*. Cambridge, MA: Harvard Law School Bernard Koteen Office of Public Interest Advising.

Wilson, J. (2005). Nation and government—from colony to nation. In *Te Ara - The Encyclopedia of New Zealand*. Wellington, NZ: Manatū Taonga Ministry for Culture and Heritage. Retrieved from http://www.TeAra.govt.nz/en/nation-and-government.

Wilson, M. J. (2013). Prime time for Japan to take another step forward in lay participation: Exploring expansion to civil trials. *Akron Law Review, 46*, 642–674.

Winick, B. (2003). Therapeutic jurisprudence and problem solving courts. *Fordham Urban Law Journal, 30*, 1054–1103.

World Justice Project. (2015). *World justice project rule of law index 2015*. Retrieved from http://worldjusticeproject.org/sites/default/files/roli_2015_0.pdf.

Worrall, J. L., & Nugent-Borakove, M.E. (2008). *The changing role of the American prosecutor*. Albany, NY: State University New York Press.

Xi Jinping's anti-graft campaign. (2015, September 22). *South China Morning Post*. Retrieved from http://www.scmp.com/topics/xi-jinpings-anti-graft-campaign.

Yin, R. K. (1989). *Case study research*. London: Sage Publications.

Youth Justice and Criminal Evidence Act UK (1999).

Yu, K. (Ed.) (2002). *The emergence of China's civil society and changes* in *governance*. Beijing, China: Social Sciences Records Publishing House.

Zhang, J. F. (2013). *History of Legal Civilization in China* (Chinese ed.). Beijing: Law Press China.

Zheng, Y., & Chen, G. (2015). China's political outlook: Xi Jinping as a game changer. *East Asian Policy, 7*(1), 5–15.

Instructions to Interviewers

Thank you for agreeing to help with this book project by interviewing a prosecutor or defense lawyer. Each interview will comprise a book chapter that should be usable to teach students in a university class/professional institute. As a book, it should be a source of knowledge and information to readers interested in legal systems, lawyers, prosecutors, and related criminal justice professionals.

The following guidelines clarify what we are looking for to attain consistency in the chapters. If you have any questions, please contact one of the editors: Jane Goodman-Delahunty, jdelahunty@csu.edu.au or Dilip K. Das, dilipkd@aol.com.

Aim of the Interviews (and the Book) and Interview Guidelines

We have listed 6 topics to cover in the interview and 25 suggested questions to address these topics. Questions on all the topic areas should be asked, but the specific questions below are suggestions. Interviews have their own dynamics. Follow the topics down their most fruitful avenues, using the suggested questions to suit the interview, taking into account that the conduct and flow of the interview will dictate the order. Feel free to add, elaborate, follow up as you see fit and necessary to clarify points, expand on ideas, or pursue an insight offered.

Since each of you will be interviewing legal advocates from different world legal systems, please adjust the list and sequence of questions as needed. For example, some questions may be more applicable to prosecutors and public defenders than to advocates working in the private defense bar. The wording of questions is of course your own. In follow-up questions, try to get specific examples or details of generalizations made. Examples are probably among the most useful information to readers.

General Themes to Cover in the Interview

The main goal of the interviews is to elicit the views and interpretations of the experienced legal advocates on legal developments and current issues in the criminal law and procedure. What do they see happening in the criminal courts and legal profession in their countries and internationally, and, how do they evaluate or interpret these developments? There are many interpretations of legal issues by scholars and policy makers who are not legal advocates. What we are seeking are insights and interpretations within this sector by advocates making critical legal decisions. We are also seeking to build personal profiles of the legal advocates interviewed, such as their career, background, influences that shaped their personality, their successes, failures, joys, temptations and frustrations in their career and in their job.

We are seeking responses on the general themes of the following:

- What legal advocates see happening in criminal law and procedure?
- What issues they consider important?
- What changes they perceive as successes or failures, what as likely lasting futures or passing fads?
- What they would like to see?

The reason for the interviews is that legal advocates do not get time to write and reflect on their experiences, views, opinions, and perspectives. We are requesting researchers like you to record their views and make them meaningful contributions to our understanding of criminal law and procedural problems of today. This may involve going beyond simple questions and answers to allow the interviewer to analyze and reflect on the issues discussed. The interviewer also needs to bear in mind that core elements of the personal profile of the interviewee should be developed. You will need to do some preliminary research on the interviewee so you can seek their candid views, probe, and follow-up.

The basic goal of the interview is to capture the views of the legal advocate not those of the interviewer. Your role is not to be too critical of or to interpret what they mean to say, but to write as accurately as possible what they tell you. When we say "reflect" we hope you reflect on what the advocate said, not on your views of the issues discussed. It is the advocates' views, based on their career, experience, and thinking, that we are interested in. We know what scholars think about legal issues, but know less about what people engaged in advocacy think, and how they evaluate trends, developments, and issues in criminal justice. It is our firm belief that legal advocates know a lot; it is that knowledge and their judgments of the legal issues that we are after. That is the important goal of the book.

The role of the interviewer is not to cross-examine. Having said that, by "not being too critical," we do not mean to suggest that you should not challenge and draw out what it is that the legal advocates tell you. We do not want the interview to consist of official rhetoric that high-level people sometimes fall back on during interviews; we want their personal views and thinking.

If you have the sense that you are getting the formal language, see if you can get the advocates to go beyond that and push them for their own views.

Before Starting the Interview

Get a sense of how much time you are likely to have and what questions you can cover during that time. In no interview will you be able to ask all the questions you have. When you write up the interview, you will have space for about 6000–8000 words. Choose your priorities. The high priorities for the book are the reflections by the legal advocates on changes experienced and the interrelations of theory and practice, as well as insights into the person.

You should, if at all possible, tape-record the interview. Chances are you will have much more information than we will have space for in writing up your interview for the proposed book chapter. Taping the interview may be critical to allow you to review what is covered, and select the priority topics for write-up.

At the Conclusion of the Interview

Be sure at the end of the interview to discuss the opportunities to follow up, for example, by phone, for clarification as needed. Discuss arrangements for sending a draft of the interview chapter to the advocate so it can be checked for accuracy before submission to the editors.

After the Interview

1. Please write a short introduction to the actual interview. The intro-duction should be as follows:
   a. Summarize highlights of the legal advocate's career. Some of this information will come from the interview and other parts from published sources or a copy of the advocate's curriculum vitae.
   b. Describe, briefly, the interview itself. Where, when, how pleasant or not, and so on.
2. Edit the interview to bring out the most important discussion and answers.
3. Write a short conclusion on your impression of the interview. What were the major themes, how well the views expressed accord with known literature, but do not be overly critical on this point, please. Again, keep it brief.

4. Write a glossary of terms or events mentioned in the interview with which a reader might not be familiar. For example, if an interview is with a German legal advocate who mentions the "Rechtstaat," describe very briefly what that is, or, if interviewing an American legal advocate and the Miranda warning is mentioned, describe what the warning is. Just select the most likely items that will be unfamiliar to readers inexperienced with that legal system.

5. Briefly describe the basic structure of the legal system in your country. You have to be the judge of how much an informed reader is likely to know about the country and how much should be explained. This information will stand alone in a separate section in the book from the interviews.

6. Send the completed chapter, the glossary of terms, and description of the legal system to the editors by email in a Word document. The total length of the interview should be 6000–8000 words (not including the glossary and legal system description).

Interview Topics and Suggested Questions

Career

Q1. Tell us a little bit about your career? (Try and include the length of service as a prosecutor/defense lawyer, organizations worked in, movements, specializations, etc.)

Q2. As your career as a prosecutor/defense lawyer developed what has surprised you?

Q3. Has your work as a prosecutor/defense lawyer proved as interesting or rewarding as you thought it would when you first started?

Philosophy of Legal Advocacy

Q4 a. What do you think should be the role of the prosecutor/(public) defense counsel in society?

b. What should be their job, functions, and responsibilities? What should be left to others?

c. What organizational arrangements work and which do not?

Q5. What policies on relations with the community, with political groups, with other criminal justice organizations work well? What hampers cooperation with other agencies and groups? (may be more relevant to prosecutors than defense lawyers)

Q6. How difficult is it for prosecutors/defense counsel to relate to the living and social conditions of those from economically deprived backgrounds who appear before them?

Q7. How can a legal advocate develop empathy for those from the lower rungs of the social division in society from which they can derive a degree of understanding why that person before them did what is alleged?

Q8. How should the criminal legal system in your country be performing? What should be the preferred priorities and strategies; hard edged crime control, prevention, services, order work, what mix for which types of problems, and so on?

Problems and Successes Experienced

Q9. In your experience what policies or programs have worked well and which have not? And can you explain for what reasons? (e.g., if someone has to plead guilty to enter drug court? What about "Probation before judgment" programs, with no criminal record if you complete them successfully?)

Q10. What do you consider to be the greatest problems and issues facing the criminal courts at this time? (caseload, plea bargaining, misdemeanors never tried, preliminary dispositions, presumption of guilt, leniency, unlimited or preventive detention, etc.)

Q11. What problems in courts do you find the most difficult to deal with?

Q12. What would be easy to change? Internal problems (culture of the organization, managerial deficiencies, allegations of corruption or gender-related problems, etc.) or externally generated problems (resources, community support, etc.)? Is anything easy?

Theory and Practice

Q13. What should be the relationship between theory and practice in legal advocacy?

Q14. What can legal practitioners learn from theory, and what can theory builders learn from legal advocates?

Q15. What is the relationship right now? Does it exist? Does it work?

Q16. What holds back collaboration or interactions?

Q17. What kind of research, in what form, on what questions would you find most useful for legal advocacy practice? If not very useful, what could or should theory builders do to make their findings more useful to you?

Q18. Where do you find theory-based information? Where do you look? What journals, books, publications, and reports?

Q19. Do you conduct supplementary research (beyond legal research required) for pending cases? If so, what are the areas, issues or questions of law researched?

Transnational Relations

Q20. Have you been affected by, and how, in the work of your organization, by developments outside your country (human rights demands, universal codes of ethics, practical interactions with legal practitioners from other countries, personal experiences outside the country, new crime threats, etc.)? (ACLU, Amnesty International, environmental crimes, trafficking, social science and law, expected relapses in drug court, etc.)

Q21. Have those interactions been beneficial or harmful? What kind of external international influences are beneficial and which ones less so?

Q22. How have developments since the terrorist attack in the United States on September 11, 2001, affected your work?

General Assessments

Q23. Are you basically satisfied or dissatisfied with the developments in criminal law and criminal procedure in your system?

Q24. What are the most likely developments you see happening and which would you like to see happening?

Q25. What is most needed now to improve legal advocacy and the justice system?

International Police Executive Symposium

The International Police Executive Symposium (IPES) was founded in 1994. The aims and objectives of the IPES are to provide a forum to foster closer relationships among police researchers and practitioners globally to facilitate cross-cultural, international, and interdisciplinary exchanges for the enrichment of the law enforcement profession, and to encourage discussion and published research on challenging and contemporary topics related to the profession.

One of the most important activities of the IPES is the organization of an annual meeting under the auspices of a police agency or an educational institution. Every year since 1994 annual, meetings have been hosted by such agencies and institutions all over the world. Past hosts have included the Canton Police of Geneva, Switzerland; the International Institute of the Sociology of Law, Onati, Spain; Kanagawa University, Yokohama, Japan; the Federal Police, Vienna, Austria; the Dutch Police and Europol, the Hague, the Netherlands; the Andhra Pradesh Police, India; the Center for Public Safety, Northwestern University, Evanston, Illinois; the Polish Police Academy, Szczytno, Poland; the Police of Turkey (twice); the Kingdom of Bahrain Police; a group of institutions in Canada (consisting of the University of the Fraser Valley, Abbotsford Police Department, Royal Canadian Mounted Police, the Vancouver Police Department, the Justice Institute of British Columbia, Canadian Police College and the International Centre for Criminal Law Reform and Criminal Justice Policy); the Czech Police Academy, Prague; the Dubai Police; the Ohio Association of Chiefs of Police and the Cincinnati Police Department, Ohio, USA; the Republic of Macedonia and the Police of Malta. The 2011 Annual Meeting on the theme of "Policing Violence, Crime, Disorder and Discontent: International Perspectives" was hosted in Buenos Aires, Argentina, on June 26–30, 2011. The 2012 annual meeting was hosted at the United Nations in New York on the theme of "Economic development, armed violence and public safety" on August 5–10. The 2013 Annual Meeting on the theme of "Global Issues in Contemporary Policing" was hosted by the Ministry of Interior of Hungary and the Hungarian National Police on August 4–9, 2013. In 2014, there were two meetings: the Annual Meeting on the theme "Policing by Consent" was hosted in Trivandrum (Kerala), India, on March 16–21, and the other on "Crime Prevention and Community Resilience" was hosted in Bulgaria's capital city Sofia (July 27–31). The 2015 summer meeting on the theme of "Police Governance and Human Trafficking: Promoting Preventative and Comprehensive Strategies" was hosted in Pattaya Beach, Thailand, on August 8–12, 2015. The 2016 Annual Meeting will be hosted in Washington DC on the theme of "Urban Security Planning: Challenges for 21st Century Global Cities."

There have been also occasional Special Meetings of the IPES. A special meeting was cohosted by the Bavarian Police Academy of Continuing Education in Ainring, Germany, University of Passau, Germany, and State University of New York, Plattsburgh, USA, in 2000. The second Special Meeting was hosted by the police in the Indian state of Kerala. The third Special Meeting on the theme of "Contemporary Issues in Public Safety and Security" was hosted by the Commissioner of Police of the Blekinge Region of Sweden and the President of the University of Technology on August 10–14, 2011. The last Special Meeting on "Policing by Consent" was hosted in Trivandrum, India, on March 16–21, 2014.

The majority of participants of the annual meetings are usually directly involved in the police profession. In addition, scholars and researchers in the field also participate. The meetings comprise both structured and informal sessions to maximize dialogue and exchange of views and information. The executive summary of each meeting is distributed to participants, as well as to a wide range of other interested police professionals and scholars. In addition, a book of selected papers from each annual meeting is published through CRC Press/Taylor & Francis Group, Prentice Hall, Lexington Books, and other reputed publishers. A Special Issue of *Police Practice and Research: An International Journal* is also published with the most thematically relevant papers after the usual blind review process.

IPES Institutional Supporters

Australian Institute of Police Management, Library, 1 Collins Beach Road RD, Manly, New South Wales 2095, Australia. Tel: +61 2 9934 4800; Fax: +61 2 9934 4780. Email: library@aipm.gov.au.

APCOF, The African Policing Civilian Oversight Forum (contact Sean Tait), 2nd floor, The Armoury, Buchanan Square, 160 Sir Lowry Road, Woodstock Cape Town, 8000 South Africa. Tel: 27 21 461 7211; Fax: 27 21 461 7213. Email: sean@apcof.org.za.

Baker College of Jackson, 2800 Springport Road, Jackson, MI 49202, USA (contact: Blaine Goodrich) Phone: (517) 841-4522. Email: blaine.goodrich@baker.edu.

Cliff Roberson, Professor Emeritus, Washburn University, 16307 Sedona Woods, Houston, TX77082-1665, USA. Tel: +1 713 703 6639; Fax: +1 281 596 8483. Email: roberson37@msn.com.

College of Health and Human Services, Indiana Universityof Pennsylvania, 216 Zink Hall, Room 105,1190 Maple Street Indiana, PA15705-1059(Mark E. Correia, PhD, Dean), mcorreia@iup.edu.Tel: 724 3572555.

Cyber Defense & Research Initiatives (contact James Lewis), LLC, PO Box 86, Leslie, MI 49251, USA. Tel: 517 242 6730. Email: lewisja@cyberdefenseresearch.com.

De Montfort University, Health and Life Sciences, School of Applied Social Sciences (Dr. Perry Stanislas, Hirsh Sethi), Hawthorn Building, The Gateway, Leicester, LE19BH, UK. Tel: +44 (0) 116 257 7146. Email: pstanislas@dmu.ac.uk,hsethi@dmu.ac.uk.

Defendology Center for Security, Sociology and Criminology Research (Valibor Lalic), Srpska Street 63,78000 Banja Luka, Bosnia and Herzegovina. Tel and Fax: 387 51 308 914. Email: lalicv@teol.net.

Department of Criminal Justice (Dr. Harvey L. McMurray, Chair), North Carolina Central University, 301 Whiting Criminal Justice Bldg., Durham, NC 27707, USA. Tel: 919-530-5204, 919-530-7909; Fax: 919-530-5195. Email: hmcmurray@nccu.edu.

Department of Psychology (Stephen Perrott), Mount Saint Vincent University, 166 Bedford Highway, Halifax, Nova Scotia, Canada. Email: Stephen.perrott@mvsu.ca.

Edmundo Oliveira, Prof. PhD 1 Irving Place University Tower Apt. U 7 A 10003.9723 Manhattan—New York, New York, Phone 407.342.24.73. Email: edmundooliveira@cfl.rr.com.

Fayetteville State University (Dr. David E. Barlow, Professor and Dean), College of Basic and Applied Sciences, 130 Chick Building, 1200 Murchison Road, Fayetteville, North Carolina, 28301 USA. Tel: 910-672-1659; Fax: 910-672-1083. Email: dbarlow@uncfsu.edu.

International Council on Security and Development (ICOS) (Andre Souza, Senior Researcher), Visconde de Piraja 577/605, Ipanema, Rio de Janeiro 22410-003, Brazil. Tel: (+55) 21 3186 5444. Email: asouza@icosgroup.net.

Kerala Police (Shri Balasubramaniyum, Director General of Police), Police Headquarters, Trivandrum, Kerala, India. Email: manojabraham05@gmail.com.

Law School, John Moores University (David Lowe, LLB Programme Leader), Law School, Redmonds Building, Brownlow Hill, Liverpool, L3 5UG, UK. Tel: +44 (0) 151 231 3918. Email: D.Lowe@ljmu.ac.uk.

Molloy College, The Department of Criminal Justice (contact Dr. John A. Eterno, NYPD Captain-Retired), 1000 Hempstead Avenue, PO Box 5002, Rockville Center, NY 11571-5002, USA. Tel: 516 678 5000, Ext. 6135; Fax: 516 256. 2289. Email: mailto:jeterno@molloy.edu.

National Institute of Criminology and Forensic Science (Mr Kamalendra Prasad, Inspector General of Police), MHA, Outer Ring Road, Sector 3, Rohini, Delhi 110085, India. Tel: 91 11 275 2 5095; Fax: 91 11 275 1 0586. Email: director.nicfs@nic.in.

National Police Academy, Japan (Naoya Oyaizu, Deputy Director), Police Policy Research Center, Zip 183-8558: 3-12-1 Asahicho Fuchu-city, Tokyo, Japan. Tel: 81 42 354 3550; Fax: 81 42 330 3550. Email: PPRC@npa.go.jp.

Royal Canadian Mounted Police (Craig J. Callens), 657 West 37th Avenue,Vancouver, BC V5Z 1K6, Canada. Tel: 604264 2003; Fax: 604 264 3547. Email: bcrcmp@ rcmp-grc.gc.ca.

School of Psychology and Social Science, Head, Social Justice Research Centre (Profs. Caroline Taylor, Foundation Chair in Social Justice), Edith Cowan University, 270 Joondalup Drive, Joondalup, WA 6027, Australia. Email: c.taylor@ecu.edu.au.

South Australia Police (Commissioner Mal Hyde), Office of the Commissioner, South Australia Police, 30 FlindersStreet, Adelaide, SA 5000, Australia. Email: mal.hyde@police.sa.gov.au.

Southeast Missouri State University (Dr. Diana Bruns, Dean), Criminal Justice & Sociology, One University Plaza, Cape Girardeau, MO63701, USA. Tel: (573) 651-2178. Email: dbruns@semo.edu.

The Faculty of Criminal Justice and Security (Dr. Gorazd Mesko), University of Maribor, Kotnikova8, 1000 Ljubl-jana, Slovenia. Tel: 386 1 300 83 39; Fax: 386 1 2302 687. Email: gorazd.mesko@fvv.uni-mb.si.

UNISA, Department of Police Practice (Setlhomamaru Dintwe), Florida Campus, Cnr Christiaan De Wet and Pioneer Avenues, Private Bag X6, Florida, 1710 South Africa. Tel: 011 471 2116; Cell: 083 581 6102; Fax: 011 471 2255. Email: Dintwsi@unisa.ac.za.

University of Maine at Augusta, College of Natural and Social Sciences (Richard Myers, Professor),46 University Drive, Augusta, ME 04330-9410, USA. Email: rmyers@maine.edu.

University of New Haven (Dr. Mario Gaboury, School of Criminal Justice and Forensic Science), 300 Boston PostRoad, West Haven, CT 06516, USA. Tel: 203 932 7260. Email: rward@newhaven.edu.

University of South Africa, College of Law (Professor Kris Pillay, School of Criminal Justice, Director), Preller Street, Muckleneuk, Pretoria. Email: cpillay@unisa. ac.za.

University of the Fraser Valley (Dr. Darryl Plecas), Department of Criminology & Criminal Justice, 33844 King Road, Abbotsford, British Columbia V2 S7 M9, Canada. Tel: 604-853-7441; Fax: 604-853-9990. Email: Darryl. plecas@ ufv.ca University of West Georgia (David A. Jenks, PhD), 1601 Maple Street, Carrollton, GA 30118, Pafford Building 2309.Tel:678-839-6327. Email: djenks@ westga.edu.

Index

Note: Page numbers followed by 'f' and 't' refer to figures and tables, respectively.